CAPONE

CAPONE

The Life and World
of Al Capone

by JOHN KOBLER

DA CAPO PRESS • NEW YORK

Library of Congress Cataloging in Publication Data

Kobler, John.
    Capone: the life and world of Al Capone / by John Kobler. — 1st Da
Capo Press ed.
        p.   cm.
    Originally published: New York: Putnam, 1971.
    Includes bibliographical references and index.
    ISBN 0-306-80499-9
    1. Capone, Al, 1899-1947. 2. Criminals — United States — Biography. I.
Title.
[HV6248.C17K6   1992]
364.1′092 — dc20   92-19640
[B]   CIP

Poem by Carl Sandburg, excerpted from "Cahoots," from *Smoke and Steel* by
Carl Sandburg, copyright 1920 by Harcourt Brace Jovanovich; copyright
1948 by Carl Sandburg, reprinted by permission of the publisher.

First Da Capo Press edition 1992

This Da Capo Press paperback edition of *Capone* is an unabridged
republication of the edition published in New York in 1971. It is
reprinted by arrangement with the author.

Published by Da Capo Press, Inc.
A Subsidiary of Plenum Publishing Corporation
233 Spring Street, New York, N.Y. 10013

For Evelyn

Contents

1.   Snorky   13
2.   A Brooklyn Boyhood   18
3.   Big Jim   38
4.   ". . . the best and dearest of husbands"   52
5.   No Christian Burial   68
6.   From Death Corner to Dead Man's Tree   76
7.   "A. Capone, Antique Dealer"   101
8.   Cicero   109
9.   "Tell them Sicilians to go to hell"   124
10.   Garlic and Gangrene   134
11.   The Fall of the House of Genna   156
12.   "I paid him plenty and I got what I was paying for"   171
13.   War   184
14.   Big Bill Rides Again   196
15.   ". . . the sunny Italy of the new world"   213
16.   "I've got a heart in me"   227
17.   Against the Wall   240

18. "Nobody's on the legit"   255

19. Case Jacket SI-7085-F   270

20. Mr. and Mrs. Alphonse Capone
    Request the Pleasure. . . .   283

21. A Murder a Day   287

22. ". . . regardez le gorille"   306

23. Paper Chase   316

24. Aggiornamento   323

25. The Reckoning   328

26. "Received . . . the body of the
    within named prisoner. . . ."   347

27. Island of Pelicans   357

28. Tertiary Stage   374

    APPENDIX: The Heritage   379

    SOURCES AND ACKNOWLEDGMENTS   387

    INDEX   395

Illustrations follow pages 64, 256, 384.

Play it across the table
What if we steal this city blind?
If they want anything, let 'em nail it down.

Harness bulls, dicks, front-office men,
And the high goats upon the bench,
Ain't they all in cahoots?
Ain't it fifty-fifty all down the line?

—CARL SANDBURG

CAPONE

1

Snorky

FOR a man of Frank Loesch's years and stature it was a galling mission. With profound distaste, the venerable corporation counsel, a founding member of the Chicago Crime Commission and, at the age of seventy-five, its president, crossed the black-and-white tessellated lobby of the Hotel Lexington and stepped into the iron-grille elevator. To compound his sense of humiliation, he was committed to the destruction of the man whose aid he sought. Among the city's "Public Enemies," a term Loesch himself had coined to dispel the romantic aura with which the yellow press had clothed gangsters, Al Capone ranked No. 1. Yet who but Capone could or would, this autumn of 1928, guarantee a free, honest election to the voters of Cook County? Not the governor of the state, an embezzler and protector of felons. Not Chicago's grotesque mayor. Not the state's attorney, who had never successfully prosecuted a single gang-ster. Not the police. Least of all the police of whom Capone once boasted: "I own the police."

Loesch recalled later: "It did not take me long after I had been made president of the Crime Commission to discover that Al Capone ran the city. His hand reached into every department of the city and county government. . . . I made arrangements to secretly meet Mr. Capone in his headquarters."

Capone's bountiful disbursements enabled him to act as if the Lexington belonged to him. The lobby was constantly patrolled by his janissaries, who at sight of any suspicious-looking or inquisitive stranger would leap to a house phone and alert their master. Other sentries kept vigil by the elevator landings, and to approach Capone's fourth-floor eyrie, the visitor had to pass between rows of bodyguards, who carried under their jackets a .45-caliber revolver in a holster, hanging, according to the prescribed style, from a shoulder halter to four inches below the left armpit.

The nerve center of Capone's multifarious activities was Room 430, the salon of his six-room suite. From there he directed—with the guidance of his porcine, Moscow-born financial manager, Jake "Greasy Thumb" Guzik—a syndicate that owned or controlled breweries, distilleries, speakeasies, warehouses, fleets of boats and trucks, nightclubs, gambling houses, horse and dog racetracks, brothels, labor unions, business and industrial associations, together producing a yearly revenue in the hundreds of millions of dollars. Cash was stacked around Room 430 in padlocked canvas bags, awaiting its transfer to a bank under fictitious names.

To enforce his will, Capone had an army of sluggers, bombers and machine gunners, 700 to 1,000 strong, some under his direct command, others available to him through allied gang chieftains. For his immunity from prosecution he relied on an intricate linkage with City Hall, involving a range of officials from ward heelers to the mayor.

Having passed inspection by the sentries, Loesch was admitted to an oval vestibule. A crest enclosing the initials A.C. had been inlaid in the oak parquet. At the left a bathroom contained an immense sunken tub with gold-plated faucets and ceramic tiles of Nile green and royal purple. An ancient Oriental rug covered the floor of the salon, and the high ceiling was embossed with an elaborate foliage design. A chandelier of amber and smoked glass shed a soft light. In an artificial fireplace a heap of artificial coal, covering light bulbs, glowed ruby red. A radio set had been built into the paneling above the mantel.

Capone was a late riser, having customarily stayed up past dawn, eating, drinking and nightclubbing, and visitors who called before noon would find him in dressing gown and silk pajamas, which, like the silk sheets he slept on, were monogrammed. He ordered the pajamas, so-called French models, from Sulka in lots of a dozen at $25 each. He preferred royal blue with gold piping. He also fancied colored shorts of Italian glove silk, costing $12. His suits, custom-made by Marshall Field at $135 each, with the right-hand pockets reinforced to support the weight of a revolver, ran to light hues—pea green, powder blue, lemon yellow—and he affected matching ties and socks, a fedora, and pearl-gray spats. A marquise diamond sparkled in his tiepin, across his bulging abdomen stretched a platinum watch chain encrusted with diamonds, and on his middle finger he wore a flawless, 11 carat, blue-white diamond that had cost him $50,000.

At the time of Loesch's visit Capone was twenty-nine but appeared considerably older. Mountains of pasta and Niagaras of Chianti had deposited layers of fat, but the muscle beneath the fat was rock-hard, and in anger he could inflict fearful punishment. He stood 5 feet $10\frac{1}{2}$ inches tall and weighed 255 pounds. He moved with an assertive, forward thrust of his upper body, the shoulders meaty and sloping like a bull's. His big round head sat on a neck so short and thick as to be almost undifferentiated from his trunk. His face looked congested, as if too much flesh had been crammed into the available frame. His hair was dark brown, the eyes light gray under thick, shaggy eyebrows, the nose flat, the mouth wide, fat-lipped and purplish. A scar ran along his left cheek from ear to jaw, another across the jaw, and a third below the left ear, mementos of an early knife fight. He was touchy about his disfigurement. He often considered plastic surgery. No hair grew through the scar tissue and to reduce the whiteness of the furrows, the whiter by contrast to his darkish jowls, he applied heavy coats of talcum powder to the rest of his face. To news photographers he would present his right, unscarred profile. He detested the sobriquet the press had fastened on him—Scarface—and nobody used it in his presence without courting disaster. He allowed his intimates to call him Snorky—slang for elegant.

Loesch found Capone in affable humor. He sat relaxed and smiling at a long mahogany desk, his back to a bay window, a cigar between his teeth. On the desk stood a French telephone, a gold-plated inkstand, a herd of miniature ivory elephants—his good-luck pieces—a pair of field glasses through which he liked to scan the headlines of the newspapers stacked on the newsstand below, and a bronze paperweight in the shape of the Lincoln Memorial. Loesch was bemused by the three portraits adorning the dark-rose stucco wall—Abraham Lincoln, George Washington and Chicago's Mayor William Hale "Big Bill" Thompson. Next to Lincoln hung a facsimile of the Gettysburg Address. The opposite wall accommodated a painting of Cleopatra, photographs of Capone's favorite movie stars, Fatty Arbuckle and Theda Bara, three stuffed deer heads, and a clock with a cuckoo that sang the hour and a quail that sang on the quarter hour.

Half a dozen henchmen milled about the room, attentive to Capone's slightest whim. When his cigar went dead, he needed neither to speak nor to gesture to have it relit. Somebody automatically sprang to his side, lighter flaring.

Loesch stated his business without preamble. He reminded Capone of the April Republican primary. In gangster parlance a bomb was a "pineapple," and the newspapers had dubbed it the Pineapple Primary. Professional terrorists on both sides, the majority of them Capone gangsters, had bombed the homes of candidates, murdered party workers, intimidated voters. The police did not intervene. Was the Pineapple Primary a foretaste of the approaching November elections?

The arrogance of Capone's reply staggered the old lawyer: "I'll give you a square deal if you don't ask too much of me."

"Now look here, Capone," said Loesch, stifling his anger, "will you help me by keeping your damned cutthroats and hoodlums from interfering with the polling booths?"

"Sure," Capone promised. "I'll give them the word because they're all dagos up there, but what about the Saltis gang of micks on the West Side? They'll have to be handled different. Do you want me to give them the works, too?"

Loesch replied that nothing could please him more.

"All right," said Capone. "I'll have the cops send over squad cars the night before the election and jug all the hoodlums and keep 'em in the cooler until the polls close."

He kept his word. He told the police of America's second-largest city what to do, and the police obeyed. On the eve of the election they spread a dragnet, rounding up and disarming many known gangsters. The following day seventy squad cars cruised the polling areas. The balloting proceeded without disorder.

"It turned out to be the squarest and the most successful election day in forty years," Loesch said later in a lecture at the Southern California Academy of Criminology. "There was not one complaint, not one election fraud and no threat of trouble all day."

It was also a display of power such as few outlaws have achieved before or since.

2.

Seldom had the three guests of honor sat down to a feast so lavish. Their dark Sicilian faces were flushed as they gorged on the rich, pungent food, washing it down with liters of red wine. At the head of the table Capone, his big white teeth flashing in an ear-to-ear smile, oozing affability, proposed toast after toast to the trio. *Saluto,* Scalise! *Saluto,* Anselmi! *Saluto,* Giunta!

On this night the Hawthorne Inn, which to all practical purposes Capone owned, as he owned the surrounding town of Cicero, had been closed to all outsiders, the doors locked and bolted, the window curtains drawn. The festivities were strictly intramural. Exuberant good-fellowship, singing, shouting, raucous joking, and laughter warmed the dining room.

When, long after midnight, the last morsel had been devoured and the last drop drunk, Capone pushed back his chair. A glacial silence fell over the room. His smile had faded. Nobody was smiling now except the sated, mellow guests of honor, their belts and collars loosened to accommodate their Gargantuan intake. As the silence lengthened, they, too, stopped smiling. Nervously, they glanced up and down the long table. Capone leaned toward them. The words dropped from his mouth like stones. So they thought he didn't know? They imagined they could hide the offense he never forgave—disloyalty?

Capone had observed the old tradition. Hospitality before execution. The Sicilians were defenseless, having, like the other banqueters, left their guns in the checkroom. Capone's bodyguards fell upon them, lashing them to their chairs with wire and gagging them. Capone got up, holding a baseball bat. Slowly, he walked the length of the table and halted behind the first guest of honor. With both hands he lifted the bat and slammed it down full force. Slowly, methodically he struck again and again, breaking bones in the man's shoulders, arms and chest. He moved to the next man and, when he had reduced him to mangled flesh and bone, to the third. One of the bodyguards then fetched his revolver from the checkroom and shot each man in the back of the head.

2

A Brooklyn Boyhood

ON May 26, 1906, Gabriel Capone, a forty-one-year-old barber of Neapolitan origin, appeared before the Kings County Court in Brooklyn, New York, to claim his final citizenship papers. He could neither speak, write, nor read English, but the new law requiring literacy as a condition of naturalization would not become effective for another month, and he left the courthouse a full-fledged American, a status which the prevailing old law automatically conferred upon his wife and children.

With his wife Teresa, née Riolia, who was eight months pregnant at the time, and their first child, Vincenzo, age six, Capone had emigrated in 1893 from the slums of Naples to the slums of Brooklyn's Navy Yard district. (The family name, pronounced in two syllables, "Cap-own," was an Americanization of the original Caponi.) They settled eventually in a flat on Navy Street in the strident, reeking chaos of the borough's biggest Italian colony. Rents in the area's two- to four-story red-brick or wooden frame tenements ran between $3 and $4.50 per room a month. None had central heating, running hot water, or bathrooms. The tenants heated water on potbellied coal stoves, which also provided their only protection against freezing weather.

After a brief, discouraging period as a grocer, Gabriel opened a barbershop at 69 Park Avenue, a few steps from his home. His progeny increased at the rate of a child about every three years to a total of nine, seven sons and two daughters. Besides Vincenzo (renamed James) and Ralph, born a month after the Capones reached America, there were, in the order of birth, Salvatore (later called Frank), Alphonse, Amadeo Ermino (later John and nicknamed Mimi), Umberto (later Albert John), Matthew Nicholas, Rose and Mafalda (named after Italy's royal princess).

The poor, uneducated Italians who had been pouring into America since the first mass migration from their country began during the 1880's proved the least assimilable ingredients of the melting pot. They were, especially the Southern Italian *contadini* and *artigiani*— the peasants and small craftsmen, who constituted the majority of the newcomers—clannish and wary of outsiders. Centuries of exploitation by both foreign invaders and rapacious domestic masters had taught them to mistrust authority. They considered politicians and police their natural enemies. The laws, they felt, had been made to protect the rich and enslave the poor. Appointment to government office seemed to them a license to steal. The early Italian immigrants tended to place loyalty to family and community above loyalty to their adopted country, and they did not necessarily condemn those who transgressed against the new society, even the hoodlum and the racketeer; sometimes, in fact, they invested the outlaw with heroic stature, as long as he kept faith with his community and, above all, remained a good family man.

The disillusionments, the hardships and brutal prejudice that the Italian immigrants endured in the promised "land of opportunity" confirmed them in their tribalism. With their lack of formal education, their language disabilities, and their past employment limited to agriculture, shopkeeping and humble crafts, they found, as city dwellers, all but the lowest-paid jobs closed to them. They became ditchdiggers, bricklayers, stonecutters; they laid pipes and railroad ties, hawked notions from street barrows and stands, ran small fruit and vegetable stores; like Gabriel Capone, they plied razor and scissors. The average male Italian in New York in 1910 earned between $9.71 and $11.28 a week, roughly $2 to $4 less than his native counterpart. Consequently, his wife and children had to work. Teresa Capone, a dour, silent, strong-jawed woman, turned her hand to dressmaking, and most of her children were doing odd jobs before they entered their teens.

Years of labor out of doors under sunny skies had endowed the typical Southern Italian immigrant with a physical stamina that could withstand the rigors of the city slums, but the health of his children suffered. Undernourished, overcrowded in foul cold-water tenements, lacking adequate sanitation and fresh air and sunlight, the first-generation Italians had the poorest health of any foreign group in New York. In Italy the percentage of youths eighteen to twenty years of age who were rejected for military service because of poor health ranged from 15 to 22 percent. In New York the percentage climbed to 35 percent. A block-by-block study of six Italian communities conducted before the First World War by Dr. Antonio Stella showed infant mortality to be almost double that of the rest of the city population. The great killers were the respiratory diseases, diarrhea and diphtheria.

Illiteracy among the Italian immigrants ran around 60 percent, by far the highest percentage of any foreign group, and because their children were obliged to work at so early an age fewer than 1 percent ever got to high school. According to a 1910 survey of fifteen nationalities in New York City schools, the Italo-Americans "led in retardation"—that is, they advanced from grade to grade at ages older than the ages of pupils in the other national groups. But contrary to a widespread canard, no survey ascribed this failure to mental inferiority. "The Southern Italian," concluded the Reverend Antonio Mangano, a Protestant minister who had closely observed the transplanted stock, "is illiterate but not unintelligent." By the second generation compulsory education had largely eliminated the illiteracy. During the boyhood of the Capone brothers, however, it was, together with truancy, the rule. Except for Matt, the youngest brother, none of the Capone brothers finished high school.

The Italian immigrants were victims of a myth that continued to plague their descendants. According to this myth, they had criminal instincts. Yet considering the hardships they bore, it is remarkable how few offenses they actually committed. With resignation and dignity, they accepted the menial tasks available to them at wretched pay, and while, in 1910, they made up approximately 11 percent of the total foreign-born population, they produced only about 7 percent of the foreign-born convicts and juvenile delinquents. Nine years later a federal study covering seventeen nationalities in prisons placed the Italian twelfth in the ratio of commitments per 100,000.

Resignation, however, was not characteristic of the younger Italians. As they grew up poor in the world's richest nation, as educational, social and economic opportunities, purportedly accessible to all Americans, eluded them, they did not, like their elders, passively accept frustration. Without yet having established legitimate values of their own, they rejected their parents' old-country traditions as irrelevant to the challenge of America. To some of them, a small minority, it appeared that only crime could open the door to the good life, and they joined the ranks of professional gunmen and bombers, extortionists, vice peddlers, labor racketeers, gambling-house operators and bootleggers.

It was this lawless first- and second-generation minority who began to combine the methods of predatory Italian secret societies like the Neapolitan Camorra, the Carbonari and the Mafia with those of American big business. From their crude, undisciplined early forays evolved one of the most efficient enterprises in the history of organized crime.

At no stage in its evolution did it represent more than a minute fraction of the Italo-American population. Crime among the latter never exceeded the average for either foreign or native populations. But the criminal few reinforced the prejudices that immigrants from other countries had brought with them. They saw the "dago," the "ginzo," as not only criminal by nature, but physically unclean and of low mentality. The effect of such vilification was to draw its victims still closer together. They formed proud, tight enclaves which no outsider could penetrate. They were further divided among themselves along traditional lines of class and regional origin just as their forebears had been in the mother country, where the urban *artigiano* looked down on the *contadino* and the educated *galantuomo* derided them both. Regardless of station, the Sicilian viewed the Neapolitan with distrust; the Roman stepped warily when dealing with the Calabrian. This insularity existed to an even greater degree at the criminal level. Not until the thirties would the Mafia, Sicilian in origin, admit a non-Sicilian. Joseph Valachi, a Mafia "soldier" turned informer, whose parents came from Naples, testifying in 1963 about organized crime before the Senate Permanent Subcommittee on Investigations, explained why, thirty-three years before, he had at first hesitated to join a Mafia family: "I refused for the simple reason when I was in Sing Sing, I met an oldtimer . . . and he used to have trouble in his days and they had wars in his time, what he terms

'Sicilians against Neapolitans,' and he was a Neapolitan, and his name was Alexander Senaro. So he was preaching to me and giving me the lowdown on this, like, for instance, he used the expression, 'If you hang out with a Sicilian for 20 years and you argue with one of his kind, well, this Sicilian will turn against you.' He made me have some fear in myself, and when they approached me, that was what I had in mind. That is the reason I sort of turned it down. . . ."

The sense of community ran so deep among some Italo-Americans that they were likely to keep in touch all their lives, no matter how widely their careers diverged; this partly explains why the pallbearers at a gangster's funeral have been known to include criminal court judges and state prosecutors, why, at testimonial dinners for a retiring city official, police inspectors have sat beside dope peddlers. Albert A. Vitale, for example, leader of the Italian-American Democratic Club, had been a New York City magistrate for ten years when, in 1930, the Appellate Division of the State Supreme Court removed him from the bench. The offense was his association with racketeers. Three months earlier his political club had given a dinner in his honor. The guests numbered seven Italo-American racketeers, among them Ciro Terranova, the "Artichoke King," so called because he terrorized merchants selling artichokes into dealing exclusively with his wholesale produce company. Vitale's ouster scarcely diminished his prestige. The guests at another dinner which the Federation of Italian-American Democratic Clubs tendered him after he returned to private law practice included General Sessions Judge John J. Freschi, State Supreme Court Justices Salvatore A. Cotillo and Louis A. Valente, Magistrates Joseph Raimo, Thomas Aurelio and Michael Delagi.

Again, in 1952, the New York State Crime Commission, investigating alliances between politicians and racketeers, subpoenaed witnesses for questioning about a meeting that took place several years earlier at the Biltmore Hotel. The five men present were Generoso Pope, publisher of the newspaper *Il Progresso Italo-Americano;* a former General Sessions judge, Francis X. Mancuso; county Democratic boss Carmine De Sapio; Judge Valente; and the racketeer Francesco Saveria, alias Frank Costello. All except Valente, a Genoese by birth, were descended from Southern Italians. The object of the meeting, it appeared, had been entirely innocent. Publisher Pope had convoked it to plan a fund-raising campaign for Italian children orphaned by war. Without embarrassment, Judge Mancuso admitted to having known Costello for about thirty-five years. "His people come from the same town my people come from," he noted. "I may say there is intermarriage in the family. My first cousin married his first cousin." Costello was also godfather to Generoso Pope, Jr. It was after dining with the publisher's son, one evening in 1957, that he was shot and wounded by an unknown assailant.

Al Capone was an atypical Italo-American in that he took scant pride in his foreign roots. "I'm no Italian," he would protest when the press gave his birthplace as Naples or Sicily. "I was born in Brooklyn." The date was January 17, 1899. On the corner of Tillary and Lawrence streets, a block from the Capone home, stood St. Michael's Church, an odd little white stucco building partly constructed below street level so that one had to descend a flight of steps to enter it. Like most of the neighborhood Italians, Gabriel and Teresa Capone worshiped at St. Michael's, and three months after Al's birth they had him baptized there by the Reverend Gioacchino Garofalo.

Life in the sector where Al lived his first ten years was harsh, but never drab, never stagnant. Hordes of ragged children gave the streets an explosive vitality as they played stickball, dodged traffic, brawled and bawled, while their mothers, dark, heavy-thighed women, bustled to and fro balancing on their heads baskets laden with supplies for the day's meals. Fruit and vegetable carts, standing wheel to wheel, made a bright, fragrant clutter along the curb. The fire escapes that formed an iron lacework across the faces of the squat tenements shook and shuddered as the El trains roared by close behind on Myrtle Avenue. The completion of the Williamsburg Bridge in 1903—up to that time, the world's greatest suspension bridge—and its opening to trains, as well as vehicular traffic, had brought vast new masses to the area, seeking cheaper housing.

The patron saint of the Capones' neighborhood was St. Michael, and in addition to September 29 (Michaelmas), the parishioners devoted May 8 to his glorification. The daylong festivities began in front of the church as St. Michael's Society, about 200 strong, assembled for a parade. At their head, flanked by bevies of white-clad little girls, solemnly stepped the bearer of St. Michael's banner, which depicted the archangel, a flaming sword in his right hand, towering triumphant over the cringing Spirit of Darkness, his left hand clasping a shield inscribed QUIS UT DEUS? ("Who is like God?"). Accompanied by Attanasio's Brass Band, they paraded down Tillary Street, past the docks on Navy Street, and circled back to their starting point via York Street. All along the line of march Italian and American flags fluttered from windows, cherry bombs burst in the gutter. (The explosions, heard afar in the surrounding foreign colonies, prompted the rumor on one occasion that a Black Hand gang was blowing up its victims' homes.) When the parade ended, Father Garofalo celebrated high mass. Attanasio and his fellow musicians then mounted the bandstand erected next to the church and shivered the air with clarion operatic overtures. The evening was given over to more music, dancing in the streets, feasting and fireworks. Hundreds of goblets containing Bengal lights dangled from telegraph poles, and as the grand finale they all went off with a mighty sizzle and hiss, casting long tongues of orange flame against the night sky.

In warm weather the corner of Sands and Navy streets was often the scene of a musical diversion, attended by hundreds. To the accompaniment of an organ grinder named Paolo Scotti, who claimed kinship to the great operatic baritone, and the tinkle of coins falling at his feet, "Signor Tutino Giovanni, Dramatic Tenor," would render Verdi arias. As he sang, he would fix some buxom girl in the crowd with a soulful gaze, clap his left hand over his heart, and stretch out the right in amorous supplication. . . . Capone acquired a passion for Italian grand opera.

Sands Street at night, all night, catered to more robust tastes, as droves of sailors piled ashore, clamoring for liquor and women. It was one of the roughest haunts in the country, the Barbary Coast of the East, where mayhem and murder constantly threatened the unwary. At the pothouse bars that sold raw liquor straight and cheap the thirsty customers lined up three and four deep. If their money ran low, there were pawnshops a step away open all night. There were tattooing parlors, gambling dives, dance halls, fleabags with rooms for rent by the hour, and a galaxy of bangled, painted whores, known by reputation in every port of the seven seas, like the Duchess, and Submarine Mary, who had a mouthful of solid gold teeth.

Capone's schooling began not far from the Sands Street stews at P.S. 7 on Adams Street. His teacher, a sixteen-year-old girl named Sadie Mulvaney, had received her pedagogic training from Catholic nuns, but despite her youth and unworldliness, she managed to enforce order among some of the borough's toughest delinquents. One of them was Salvatore Lucania, better known in later life as Lucky Luciano. He and Al took to each other, and they remained lifelong friends. Miss Mulvaney would remember Al as "a swarthy, sullen, troublesome boy," though no more troublesome than many of her other pupils. He was big and strong for his age, quick to anger, and then murderous. In winter his nose tended to run, a weakness for which his schoolmates, at risk of severe injury, ridiculed him. The fight-loving Irish boys called him Macaroni.

After school hours he liked to loiter on the docks, gazing at such nautical wonders as the Navy's 100-ton floating crane. He never wearied of watching the change of U.S. Marine guards behind the main Navy Yard gate. Many of them were raw recruits still needing elementary drill, and before they could fall out when relieved, they had to mark time in drill formation. If a recruit was out of step, the commanding corporal would keep the entire detail marking time until the blunderer caught on. One afternoon Al, who was then about ten, but looked fourteen, arrived at the gate with several companions. Having observed the routine for weeks, he understood the corporal's strategy. On this occasion there was an exceptionally obtuse guardsman. The detail had been marking time for three or four minutes, and still no light dawned. At length Al yelled at him: "Hey, you long-legged number three there! Get in step! You're holding 'em up." The recruit changed step, and the detail was dismissed. Crimson with shame and anger, the recruit ran up to the gate, making as if to spit at the boy through the bars. Al flew into a rage and, though the recruit was twice as big, challenged him to a fight. The corporal intervened, ordering the recruit back to the guardhouse. "You got his goat for sure," he told Al. "But if he really spits on you, I'll put him on report."

"Don't do any reporting," said Al. "Just let the big so-and-so step outside the gate. I'll take care of him." And fists clenched, eyes blazing, he swaggered up and down before his awed companions.

Not long after, discussing the cocky little Italian with the sergeant of the guards, the corporal remarked: "If this kid had a good Marine officer to get hold of him and steer him right, he'd make a good man for the Marines. But if nothing like this will happen, the kid may drift for a few years until some wise guy picks him up and steers him around and then he'll be heard from one day." *

The prophecy came true sooner than the corporal imagined. Capone fell under the influence of a Navy Street Neapolitan gangster seventeen years his senior. John Torrio, born in Naples in 1882, was already an underworld figure of some note. "Terrible John," his followers called him, but more commonly "Little John." He stood no higher than Capone's chest, a pallid, round-faced, button-eyed man, with small, delicate hands and feet. But his size and surface mildness were as deceptive as those of a slumbering pit viper. He had belonged to Manhattan's historic Five Pointers for seven years until that gang of eye-gouging, skull-bashing desperadoes began to vanish into prisons or the grave. He then formed an affiliated gang with headquarters nearby in a saloon he ran on James Street. Torrio was a calm, reflective man. While he had no moral compunctions about murder and would unhesitatingly order the execution of an adversary, he himself shrank from physical violence. He claimed that he had never fired a gun in his life. He had practical objections to violence. He considered it a poor solution to problems of business rivalry. He preferred diplomacy, palaver, alliances. There was, he felt, enough profits in racketeering for all to share peaceably without risking injury or death. In this he anticipated the more sophisticated outlook of the midcentury racket chieftains. Torrio, in his heyday, was the nearest equivalent to a true mastermind criminal outside the pages of detective fiction, and he enormously influenced the policies and tactics of his younger friend and protégé. "I looked on Johnny like my adviser and father," said Capone in middle age, "and the party who made it possible for me to get my start."

In 1907 the Capones moved to another Italian community about a mile south of Navy Street. They squeezed themselves, eight of them, into a flat on the second story of a two-story cold-water tenement at 38 Garfield Place. The oldest son, James, had meanwhile vanished at the age of sixteen, and many years would pass before his family learned what had happened to him.

Torrio became a figure as familiar to Capone in the new neighborhood as he had in the old, for on the corner of Fourth Avenue and Union Street, above a restaurant within sight of Garfield Place, he

---

* The corporal recounted the episode in a letter to the Brooklyn *Eagle*, September 27, 1947.

started a "social club" with the name in gilt letters on the windows: THE JOHN TORRIO ASSOCIATION. Capone passed it every day going to and from school.

He entered the second grade at P.S. 113 on Butler Street, a six-block walk from his home. Up to the sixth grade he maintained a B average. He then fell behind in arithmetic and grammar, mainly because of truancy, and he had to repeat the grade. That year, his fourteenth, his attendance dropped to thirty-three days out of a possible ninety. When a teacher reproved him, his volcanic temper erupted, and he struck her. Thrashed by the principal, he quit school, never to return. He worked sporadically first as a clerk in a candy store at 305 Fifth Avenue, next as a pinball setter in a bowling alley, then as a paper and cloth cutter in a bindery. There was a poolroom at 20 Garfield Place where Capone father and son both played and Al became the neighborhood champion.

He could not roam very far from home without crossing territory overrun by bellicose, adolescent street gangs. Any stranger was apt to arouse their hostility, a reaction that reflected the prejudices of their elders. The easterly stretch of Flushing Avenue, near Capone's former home, was unhealthy for Neapolitans, being a Sicilian stronghold. Vicious knife fighters, the Sicilian gangs had adapted to Brooklyn street combat the ancient island practice of disfiguring an enemy, particularly an informer. They would slit his face from eye to ear. This "rat" work became so widely recognized as a Sicilian practice that non-Sicilian gangs took to imitating it after felling their prey in order to divert suspicion from themselves. Not that the other Italian gangs were benign. They, too, fought with knives to maim and sometimes to kill.

Northwest, up to the Navy Yard wall, the Irish predominated. To them, especially those who worked on the docks where their leaders strove to monopolize the labor market, the hungry "greasers" were cheap competition, threatening their livelihoods. The preferred weapons of the Irish gangs were fists, bricks and stones, hauled to the field of battle in onion sacks. For shields they used covers filched from garbage cans.

The Jews, occupying territory northeast, in the Williamsburg section, despised the Italian for what they considered his excessive individualism and lack of social consciousness, which left him indifferent to group efforts toward the general betterment. The Jewish gangs, however, showed less belligerence than most. Dread exceptions were the Havemeyer Streeters, who waged implacable warfare against all Gentile gangs. They repeatedly smashed the windows of the Williamsburg Mission for Jews because it sought to convert Jews to Christianity.

Street gangs proliferated in every slum of every city, and the greater the foreign influx, the more numerous the gangs. They were a symptom of the disorganization that afflicted so many uprooted families. In the small towns and rural villages from which the majority came society was stable, changeless, stratified, its traditions and code of conduct long fixed and unchallenged. Whatever problem might confront the head of the family, there were time-hallowed precedents to guide him. But in the maelstrom of the vast, ever-expanding American metropolis, with its continual swift changes, its ebb and flow of polyglot masses, its ethnic collisions, the old, familiar standards were unavailing. The baffled parents were hard put to comprehend their children's needs, let alone to respond to them, and as a result they lost authority. They could no longer command their children's unquestioning obedience, no longer control them. The breach widened as the children learned the language and the strange, new American ways, while the parents stubbornly clung to their Old World values.

The daily abrasions of tenement life further eroded family unity. What boy would want to linger an instant longer than necessary where eight, ten, twelve people ate and slept, washed and dressed in two or three dank, dingy rooms, where the fetor of excrement from rotten drains filled the hallways and vermin feasted on the garbage dumped out of windows, where you either froze or sweltered, where the grown-ups, in their distress and bewilderment, constantly screamed at one another and at you and whipped you for the least offense?

The street gang was escape. The street gang was freedom. The street gang offered outlets for stifled young energies. The agencies that might have kept boys off the street, the schools and churches, lacked the means to do so. Few slum schools had a gym or playground or any kind of after-class recreation program. The average teacher was badly trained, unimaginative and chronically irritable, and the curriculum deadly dull. Still less were the churches equipped to provide activities that might have competed with the lure of the streets, and religion as taught in the slum parishes failed to reach the young.

They formed their own street society, independent of the adult world and antagonistic to it. Led by some older, forceful boy, they pursued the thrills of shared adventure, of horseplay, exploration, gambling, pilfering, vandalism, sneaking a smoke or snuff or alcohol, secret ritual, smut sessions, fighting rival gangs. In his classic study of 1,313 Chicago boys' gangs, Frederic Thrasher quoted a member of the Bimbooms as follows:

"When I first moved into the neighborhood I met two brothers who took me one night with the rest of the gang—about thirteen boys eleven to twenty-two years old. We stayed out till nine, pitching pennies on the corner. They showed me their hang-out up in a barn, where there was an electric light, and we began to stay out till two or three every morning.

"We used to bring up pop and candy to eat, and play cards. It was a big room, with furniture and everything. The people had stored an old dining-room set, a library table, a kitchen table, and an army bed up there. It was not really a club, just a hang-out. Some of the big fellows got to bossing it, and we called them the 'Bimbooms.' Then they called the whole gang the 'Bimbooms.'

"We loved baseball and sometimes we would all play hooky from school to go to a game. When we had our own team, we called it the 'Congress Athletic Club.'

"On the corner, we would pitch pennies and then it got to be quarters. We played Rummie and Seven-and-a-half for money. I wanted to learn how to play Stud-poker, but no one would teach me. Oftentimes we shot dice for pocket-trash. Sometimes when we were hollering and playing games, the flying-squad would chase us away. The horse-cop would run us like anything, but we were too fast for him. Then he'd throw his club and we'd throw it back again at his horse's feet to make him prance. We'd call him 'Old Mickey Cop.'

"In the wintertime, we'd hitch boards to street cars, and it was a lot of fun to see the fellows hit a switch and get spilled off. I never liked to go to Union Park with the family, but to go with the gang on the 'L' platform and blow up pigeons through their beaks or smash stolen eggs in the kids' pockets.

"We used to keep pretty much to ourselves, and if another gang got fresh with us, a couple of guys would go down and get the Winchesters to come up and help us. One gang of fifteen or sixteen kids would try to run us off our corner just to be smart. They had a double-barreled shotgun which they would load with rock salt. And when it hit you, would it hurt! You tell 'em, boy!

"We built a fort in a vacant lot on the corner to keep them from shooting us. Then they'd throw rocks and knock the boards off, so they could hit us. They would usually come around raiding about three times a week. We had beebee guns and a 22-rifle, in which we shot blanks to scare them, but we might have shot something else if we'd had it."

The supreme thrill—and an activity important to the cohesion of the gang—was fighting. The captains would stake out a block or two as their gang's domain and declare war on any other gang that attempted to set foot inside the boundaries. Or they would mount a raid against a rival gang's territory.

"Jimmie, the leader of the gang, is a bad actor. He would kill a policeman, if necessary, to get away. Most of the bunch are getting rounded up now, on account of their robbing expeditions. The greatest spirit of the gang is fighting and Jimmie would lead the boys to battle on the least pretext.

"One fourth of July the bunch had a big fight with Danny O'Hara's gang. We had about two hundred on our side, and there were about as many there for Danny. Danny got hard with Jimmie and told him that he was trying to start a fight or something. First Jimmy busted Danny in the nose and then the whole gang started fighting. We had the traffic blocked on the boulevard for a long time, and finally the patrol wagon came, but they did not get any of the gang.

"We had wars with lots of other gangs. We fought the Deadshots and there were about a hundred in the fight. Jimmie got bounced on, and when he saw our enemies were too big for us, he beat it.

"We fought the Jews from Twelfth Street, but they had too many for us. They're pretty good fighters. We knew they had more than we did, so we went down with clubs and everything.

"Another time we went to Garfield Park to lick the Thistles. We had only about seventy-five guys. They had said they could lick Jimmie and the rest of the gang and right away he wanted to go down there and fight them, but he got beat up as usual. There were too many of them for us, and half of them were about twenty years old.

"We also had a war, starting over a baseball game at the park, with the Coons from Lake Street."

Not all gangs were as belligerent as the Bimbooms. Not all were criminal. Some developed into social or athletic clubs, approved and aided by the adults of the community. For many boy gangs, however, it was a short step from random mischief to professional criminality. Practically every racketeer, Capone included, spent his formative years on the prowl with a gang.

Nearly always the delinquent gang enjoyed the protection of some ward boss, for its members need not have reached voting age to render valuable services during elections, to intimidate, slug, kidnap, steal ballots, recruit repeaters. The bosses spared no effort to secure such allies. They would lease a clubhouse for them, buy them sporting equipment and uniforms, give them beefsteak dinners, picnics, tickets to prizefights and ball games. If arrested, a gang member could count on the ward boss to furnish bail and a lawyer; if convicted, to get his sentence reduced or quashed.

The gang Capone joined during his mid-teens, as did Lucky Luciano, was the Five Pointers, into which Torrio may have introduced them both. It was based on the Lower East Side of Manhattan. Its name derived from an intersection at the heart of the "Bloody Ould Sixth Ward" between Broadway and the Bowery, a warren of decaying tenements, gin mills and dance halls built on swampy land that emitted foul gases. Though the section had undergone some physical improvements, it was almost as noisome, its moral climate as debased, as when Charles Dickens, in his *American Notes,* three-quarters of a century earlier, described "these narrow ways . . . reeking everywhere with dirt and filth . . . hideous tenements which take their names from robbery and murder; all that is loathsome, drooping and decayed. . . ."

For nearly a century the Five Points spawned the most feral gangs ever to terrorize the city. Following the Forty Thieves, the first gang from that district (*circa* 1825), came the Shirt Tails, so dubbed because they wore their shirttails outside their trousers; the Plug Uglies, mammoth Irishmen who protected their heads during combat under leather-reinforced plug hats, felled their victims with bludgeons, and stamped them to death with hobnailed boots; the Dead Rabbits ("rabbit," in the slang of the day, meaning ruffian; "dead rabbit" a super-tough brawny ruffian), whose standard-bearers led them into the fray behind a dead rabbit stuck on a spear. After the Civil War there emerged the Whyos. Legend ascribes the origin of the name to a cry they uttered when fighting. Legend further holds that a qualification for membership in the Whyos was the commission of at least one murder. Filling contracts for murder and mayhem was the Whyos' main business, and to potential clients they presented a printed price list:

Punching	$ 2
Both eyes blacked	4
Nose and jaw broke	10
Jacked out [knocked out with a blackjack]	15
Ear chawed off	15
Leg or arm broke	19
Shot in leg	25
Stab	25
Doing the big job	100

Every gang tolerated, when it did not actively recruit, a following of imitative juveniles. Thus, there were the Forty Little Thieves, the Little Dead Rabbits, the Little Whyos, and though some members were barely eight years old, they robbed, slugged, and occasionally killed with as much exuberance as their seniors.

The word "racket" in its criminal sense probably comes from a device adopted by the old New York gangs. It was common practice for social and political clubs of the era to sponsor benefit galas in their own behalf. These were noisy affairs, what with the brass band and the general boisterousness stimulated by heavy drinking, so that they came to be known as rackets. Grasping the opportunity for easy and, to all outward appearance, licit profit, a gangster would organize a benevolent association of which he was the sole member, announce a racket, and with threats of demolishing their premises compel the neighborhood shopkeepers and businessmen to purchase blocks of tickets. James "Biff" Ellison, a Five Pointer dandy, who drenched himself with perfume, founded the Biff Ellison Association, and its rackets, held three times a year, netted him $3,000.

The Five Points gang, successor to the Whyos, reached its zenith at the turn of the century under the generalship of an ex-bantamweight prizefighter, Paul Kelly (real name: Paolo Antonini Vaccarelli). From his New Brighton Dance Hall in Great Jones Street, one of Manhattan's brassiest, wickedest fleshpots, he mapped the operations of some 1,500 Five Pointers and laid claim to all the territory bounded by the Bowery and Broadway, Fourteenth Street and City Hall. A quiet, urbane man, Kelly was better educated than any of his fellow gangsters. He spoke Italian, French and Spanish, dressed with impeccable taste, and generally exhibited the appearance and manners of polite society. No gang chieftain could long retain power unless he proved politically useful, and Tammany Hall was beholden to Kelly for the help his hearties frequently gave its candidates at the hustings.

By the time Capone joined the Five Pointers Kelly's prestige had somewhat deteriorated. Years of warfare with the apelike Monk Eastman's Bowery gang had strained his resources. Then his own henchman, the aromatic Biff Ellison, grew to resent his leadership. One winter night in 1905 Ellison and a member of the rival Gopher gang burst into the New Brighton, a gun blazing in each hand. A Five Pointer named Harrington went down with a bullet through his head. Kelly stopped three bullets. He survived, however, and after months of convalescence opened another dance hall, Little Naples. A reform group, the Committee of Fourteen, managed to have it padlocked. Kelly withdrew to Harlem, where he developed a new source of profit. He organized first the ragpickers, then the garbage scow trimmers into unions and served as their business agent. Eventually he became vice-president of the International Longshoremen's Association, AFL.

Kelly did not sever his connections with the Five Pointers, what was left of them. Though the membership had drastically dwindled, the remnants included a core of battle-seasoned roughnecks whose fealty a man with Kelly's business and political aspirations found worth preserving. On Seventh Avenue, close to the Broadway theater district, he set up new headquarters for them, naming it quaintly the New Englander Social and Dramatic Club. Seldom did a front so innocent mask exploits so nefarious. In vain the police, investigating an epidemic of knifings, bludgeonings and shootings, repeatedly raided the place. They discovered nothing more sinister than a few club members enjoying a game of cards or checkers. They arrested Capone three times during his salad days as a Five Pointer, once for disorderly conduct and twice on suspicion of homicide, but they could support none of these charges.

What enhanced the usefulness of some Five Pointer veterans in Kelly's estimation were their affiliations with other gangs and gang leaders. The Sicilian Frank Uale, alias Yale, of Brooklyn, for example, had the respect of John Torrio and his James Street boys; he knew Ciro Terranova intimately. At twenty-five Yale was making his mark in the Brooklyn rackets, and before long he would dominate them. His basic specialty was murder contracts, and he made no bones about it. "I'm an undertaker," he said. But he believed in diversification. He owned a dine-and-dance dive, the Harvard Inn, on the Coney Island waterfront, and a strategic location it turned out to be when, with Prohibition, he became one of the first New York racketeers to distribute liquor from coastal rum-running fleets. Yale also built up a stable of hooligans for hire in labor-management disputes. They were available to both sides as either strikebreakers or union goons. Inspired perhaps by Terranova's success with artichokes, Yale proceeded to force upon Brooklyn tobacconists cigars of his own crude manufacture. His portrait adorned each box—jet-black hair parted far on the left, stolid, squarish face above a stiff white collar and black necktie—together with the price, "20¢, 3 for 50¢." The price bore so little relation to the quality of the product that a "Frankie Yale" came to mean in the borough slang a cheap bad smoke. Racehorses, prizefighters, nightclubs, a funeral parlor—all fell within reach of Yale's grasp. But his single greatest source of profit and power was the Unione Siciliane.

Conflicting accounts by police, press and its own officers have obscured the nature of the Unione Siciliane, or Italo-American National Union, as it was renamed in the twenties. Some accounts describe it as a secret criminal society with close ties to the Mafia, founded and run from its inception by gangsters; others, as a much maligned fraternal association. The Unione Siciliane did indeed originate as a lawful fraternal association, one of the first to advance the interests of Sicilian immigrants. The place was New York; the time, the late nineteenth century. For modest dues its members received life insurance and various social benefits. Branches sprang up wherever there was a sizable Sicilian community. Gradually the association developed enough strength to swing an occasional district election. By the twenties the Chicago area, which contained the biggest chapter, had 38 lodges and more than 40,000 members.

Meanwhile, a cadre of New York hoodlums had begun to infiltrate and pervert the Unione Siciliane. Their leader, a kinsman by marriage of Ciro Terranova, was Ignazio Saietta, known as Lupo the Wolf, a pathological killer. Largely through Saietta's maneuvers, begun in New York and extended to branches in other cities, the association acquired a dual character: the one side open and respectable, doing good works among needy Sicilians; the other, hidden and malevolent, linked to the Mafia, dealing in white slavery, extortion, kidnaping, industrial and labor racketeering, bank robbery, murder. Invariably, the president was also a Mafioso. During a six-year period the U.S. Secret Service traced sixty murders to members of the Unione Siciliane. Saietta himself maintained a "murder stable" in Harlem with meathooks from which he hung his victims and a furnace in which to burn them alive. According to one of the few Unione members whom the police ever persuaded to talk, the neophyte had to submit to a blood ritual. Led to an altar where a stiletto lay, the point toward him, he would prick his finger on it and swear eternal fidelity and secrecy.

The more or less reputable officers of the Unione Siciliane, the businessmen, judges, state and city officials, professed to know nothing of how gangsters were exploiting it. They owed the association too great a debt to endanger it. The frequent fund-raising festivities, moreover, provided opportunities for politicians to meet and make deals with people in whose company they could not otherwise afford to be seen.

The change of name to the Italo-American National Union effected no change of character, and the police greeted with skepticism the disclaimers issued by executive officers like Constantino Vitello, vice-president of the mother chapter in Chicago. "Crime?" Vitello protested in 1927. "It is heart sickening to us who for the sake of our Italian brothers and our American future spend our time without any remuneration, day after day, and then are told by those who know nothing about us that we are breeders of crime and disorder in Chicago. . . . Our president is former Judge Bernard Barasa. Our officers are strong business and professional men. Our members are honest Americans. The constitution of the Unione, strictly enforced, declares that: No man who has a blot on his character may enter and those who are proved to have committed a felonious act while members will be expelled. . . ."

For nearly a decade the national head of the Unione Siciliane had been Frank Yale.

Yale hired Capone as a bouncer and bartender for his Harvard Inn, functions to which the younger Five Pointer brought excep-

tional endowments. When required to subdue obstreperous carous-
ers, his huge fists, unarmed or clutching a club, struck with the impact of a pile driver. He was also fast and accurate with a gun, having
perfected his marksmanship shooting at beer bottles in the basement of Brooklyn's ramshackle Adonis Social Club, a favorite Italian
hangout.

Capone did not emerge triumphant from every fracas that erupted
at the Harvard Inn. He suffered a notable defeat there one night
when Frank Galluccio, a Brooklynite and petty felon, dropped in
with his sister. Capone made an offensive remark to her. Galluccio
unclasped a pocket knife and went for the bartender's face. When
the wounds healed, there remained (in the words of the Capone dos-
sier compiled through the years by federal agents) an "oblique scar
of 4" across cheek 2" in front left ear—vertical scar $2\frac{1}{2}$" on left jaw—
oblique scar $2\frac{1}{2}$" under left ear on neck." Capone, normally vindictive, chose to forgive Galluccio. Some years after, in one of those mag-
nanimous gestures which, he had learned, could win him quick, easy
admiration, he hired him as a bodyguard at $100 a week. Accord-
ing to the story Capone later invented to explain his scars, he was
wounded by shrapnel fighting in France with the famous "Lost Bat-
talion" of the Seventy-seventh Division. But he got no closer to war
than his draft board and was never called upon to serve in any
capacity.

It was the style among the young bucks of Capone's milieu to start
a cellar club. This usually consisted of a rented storefront where,
behind drawn blinds, the members gambled, drank and entertained
girls. In 1918, during a party in a Carroll Street cellar club, Capone
met a tall, slim girl named Mae Coughlin. She was twenty-one, two
years older than Capone, and worked as a sales clerk in a neighborhood department store. Her parents, Michael Coughlin, a construction laborer, and Bridget Gorman Coughlin of 117 Third Place,
were respected in the Irish community for their industry, rectitude,
and religious devotion.

Despite the antagonisms that persisted between the Irish and the
Italians, many Irish girls showed a distinct preference for Italian boys
because the latter did not shrink from early marriage, whereas the
Irish boys tended to wait until they felt settled and secure in their
occupation. Johnny Torrio married an Irish girl from Kentucky,
Ann McCarthy. Capone was so eager to marry Mae Coughlin that

he obtained a special dispensation from the church, eliminating the necessity to publish banns. Presumably the difference in ages embarrassed the bride; on the certificate of marriage registration she lowered her age by one year and Capone raised his by one. The ceremony was performed on December 18, 1918, by the Reverend James J. Delaney, pastor of St. Mary Star of the Sea Church, where the Coughlins worshiped. The bride's sister Anna and a friend of Capone's, James De Vico, acted as witnesses. The following year Mae Capone bore her first and only child, Albert Francis, nicknamed Sonny. Torrio was the godfather, and on each of Sonny's birthdays he bought him a $5,000 bond. "I'd go the limit for Johnny," Capone said in later years.

Torrio had been spending more and more time in Chicago ever since 1909, when his uncle, James "Big Jim" Colosimo, first fetched him there, and though he continued to pursue various joint ventures in New York with Paul Kelly, Frank Yale and others, Chicago was now his base. Capone's fortunes, meanwhile, had not progressed. The money he craved to pamper his wife and son eluded him. Already suspected of two murders, he faced indictment for a third, if a man he had sent to the hospital after a barroom brawl should die. The man lived, but this Capone did not wait around to learn. A message came from Torrio, summoning him to Chicago. He needed no urging. With his wife and son he fled New York.

3

Big Jim

THE capstone of his career was Colosimo's Café. Opened in 1910 at 2126 South Wabash Avenue and remodeled four years later, it had become the *ne plus ultra* of Chicago night life. No other pleasure palace in the city could compete with the talent of its star entertainers, the beauty of its chorus girls or the virtuosity of its orchestra, which alternated "jass," or "jaz" (as they spelled it then), with operatic medleys. Nor could any Chicago restaurant boast a more accomplished chef than Colosimo's Antonio Caesarino or a wider choice of vintage wines. Ben Hecht, at the time a columnist on the Chicago *Daily News,* marveled at the quantity and diversity of Big Jim's collection of imported cheeses.

For the bon ton from the North Side "Gold Coast" who patronized the cabaret its location added piquancy to the trip downtown. They had to venture deep into the wicked Levee. Bounded north and south by Twenty-second and Eighteenth streets and east and west by Clark and Wabash, the Levee had one of the world's heaviest concentrations of crime and vice. Colosimo's place was all gaudy opulence from its gilded portals to its immense mahogany and glass bar. Green velvet covered the walls. Gold and crystal chandeliers hung from a sky-blue ceiling where rosy, dimpled seraphim gamboled on cotton-candy clouds. Wherever the eye fell, it was dazzled by gold-framed mirrors, murals depicting tropical vistas, tapestries. At the flick of a switch hydraulic lifts raised or lowered the dance floor on which bobbed-haired women with calf-length skirts and their tuxedoed escorts performed whatever gyrations the current fad dictated—one-step, two-step, Boston, turkey trot, fox trot, grizzly bear, bunny hug, Castle walk—to the beat of "Tiger Rag," "Ja-da," "Pretty Baby," "Dardanella," "Oh! How She Could Yacki, Hacki, Wicki, Wacki, Woo." The festivities, which seldom got up full steam before midnight, sometimes went on past dawn. In a suite of rooms on the second floor gamblers could find any game they fancied from faro to chuck-a-luck at any stakes they cared to hazard.

Colosimo's Café enjoyed national renown, and the nightly throng was a miscellany of sporting figures, big businessmen, collegians, gangsters, journalists, politicians, the rich, the chic, the famous and infamous, the tourists. At Big Jim's insistence the tables were wedged close together to promote an atmosphere of warmth and intimacy. Thus, a Potter Palmer or a Marshall Field might find himself rubbing elbows with such underworld celebrities as Mike Merlo, the Sicilian boss, head of the local Unione Siciliane; Mont Tennes, the racetrack gambling czar, whose complete life history, if known, would (according to the Illinois Crime Survey) "disclose practically all there is to know about syndicated gambling as a phase of organized crime in Chicago in the last quarter century"; the gambler Julius "Lovin' Putty" Annixter; "Mike de Pike" Heitler, merchant of vice, who looked like a Surinam toad, and his wizened confederate, "Monkey Face" Charlie Genker; Dennis "the Duke" Cooney, suave whoremaster whose notorious Rex Hotel was a favorite playground of gangdom; Joey D'Andrea, president of the Sewer Diggers and Tunnel Miners' Union, who was believed to have introduced to Chicago labor racketeering the peonage system of exploiting immigrant Italian workers; the labor thug "Izzy the Rat" Buchalsky; the Black Hander Vincenzo "Sunny Jim" Cosmano; Dion O'Banion, jack-of-all-crimes and chieftain of Chicago's most redoubtable strong-arm gang. . . . There were the political sachems, notably the two First Ward Democratic aldermen to whose protection Big Jim owed his rise, Michael Kenna, nicknamed Hinky Dink because of his puny size, and John Joseph "Bathhouse John" Coughlin, a chesty six-footer with a handlebar mustache, who once worked as a rubber in a Turkish bath. Between them they ruled the Levee, exacting a percentage of the profits from every illegal enterprise that flourished there. . . . Few headliners who played Chicago failed to put in an appearance at Colosimo's Café after the show. The celebrities in the late-supper crowd might include Al Jolson, George M. Cohan, John Barrymore, Sophie Tucker, whose "coon-shouter" song with gestures, "Angle Worm Wriggle," had caused the normally permissive Chicago police to arrest her. . . . Big Jim loved opera, and no matter how packed the place was, he would always find a table for the resident or guest artists of the Chicago Civic Opera Company—Mary Garden, Luisa Tetrazzini, Amelita Galli-Curci, Titta Ruffo, John McCormack, the conductor, Maestro Cleofonte Campanini. He counted Caruso among his personal friends.

Not the least distinctive feature of Colosimo's Café was Colosimo himself. He had a verve, a bluff, zesty Southern Italian humor. A big, fleshy man, he would move with ursine tread from table to table, gesticulating grandly, charming the women and amusing the men, ordering champagne and cigars on the house. He was the glass of Levee fashion. His pomaded black brush of a mustache and luxuriant black hair gleamed like onyx. His winter wardrobe ran to two-button sack suits with flaring lapels, white shirts embroidered with blue elephants or horses and striped knit neckties. His season of fullest sartorial flower was summer, when he appeared swan white in immaculate linens. He had a diamond fetish. By comparison the personal ornamentation of other gangsters was lackluster. Not only did Big Jim festoon his bulky person with the precious stones, wearing them on several fingers, on his belt, suspender and garter buckles, his tiepin, watch fob, shirt bosom, cuffs and vest, to which he fastened a sunburst the size and shape of a horseshoe, but he also carried about with him chamois bags full of unset diamonds. In idle moments he would empty the bags onto a square of black felt, count his treasures, toy with them, rake them up into little heaps.

Profitable though Colosimo's Café was, it produced but a fraction of the fortune that enabled Big Jim to maintain two limousines, each driven by its own uniformed chauffeur, a sumptuous house for his father and another for himself, crammed with chinoiserie, bronze and marble statuary, deep rugs, yard upon yard of unopened books bound in full morocco, rare coins, a wife and a mistress. Gamblers sometimes called him Bank because he would advance losers a fresh stake from a billfold bulging with $1,000-dollar notes. The chief sources of his annual income, which averaged about $600,000, were white slavery and a chain of brothels.

On the lowest stratum of Levee life, at the corner of Nineteenth Street and Armour Avenue, sprawled Bed Bug Row, a malodorous cluster of twenty-five-cent cribs inhabited by Negro whores. It faced the Bucket of Blood, a combination saloon and whorehouse. Only slightly higher up the scale, on Dearborn Street, stood the California, run by "Blubber Bob" Gray, who weighed 300 pounds, and his wife, Therese. The tariff here was $1, and the inmates, wearing transparent shifts, flaunted their charms at the windows. The customers made their choices sitting on wooden benches in the otherwise barren reception room while the girls sashayed up and down before them and Madame Therese screamed at them: "Pick a baby, boys! Don't get stuck to your seats." Black May's, between Dearborn and Armour avenues, also offered Negro women, but only to white clients, and it staged "circuses" renowned for their depravity. Opposite Black May's was a Japanese and a Chinese bagnio and a few doors south, the House of All Nations which, like the famous Paris lupanar of the same name, claimed it could provide girls from every country in the world. The stretch between Twenty-first and Twenty-second streets enclosed some of the better-class brothels: French Emma's, featuring mirrored bedrooms, Georgie Spencer's, Ed Weiss', the Casino, the Utopia, the Sappho, and the most luxurious, stylish, profitable and celebrated bawdy house in the country, if not the world—the Everleigh Club.

Few successes in the annals of whoredom compare with the achievement of the two handsome, queenly sisters from Kentucky, Ada and Minna Everleigh. With no previous experience in the field, their private lives having been above reproach, they opened their first bordello in Omaha when Ada was twenty-two and Minna twenty. A lawyer's daughters, they had been genteelly reared and educated at a private Southern school, had married brothers who maltreated them, and had run away with a barnstorming theatrical troupe which brought them to Omaha shortly before the 1898 Trans-Mississippi Exposition. Having inherited $35,000, they decided to invest it in an enterprise likely to attract the males who visited the exposition, and close by they opened their first brothel. With their substantial profits they then moved to Chicago, where they bought and redecorated the late Lizzie Allen's bordello at 2131–3 South Dearborn, a three-story mansion of fifty rooms.

From the day the Everleigh Club admitted its first customers, Feb-

ruary 1, 1900, to its closing eleven years later, it was the wonder of
the Levee. In addition to the purchase price of $50,000, the sisters
spent almost $200,000 on new furnishings. Twin entrances opened
into hallways massed with exotic shrubbery and marble Greek dei-
ties. Greeted by Minna or Ada, gowned and jeweled like empresses,
one mounted mahogany stairs to a maze of public rooms with par-
quets of rare woods, brocaded draperies, damask-upholstered divans,
pianos, one of which, fashioned of solid gold, cost $15,000. Food pre-
pared by a *cordon bleu* chef and wine at $12 a bottle were served, ac-
cording to the client's whim, in the walnut-paneled dining room
whose mahogany refectory table could seat fifty, in a private parlor
or in a bedroom. The cutlery was gold and silver, the dishes gold-
rimmed china, the glassware crystal, the tablecloths and napkins of
handwoven linen. Each private parlor embodied a different decora-
tive theme. There was the Copper Room, its walls paneled in beaten
copper, the Moorish and Turkish rooms, where one reclined against
hassocks and silken bolsters, the Chinese, Egyptian, and Japanese
rooms, heady with incense. . . . Each of the parlors had a gold spit-
toon and a fountain that sprayed perfume.

No lineup of wriggling seminaked girls marred the refinement of
the Everleigh Club. Handpicked by the sisters (without the inter-
mediate agency of any pimps, whom they scorned) for their beauty,
good health, freedom from addiction to drugs or alcohol, taste in
clothes, ladylike manners and sexual artistry, the Everleigh Paphians
sauntered casually through the parlors with the aplomb of a guest at
a Gold Coast soiree. When a gentleman expressed his preference,
one of the sisters would introduce him, observing all the amenities
prescribed by etiquette.

Such pleasures were not cheaply procured, and only the rich could
afford to spend many evenings at the Everleigh Club. A meal with
wine began at $50, and the cost rose according to the rarity of the
dishes ordered. The price of a girl ranged from $10 to $50, depending
on the length of time and the nature of the favors her companion
demanded. For a circus the price was determined by the number of
performers and the degree of lasciviousness—$25 to $50 a spectator
with a minimum of five spectators.

No Levee brothel could survive without tribute to the Dink and
the Bath. To refuse to buy protection was to invite police raids and
a listing on the police register of known vice resorts. In eleven years

the Everleigh sisters, whose gross nightly profit averaged between $2,000 and $2,500, enriched the aldermen by about $100,000.

During the first decade of the century the number of Chicago brothels reached a total, estimated by the Chicago Vice Commission, of 1,020, employing about 5,000 madams, servants and prostitutes, most of them situated within the Levee. The commission put the gross revenue in 1910 at $60,000,000 and the net at more than $15,-000,000. These figures did not include the myriad independent call girls and streetwalkers working out of hotel rooms or rented flats—again, mainly in the Levee. Their earnings probably exceeded $10,-000,000 a year.

In addition to the harlots, the Levee crawled with homosexual hustlers, pimps, procuresses, white slavers, dope peddlers, thieves, killers for hire. Hundreds of the pimps banded together as the Cadets' Protective Association, while the madams formed their own cartel, the Friendly Friends, which raised a slush fund for police payoffs. There were peep shows catering to adolescents, agencies that supplied performers for stag parties, burlesque houses like Harry Thurston's Palace of Illusion with its chorus line of Negro girls performing obscene dances, "stockades," where white slaves were held captive, "broken in"—that is, raped—and sold into prostitution. In one stockade, run by a young Negress, the specialty was teaching novices a repertory of sexual tricks.

Such was the environment in which James, son of Luigi Colosimo, grew to manhood. Papa Luigi, a native of Cosenza, in Calabria, thrice married, with two other sons and two daughters, came to the Levee in 1895, when Jim was seventeen. He brought with him an heirloom, an ancient sword whose continued possession—as Big Jim liked to tell the story—guaranteed that some Colosimo someday would attain great power. Big Jim professed to believe himself to be the elected one, and after he did attain power, he hung the talisman on the walls of his office at the rear of Colosimo's Café. There he also kept a Bible upon which he swore his lieutenants to fealty.

In his boyhood Big Jim constantly shifted back and forth between crime and spasms of honest toil, the latter probably brought on by the chastening effect of police pursuit. He had many narrow escapes. He started as a newsboy and bootblack. He also stole. He hauled drinking water for a railroad section gang laying tracks through the First Ward and developed a deft touch as a pickpocket. At eighteen,

muscular, dashing, radiating animal magnetism, he became a pimp
and acquired a stable of diligent girls. Then, reduced to poverty and
penitence after a brush with the law, he went to work as a street
sweeper. Promoted to foreman, he organized his fellow sweepers into
a social and athletic club. Like every denizen of the Levee, Big Jim
recognized the sovereignty of Aldermen Coughlin and Kenna, and
he set out to ingratiate himself with them by delivering the club
votes to their political machine. In return they made him a precinct
captain, an office that conferred virtual immunity from arrest. It
was the first of numerous *quid pro quos*. Under the aldermen's patronage Big Jim rose to poolroom manager, saloonkeeper and—the
juiciest plum—one of their brothel bagmen. In the last capacity he
established his effectiveness once for all when he called on Georgie
Spencer to notify him that the cost of protection was about to go up.
Georgie balked and in the ensuing argument reached for a knife.
Slipping on brass knuckles, Big Jim battered him to a jelly, lifted
$300 from his billfold, the assessment due, and left him at death's
door. Collections flowed smoothly thereafter. During a vice investigation ten years later Minna Everleigh identified Big Jim as the
agent through whom she had paid Coughlin and Kenna $100,000.

In 1902, while fulfilling his bagman's duties, Big Jim made the acquaintance of Victoria Moresco, a fat, homely, middle-aged bawd
who operated a second-rate brothel on Armour Avenue. She was
devastated by his dark Latin virility. She offered him the post of manager, which he eagerly accepted. Two weeks later they were married.
Under Colosimo's management and the benevolence of his aldermanic
protectors, the brothel prospered. In his bride's honor he named it
the Victoria. Presently he acquired a brothel of his own, then another, and before long he owned or controlled scores, most of them
$1 and $2 cribs, though the Victoria and later the Saratoga came to
rank among the Levee's fancier vice resorts. Out of every $2 his girls
earned Colosimo kept $1.20. Like most of his colleagues, he also ran
a number of saloons near, or connected by, passageways to his bordellos.

The supply of prostitutes never quite met the demand. The turn-
over was too rapid. The average parlor house whore seldom lasted
more than five years. Aging fast, she would sink to cheaper and
cheaper houses until she hit bottom on Bed Bug Row or took to the
streets. Drink, drugs or disease usually completed her destruction.

To replenish their "stock," the whoremasters resorted to white slavery.

The origin of the term "white slave" is sometimes associated with Mary Hastings, a Chicago madam of the nineties who prowled through the Midwest seeking seducible young girls. She preferred those between the ages of thirteen and seventeen. By promising them a job in Chicago, she gulled many of them into returning with her. Once inside her three-story brothel on Custom House Place, they were stripped, locked in a top-floor room, and abandoned to professional rapists. The broken-in girls whom Mary Hastings did not employ herself she sold to other brothelkeepers at prices ranging from $50 to $300, depending on their age and looks. One victim managed to scrawl on a scrap of paper, "I'm being held as a slave," and tossed it out of her prison window. Found by a passerby and taken to the police, who raided the brothel and rescued the prisoner, the note supposedly inspired a newspaper reporter to coin the term "white slave." (The raid evidently caused Mary Hastings no serious damage since she continued to do business at the same address for several more years until four captives escaped and brought about her downfall.)

The countrywide scope of white slavery was never statistically determined. Without arriving at any national figures, the Chicago Vice Commission did uncover evidence indicating that while no well-organized syndicate existed, there were numerous small, loosely affiliated gangs of white slavers. The interstate traffic was heavy enough to warrant federal action. In 1910 Congress passed the White Slave, or Mann, Act, making it punishable by five years' prison to transport a woman across state lines for immoral purposes. This legislation, together with state antivice laws, crippled but did not end the traffic for a good many years. Between 1910 and 1914 the Vice Commission documented seventy-seven local cases, of which the following typified the *modi operandi* of the more brutal white slavers:

> *Case 5a.* M.B., 18 . . . came to Chicago from a small Wisconsin town, April 1911. M.B. claimed she came to stay with her aunt, held a position in general housework and sewing for two months, met F. at a saloon, took her to J.'s place (a resort) , F. promised to marry her, stayed with him there that night, next morning J. (the woman keeper) told the girl she could make $65 per week and she could have half of what she made, girl refused . . . social worker

takes girl back to her aunt's, 3 days later met F. again and took girl back to J.'s place where she practiced prostitution for 5 months, girl was whipped with rawhide by J.'s husband, J. took all money girl earned, an opium joint in the place. . . .

Case 39. . . . born in Hungary, came to the United States in 1908, married in New York City 5 months after arrival, lived with him 6 months, left him because he turned out to be a drunkard and because he beat her, came to Chicago, worked as a waitress in northside restaurant, met G (Bohemian evidently) at her rooming house in the Bohemian area, he was 50 years of age and a cripple, he sent a woman to see her, H. got on friendly terms with girl, taken by H. to South Chicago vice district on promise of better work, this was a ruse evidently and the better work was at a resort, forced to stay with men, prevented from leaving. . . .

In his recollections of the early Chicago gangsters, *The Dry and Lawless Years,* Municipal Court Judge John H. Lyle described a case in which he intervened when he was a young alderman.

One evening a youth living in my ward came to see me for help. His 16-year-old sister had been missing for weeks. She had sent a letter, postmarked St. Louis, stating that she was happy in a new job. The brother was sure something was wrong. His anguish stirred my sympathy.

I hired a detective who found the girl in a bawdyhouse. He brought her back to Chicago. Her wretched condition supported her story. This beautiful high school student had gone into the Levee seeking a real estate office where she was to make a payment on the family home.

She asked a man for directions. He persuaded her to enter a restaurant. A knock-out drop was slipped into her coffee. She was taken to a resort where the man seduced her and then sold her to the keeper for $200. Repeated use of drugs clouded her mind. She was used as a prostitute for several days and then resold for $400 to a bagnio in St. Louis.

One of the Levee's leading panders was Maurice Van Bever, a preening dandy who rode around in a carriage driven by a top-hatted coachman. With his wife, Julia, he ran two whorehouses on Armour Avenue. In 1903 Van Bever and Colosimo combined forces. They organized a gang to handle fresh stock, established connections with white slavers in New York, St. Louis and Milwaukee, and during the next six years imported hundreds of girls, either booking them into their own establishments or selling them to their fellow whore-masters.

It was inevitable that an Italo-American as conspicuously *nouveau riche* as Colosimo would attract the attention of Black Handers.

The Black Hand was not, as some writers have misrepresented it to be, a nationwide criminal conspiracy. Contrary to what its victims, too, imagined, it was not synonymous with the Mafia, the Camorra, the Unione Siciliane or any other secret society. It was simply a crude method of extortion with a long Italian—chiefly Sicilian—tradition, transplanted to America during the mass migrations of the eighties. The majority of its early practitioners in America were Italians with criminal records in their native land who had joined the movement westward to victimize their compatriots. Individually or in small community gangs of five to ten members, long experienced in the use of the Black Hand, they preyed mainly on the *cafoni,* the igno-rant Southern Italian peasants. About the only thing they had in common with the Mafia was their technique of terrorism, but they fostered the delusion that Black Hand and Mafia were identical be-cause of the fear the latter had always aroused among Italians, a fear so ingrained that few victims dared even breathe the word.

In the Little Italy of America to display any sign of affluence, such as expensive jewelry or an automobile, was to arouse the malign in-terest of the Black Hand. For that reason many Italo-Americans hesi-tated to buy property and if they did, few banks would mortgage it. Having selected his victim, the Black Hander would send him an anonymous letter, demanding money, signed *La Mano Nera* and usu-ally garnished with sinister symbols—daggers, skull and crossbones, a hand imprinted in black ink. The letters were sometimes blunt, sometimes couched in the flowery idiom of old-world courtesy.

Mrs. Joseph Lupo, for example, a resident of Chicago's North Side Little Italy and a real estate investor, bought a small apartment build-ing for $25,000. At the same time her daughter also bought one nearby. Six weeks later Mrs. Lupo received the following note:

> Place $4000 in a red handkerchief and put it with $4000 from your daughter. Place it at the west end of the Chicago avenue bridge at midnight Thursday. We have looked at your new build-ing on Park Avenue and have found a nice spot where a bomb could do a great amount of damage if you don't obey. Don't notify your son-in-law, Marino Modeni.

Ignoring the warning, Mrs. Lupo appealed to Marino, who, though terrified, went to the police. Two plainclothesmen kept watch by the bridge all through the appointed night, but the Black Handers never showed up.

In the courtly epistolary vein, another Chicago Black Hander wrote to a Sicilian named Silvani:

> MOST GENTLE MR. SILVANI—
>
> Hoping that the present will not impress you too much, you will be so good as to send me $2000 if your life is dear to you. So I beg you warmly to put them on the door within four days. But if not, I swear this week's time not even the dust of your family will exist. With regards, believe me to be your friend.

Silvani, too, mustered the courage to go to the police. They traced the letter to one Joseph Genite, raided his home on South Racine Avenue, in Little Italy, and uncovered a cache of revolvers, shotguns, and dynamite. Despite the evidence, they failed to establish Genite's guilt.

No accurate tally of Chicago's Black Hand crimes was possible. The police found it convenient to ascribe every unsolved crime involving Italians to Black Handers. Still, the frequently quoted figure of 400 Italians killed by bullets, knives, bludgeons or bombs between 1895 and 1925 was probably not excessive. How many people survived injuries inflicted by Black Handers during the three decades of their greatest activity and how many quietly yielded to threats were incalculable. On May 25, 1913, the Chicago *Daily News* speculated:

> In the first ninety-three days of this year, 55 bombs were detonated in the spaghetti zone. Not one of the 55, so far as can be determined, was set for any reason other than the extraction of blackmail. A detective of experience in the Italian quarter estimates that ten pay tribute to one who is sturdy enough to resist until he is warned by a bomb. Freely conceding that this is all guess work, then 550 men will have paid the Mano Nera since January 1. The Dirty Mitt never asks for less than $1,000. If a compromise of $200 was reached in each of the 550 cases, "Black Handers" profited by $110,000 in 93 days. That's an average of $1,111 a day, which is fair profit for the expenditure of five two-cent stamps, a dollar's worth of gunpowder and 15 quarts of wood alcohol chianti, that being the usual ration. Perhaps these figures are inaccurate in detail, but they are conservative enough en masse. Well informed Italians have never put the year's tribute to the "Black Hand" at less than half a million dollars.

When a Black Hander was arrested, mutism afflicted the neighborhood. Family, friends, and witnesses would receive letters promising swift and terrible retribution should they break their silence. If the case got as far as the courtroom, threats deluged the district attorney, judge, and jury. On June 22, 1909, Joseph Bertucci stood trial for a Black Hand killing. Bruno Nordi, who had been indicted as an accomplice, turned state's evidence, and his wife also agreed to testify. As Nordi mounted the witness stand, a man slipped into the courtroom, waved a red handkerchief and vanished. After that nothing could prevail upon either Nordi or his wife to utter a word. The case was dismissed.

On January 8, 1910, a sixty-year-old Italian named Beneditto Cinene, living at 500 Oak Street, was shot to death in bed. To every question put by the police sergeant from the Chicago Avenue Station the murdered man's relatives all replied with the same three words: "Me don't know." His son-in-law simply shrugged.

The hostility of native Americans to immigrants was, in the case of the Italians, intensified by the depredations of Black Handers. Demagogues and irresponsible journalists revived all the old nonsense about instinctive Italian criminality. In *McClure's Magazine* for May, 1912, Arthur Train, a former New York City assistant district attorney, contributed his bias after a six-month tour of Italy. "The Italians from the extreme south," he declared, ". . . are apt to be ignorant, lazy, destitute, and superstitious. . . . The number of South Italians who now occupy positions of respectability in New York and who have criminal records on the other side would astound even their compatriots. . . ."

The truth was that in Chicago, as in New York, the Italians—the majority of Neapolitan, Calabrian, or Sicilian origin—had a percentage of arrests and convictions far lower than their ratio of the population. In 1913 the Italians totaled approximately 59,000. That year 2,972 were arrested for misdemeanors and 1,333 convicted; 392 were arrested for felonies and 108 convicted. The combined convictions represented slightly more than one-tenth of 1 percent of the Italian proportion of the population, which was, as the City Council Committee on Crime observed, "surely so small as to be negligible."

In 1907 the worthies of Chicago's Italian colony organized, under the leadership of the Italian consul, Guido Sabetta, the White Hand Society, with the double object of stamping out Black Hand crime and counteracting the slander against their people. They set an example which was followed by Italian community leaders in other cities. Hiring attorneys and private investigators to assist the authorities, the society brought about the conviction of several Black Handers and drove from the city what it claimed to be the 10 most dangerous. But after this impressive start it met frustration at every turn. In 1910 the Black Handers killed 25 people; in 1911, 40; in 1912, 31. Though the police arrested many suspects—194 following the shooting of one supposed informer—bribery and terrorism continued, and they solved not a single murder. The few imprisoned culprits whom the White Hand had brought to justice were, one after the other, paroled, their co-conspirators having provided the money with which to suborn officials. The society's members began dropping away, unwilling to sacrifice further sums for futile prosecutions. At the same time rank-and-file Italians had come to feel that by publicly acknowledging the existence of crime in their midst the White Hand was bringing opprobrium upon the whole community, and they, too, withdrew their support. As for the native Americans, they had never given the society any support, for they considered the Black Hand atrocities no concern of theirs as long as they were confined to Italians. By 1913 the White Hand had disbanded and the Black Handers extended their reign of terror.

What finally stopped the flow of extortion letters in the twenties was what reduced white slavery: federal intervention. For using the mails to defraud, the federal law set penalties of up to five years' prison and $1,000 fine. The game seemed too hazardous after several Black Handers drew the maximum sentence and were removed beyond reach of corrupt local officials to Leavenworth Penitentiary.

Extortion, however, far from languishing, expanded in new directions. Threats were conveyed by other means. The dread letter signed *La Mano Nera* was replaced by a voice on the telephone or a personal visit. The character of the victim changed, too. The supply of simpleminded, malleable *cafoni* began to dwindle after 1914, when new regulations restricted immigration. By then far richer opportunities were beckoning to the professional extortionists in the city which Lincoln Steffens described as "first in violence, deepest in dirt, loud, lawless, unlovely, ill-smelling, irreverent, new, an overgrown gawk of a village, the 'tough' among cities, a spectacle for the nation." The skill developed in three decades of bomb throwing and marksmanship with revolver and shotgun was not wasted. Many an ex-

Black Hander became a prized technician in the swelling ranks of gangdom.

Bombing as a business thrived. Contractors in the field were retained by labor and business racketeers to discipline tradesmen who declined to pay tribute. During the twenties some 700 bombs destroyed millions of dollars' worth of Chicago property. The contractors established a price list:

> Black powder bombs—$100
> Dynamite bombs—$500 to $1,000 (depending on the risk)
> Guaranteed contracts—$1,000 and up

Joseph Sangerman, an officer of the Chicago Barbers' Union, directed one of the busiest bombing crews. His ace was George Matrisciano, alias Martini, a Neapolitan barber's son and a veteran of Little Italy terrorism, who manufactured his own black powder bombs. When a barbershop owner defied the union's dictates, Matrisciano and his four teammates would reduce the shop to rubble.

Colosimo knew what to expect. In his youth he had turned a Black Hand trick or two himself. At first he submitted. He met demands for as much as $5,000. But as the extortionists kept after him, raising the amount each time, he prepared to fight. He commanded plenty of muscle in such subalterns, who had sworn on his Bible to defend him, as his brother-in-law, Joe Moresco; Mac Fitzpatrick, alias W. E. Frazier, a gunman from San Francisco; Billy Leathers; "Chicken Harry" Gullet; Joe "Jew Kid" Grabiner. At the next attempted levy Colosimo wrapped up a bundle of blank paper, armed himself with a revolver, and, accompanied by a brace of his gorillas, concealing sawed-off shotguns, set out for the rendezvous under a South Side bridge well in advance of the appointed hour. After depositing the bundle as instructed, they fell back into the shadows across the street. At midnight three men approached the bundle. They had scant opportunity to verify its contents. The hidden foe opened fire, killing them all.

Colosimo enjoyed tranquillity for a while. Then he heard from still another Black Hand gang. He decided he needed an adjutant wilier than any available to him in Chicago. He thought of his sharp-witted, ruthless little nephew.

4

" . . . the best and dearest
of husbands"

TORRIO was thirty-one when he came to Chicago in
1909. Not long after, three more of Colosimo's tormentors were ambushed under the Rock Island Railroad overpass on Archer Avenue
and shot to death. Torrio, with his aversion to bloodshed, had taken
no direct hand in the massacre. He had only arranged it. He arranged other killings in behalf of his beleaguered uncle. The time
for treaties and coalitions was not yet.

The lesson was lost on Sunny Jim Cosmano. He thought he could
extract $10,000 from Big Jim. The misjudgment cost him a nearly
mortal stomach wound inflicted by buckshot at close range. Two
policemen stood guard by his hospital bed, waiting to remove him for
questioning to headquarters as soon as he recovered, a trip Cosmano
contemplated with no relish. His confederates, wondering how they
could spare him the ordeal, consulted "Big Tim" Murphy, one of the
few important Irish racket bosses whom the Italian underworld es-
teemed. Big Tim's advice was succinct: "Knock the cops on the head
and carry him out." Four of Sunny Jim's friends paid him a visit,
bearing flowers and candy. They also carried guns. They disarmed the
policemen. They roped them together back to back, helped the patient dress, and smuggled him out of the hospital to a hideaway, where
he convalesced, untroubled by interrogators.

Torrio's mother, Maria Caputa, was living with him in Chicago,
and when Big Jim bought the restaurant that became famous as

Colosimo's Café, she lent her name to the deeds. For a time Mama Maria and Papa Luigi Colosimo ran the place. Torrio had a small interest in it, which he sold to Mary Aducci, the wife of a Colosimo lieutenant. She remained Big Jim's partner for many years. He later took in a third partner, "Mike the Greek" Potzin, a gambler and whoremaster.

Torrio's services to Colosimo went far beyond planning the liquidation of Black Handers. He was an organizational genius. Years later Elmer L. Irey, chief of the Enforcement Branch of the U.S. Treasury, called him "the father of modern American gangsterdom." With the cool, soft-spoken little New Yorker as his gray eminence, Big Jim consolidated his holdings to become the foremost Chicago racketeer of his era. Starting with the Saratoga, of which his grateful uncle had made him the manager, Torrio was soon supervising all the Colosimo brothels, and he put them on a sounder business footing. He next reorganized the adjunctive saloons and gambling dives. Under his guidance the Colosimo-Van Bever white slave ring captured the Levee market. Torrio saw personally to the greasing of police and political palms. When Colosimo branched out into the protection racket, Torrio collected the dues, using no persuasion other than a quiet word of warning, a thin smile, and an icy stare. He suffered a slight setback when he was arrested along with several members of the white slave ring, following the transportation of a dozen girls from St. Louis to Chicago. Maurice Van Bever and his wife, Julia, paid a $1,000 fine and went to jail for a year. Five others received lesser sentences, among them the prosecution's star witness, Joe Bovo, the pimp who had delivered the St. Louis cargo. But the court freed Torrio because Bovo would not testify against him. It was Torrio's first court appearance. Colosimo, shielded by Coughlin and Kenna, was not even questioned.

The year Torrio came to Chicago the armies of reform were beginning to gather strength. Crisis after crisis shook the Levee, toppling some of its vice lords, but Torrio steered his uncle safely through all of them. On the night of October 18, 1909, the English evangelist Gipsy Smith, accompanied by three Salvation Army bands, led 2,000 faithful to the red-light district. By the time they got to Twenty-second Street 20,000 curious Chicagoans were marching with them. As the harlots and their madams looked on in stunned disbelief from behind closed shutters, the bands struck up and the congregation joined Smith in the hymn "Where He Leads Me I Will Follow." Marching back and forth through the Levee, they knelt before the most notorious brothels like the Everleigh Club and Colosimo's Victoria, recited the Lord's Prayer and sang "Where Is My Wandering Boy Tonight?" Smith climaxed the invasion with a prayer for all of the Levee's fallen women.

One immediate result was not what the evangelist intended. Many of the youths in the great throng, who might never have set foot inside "this hellhole of sin" had not Gipsy Smith led them there, remained to taste the forbidden fruits. The district had never been livelier. "We are glad of the business, of course," said Minna Everleigh, wickedly, "but I am sorry to see so many nice young men coming down here for the first time."

The long-range repercussions, however, advanced the cause of rectitude. The evangelist had focused the attention of powerful church and civic groups on the extent of prostitution and white slavery in Chicago. Two months after Smith's march the Federated Protestant Churches, representing 600 parishes, passed a resolution demanding the appointment of an investigative Vice Commission. The Republican mayor, Fred A. Busse, an obese barroom brawler and crony of racketeers, found it expedient to comply. The commission's blunt 400-page report, published the following year, enumerating the city's brothels and estimating their enormous profits, jolted the normally apathetic citizenry. The newspapers joined in the clamor for reform.

Busse, meanwhile, had been succeeded by a cultivated, debonair Democrat, Carter H. Harrison, Jr. Like most of Chicago's officials, whether corrupt or honest, like Busse before him, Mayor Harrison believed that a red-light district, tolerated though not legalized, offered the best chance of containing and controlling prostitution. Abolition, they argued, would not eliminate the evil; it would only disperse it. But to appease the reformers, Harrison ordered the police to clean out the flats and houses of assignation along South Michigan Avenue skirting the Levee. Inside the Levee the only major casualties were the Everleigh sisters, who had been brash enough to distribute a glossy illustrated brochure advertising their establishment ("Steam heat throughout, with electric fans in summer, one never feels the winter's chill or summer's heat in this luxurious resort. Fortunate indeed, with all the comforts of life surrounding them, are the members of the Everleigh Club . . ."). Incensed, Mayor Harrison determined upon the immediate extinction of the bagnio. The sisters quit Chicago and the brothel business forever, settling eventually on New York's Central Park West, where they lived in affluence and dignity to an old age.

The reform movement in Chicago coincided with a sweeping governmental investigation of white slavery throughout the country. In New York a girl who had traveled the Colosimo-Van Bever circuit defied threats of death and publicly exposed the system. Pending indictments against the white slavers, she was whisked away for safekeeping to a hideout in Bridgeport, Connecticut. There, according to neighborhood witnesses, two men called for her in a car, showing Department of Justice credentials and saying they required an affidavit from her. The next morning her body, torn by a dozen slugs, was found sprawled across a grave in a cemetery outside Bridgeport. From the neighbors' descriptions the investigators identified the two callers as members of Torrio's old James Street gang, but they could prove nothing. The case against Colosimo collapsed. Upon this happy denouement Big Jim handed Torrio a percentage of all his brothel and gambling interests.

After routing the Everleigh sisters, the Chicago police relapsed into inertia. Torrio, however, harbored no false optimism. He convinced Colosimo that the days of the Levee as a center of unbridled crime and vice were numbered and that they should plan for the future. What prompted their first major step was the new mobility of the American pleasure seeker. In six years, from 1908 to 1913, the registration of motor vehicles in the United States increased tenfold to a total of 1,192,262, and they were used a great deal more for pleasure than for business. One by-product was the roadhouse. It occurred to Torrio that the hinterland, with its meager police force, offered scope for the expansion of the vice industry. Colosimo agreed. All they needed was the compliance of rural officials.

They established their first suburban foothold in tiny Burnham, 18 miles from the Levee, on the Illinois-Indiana border. The president of the incorporated village, or "boy mayor," as everybody referred to him because he had taken office before the age of twenty, having run a Burnham saloon since his fourteenth year, was John Patton. He proved a willing pawn so that by the time a second reform wave smote the Levee Torrio and Colosimo were ready to launch their first country brothel.

In October, 1912, under the renewed pressure of church and civic groups, the hitherto laissez-faire state's attorney, John E. W. Wayman, mounted a massive attack against the Levee. After the first day of arrests and padlockings, the principal brothelkeepers organized their own committee, with Colosimo as chairman. A meeting at Big Jim's café was followed by a phenomenon that momentarily paralyzed the hand of reform. Obeying their masters' instructions, the Levee girls donned their gaudiest finery and scattered through Chicago's respectable residential districts. Hips swaying, raucous as macaws, they preempted tables in the most sedate restaurants, tried to book rooms in the most elegant hotels, rang private doorbells and begged for lodging. . . . Even the Vice Commission had to concede that sudden mass eviction from the Levee might be a mistake, and the raids were suspended.

The reformers were not so easily put off. They persisted until, in November, 1912, Chicago became the first American city to close its red-light district. But just as the advocates of toleration had forewarned, the measure did not thwart the vice magnates. New resorts sprang up elsewhere in the city and the suburbs. (The Vice Commission survey twenty years later showed that 731 Chicago brothels were still in operation, only about 300 fewer than in 1912.) Nor did the Levee red-light district stay closed. Although it never quite recovered its pristine blatancy, many of the brothelkeepers either reopened their original premises as soon as the raids slackened or camouflaged them as hotels, saloons, and cabarets.

Colosimo's first Burnham roadhouse kept open twenty-four hours a day with ninety girls working in three shifts. It earned $9,000 a month, of which Torrio took half. They next acquired the Speedway Inn, putting Jew Kid Grabiner in charge, then the Burnham Inn, which Torrio supervised. None of these roadhouses stood more than a few feet from the Indiana line so that in the event of a raid the girls and their guests could avoid arrest by scurrying across it. Warnings came through a network of gas station attendants, short-order cooks, roadside fruit sellers and the like, posted along the approaches to Burnham. When danger threatened, they would press a buzzer connected by electric wiring to an alarm in the roadhouse. The customers, mostly laborers in the area's steel mills and oil refineries, tended to be uncouth types, destructive as rampaging rhinoceroses when drunk, and it was common practice to nail down the chairs and tables lest they brain one another with them.

Other vice entrepreneurs set up shop under the protective wing of the boy mayor until Burnham, which measured barely one mile square, was a citadel of boozing, gambling and whoring. Nobody did business there for long, however, without Torrio's consent. When a pot-valiant hoodlum known as "Dandy Joe" Fogarty, who resented the Italian's supremacy, staggered out to the middle of the Burnham Inn dance floor one night and shouted loud enough to be heard above the jazz band: "I'll get that wop!" bullets silenced him. Two Torrio lieutenants, "Sonny" Dunn and Tommy Enright, were detained by the local constabulary, but only for an hour or two.

The affairs of Colosimo and Torrio were not progressing quite as smoothly in the Levee. One police inspector had been sentenced to the Joliet Penitentiary, two others suspended, and a superintendent of police dismissed for graft. Mayor Harrison had then appointed a retired Army officer, Major Metellus L. C. Funkhouser, to the newly created post of Second Deputy Police Commissioner, with the power to investigate and prosecute vice offenders independently of the regular police. Funkhouser established a Morals Squad and chose as its director Inspector W. C. Dannenberg, whose past feats included the jailing of Maurice and Julia Van Bever.

Deeply disturbed by these appointments, the Levee vice bosses convened again under Colosimo's chairmanship. They agreed that the Morals Squad must be stopped if not with money, then with murder. Chicken Harry Gullet was delegated to offer Dannenberg $2,200 a month to protect the brothels. The inspector arrested him for attempted bribery. During the following weeks his Morals Squad arrested about 2,000 panders and their women, and he brought charges of graft against the regular police assigned to the Levee. The latter, captained by one Michael F. Ryan, circulated Dannenberg's photograph among the brothelkeepers so that they could spot him during raids. Colosimo and his colleagues voted to kill Funkhouser, Dannenberg, and various members of the Morals Squad. At about this time Torrio sent for Roxie Vanilli, his cousin and a veteran of New York's Gyp the Blood gang.

Among those attending the whoremasters' conclave had been Roy Jones, who ran a saloon at 2037 South Wabash Avenue. On an April night in 1914 a man named Isaac Henagow, whom the Levee suspected of being a Morals Squad stool pigeon, dropped in for a drink. Shortly, Jim Franche, popularly known as Duffy the Goat, a Colosimo minion, walked up to him with a drawn revolver, shot him through the heart, and bolted.

Mayor Harrison revoked Jones' license. When the Levee politicians failed to get it restored, the saloonkeeper concluded that he had been double-crossed. Embittered, he took to drink and in his cups would prattle about the plot to decimate the Morals Squad. Colosimo offered him $15,000 to leave the country. Jones refused. Colosimo tried to frame him on a white slavery charge. Jones finally fled to Detroit. By that time his drunken revelations had reached Inspector Dannenberg's ears.

Later in April, a police sergeant from the Morals Squad was knifed to death while investigating Henagow's murder. Then, on July 16 Dannenberg led a raid against the Turf, a brothel at 28 West Twenty-second Street. When he and his men left the scene, after packing the girls into a patrol wagon, they found themselves surrounded by a mob of howling hoodlums. They started to walk toward Michigan Avenue. The mob followed, throwing stones at them. Behind the mob rolled a big red automobile, and inside sat Torrio, flanked by Roxie Vanilli and Mac Fitzpatrick. As the mob grew more menacing, the raiders halted and drew their guns, all but Dannenberg, who went on to the station house to book the prostitutes. At that moment two sergeants from the regular police, Stanley J. Birns and John C. Sloop, came around the corner of Michigan and Twenty-second. Mistaking Dannenberg's men for thugs, they, too, whipped out their revolvers. The red car braked, and its passengers got out. Who fired first and at whom was never established. But when the combatants ceased fire, Birns lay dead, and three of Dannenberg's men were bleeding from multiple wounds. The red car was gone. A third officer from the Twenty-second Street Station, Sergeant Edward P. O'Grady, arriving after the shooting, ran into Torrio and Fitzpatrick as they were helping Vanilli, who had also been wounded, climb back into the car. They disclaimed any knowledge of the skirmish, and he let them drive away. Other witnesses, however, reported that they had seen shots fired from the red car. An autopsy performed on Birns seemed to confirm this. The bullets extracted from his body were dumdums, a type commonly used by gangsters, whereas the regulation police issue were .38-caliber bullets. In all probability Birns had been accidentally killed by dumdums intended for Dannenberg. Commenting editorially, the Chicago *Tribune* explained:

There are three reasons why the tragedy of the levee could not have been avoided. First, is Alderman "Hinky Dink" Kenna. . . . The levee exists because it is by the denizens of the levee that he rolls up the voting power which causes such men as Carter Harrison and Roger Sullivan [state Democratic boss] to consult him as a political peer, and County Judge Owens to have him as a trimmer.

Second, is "Bath-house" John Coughlin. . . .

Third, is Captain Michael Ryan of the Twenty-second Street Police Station. He is the Chief of Police of the First Ward. The "Hink" put him there. The "Hink" and the "Bath" keep him there. He has been denounced as either notoriously corrupt or incompetent. But Funkhouser, Dannenberg, Gleason [the Chicago chief of police] and Hoyne, himself [the new state's attorney], cannot budge Ryan from that station. They have all tried and failed.

When State's Attorney Wyman closed the levee, there was one set of dividing lines he could not touch. They were the lines marking out the police district. They are there now. Captain Ryan's instructions to his subordinates are their only instructions—they are the instructions carried out. Chief Gleason and First Deputy Schuettler may send the Funkhouser squads and the Dannenberg squads to make raids, but they cannot force Ryan to make raids. And no matter how many raids they make and how they show Ryan up, he is still on the job, in complete control of his precinct lines.

In other cities the one "ring" has been found to be a clique of gambling kings who ruled the situation; in Chicago the "ring" is extended to the formation of a complete wheel.

Ryan is the hub. His plainclothes policemen, his confidential men, are the spokes, and sections of the rim are the "Big Four" or the "Big Five" as conditions happen to be at the time, the dive owners and keepers controlling strings of saloons and resorts that travel along without interruption.

But more important than any or all of these parts—the one thing without which the wheel could not revolve—is the axle, and this axle is the "little fellow" to every denizen of the district, or "Hinky Dink." Men in uniform in Ryan's district are told to keep their eyes straight, ignoring what is going on behind doors and windows, and watching only for disturbances in the street. They are told to do police duty as if the social evil did not exist around them.

For the first and last time in his life Colosimo was jailed. He spent half a day in a police station lockup before the Magistrates' Court accepted bail. The police also arrested Van Bever, Joe Moresco, and Vanilli, among others, and the court released them the same day. No indictments followed. Faced with the usual wall of silence, the state's attorney dropped all but one of the cases for lack of evidence. The single exception was Duffy the Goat. He actually stood trial for the murder of Isaac Henagow. The jury found him guilty, and the judge sentenced him to hang. He obtained a new trial because of some technical irregularities. This time the jury acquitted him on his plea of self-defense, despite the testimony of eyewitnesses that Henagow never raised a hand against him.

One of Mayor Harrison's last important official acts was to transfer Captain Ryan to a precinct remote from the Levee and replace him with Captain Max Nootbar, who proceeded to purge the Levee with such vigor that one veteran brothelkeeper declared: "I've seen reform come and reform go, but this is honestly the first time since the closing of the old Custom House Place and Federal Street tenderloin that it looked as if it might stick."

Harrison also withdrew the liquor license recently granted to Colosimo for his refurbished establishment on South Wabash Avenue. But the splendrous café did not long remain dark. The mayoral election of 1915 swept into office a Republican candidate in whom were conjoined about equal parts of ineptitude, buffoonery and rascality. William "Big Bill" Hale Thompson, Jr., was destined to become the hero of every pimp, whore, gambler, racketeer and bootlegger in Chicago.

In 1900 the nonpartisan Municipal Voters' League, an organization dedicated to the overthrow of predatory politicians, was seeking a nominee it could support for Second Ward alderman. One Republican citizens' group proposed Bill Thompson, a towering athlete with a snaggled front tooth who had brought glory to the Chicago Athletic Association in half a dozen different sports. By way of recommendation the chairman of the sponsoring group pointed out: "The worst you can say about Bill is that he's stupid."

Thompson, who was then thirty-five, harbored only the feeblest interest in government. He had agreed to run to win a $50 bet. Born in Boston and reared in Chicago, he came from a line of New England military and naval officers. His father amassed a fortune as a Chicago real estate dealer. He wanted the same kind of gentleman's education for his son that he himself had received back East, but mental effort pained Billy. The only reading he enjoyed were dime thrillers about the Wild West, and they filled him with longing for the life of a cowboy. He struck a bargain with his father: He would spend part of every winter at school in Chicago and the rest of the year on the Western range. He quickly adopted the idiom, manners and drinking habits of a frontiersman, and he never entirely discarded them. Between trips to Utah, Wyoming and Nebraska he attended a Chicago preparatory school, then a business college. His father's death in 1891 ended the *Wanderjahre*. He stayed home to keep an eye on the family real estate business. It was during his leisure hours—actually, most of the day—that he distinguished himself as an all-star athlete, the idol of Chicago youth.

As the Republicans' victorious "reform" alderman, Thompson was conspicuous by his absence. He had added sailing to his sporting skills, and he preferred racing a yacht on Lake Michigan to the tedium of aldermanic responsibilities. At what point political ambition seized him is not clear, but in 1902 he appeared on the Republican slate as a candidate for Cook County commissioner. He developed a natural gift for campaign tent oratory. He knew instinctively how to tickle the prejudices of ethnic and national groups. Though his bull-roaring platform speeches ranged in content from the banal to the inane, Chicago's Irish and Italian voters responded enthusiastically when he vilified the British, calling them "seedy and untrustworthy." He won the election.

His rise in the Republican ranks was slow but steady, with an occasional minor setback caused by the exposure of some peccadillo, as when the Amateur Athletic Union suspended him and other CAA football players for professionalism or when, testifying in a separation suit brought by a woman against a friend of his, he had to confess that he used to frequent the Levee dives. He was forty-eight, running to paunch and jowl, his voice whiskey-hoarse, when the party elders began to see mayoral timber in him. "He may not be too much on brains," said Congressman Fred Lundin, their shrewdest strategist, "but he gets through to people." Lundin had once roamed the city as a medicine man, peddling nostrums of his own brew. He sold Thompson to the voters and taught Thompson how to sell himself.

The Democratic opponent was a Catholic of German extraction, Robert M. Sweitzer.

Practically every plank in Big Bill's platform invalidated some other plank. It depended where he was campaigning. The war overseas had broken out four month before, and in German neighborhoods, the Chicago *American* reported, he sounded like "Kaiser Bill." In the German-hating Polish districts, meanwhile, his campaign workers were circulating handbills deriding "Sweitzer, the German candidate," and in the Protestant wards they warned that a vote for Sweitzer was a vote for the Pope. In the Irish wards Thompson lashed out at the English. Addressing native American audiences, he would wrap himself in the Stars and Stripes and invoke the spirit of George Washington.

He promised the reform groups strict enforcement of the anti-gambling laws, and he promised the gamblers a wide-open town. Speaking to the Negroes of the Second Ward: "If you want to shoot craps, go ahead and do it. When I'm mayor, the police will have something better to do than break up a friendly little crap game."

He further promised the Negroes: "I'll give you people jobs. . . . Only a good cowboy like Jess Willard [who had just defeated the Negro heavyweight champion, Jack Johnson, in Havana] could beat a good man like Johnson. Tomorrow the cowboy will be on your side."

To the wives and mothers of the silk-stocking wards: "I'll clean up this city and drive out the crooks! I'll make Chicago the cleanest city in the world! . . . I'll appoint a mother to the Board of Education! Who knows better than a mother what is good for children?"

He promised the drys he would uphold the state's blue law prohibiting the sale of liquor on Sunday. He promised the wets he would oppose all Sunday blue laws, and he wooed the saloon owners by signing a pledge to that effect. "I see no harm in a friendly little drink in a friendly little saloon," he said.

Big Bill Thompson won the 1915 mayoralty by the biggest plurality ever registered for a Republican in Chicago.

Within six months he had violated every campaign promise but one. He did keep Chicago wide open. After a flurry of token arrests in the Levee and elsewhere, a live-and-let-live policy prevailed anew. Slot machines manufactured by Chicago's Mills Novelty Company clicked and clattered away all over the city, with the bigwigs of City

Hall getting a cut of the profits. The Sportsmen's Club, a Republican organization, was used as a collection agency for the graft. Not only gamblers, but saloon- and brothelkeepers received solicitations for $100 "life memberships" on club letterheads bearing the mayor's name. The members included Thompson's chief of police, Charles C. Healey; Herbert S. Mills, president of the slot machine company; Mont Tennes, the gambling magnate; Jim Colosimo, whose liquor license the mayor restored.

In preference to the big, easily raided whorehouses the principal vice mongers now maintained numerous discreet "call flats." The whores would seek their customers in dance halls, also owned by the panders, and take them to the flats. In an exposé of the system Major Funkhouser put the total number of flats at 30,000. Thompson stripped him and his Morals Squad of all authority.

The first eight months of the Thompson regime produced twice as many criminal complaints as the entire preceding year. "The police department is just a big sewing circle," said Alderman Charles E. Merriam, a political science professor at the University of Chicago and the leader of a reform faction. Chief Healey, who had begun his tenure with a declaration of war against the underworld, ended it exposed as the boss of the city's biggest graft ring, an associatee of malefactors like Mike de Pike Heitler. In January, 1917, he was indicted for graft and bribery along with three other members of the department, four underworld magnates and an alderman. As its main exhibit at the trial, the prosecution introduced a notebook which had been found in the possession of a North Side police lieutenant. The first pages listed shady hotels and their weekly tributes of $40 to $150. Next came brothels, houses of assignation and gambling dives, some marked "the chief's places," indicating that all the payoff money went directly to Healey, others marked "three ways," which meant that Healey shared the loot with Police Captain Tom Costello, Heitler and one Billy Skidmore, a bondsman, gambler and saloonkeeper. A fourth list named the saloons the police allowed to operate illegally after 1 A.M. and on Sunday. A fifth list of gambling houses and disorderly hotels was headed "Can't be raided" and a sixth, "Can be raided."

Healey retained two of Chicago's most successful criminal lawyers, Clarence Darrow and Charles Erbstein, and they won an acquittal. The jury, in fact, acquitted all nine defendants.

"Chicago is unique," said Professor Merriam. "It is the only completely corrupt city in America."

The contrast between Torrio's professional and private life amazed the few associates familiar with both. Catering to the vices of others, he himself had none. By temperament ascetic, he never smoked, drank or gambled. He ate sparingly. He eschewed profane and obscene language and disliked hearing it. He took no interest in any woman but his wife, Ann. With his small, dark, watchful eyes and thin, compressed lips, he seemed perpetually to be deploring the sinful ways of man.

In his daily routine he observed a clocklike regularity. Early every morning, attired in a suit of sober hue and cut, wearing no jewelry save his wedding ring, he would tenderly embrace his wife and either walk the three blocks from their flat on Nineteenth Street and Archer Avenue to his office on South Wabash or drive to Burnham. Then, for the next nine or ten hours he would attend to the minutiae of the brothel business, routing the whores from house to house in order to ensure the regular customers a continual change of faces, cutting corners on the whorehouse food, drink and linens, calculating the previous night's profits. He ascribed no humanity to the girls he handled. He regarded them simply as commodities, to be bought, sold and replaced when worn out.

Barring some crisis, Torrio would return home at six and, except for an occasional play or concert, not leave it again until morning. His wife would bring him slippers and smoking jacket. After supper they would play pinochle or listen to the phonograph. Torrio loved music and knew a good deal about it. He could follow a score and hold his own in a discussion with professional musicians. "He is the best and dearest of husbands," said his wife. "My married life has been like one long, unclouded honeymoon. He has done everything to make me happy. He has given me his wholehearted devotion. I have had love, home and contentment."

Colosimo found Torrio exemplary as a business manager. Between his nephew's efficiency and the lenience of Mayor Thompson he had become top dog among Chicago vice kings. His political value extended far beyond the Levee. With his City Hall connections, he no longer depended on Aldermen Coughlin and Kenna for protection. The roles were reversed. They went to him.

Garfield Place, Brooklyn, where the Capone children grew up.

Johnny Torrio (right), at the age of twenty-nine, shortly after his Uncle Jim Colosimo brought him to Chicago. Big Jim's father sits between them.

In its heyday,
Chicago's plushiest
pleasure palace.
The second story
was given over to
gambling.

*Chicago Historical
Society.*

Colosimo took up
horseback riding to
please his adored
wife, Dale.

*United Press
International.*

Big Jim, shot down
by an unknown
assassin in the
vestibule of his
restaurant.

Above left:
Dion O'Banion, flower lover, wearing a sprig of lily of the valley in his buttonhole.

International News.

Above right:
George "Bugs" Moran, third in line of succession as leader of the O'Banionites.

Wide World Photos.

Right:
Leland Verain alias Three-Gun Louis Alterie.

Below left:
Vincent "Schemer" Drucci.

United Press International

Below right:
Hymie Weiss, who succeeded O'Banion as gang leader.

United Press International.

O'Banion's flower shop at 738 North State Street where he was killed. A crowd gathers outside after the killers fled.

The Terrible Gennas dine *en famille*. Left to right: Sam, Angelo, Peter, Tony, Jim.

The funeral of Angelo Genna.

The Capones' Chicago home, 7244 South Praire Avenue (center).

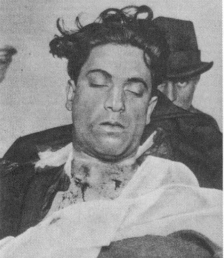

Brother Frank—killed in a gun battle with police when he and his fellow gangsters terrorized voters in the 1924 Cicero elections.

Frank Capone's funeral.

FAMILY ALBUM

Chicago Tribune.

Mama Teresa and Al.

Wide World Photos.

Mae Capone, despair of press photographers.

Left:
Brother Matt.

United Press International.

Right:
Brother John.

Wide World Photos.

Below left:
Brother Ralph.

Below center:
Brother James.

United Press International

Below right:
Brother Albert.

Frank "the Enforcer" Nitti, treasurer.

Machine Gun Jack McGurn, chief triggerman.

Murray "the Camel" Humphries, robbery expert.

William "Three-fingered" White, triggerman.

Charlie Fischetti, triggerman.

THE ORGANIZATION

Mike "de Pike" Heitler, whoremaster.

United Press International.
Al.

Frank Maritote, alias Diamond.

Chicago Sun-Times.

Accardo Giancova, bodyguard.

Johnny Torrio, president emeritus.

Sam Hunt.

Tony "Joe Batters" Accardo, triggerman.

Acme Photo.

Phil D'Andrea, chief bodyguard.

Jake "Greasy Thumb" Guzik, business manager.

United Press International.

Ralph Capone, sales manager.

Tony Lombardo, *consigliere*.

Chicago Tribune.

His pride and joy was his café, where he could truckle to celebrities and be flattered and fussed over by them. In his dedication to the resort he gave Torrio virtual autonomy in the management of everything else. This was his first grave mistake, for it emboldened Torrio to strike out on his own; it created a conflict of interest. The second mistake was a romantic one.

One evening in 1913 a Chicago *News* reporter, Jack Lait, came into Colosimo's Café lyrical over a girl he heard singing with the choir of the South Park Avenue Methodist Church. She had, he told Colosimo, beauty and talent, and she deserved a better opportunity to display them. Why didn't he put her in his floor show? Big Jim agreed to audition this paragon, and the next evening Lait introduced him to a demure, slender brunette with blue eyes and skin like white rose petals.

Dale Winter was nineteen, an Ohioan by birth, who dreamed of an operatic career. Her father died when she was five. After high school, where she shone in the glee club, her mother took her to New York. She auditioned for the producer George Lederer, who was casting a road company version of the operetta *Madame Sherry*, a smash hit, with its saucy song "Every Little Movement Has a Meaning All Its Own." He assigned Dale the ingenue role. Chaperoned, as always, by her mother, she traveled across country to San Francisco, where the tour ended. With another actress she then contrived a vaudeville sketch, sold it to a company about to take off for Australia, and went along to play the main part. In Australia the venture collapsed, stranding mother and daughter 6,000 miles from home. Borrowing money from a kindly actor, they got back to San Francisco. A booking agent sent them on to Chicago, where, he assured them, Dale would find work with a newly organized light opera company. They arrived penniless only to learn that the company had disbanded without giving a single performance. The South Park Avenue Methodist Church saved them from starvation by employing Dale as its soloist.

Big Jim found Dale Winter as delectable as Lait had pictured her, and he needed no persuasion to hire her. She became his star attraction, enchanting the customers every night with a repertoire of light operatic arias. She did not want to leave the church choir, however, and she continued to sing hymns by day until the congregation discovered her connection with Colosimo's Café. The churchgoers were scandalized. They demanded her immediate dismissal. The pastor was more tolerant. As the text for his next sermon he chose John 8:7: "He that is without sin among you, let him first cast a stone at her." But the congregation was unmoved. He had to let Dale go.

The Levee was hardly a congenial environment for such a girl, and she promised herself she would quit the moment she had saved enough money to return with her mother to New York. Grand opera was still her dream. As the star of Colosimo's floor show, she encountered no dearth of better job opportunities. The Broadway impresario Morris Gest offered her a contract. So did the mighty Florenz Ziegfeld. She turned them both down, for by then Colosimo had fallen in love with her and she with him. Big Jim left his wife, Victoria. "This is the real thing," he assured Torrio. "It's your funeral," said Torrio.

Under Dale's gentle prodding Big Jim acquired some slight polish. He learned to modulate his bull horn of a voice and to use politer language. He hired a tutor to teach him correct English. He dressed more conservatively, adorning himself with fewer diamonds. He neglected the politicians and underworld characters among his clientele in favor of the artists and the swells from uptown. Dale liked to ride horseback through the city parks, and Big Jim, attired in equestrian togs, would trot along beside her.

Her ambition became his. He badgered his friend Caruso for an opinion of her voice. The great tenor pronounced it pleasing and asked Maestro Campanini to grant her an audition. The conductor, too, liked her voice but felt it required retraining. At his suggestion Colosimo enrolled her in the Chicago Musical College.

The irony was that Dale Winter, the only decent girl with whom he had ever had a close relationship, should be an instrument of his destruction, for in the pecking order of the underworld such emotional vulnerability was an invitation to rebellion. The word went around: "Big Jim's getting soft. Big Jim's slipping." The extortionists resumed their demands, but he no longer fought them. He paid up, probably because they also threatened Dale, and they plagued him to his dying day.

Torrio, meantime, while continuing to administer his uncle's domain, slowly and quietly built his own organization. He prepared the ground for other outposts of vice besides Burnham. He found the officials of Stickney, a village eight miles west of the Levee, equally amenable. In the Levee itself, a block from Colosimo's Café, he took title to a four-story red brick building thereafter known as the Four Deuces because of the address—2222 South Wabash Avenue. On the first floor he installed a saloon and office, separated by a steel-barred gate. Solid steel doors led to gambling rooms on the second and third floors, and on the fourth floor he installed a brothel. It was at about this time, in late 1919, that Torrio sent for Al Capone.

Capone's initial duties were varied and humble—bodyguard, chauffeur, bartender, capper for the brothel. "I saw him there [in front of the Four Deuces] a dozen times," the journalist Courtney Ryley Cooper remembered, "coat collar turned up on winter nights, hands deep in his pockets as he fell in step with a passer-by and mumbled: 'Got some nice-looking girls inside.' "

The cellar had an unusual feature, whose purpose was revealed to Judge Lyle. "I got some first-hand information on the resort from Mike de Pike Heitler who bitterly resented the mob's invasion of his field," the judge wrote. "Shuffling into my chambers one afternoon, he told me: 'They snatch guys they want information from and take them to the cellar. They're tortured until they talk. Then they're rubbed out. The bodies are hauled through a tunnel into a trap door opening in the back of the building. Capone and his boys put the bodies in cars and then they're dumped out on a country road, or maybe in a clay hole or rock quarry.' "

Years later a retired police lieutenant, who had once patrolled the neighborhood, took Judge Lyle through the now-abandoned building. They came upon the tunnel and the trap door. The policeman said that at least twelve gangsters had been killed in the Four Deuces.

Soon after Al Capone, or Al Brown, to use his favorite alias, moved to Chicago, there occurred a momentous event. The foresighted Torrio had long been planning for it. He had been urging Colosimo to marshal all his resources to exploit it. The profits, Torrio was certain, would dwarf everything they had ever made from vice. But Big Jim, torpid with love, could muster no energy for new ventures. Whoremongering and gambling had brought him a fortune. They were still lucrative. Why risk the unknown? Besides, this crazy new situation couldn't last. Torrio knew then that his uncle's sun was setting.

5

No Christian Burial

THE National Prohibition Act, popularly known as the Volstead Act, after the tobacco-chewing Republican Representative from Minnesota who introduced it into the House, went into effect at 12:01 A.M. on January 17, 1920. Volstead was serene in his conviction that "law does regulate morality, has regulated morality since the Ten Commandments." The first recorded violation occurred at fifty-nine minutes past midnight in Chicago. A truck rolled into a railroad switching yard. Out leaped six masked men, brandishing revolvers. They bound and gagged a watchman, locked six engineers in a shed, and, breaking into two freight cars, removed $100,000 worth of whiskey stamped FOR MEDICINAL USE. At approximately the same hour another Chicago gang stole four barrels of alcohol from a warehouse, while a third gang hijacked a truck loaded with whiskey—the first known instance of what would become common gangster practice. Nobody was ever arrested for any of these forays.

Torrio surveyed the scene with impatience. No fairer prospect of profits had ever beckoned to him, yet he could not rouse Colosimo from his amorous torpor. Most of the saloons and roadhouses had stayed open in expectations of obtaining liquor somehow, and the risk of supplying it seemed trifling compared to the rewards. To cover the entire state, as well as Iowa and part of Wisconsin, the Prohibition Unit had assigned a measly force of 134 agents. As for the Chicago police, Torrio anticipated no more difficulty securing their protection for bootlegging than he had for whoremongering or gambling. (He was right. Charles C. Fitzmorris, Chicago's chief of police during the early Prohibition years, publicly admitted: "Sixty percent of my police are in the bootleg business.") Best of all, there was Big Bill Thompson, paladin of the wide-open policy. When he began his term, the city treasury had a $3,000,000 surplus. Four years later it had a deficit of $4,500,000. The crudity of Thompson's speech and behavior, his xenophobia and know-nothing isolationism, which he trumpeted throughout World War I, made him an international laughingstock. When Marshal Joffre, the hero of the Marne, and René Viviani, the French minister of justice, undertook a goodwill tour of America after it had entered the war, Mayor Thompson refused to invite them to Chicago. "Are these distinguished visitors coming here to encourage the doing of things to make our people suffer or have they some other purpose?" he asked. The shamefaced City Council issued its own invitation. But despite his gaucheries and misrule Big Bill retained the support of the most powerful political machine in Chicago's history and with it a fat campaign chest to which his thousands of civil service appointees were compelled to contribute. By a slim margin he managed to win a second term.

Altogether a situation fraught with promise, and Torrio was not the only one to appreciate it. Most gang leaders were going into bootlegging. Some had laid away stocks months before the Volstead Act became law. (The Dink and the Bath accumulated a million dollars' worth of bourbon and were offering it for sale at twice the original price.) Others had arranged for deliveries from moonshiners and smugglers. Torrio planned, characteristically, to obviate wasteful hostilities by working out among the gang chieftains a series of multilateral trade agreements guaranteeing to each unchallenged sovereignty in his own territory. Colosimo neither opposed nor actively supported the proposal. Content as long as he received his share of earnings from the enterprises Torrio was directing in his name, he left him free to act as he thought best. But what was needed to bring everybody into line was a reassertion of Big Jim's old forceful leadership, a recovery of his prestige. Passive acquiescence was dangerous. It could only encourage the jackals to turn on the lion and divide up his kingdom. But the lion would not stir. Plainly, the time had come for Torrio to assume authority in name, as well as in fact.

Big Jim, who had been living apart from Victoria Moresco for three years, offered her a settlement of $50,000 not to contest a divorce action. "I raised one husband for another woman," the fat and aging procuress said later, "and there's nothing to it." The decree became final on March 20, 1920. The grounds: desertion. Within three weeks Victoria had married a Sicilian hoodlum twenty years her junior named Antonio Villani, and Big Jim had married Dale. After a honeymoon in the fashionable Indiana spa of French Lick, Big Jim brought his bride back to his ornate mansion at 3156 Vernon Avenue and invited her mother to live there, too.

A week later, on Tuesday, May 11, Torrio telephoned to announce the delivery at the café of two truckloads of whiskey. He was very precise about the time—4 P.M. Big Jim left the house a few minutes before the hour, ablaze with diamonds, a red rose in his buttonhole, a homburg perched jauntily on his large head. In his right hip pocket he carried a .28-caliber pearl-handled revolver. His car, driven by a chauffeur named Woolfson, was standing at the curb. Dale asked him to send the car back so that she and her mother could go shopping. He promised to do so, kissed her good-bye, and climbed into the back seat. Woolfson recalled later that Big Jim kept muttering to himself in Italian all the way to the café.

There were two entrances on South Wabash Avenue about 50 feet apart. Woolfson deposited Big Jim at the arched north entrance and drove back to Vernon Avenue. Big Jim pushed open a glass-paneled door and crossed a small porcelain-tiled vestibule, passing a cloakroom, a phone booth and a cashier's cage, walked the length of the main dining room, went through an archway into a second dining room used for overflow crowds, and entered his office at the rear. Presently, a porter, coming up from the basement, noticed a stranger going into the vestibule. The porter returned to his duties below, where four other employees were working.

In the office, standing beneath the Colosimo family sword, Big Jim's secretary, Frank Camilla, and Chef Caesarino were discussing the day's menu. Big Jim asked them if anybody had called. Nobody had. This appeared to trouble him. He tried unsuccessfully to reach his lawyer, Rocco De Stefano, on the phone. After chatting a while with Camilla and Caesarino, he walked back toward the vestibule through the auxiliary dining room. They had the impression that he intended to wait for his caller there or on the sidewalk. They glanced at a wall clock—it showed 4:25—and resumed their discussion of the menu. A moment later they heard two sharp reports. Caesarino dismissed them as backfire, but Camilla decided to investigate. He found Big Jim lying facedown on the porcelain tiles of the vestibule, blood streaming from a bullet hole behind his right ear. A second bullet had cracked the cashier's window and buried itself in the plaster wall opposite. Big Jim was dead.

In response to Camilla's call, Chief of Police John J. Garrity arrived from headquarters with Chief of Detectives Mooney. The state's attorney sent several of the detectives attached to his office. When Camilla called Dale Colosimo, she fainted.

From the angle of fire the police deduced that the killer had waited for his victim in the cloakroom. On the phone booth shelf they found a note in Big Jim's handwriting.

> Swan [it said] I made out the statement. You fill in the rest as you see fit. Tell the man to look out after the drugstore and see that he finds out where to find the stuff for me. Don't keep over thirteen men. If you've got more, ask someone to lay off. Bank. P.S. Anything you make over $50 belongs to me.

When Big Jim wrote the note, how it came to be left in the phone booth, what it meant, who Swan was—the police never discovered.

They questioned more than thirty suspects, including Torrio and Capone, both of whom could prove that they were occupied elsewhere at the time of the shooting. Torrio's eyes filled with tears, an unheard-of display of emotion. "Big Jim and me were like brothers," he said. Had Joe Moresco pulled the trigger to avenge his scorned sister? He, too, furnished an unbreakable alibi. Victoria herself and her Sicilian husband were in Los Angeles when Big Jim died.

The state of the dead man's finances deepened the mystery. Rocco De Stefano had expected to find at least $500,000 in cash and diamonds. An exhaustive search turned up $67,500 in cash and bonds, $8,894 worthy of jewelry and 15 barrels of whiskey. According to a rumor nobody could confirm, Colosimo left his home on May 11 with $150,000 cash in his pockets, but they contained no such sum when the police reached the scene of his death. De Stefano ascribed the dwindling of his client's fortune to the tribute paid to extortionists. Several Black Handers fell under suspicion, particularly Sunny Jim Cosmano, but Sunny Jim happened to have spent May 11 in jail.

Yet there were developments that suggested the solution. Chance, underworld rumor and the testimony of the café porter produced them. Into a police dragnet the day of the murder blundered the veteran Five Pointer and executioner Frankie Yale. He had been in town a week and was about to board an eastbound train when the police stopped him. They could not connect him with the murder at that time, however, and they let him go on to New York. Then the porter came forward with a description of the stranger he saw entering the café on Colosimo's heels. It fitted Yale. Finally, a stool pigeon passed along the underworld rumor that Torrio had paid Yale $10,000 to rid him of Colosimo. At the request of the Chicago authorities the New York police picked up Yale, and the porter was brought to New York. Face-to-face with the killer, the witness froze. He swore he could not identify him. The investigation foundered there, but the police of both cities doubted neither Yale's guilt nor Torrio's.

Big Jim, first of Chicago's great gangster overlords to be slain, was buried on May 14. The lavishness of the floral tributes (with wreaths "from Johnny" and "from Al" among the showiest), the costly bronze casket, the size and the composition of the cortege set the style for gangster funerals. No rites were performed in a Catholic church or a Catholic cemetery, because Archbishop George Mundelein forbade them.

> His Eminence makes it plain to his pastors [so a diocesan spokesman later interpreted injunctions of this kind] that any gangster who, because of his conduct, is looked upon as a "public" sinner or who by his refusal to comply with the laws of his church regarding attendance at church services and Easter duty . . . such a man is to be refused Christian burial.
>
> Therefore, it cannot be assumed that the fact of one's being a gangster or bootlegger is alone the cause of his being refused Christian burial, for each individual case must be considered. . . .

The only offense specified in Big Jim's case was neither whoremongering nor murder, but divorcing his wife to marry Dale Winter.

In the end a Presbyterian minister, the Reverend Pasquale De Carol, was found to perform the funeral rites in the Vernon Avenue mansion. The Apollo Quartet sang the hymns. As they began "Nearer My God to Thee," Dale Winter Colosimo appeared, barely able to stand, supported by De Stefano and the Dink. Before the casket was closed, the Bath knelt beside it, recited Hail Marys and the Catholic prayer for the dead. Ike Bloom, who managed one of the Levee's most disreputable dance halls, delivered a eulogy. "There wasn't a piker's hair in Big Jim's head," he said, uttering the underworld's ultimate accolade. "Whatever game he played, he shot straight. He wasn't greedy. There could be dozens of others getting theirs. The more the merrier as far as he was concerned. He had what a lot of us haven't got—class. He brought the society swells and the millionaires into the red-light district. It helped everybody, and a lot of places kept alive on Colosimo's overflow. Big Jim never bilked a pal or turned down a good guy and he always kept his mouth shut."

Capone observed an ancient Italian mourning custom: During the three days between Big Jim's death and his burial he didn't shave.

A thousand First Ward Democrats preceded the cortege as it wound through the Levee on its way to the nonsectarian Oakwood Cemetery. They paused before the crepe-draped portals of Colosimo's Café while two brass bands played a dirge. Dale Colosimo and De Stefano rode behind the hearse in a car with drawn curtains. Five thousand mourners followed. The fifty-three pallbearers and honorary pallbearers included, in addition to criminals of every stripe, nine aldermen, three judges, two Congressmen, a state senator, an assistant state's attorney and the state Republican leader. The Bath had tried to persuade Judge Lyle, then a Republican alderman, to join the pallbearers, but he declined.

"Jim wasn't a bad fellow, John," the Dink pleaded. "You know what he did. He fixed up an old farmhouse for broken-down prostitutes. They rested up and got back in shape and he never charged them a cent."

"Well," said Lyle, "now that he's dead, who's going to run this convalescent camp?"

"Oh, Jim sold it. Some of the girls ran away after they got back on their feet. Jim got sore, said they didn't have no gratitude."

The Chicago *American* reported:

"No matter what he may have been in the past, no matter what his faults, Jim was my friend and I am going to his funeral."

These and similar words were heard today from the lips of hundreds of Chicagoans. They were heard in the old Twenty-second Street levee district, over which Jim for so many years had held undisputed sway, they dropped from the mouths of gunmen and crooks, while many a tear ran down the painted cheeks of women of the underworld.

They were heard from many a seemingly staid businessman in loop skyscrapers and from men famous and near-famous in the world of arts and letters, who had all mingled more or less indiscriminately with the other world which walks forth at night.

Referring to gangster funerals in general, the perceptive Illinois Crime Survey illuminated the nature of the relationship between crime and politics:

> *Political power in a democracy rests upon friendship.* A man is your friend, not merely because he is kind to you, but because you can depend on him, because you know that he will stick and that he will keep his word.
>
> Politics in the river wards, and among common people elsewhere as well, is a feudal relationship. The feudal system was one that was based not on law but upon personal loyalties. Politics tends, therefore, to become a *feudal system.* Gangs, also, are organized on a feudal basis—that is, upon loyalties, upon friendships, and above all, upon dependability. That is one reason why politicians and criminal gangs understand one another so well and so frequently enter into alliances with each other against the more remote common good.
>
> . . . the rule which Colosimo established and maintained was a rule outside of and antagonistic to the formal and established order of society . . . for it is an undoubted fact that friendship . . . frequently does undermine the more formal social order. Idealists are notoriously not good friends. No man who is more interested in abstractions like justice, humanity and righteousness than he is in the more common immediate and personal relations of life, is likely to be a good mixer or a good politician. . . .
>
> The city of Chicago, if we look at the map, is clearly divided into two regions, the east side and the west side—the lake front and the river wards. On the lake fronts are idealists and reformers, and in the river wards party politics based on friendly relations. This contrast between the two sides of the city, with their different social systems, is part of the problem of the interlocking relationships of crime and politics; and the repeated failures of the public in its attempts to break the alliance is an indication of the extent and persistence of these relations. In the practical work-a-day world

in which Colosimo lived, the clear demarcation between right and wrong, as defined by law and public policy, did not exist.

Politics, particularly ward politics, is carried on in a smaller, more intimate world, than that which makes and defines the law. Government seeks to be equal, impartial, formal. Friendships run counter to the impartiality of formal government; and, vice versa, formal government cuts across the ties of friendship. Professional politicians have always recognized the importance, even when they were not moved by real sentiment, of participating with their friends and neighbors in the ceremonies marking the crises of life—christenings, marriages, and deaths. In the great funerals, the presence of the political boss attests the sincerity and the personal character of the friendship for the deceased, and this marks him as an intimate in life and death.

Dale Colosimo lay grief-stricken for ten days. She learned that she had not been Big Jim's wife under Illinois law, which at that time required a year's interval between divorce and remarriage. She therefore had no claim to what remained of his estate. His family nevertheless granted her $6,000 in bonds and diamonds and to Victoria Moresco, $12,000. The rest went to Papa Luigi.

Dale tried briefly to manage Colosimo's Café until Mike the Greek Potzin took it over. She and her mother then returned to New York. Since November, 1919, the musical comedy *Irene* had been sending capacity audiences home from the Vanderbilt Theater humming and whistling "In My Sweet Little Alice Blue Gown." Resuming her maiden name, Dale succeeded Edith Day in the title role and for several years sang it in New York and on the road. (*Irene* was the longest-running show in Broadway history up to that time.) In San Francisco, in 1924, she married an actor, Henry Duffy, and they played in stock together until the thirties, when Dale finally left the theater and disappeared from public view. Her story, meanwhile, had furnished Jack Lait and a collaborator, Jo Swerling, with the inspiration for a play entitled *One of Us*.

6

From Death Corner to
Dead Man's Tree

IMMEDIATELY after Colosimo's death Torrio, assisted
by Capone, embarked upon his grand design for territorial expansion.
In the initial phase he sought to win recognition as Big Jim's successor in the Levee. Aldermen Kenna and Coughlin bestowed their
approval, and none of the other key Levee figures raised any serious
objections. Next, having secured their home base, Torrio and Capone
proceeded to expand their suburban gambling and whorehouse interests. Bribery was their principal tool. Town and village officials
readily succumbed. Property owners near the site of a prospective dive
might protest, but resistance usually melted when Torrio offered
them money to pay off the mortgage, repair the roof, buy new furniture. . . . Within two years corruption transformed a long chain of
once placid law-abiding communities, stretching from Chicago
Heights, south of the city, to Cicero, west of it, into sinkholes of vice.
In Chicago Heights Torrio opened the Moonlight Café. To his two
thriving roadhouses in Burnham, the Burnham Inn and the Speedway, he added the Coney Island Café and the Barn. In Posen he established the Roamer Inn under the management of Harry Guzik,
one of three Moscow-born brothers, and his wife, Alma. In Blue
Island it was the Burr Oak Hotel (manager: Mike de Pike Heitler);
in Stickney, the Shadow Inn; in Cicero, a string of cabarets and
gambling houses.

The Roamer Inn was the prototypal suburban bagnio. The Chicago-born jazz clarinetist, Milton "Mezz" Mezzrow, an habitué in his youth, described it in his autobiography, *Really the Blues:*

> . . . There was a big front room with a long bar on one side and quarter slot machines lined up along the wall. In back there was a larger one, with benches running all around the walls but not tables. The girls sat there while the johns (customers) moped around giving them the once-over. Those girls were always competing with each other: one would come up to you, switching her hips like a young duck, and whisper in your ear, "Want to go to bed, dear, I'll show you a good time, honey, I'm French," and a minute later another one would ease along and say coyly, "Baby, don't you want a straight girl for a change?" . . .
>
> The girls we knew were all on the dogwatch, from four to twelve in the morning. . . . They paraded around in teddies or gingham baby rompers with big bows in the back, high-heeled shoes, pretty silk hair ribbons twice as big as their heads, and rouge an inch thick all over their kissers. When a john had eyeballed the parade and made his choice he would follow her upstairs, where the landlady sat at a little desk in the hall. This landlady would hand out a metal check and a towel to the girl, while the customer forked over two bucks. Then the girl was assigned a room number. All night long you could hear the landlady calling out in a bored voice, like a combination of strawboss and timekeeper, "*All* right, Number Eight, *all* right, Number Ten—somebody's waiting, don't take all night." She ran that joint with a stopwatch.
>
> The girls explained to me that they got eighty cents a trick, one payment for each metal check. . . . Twenty cents went for protection, and the other dollar belonged to the house. . . .
>
> Those girls worked hard—some of them didn't even knock off for a single night, hiding their condition with tricks I won't go into now. . . .

It may have been at the Roamer Inn that Capone contracted gonorrhea in 1925.

The strength of Torrio's political connections underwent a stringent test in 1921, following an incident at the Roamer Inn. The Guziks advertised for a housemaid. When a pretty farm girl applied, they made her a prisoner, took away her clothes, and had her broken in as a prostitute. After five months of captivity she managed to get word to her family. By the time her brothers rescued her she was physically and mentally destroyed. In court her father told how the Guziks had tried to bribe him not to testify. They were convicted and sentenced to the penitentiary. While free under bail, pending an appeal to the Illinois Supreme Court, they looked to Torrio for deliverance. He approached Walter Stevens, dean of Chicago's gunmen.

Stevens was fifty-four, an advanced age for one with his occupational hazards. As a lieutenant of Maurice "Mossy" Enright, a pioneer in labor union racketeering, he had slugged, bombed and slaughtered numerous victims during the industrial strife of the early 1900's. His price scale ran from $24 for laying open a skull to $50 for murder. He was the last survivor of the Enright gang, Mossy himself having been liquidated in 1920 by Sunny Jim Cosmano as a favor to a rival union racketeer, Big Tim Murphy. In certain respects Stevens resembled Torrio, that "best and dearest of husbands." He worshiped his wife, and when she became incurably ill, he nursed her for twenty years until the day she died. He adopted three children and sent them all to good schools. He himself was an educated man, a student of military history, who greatly admired Ulysses S. Grant and Bismarck, and a voracious reader, whose favorite authors included Robert Louis Stevenson, Robert Burns and Jack London. Like Torrio, he had a puritanical streak. He never touched a drop of liquor and rarely smoked. He forbade his adopted daughters to wear short skirts or use cosmetics. Before permitting them to read the classics, he excised any passages he considered indecent. He constantly preached old-fashioned morality and idealism and denounced the "flaming youth" of the era typified by Clara Bow, Hollywood's "It" girl.

When Mossy Enright died in 1920, Stevens moved into the Torrio-Capone camp. His greatest asset was the gratitude of Governor Len Small. A few months after Small, a farmer from Kankakee and a Thompson puppet, took office in 1921, a grand jury indicted him for embezzling $600,000 while state treasurer. Working behind the scenes for the defense were Stevens; "Jew Ben" Newmark, former chief investigator for the state's attorney, but more successful as a thief, counterfeiter and extortioner; and Michael J. "Umbrella Mike" Boyle, business agent for Electrical Workers' Union No. 134. Boyle's nickname derived from his practice of standing at a bar on certain days of the month with an unfurled umbrella into which contractors who wished to avoid labor trouble would drop their cash levy. As the governor's trial progressed, the trio undertook such delicate missions as bribing and intimidating jurors. Small was acquitted. He did not forget his deliverers. When they went to jail, Newmark and Boyle for jury tampering and Stevens for an old murder, he pardoned them. During his first three years in office he pardoned or paroled almost 1,000 felons. Stevens now drew his attention to the Guziks' plight, and before the State Supreme Court handed down its decision, the governor pardoned them. Within three months they were operating a new brothel, the Marshfield Inn, just beyond the city's southern limits.

In the third phase of their expansionist campaign, the bootlegging phase, Torrio and Capone faced a formidable array of gangs without whose concurrence they could not hope to succeed. On the Northeast Side, between the Chicago River and the lake, there was Dion O'Banion's gang. "Who'll carry the Forty-second and Forty-third wards?" Every Chicagoan knew the old quip. "O'Banion in his pistol pockets." "Deany's" suits did, as a matter of fact, conceal three extra pockets for firearms—one under the left armpit of the coat jacket, another on the outside left, and a third on the center front of the trousers like a codpiece. He could shoot accurately with either hand. A fellow Irishman named Gene Geary taught him how. O'Banion had a sweet, choir-trained voice, and when raised in "Mother Machree" or "When Irish Eyes Are Smiling," it brought tears streaming down his mentor's cheeks. A criminal court later committed Geary to an insane asylum as a homicidal maniac. In the act of murder O'Banion's own blue eyes were usually smiling, his lips parted in a boyish grin, with what a psychiatrist once called his "sunny brutality."

He never shook hands with strangers. If anybody he didn't know approached him, he would face him, feet firmly planted apart, hands on hips, poised to draw a gun at the faintest hostile move. He had good reasons for caution. "Chicago's arch criminal," Chief of Police Morgan Collins said of him, "who has killed or seen to the killing of at least twenty-five men." He would fire on slight provocation, sometimes out of sheer nervousness. He once asked Edward Dean Sullivan, a *Herald-Examiner* reporter, to recommend a good cigar for a convalescing hospital patient. "Who's sick?" Sullivan asked. O'Banion showed him a clipping from the afternoon edition. A laborer, Arthur Vadis, had been shot in the leg by an unknown assailant. "This morning," O'Banion recounted, "I'm going across the Madison Avenue Bridge and I got plenty on my mind. Somebody's been trailing me lately. An automobile crossed the bridge and backfired. I didn't know what it was. I took a pop at the only guy I saw. I got to send some smokes over to him."

A fancied slight prompted O'Banion to attempt a murder in the lobby of the La Salle Theater. Exactly what Davy "Yiddles" Miller, a prizefight referee, had said or done to offend him was never clear, but having spotted him in the audience, O'Banion waited for him outside after the performance and before hundreds of witnesses put a bullet through his stomach. A younger brother, Max Miller, leaped to the fallen Davy's rescue, whereupon O'Banion fired at him. The bullet glanced off Max's belt buckle. Smiling, the marksman swaggered out into the night. The police arrested him, but neither Davy, who recovered, nor Max cared to prosecute. "I'm sorry it happened," said O'Banion. "It was just a piece of hotheaded foolishness."

He never spent a day in jail for shooting anybody. His political usefulness was too great. Just as Big Jim Colosimo had controlled the Italian vote in his part of town, so Deany O'Banion controlled the Irish vote in his. Cajolery and bounty normally sufficed to swing it any way O'Banion chose, but if they failed, he and his cohorts never hesitated to slug, shoot or kidnap. "I always deliver my borough as per requirements," he declared and he always did. So highly did the Democratic bosses of the Forty-second and Forty-third prize O'Banion's vote-getting ability that when they heard he might shift to the Republicans, they gave him a testimonial dinner at the Webster Hotel, climaxing it with the gift of a gem-encrusted platinum watch. Among those present were Colonel Albert A. Sprague, Cook County commissioner of public works and Democratic candidate for the U.S. Senate; Robert M. Sweitzer, then Cook County clerk; and Chief of Police Michael Hughes. The guest of honor went Republican anyway.

O'Banion loved flowers, and he loved the church, and he was overjoyed to acquire a half interest in William Schofield's flower shop at 738 North State Street, directly opposite Holy Name Cathedral, where he once served as an acolyte and choirboy. Most days, between 9 A.M. and 6 P.M., he could be found in the shop, a sprig of lily of the valley or a white carnation in his buttonhole, happily breathing in the perfumed air as he bustled about, potting a plant here, nipping an excess bud there, arranging a wedding bouquet or a funeral wreath. He became gangdom's favorite florist, a lucrative situation, because underworld etiquette required the foes, as well as the friends, of a fallen gangster—including those who felled him—to honor him with an elaborate floral creation. To order funerary flowers from any florist but O'Banion would have been as egregious a *faux pas* for a gangster as it would for a Gold Coast matron to have invitations to her daughter's debut engraved by other than a Cartier or a Tiffany. O'Banion never needed to wait until the mourners actually placed their orders. The moment word of a gangster's demise reached him he knew how many flowers to buy from the wholesalers. It depended on the dead man's rank in the underworld hierarchy. Even before the calls started coming in and while the embalmer was still plugging up the bullet holes in the corpse, O'Banion and his staff would be at work composing floral wreaths, blankets and horseshoes and choosing suitable sentiments to be sewn in gilt letters to the ribbons—"Sympathy from the boys—We'll miss you, dear old pal. . . . Gone but not forgotten." All the caller had to do was identify himself and name the amount he wanted to spend—"This is Charlie. Five grand." *

By night O'Banion and his crew devoted themselves to other employment, consisting variously of banditry, burglary, safecracking, hijacking and, after 1920, bootlegging. O'Banion's adoring wife, Viola, maintained, with the willed blindness necessary to most gangsters' wives: "Dean loved his home and spent most of his evening in it. He loved to sit in his slippers, fooling with the radio, singing a song, listening to the player-piano. He never drank. He was not a man to run around nights with women. I was his only sweetheart. We went out often to dinner or the theater, usually with friends. He never left home without telling me where he was going and kissing me good-bye."

A childless couple, they occupied a twelve-room apartment on North Pine Grove Avenue, a short spin from the flower shop in O'Banion's late-model Locomobile. His proudest home possessions were the player-piano, for which he had paid $15,000, and a Victrola, and he was constantly setting them both to playing the same tune and trying to synchronize them.

"We're big business without high hats," O'Banion once remarked to his second-in-command, Earl "Little Hymie" Weiss, after they had hijacked a liquor truck. He nevertheless aped the dress and manners

---

* Schofield's sons continued to run the shop up to 1960, when it was razed to make way for a parking lot. At last reports they had a flower shop at 714 North State, half a block south of the old address. Holy Name Cathedral remains.

of the Gold Coast high-hatters, wearing a tuxedo when he attended a dinner or theater and minding his grammar and etiquette, and he insisted that his cohorts restrain their natural impulses. O'Banion popularized formal attire among gangsters, and owing partly to his example, their general social behavior distinctly improved.

He limped, his left leg being shorter than his right, the aftermath of a boyhood fall from a streetcar. He was otherwise a prime physical specimen, broad-shouldered and lean-hipped. He had slender hands, with long, tapering fingers, which he submitted regularly to a manicurist's care. He parted his brown, silken, wavy hair low on the left side. His face was round, his chin cleft, and his normal expression one of geniality and goodwill toward men.

He was born Charles Dion O'Banion twenty-eight years before Prohibition to an immigrant Irish plasterer and house painter in Aurora, Illinois. His mother died when he was five, but he retained a glowing memory of her, speaking of her frequently as the maternal ideal. One Memorial Day, as his customers were ordering flowers to decorate the graves of their loved ones, he was moved to such transports of filial piety that he jumped into his Locomobile and drove 150 miles to his mother's grave in the tiny village of Maroa, Illinois. Finding her tombstone with difficulty because of the weeds overgrowing it, he had it replaced by a huge monument visible at a distance. When his father grew too told to work, O'Banion settled a sum on him large enough to take care of him for the rest of his life. There was also a married sister in Coldwater, Kansas, to whom he regularly sent money.

"Deany was a fighter as a boy but a good worker," said his father. In his infancy the family left Aurora for Chicago and a tenement flat on the edge of the North Side's Little Sicily, a maze of narrow, garbage-strewn streets, overrun by dogs and rats, the air hazy and reeking with the smoke of surrounding factories. The flames from a gasworks chimney that reddened the sky at night gave the area its nickname—Little Hell. It was formerly an Irish shantytown called Kilgubbin, and about 1,000 Irish remained, but the "dark people"—the Sicilians—had been coming since 1900, and now they were in the majority. Though barely half a mile square, Little Hell surpassed even the Levee in the incidence and diversity of its vice and crime. Every year for twenty years between twelve and twenty violent deaths occurred in Little Hell. One spot, the intersection of Oak and Milton streets, became known as Death Corner after thirty-eight people had been gunned down there in little more than a year. Thirteen of those murders were attributed to a single Black Hander, identity never discovered, whom the press dubbed the Shotgun Man.

For the boy O'Banion this baneful environment was partly offset by the influence of Father O'Brien at Holy Name Cathedral. During four years as a chorister and altar boy Deany developed such religious zeal, his conduct was in all ways so estimable, that the pastor hoped he might someday qualify as a novitiate. But before his voice changed, the choirboy was attracted to a gang of juvenile Little Hellions, the Market Streeters, and though he continued to observe religious ritual, Father O'Brien's moral precepts soon went by the board. At ten he was peddling newspapers and thieving. At sixteen he was a singing waiter in McGovern's Saloon, one of the lowest North Side dives, reducing the drunks to maudlin tears and picking their pockets or, if they became altogether helpless, a condition he frequently hastened by slipping them Mickey Finns, jackrolling them. By his seventeenth year he had enlisted as a slugger in the newspaper circulation wars on the side of the *Herald-Examiner,* overturning the competition's delivery trucks, burning newspapers, and beating up dealers who sold them. As leader of his own gang, he turned to burglary, safecracking and highway robbery. In 1909 he served three months in the House of Correction and two years later, another six months for blackjacking his prey. Those six months constituted his total prison record. Having demonstrated his efficiency as a ward heeler, he could rely on political patrons to keep him out of prison.

Had he been a subtler safecracker his name might never have appeared on a police blotter at all, but his guilt was usually glaring. In attempting to open a safe with a charge of dynamite, he once blew out the entire side of an office building, but hardly scratched the safe. In 1921 a Detective Sergeant John J. Ryan caught O'Banion, Hymie Weiss and two lesser satellites *in flagrante* as they started to blast open a Postal Telegraph safe. With his sweetest smile, O'Banion explained that Ryan had misinterpreted their presence; they were there simply to apply for jobs as apprentice telegraph operators. An alderman furnished the $10,000 bail bond for O'Banion, and it cost $30,000 in bribes to have the case nolle prossed. Not long after, the police raised the fingerprints of O'Banion, Weiss and Vincent "Schemer" Drucci on the dial of a safe they had emptied in the Parkway Tea Room. The jury acquitted them. "It was an oversight," O'Banion remarked to a reporter as he strutted out of the courtroom. "Hymie was supposed to wipe off the prints, but he forgot."

Every good ward heeler knew when and where to scatter bounty, and O'Banion was no exception; but as his fortunes soared, his charity went beyond self-interest. He genuinely pitied the outsider, the derelict, the disenfranchised such as he and his parents had been. O'Banion often visited the slums, his car laden with food and clothing. He gave money to the aged poor and to the orphaned young, paid their rent and their medical bills. He once sent a crippled boy to the Mayo Clinic and, when told that neither surgery nor medication could cure him, undertook to support him as long as they both should live. "No high-salaried organization to distribute my doles," he said. "My money goes straight to those who need it."

O'Banion's general staff consisted of criminals no less individualistic. Hymie Weiss, born Wajiechowski of Polish parentage, invented one of gangland's favorite murder methods and coined the phrase for it—"taking him for a ride." The victim was lured into the front seat of a car, the back of his head exposed to the gunman behind him. Gangsters considered the cerebellum an ideal target because the bullet was unlikely to "take a course"—that is, to be deflected from a vital area. The killers would fire when the car reached a desolate spot, fling open the door, and eject the corpse. The first one-way ride victim, executed by Weiss himself in July, 1921, was another Pole, Steve Wisniewski, who had hijacked a beer truck belonging to O'Banion.

Like O'Banion, Weiss attended Holy Name Cathedral. He wore a crucifix around his neck and frequently fingered a rosary. Thin and wiry, with hot black eyes set far apart, tense, tempestuous, vindictive, he was the brainiest member of the gang and the cockiest. He once sued the federal government. A U.S. marshal, armed with a warrant for a violation of the Mann Act, broke into the apartment Weiss shared with a *Ziegfeld Follies* chorine named Josephine Libby. Weiss forced him to leave at the point of a shotgun. Returning with a raiding party, the marshal seized a bottle of knockout drops, handcuffs, revolvers, shotguns and a dozen cases of whiskey, brandy and champagne. Weiss brought an action in federal court to recover some silk shirts and socks which, he claimed, the raiders had also confiscated. Nothing came of either Weiss' civic suit or the government's criminal charges.

On behalf of whichever political party happened to be sponsoring the gang during municipal elections Weiss would go swashbuckling from poll to poll with a revolver and hold off the officials while his fellow thugs stole ballot boxes. He had a tigerish temper. "I saw him only once in the last twenty years," said his brother Frank, who drove a newspaper delivery truck during Chicago's circulation wars. "That was when he shot me."

Josephine Libby's opinion of her lover was practically interchangeable with Viola O'Banion's opinion of her husband. "Earl was one of the finest men in the world," she said, "and I spent the happiest time of my life with him. You'd expect a rich bootlegger to be a man about town, always going to nightclubs and having his home full of rowdy friends. But Earl liked to be alone with me, just lounging about, listening to the radio or reading. He seemed to me pretty well read. He didn't waste time on trash, but read histories and law books. If you hadn't known what he was, you might have mistaken him for a lawyer or college professor. He was crazy about children. 'I like 'em, Jo,' he said. 'I want a boy of my own some day. I don't amount to much, but maybe the youngster would turn out all right.' "

On safecracking sorties O'Banion and Weiss usually took along Schemer Drucci and George "Bugs" Moran. Drucci's sobriquet stemmed from his imaginative but impractical schemes for robbing banks and kidnapping millionaires. He made his underworld debut looting telephone coin boxes. Bugs Moran had committed twenty-six robberies and served three prison sentences, totaling two years, before his twenty-first birthday. A Pole from Minnesota, the Irish name notwithstanding, he married the sister of another O'Banionite, James Clark, alias Albert Kashellek, a full-blooded Sioux Indian. Moran was a moonfaced 200-pounder with a cleft chin, whom O'Banion tended to treat like a court jester. He had a certain rueful wit. His misdeeds often brought him for arraignment before Judge Lyle, whose threshold of tolerance for gangsters was low, and he invariably requested a change of venue. "Don't you like me, Moran?" the judge once asked him. "I like you, Your Honor," Moran replied, "but I'm suspicious of you."

Running into Lyle at a baseball game one afternoon, Moran remarked: "Judge, that's a beautiful diamond ring you're wearing. If it's snatched some night, promise me you won't go hunting me. I'm telling you now I'm innocent."

As a killer Moran, too, had an innovative flair. He introduced the motorcade system—gunmen in half a dozen cars enfilading the victim's home as they sped past it.

O'Banion's most devoted follower was Leland Varain, alias Louis Alterie. A product of the Colorado plains, he wore a ten-gallon hat and rejoiced in the nicknames Cowboy and Two-Gun. (Actually, like his leader, he always packed three firearms—two nickel-plated .38's with maple-wood handles and a blue-steel snub-nosed revolver.) Before coming to Chicago, Varain fought as a heavyweight in small-town prize rings under the pseudonym "Kid Haynes." In Chicago he doubled as O'Banion's bodyguard and as a slugger for the Theatrical and Building Janitors' Union. With Hymie Weiss he perfected yet another widely imitated murder technique—the rented ambush. They would rent a flat within shotgun range of an address that the marked man frequently visited and keep vigil at the open window until they held him squarely in their gunsights.

Two-Gun Louis had a predilection for blondes so pronounced that when he discovered a girl with whom he was journeying West to be a bleached blonde, he threw her off the train. The parting occurred en route to a 3,000-acre cattle ranch he owned near Gypsum, Colorado. He often hid out fugitive criminals there, and to Gypsum every autumn, during the open season on deer, he would invite O'Banion, Weiss *et al.* for a week or so of hunting. Among his favorite hunters was Samuel J. "Nails" Morton, one of the gang's few Jewish recruits. A war hero, he had risen from the ranks of the 131st Illinois Infantry to first lieutenant, and for leading a squad over the top despite two bullet wounds the French awarded him the Croix de guerre. On the Gypsum ranch Morton learned to love horseback riding. In Chicago he outfitted himself with jodhpurs, a red velvet jacket and a black derby, rented a spirited mount from a Clark Street stable, and began a daily program of riding through Lincoln Park. One day the horse threw him and kicked him to death. The O'Banionites demanded a reprisal. With Alterie at their head, they broke into the stable after dark, kidnapped the guilty horse, led him to the bridle path where Morton had fallen, and pumped him full of lead. Alterie then telephoned the stable manager. "We taught that horse of yours a lesson," he said. "If you want the saddle, go get it." OBanion celebrated the act of vengeance with a gala party.

On the West Side, between Chicago Avenue and Madison Street, there were the O'Donnell brothers—William "Klondike," Myles and Bernard—and their all-Irish gang. They bore the Italians no love, least of all rank outsiders from the East like Torrio and Capone, whom they anticipated in the invasion of Cicero.

On the South Side, in Little Italy, the Genna brothers, the six swarthy, jet-eyed, jet-haired "Terrible Gennas"—Sam; Vincenzo, or Jim; Pete; Angelo ("Bloody Angelo") ; Antonio ("Tony the Gentleman, "Tony the Aristocrat") ; and Mike ("Little Mike," "Il Diavolo," "Mike the Devil"). If you walked a block north from the Four Deuces, then west on Taylor Street for two blocks, you came to the heart of the Genna fief. Here the father, a railroad section hand from the Sicilian port of Marsala, had brought his brood in 1894 when Sam, the eldest, was ten and Mike, an infant. Both parents died young in squalor, leaving the boys to fend for themselves. They clawed their way up fast in the underworld. Through Black Hand extortion they built up the bankroll, and through service to the ward bosses the political connections needed to operate a gambling den, a poolroom, a blind pig, a cheese and olive import firm, and the biggest bootleg alcohol plant in Chicago. They were ardent family men and zealous churchgoers.

In their proliferating enterprises each brother assumed a different function. Sam was chief organizer and business manager. Jim and Pete Genna saw to the technical aspects of moonshining; Angelo and Mike to the dirty work—the political assassinations, the reprisals, the chastisement of territorial invaders. Tony the Gentleman, thin, sharp, stylish in contrast with his gross, overfed brothers, a Dapper Dan who manicured his toenails, acted as family *consigliere,* helping chart every move they made from bootlegging to murder, but taking no direct hand in any. He occupied a suite in the Congress Hotel, remote from Little Italy, which he shared with Gladys Bagwell, from Chester, Illinois, a cabaret pianist and the daughter of a Baptist minister. The only educated Genna, Tony studied music and architecture and, eager to improve the lot of Chicago's poor Sicilians, built for them a low-rent, model-housing community at Troy and Fifty-fifth Streets. He maintained a seasonal box at the opera and loved to entertain the singers.

The Gennas recruited several bodyguards of Sicilian origin. Samuzzo "Samoots" Amatuna was a professional fiddler, a member of the Musicians' Union, whose business agent he and three other members attempted unsuccessfully to kill with weapons concealed in their instrument cases. A fop, with a wardrobe containing 200 monogrammed silk shirts, Samoots, too, once wreaked vengeance upon a horse. When the horse-drawn delivery wagon from the Chinese laundry to which he entrusted his shirts returned one scorched by an iron, he pursued it through the streets, aimed his revolver at the driver, then, changing his mind, shot the horse dead instead. One of the Gennas' most dependable terrorists was Orazio "the Scourge" Tropea. Lean, swarthy, and hawk-nosed, he seldom required much muscle to enforce his will. Usually a single piercing glance sufficed, for Tropea was reputed to possess *il malocchio*—the evil eye. As ignorant as the poor Sicilian immigrants upon whom he preyed, Tropea believed himself to be a sorcerer. In his extortionary missions on behalf of the Gennas he was abetted by a small group of younger predators that included Ecola "the Eagle" Baldelli, a former postal van driver who served as his chauffeur; Vito Bascone, a wine bootlegger; Felipe Gnolfo; and Tony Finalli. Giuseppe Nerone, alias Antonio Spano alias Joseph Pavia, and popularly known as *Il Cavaliere* because of his courtly manner, had graduated from the University of Palermo and taught mathematics before he turned to crime, fled the Sicilian police, and escaped to America. After joining the Gennas, he came to consider himself a financial genius largely responsible for their prosperity, an opinion from which they dissented. They valued him chiefly as a torpedo. John Scalise and Albert Anselmi also left Sicily a step ahead of the law, and since they hailed from the Gennas' native Marsala, the family extended a welcoming hand. They were the Mutt and Jeff of murder, Scalise tall and lean, Anselmi short and fat. They subscribed to the curious belief, common among Sicilian assassins, that bullets rubbed with garlic would cause gangrene if they failed to kill the victim outright. Garlic has no such toxicity; but Scalisi and Anselmi so treated all their bullets, and the practice spread through gangland.

Early in 1920 the Gennas' political pull enabled them to obtain a government license for handling industrial alcohol. They acquired a three-story warehouse at 1022 West Taylor Street, about 600 feet from the Maxwell Street police station, and started with $7,000 worth of denatured alcohol purchased legitimately from federal sources. They distributed a token quantity to legitimate users. The bulk they redistilled, colored and flavored to imitate whiskey, brandy or what's your pleasure and sold it through bootleg channels at $6 a gallon for 190 proof, $3 cut to 100 proof.

Their manufacturing methods created dreadful dangers for the consumer. To eliminate completely the denaturants, chiefly wood alcohol, required not only a great deal more chemical knowledge than the Gennas possessed, but more time than they deemed it worthwhile to invest. As a result of ignorance and haste, the end product retained a poison which could, depending on the amount, produce excruciating pain lasting three or four days, cause permanent blindness, kill. The coloring and flavoring process increased the dangers. Good whiskey gets its amber hue by slowly absorbing the rosin and tars from the charred casks in which it is aged, a matter of years. The Gennas obtained instant color with coal tar dyes. For flavor they added fusel oil. This substance—the word "fusel" is German, meaning "bad liquor"—occurs naturally during fermentation, but aging removes most of it. Whiskey with a high fusel content, such as the Gennas marketed, was believed to account for a distinct new form of insanity characterized by sexual depravity, hallucinations, paranoia and homicidal impulses.

However noxious the Gennas' liquor, their Taylor Street plant could not begin to supply the demand for it. Their solution to this problem convulsed the district economy. They persuaded hundreds of tenement dwellers and shopkeepers to let them install portable copper stills in their kitchens. They provided corn sugar and instructions on how to extract alcohol from it. The crude techniques they used had been developed by Henry Spingola, a young neighborhood lawyer and the brother of Angelo's intended, Lucille. The inducement was $15 a day, a fortune compared to what most inhabitants of Little Italy earned as laborers or peddlers. Not many rejected the offer. Those who did the Gennas either won over or put to flight with Black Hand terrorism. They also stimulated a minor immigration wave by guaranteeing a livelihood to Sicilians who would tend their stills. Alky cooking became the cottage industry of Little Italy. The tenement flats, houses and back rooms of stores with the required apparatus ran into the thousands, and over the entire community hung the stench of fermenting mash.

The alky cooker shouldered no very onerous chores. He could fulfill most of them as he lolled beside his still, smoking a pipe or sipping a glass of wine. All he had to do for his $15 a day was keep the fire burning under the still and skim the distillate. The Gennas' truck drivers collected the alcohol in five-gallon cans. To be sure, the careless alky cooker ran grave risks. If he used gas for fuel, he might have to steal it by tapping a main, not because the Gennas wouldn't pay for it, but lest the abnormal consumption arouse the suspicion of the meter reader, who might then demand hush money. Clumsy main-tapping sometimes released a rush of gas that asphyxiated the thief. It sometimes happened, too, that a still would explode, scalding him to death.

The physical conditions of the average tenement threatened the consumer with appalling health hazards. While the alky cooker dozed next to his still, vermin, drawn by the reek of fermenting yeast and sugar, would tumble into the mash. When Captain John Stege, a policeman who tried to uphold the Prohibition laws, confiscated 100 barrels of Little Italy mash, he found dead rats in every one.

The Gennas' profits were enormous. A home still would yield on the average 350 gallons of raw alcohol a week at a cost of 50 to 75 cents a gallon, depending on the fluctuating price of corn sugar and yeast. After redistillation to eliminate the grosser impurities, the Gennas wholesaled the stuff at $6 a gallon. The retailer—the speakeasy proprietor—would reduce the alcoholic strength by half with water, thereby doubling his reserves. Each gallon yielded 96 bar drinks, and he charged his customers 25 cents a drink. Thus, he realized a profit of $40 a gallon. The Gennas' gross sales climbed to $350,000 a month and their net earnings to $150,000.

They earmarked a substantial part of their gross for graft. They paid off the Maxwell Street cops at the monthly rate of $10 to $125, according to importance and service. The payees eventually numbered about 400, not counting 5 police captains, scores of plainclothesmen and special detectives assigned to the state's attorney. The transactions were conducted so openly that the neighbors called 1022 Taylor Street "the police station." On the monthly paydays, all day, police in and out of uniform would swarm through the warehouse, some casually pausing on the sidewalk to count their graft.

To foil police from other precincts who might try to misrepresent themselves as Maxwell Streeters, the police captains sent the Gennas a monthly list of the numbered badges against which they could verify the names of the deserving. Occasionally, a truckload of alcohol consigned to a distant part of the city would be intercepted by police en route. On the Gennas' complaint a protective system went into effect. Before undertaking a long haul through strange territory, the Gennas would notify the Maxwell Street Station. A uniformed squad would then convoy the truck through the danger zones. Not every home still in Little Italy operated under Genna auspices, but to avoid paying off an inquisitive cop, many of these competitors would claim that they did. The Gennas countered such imposture by distributing lists of every installation they owned to the Maxwell Street captains. Thereafter, when the police found an unlisted still, they destroyed it.

The Gennas could not, however, maintain their dominion by bribery alone. They required the support of the ward bosses as well. This they won during the aldermanic wars of the Nineteenth Ward—the "Bloody Ward"—that encompassed Little Italy. Before those wars ended, thirty men died in the streets. They usually died after the killer, in a rite designed to shatter the victim's nerve, had tacked his name to "Dead Man's Tree," a poplar growing on Loomis Street.

In the 1921 municipal elections the principal contenders for Nineteenth Ward alderman were Anthony D'Andrea, a nonpartisan candidate, and the Democratic incumbent, John "Johnny de Pow" Powers. Both men owed their public careers to a confederacy of crime and politics. Powers, a saloonkeeper and protector of criminals, gloried in the epithet conferred by his detractors, Prince of Boodlers. In and out of office he had ruled the Nineteenth Ward since 1888, when his constituency was mainly Irish. The Italians came to predominate and by 1918 composed 80 percent of the voting population. Powers wooed a majority of the Italians as successfully as he had the Irish. According to the Chicago *Times,* "The only way he can get votes is by hypocritical posing as a benefactor by filling the role of a friend in need when death comes. He has bowed with aldermanic grief at thousands of biers. He is bloodless, personally unattractive. His demeanor is one of timid alertness and anxiety to please, but he is actually autocratic, arrogant and insolent."

In 1914, when Tony D'Andrea entered politics as a Democratic candidate for county commissioner, he was one of Chicago's most prominent and popular Italians. As a lawyer he had accumulated a small fortune. Two of his daughters had graduated from the University of Chicago, and a third would shortly start her freshman year there. D'Andrea himself was a University of Palermo alumnus, a scholar and a linguist. During his early Chicago years he had privately tutored various Gold Coast ladies in Italian. When his brother Joey, Big Jim Colosimo's labor racketeering crony, was killed in a fight over city construction contracts, Tony replaced him as head of the Sewer Diggers' and Tunnel Miners' Union. (Another brother, Horace, was a priest.) He later succeeded to the presidency of the Macaroni Manufacturers' Association, then of the International Hod Carriers' Union and, finally, of the Unione Siciliane, offices which carried enormous prestige among Italian voters.

During the 1914 campaign the opposition, rooting around in D'Andrea's past, came up with some startling revelations. The attorney, they discovered, was an unfrocked priest, a convicted bank robber and counterfeiter, who had served thirteen months in Joliet Penitentiary before President Theodore Roosevelt pardoned him upon the intercession of one of D'Andrea's Gold Coast pupils.

Far from disaffecting his followers, the exposure infuriated them with the opposition, who, they felt, had struck a low blow. D'Andrea lost the election but made great gains in influence. At his next try, two years later, running against a Powers puppet, James Bowler, for Democratic alderman nominee, he split the Nineteenth Ward Italian vote and started a miniature civil war.

The first casualty was Frank Raimondi, a Powers ward heeler. On February 21, 1916, a gunman shot him down in a Taylor Street saloon. His daughter held the D'Andrea faction responsible. D'Andrea, she said, had long "lorded it over a stricken ward, too afraid of his power to cross him." The press agreed. As for the actual killers, the name most frequently whispered was "Genna."

D'Andrea again lost the election. He returned to the fray in 1921 as a nonpartisan candidate against Johnny de Pow. The hostilities opened with bombs, one exploding on Powers' front porch, another at a D'Andrea rally, seriously injuring five people, a third and fourth in D'Andrea's home and headquarters. "Conditions in the Nineteenth Ward are terrible," proclaimed Alderman Bowler. "Gunmen are patrolling the streets. I have received threats that I was to be bumped off or kidnaped. Alderman Powers' house is guarded day and night. Our men have been met, threatened and slugged. Gunmen and cutthroats have been imported from New York and Buffalo for this campaign of intimidation. Alderman Powers' forces can't hold meetings except under heavy guard. Owners of halls have been threatened with death or destruction of their buildings if they rent their places to us. It is worse than the Middle Ages."

D'Andrea's third defeat did not bring a truce. It merely left a lot of old scores to be settled. At 9 A.M. on March 9 Paul Labriola, a Powers true blue, set forth from his home on Halsted Street for the Municipal Court in City Hall where he worked as a bailiff. His wife watched apprehensively from the doorway until he passed out of sight, for he had been receiving Black Hand threats. At the corner of Halsted and Congress streets he ran into a group of D'Andrea followers, among them Angelo Genna, Samoots Amatuna, Frank "Don Chick" Gambino and Johnny "Two-Gun" Guardino. The exchange of greetings was frosty. As Labriola started to cross the intersection, a volley of revolver shots dropped him to the pavement. Walking up to the body, Genna stood over it, straddle-legged, and fired three more bullets into it. With his companions he then got into a car and drove off.

At 1 P.M. the same day the four men entered Harry Raimondi's cigar store on Taylor Street. Raimondi was a renegade from the D'Andrea ranks, suspected of having betrayed the leader's criminal record to the enemy. When his vistors left, he lay dead behind his counter, five bullets in his back. The next Powers partisans to go were Gaetano Esposito, his body dumped from a car to the sidewalk; then Nicolo Adamo, whose wife identified Jim Genna as the assassin; then Paul Notte, who named Angelo on his deathbed. Notte's statement was later disqualified by a magistrate because it had been uttered while the dying man was under the influence of an opiate administered to relieve his pain.

The militant arm of the Powers faction was not idle either. In swift retaliation it struck down two D'Andrea henchmen, Joe Marino and Johnny Guardino, the latter with a revolver as he stood on a street corner watching some small boys playing ball. At about the same time a car full of Powers hoodlums, cruising Little Italy in search of the foe, halted outside a Taylor Street poolroom and emptied shotguns into it.

Even though D'Andrea, appalled by the slaughter and fearful for his own life, had renounced Nineteenth Ward politics, the war raged on. A man named Abraham Wolfson, who lived across the hall from the D'Andrea apartment on the ground floor of 902 South Ashland Avenue, received a series of Black Hand-like notes. "He killed others," the first message stated. "We are going to do the same. [signed] Revenge." Then: "You are to move in fifteen days. We are going to blow up the building and kill the whole D'Andrea family. He killed others and we are going to do the same thing. We mean business. You better move and save many lives." After showing D'Andrea the notes, Wolfson moved.

On the night of May 11, 1921, while D'Andrea's wife and daughters were asleep and D'Andrea was playing cards in a neighborhood restaurant, a car carrying three men parked near an alley behind 902 Ashland. Two of them got out, pried open a basement window with a chisel, crept through it into a coal bin and thence upstairs to the now-vacant Wolfson apartment. There they waited by a window next to the front door. Presently D'Andrea's car, driven by his bodyguard, Joe Laspisa, drew up. Laspisa watched his boss climb the steps of 902 to a stone porch and drove away. As D'Andrea approached the front door, two shotgun blasts caught him full in the chest. He fell, reaching for his revolver, and from the floor fired five times through the shattered porch window. The killers, escaping the way they came, left behind a note pinned to a $2 bill: "This will buy flowers for that *figlio di un cane*." D'Andrea died in Jefferson Park Hospital, murmuring to his wife and daughters, "God bless you."

The aldermen's war ended after two more killings. Laspisa and his Sicilian "blood brother," Joe Sinacola, had sworn on D'Andrea's bier to avenge him. They never got the opportunity. Laspisa died on June 24 at the wheel of his car on Death Corner, within sight of the Church of San Filippo Benzi. The next day the pastor, Father Louis Giambastiani, posted an appeal beside the church portals: "Brothers! For the honor you owe God, for the respect of your American country and humanity—pray that this ferocious manslaughter, which disgraces the Italian name before the civilized world, may come to an end." From the pulpit he implored any parishioners with knowledge that might lead to the arrest of the killers to report to the police. None did.

Of the thirty murders committed during the aldermen's war only one resulted in a trial. Angelo Genna was prosecuted for the murder of Paul Labriola. He was defended by an assistant state's attorney, an inhabitant of Little Italy, Stephen Malato, who resigned his office in order to plead the case. He won it owing chiefly to the scarcity of

prosecution witnesses. As Dion O'Banion observed in similar circumstances, "We have a new disease in town. It's called Chicago
amnesia."

Another neighborhood potentate who loaned the Gennas a helping hand on their way up was the Republican ward committeeman,
Giuseppe "Diamond Joe" Esposito, a clownish, keg-shaped Neapolitan, rivaling Big Jim Colosimo in the splendor of his jeweled trap-
pings. Fixer for bootleggers, gamblers and vicemongers, illiterate but
canny, speaking mangled English but a redoubtable labor union
agent, owner of the Bella Napoli Café, Lucullan rendezvous of politicians and gangsters, and lord bountiful to the ward's Italian poor,
Esposito controlled a substantial block of votes. These he placed at
the service of the Republican Senator from Illinois, Charles S. Deneen, whom he greatly admired, even though the Senator carried the
banner of reform and professed to be an uncompromising dry.

On the West Side, between Little Italy and Cicero, there was the
Druggan-Lake or Valley gang. Both wearing fedoras and horn-
rimmed glasses, Terry Druggan, wizened and dwarfish, Frankie Lake,
big and bull-like, were the comic turn of Chicago gangland, a vaudeville brother act about to break into a song-and-dance routine. Lake
had been a railroad switchman, then a member of the Chicago Fire
Department, from which he resigned in 1919 to become Druggan's
partner. They both belonged to the Valley Gang, one of Chicago's
oldest, dating from the 1890s. Evolved under such leaders as "Big
Heinie" Miller, a peerless cracksman; the ferocious brawlers "Paddy
the Bear" Ryan and Walter "the Runt" Quinlan; and, before he
switched to the O'Banion gang, Two-Gun Louis Alterie, the Valley
gang specialized in burglary. Establishing a joint captaincy, Druggan
and Lake guided the members into broader, more remunerative
fields. They took over the North Side cabaret Little Bohemia. Turning to bootlegging, they decided to traffic exclusively in beer, and they
began looking for breweries to buy. Models of piety, the two Irishmen
would brook no slight to religion. They once hijacked a beer truck
standing in front of a church, and upon recognizing the pair in the
front seat as Jewish gangsters, Druggan shouted at them: "Hat's off,
you Jews, when you're passing the house of God or I'll shoot 'em
off!"

On the Southwest Side, the Saltis-McErlane gang. Joe Saltis was a hulking, slow-witted Pole, a saloonkeeper, so enriched by Prohibition that he bought a summer estate in Wisconsin's Eagle River Country, the playground of millionaire sportsmen. If opposed in his efforts to enlarge his speakeasy holdings, he used primitive methods of persuasion. When a woman who owned an ice-cream parlor refused to convert it into a speakeasy under his control, he clubbed her to death. His principal associates were John "Dingbat" O'Berta, another Pole from the Thirteenth Ward, and Frank McErlane. Dingbat, so nicknamed by his schoolmates after a comic strip character, combined labor racketeering with politics. The apostrophe did not belong to Oberta. He added it to Celticize his name because the Thirteenth Ward numbered thousands of Irish voters.

Frank McErlane was an alcoholic and a compulsive killer. The Illinois Association for Criminal Justice pronounced him "the most brutal gunman who ever pulled a trigger in Chicago." He had the build of a Chinese wrestler, a red face and the beady eyes of a wild boar. When he was drunk, his eyes went glassy, a sign which usually portended some act of violence. He was glassy-eyed one night in a Crown Point, Indiana, barroom when an equally drunken companion challenged him to demonstrate his skill with a revolver. McErlane drew a bead on a stranger picked at random, an attorney named Thad Fancher, and sent a bullet through his head.

The killer outraced the Indiana police to the state line and successfully fought extradition for a year. When he was finally brought to trial, the prosecution could no longer call its star witness, one Frank Cochran. His skull had been split with an ax. McErlane was acquitted.

The Saltis-McErlane gang was the first to adopt the weapon that a *Collier's* crime reporter described as "the greatest aid to bigger and better business the criminal has discovered in this generation . . . a diabolical machine of death . . . the highest-powered instrument of destruction that has yet been placed at the convenience of the criminal element . . . an infernal machine . . . the diabolical acme of human ingenuity in man's effort to devise a mechanical contrivance with which to murder his neighbor." This was the Thompson submachine gun—the "tommy gun," "chopper," "typewriter," "Chicago piano"—named after its co-inventor, Brigadier General John T. Thompson, director of arsenals during World War I. Developed too late (1920) for its intended use in trench warfare ("a trench broom," Thompson called it), it was placed on the open market by the New York corporation Auto Ordnance. It met with scant success among the hoped-for customers. Few military agencies, in the United States or abroad, cared to invest in a firearm that fitted no traditional category,* neither a pistol proper nor a rifle, but something of both. Most law enforcement agencies rejected it as a danger to the innocent bystander. To the general's dismay, however, the tommy gun fascinated the underworld.

Light enough ($8\frac{1}{2}$ pounds) for a small boy to operate, the new weapon could fire up to a thousand .45-caliber pistol cartridges a minute; penetrate, at a range of 500 yards, a pine board 3 inches thick; and at closer ranges cut down a tree trunk 23 inches thick, drill through $\frac{1}{4}$-inch steel armor plate, reduce a heavy automobile to junk.

By 1923 Model 21 A, complete with a 20-cartridge capacity box magazine, was retailing at $175. Extra box magazines cost $3 apiece and a 50-cartridge capacity drum magazine, $21. While most cities and states had enacted legislation similar to New York's 1911 Sullivan Law, prohibiting the possession of small, easily concealed firearms, they placed no restrictions on tommy guns. Anybody could buy as many as he liked either by mail order or from a sporting goods store. The seller was required only to register the purchaser's name and address.

The tommy gun became the indispensable accessory of every self-respecting gangster, his ideal weapon of offense and defense and his status symbol. When stricter controls were finally instituted, in the late twenties, he either bought his tommy guns through black market channels at prices as high as $2,000 each or stole them from one of the few police or military arsenals that stocked them.

On the South Side, Ragen's Colts. Here was an archetypal instance of the gangster-politician symbiosis. Predominantly Irish from the Stockyards district, in ages eighteen to thirty, Ragen's Colts—formally, the Ragen's Athletic and Benevolent Association—started as a baseball team, the Morgan Athletic Club. The star pitcher was a lusty boyo with a highly developed political sense named Frank Ragen. By 1902 the club, numbering 160 members, had broadened its inter-

---

* Until World War II, when the United States and its allies bought almost 2,000,000. Today the tommy gun is obsolete.

ests to embrace soccer, football, wrestling, track and miscellaneous social activities. It held an annual fund-raising minstrel show, a picnic and a ball (which citizens' reform groups regularly denounced for its "debauchery and drunkenness"). The proceeds, augmented by contributions from Ragen and other Democratic Party faithful, paid for a building on South Halsted Street that contained a gym, ballroom and pool hall. The change of name in 1908 followed a Donnybrook that broke out during the annual outing in Santa Fe Park over who should head the club. Ragen won the presidency. The baseball team then became Ragen's Colts, a label which the press and public extended to the general membership of the club.

Through a combination of Celtic charm and ruthlessness, Ragen rose high in the Democratic Party and was elected city commissioner, one of Cook County's principal governing officers. The club, which he molded into a powerful party arm, grew to such proportions that it adopted the motto "Hit Me and You Hit 2,000." In addition to notable ballplayers, it turned out aldermen, county treasurers, police captains, sheriffs and sundry officeholders. It also turned out a gallery of criminals. They included Harry Madigan, owner of the Pony Inn, a Cicero saloon, who accumulated eight charges of kidnapping and assault to kill during elections, none of them ever prosecuted, thanks to the club's protection; Joseph "Dynamite" Brooks, another saloonkeeper, a barrel-bellied clodhopper, usually drunk and often homicidal; William "Gunner" McPadden, wanted for numerous murders; Danny McFall, appointed deputy sheriff despite his murder of two business competitors; Yiddles Miller, the prizefight referee, a white supremacist as brutish as any Southern red-neck; Hugh "Stubby" McGovern, gambler, larcenist and triggerman, with a record of seven arrests and only two penalties—both trifling fines for petty larceny and carrying concealed weapons; Ralph Sheldon, who organized his own splinter gang.

At every stage of Ragen's rise the Colts backed him with muscle and firepower. Nor did they confine their operations to a single precinct or candidate. Many politicians all over Chicago, candidates for every office from City Council to the state legislature, owed their victory or defeat to the rampaging Colts. "When we dropped into a polling place," one of them bragged, "everybody else dropped out."

Racists and 110 percent Americans, the Colts further served as protector of Chicago's white population against the encroachments of

Negroes. On a blistering July afternoon in 1919 a Negro boy, swimming off a South Side beach, crossed into segregated waters. From the lakeshore a crowd of white bathers began hurling rocks at him. The boy scrambled aboard a float. A rock knocked him back into the lake, and he drowned. That night the long-smoldering racial tensions of the South Side erupted. Shortly before the first blow was struck, a swaggering youth from Halsted Street warned a group of Negroes (according to their subsequent testimony before a coroner's jury): "Remember it's the Ragen Colts you're dealing with. We have two thousand members between Halsted and Cottage Grove and Forty-third and Sixty-sixth streets. We intend to run this district. Look out." In the ensuing riot the Colts tore through the Black Belt with guns, bombs and torches, shot Negroes on sight, dynamited and set fire to their homes, looted their shops. The Negroes, many of them war veterans armed with their old service revolvers, returned the attack, toppled over automobiles and streetcars carrying whites, wrecked white property. Before the fury burned itself out four days later, 14 Negroes and 20 whites had been killed and on both sides more than 500 injured.

With Prohibition the Ralph Sheldon wing of Ragen's Colts added bootlegging to their exploits.

On the far South Side, the O'Donnell brothers (no relation to the West Side O'Donnells) —Ed "Spike," Steve, Walter and Tommy. Versatile outlaws since boyhood, they were proficient as pickpockets, second-story men, muggers, labor sluggers, bank robbers, political terrorists. Spike, the eldest and the head of the gang, was a raffish, whimsical joker, given to polka-dot bow ties, who had been twice tried for homicide and was suspected of half a dozen other killings. "When arguments fail," he would exhort his troops, "use a blackjack." St. Peter's Catholic Church had no communicant more devout.

The O'Donnells were a force Torrio should have reckoned with in his blueprint for citywide, intergang organization, but he left them out of his calculations, a rare strategic error that would prove costly. He ignored them because they were leaderless and drifting, Spike O'Donnell, without whom they never ventured a coup, having been confined to Joliet Penitentiary for complicity in the $12,000 daylight robbery of the Stockyards Savings and Trust Bank. Spike, however, had no intention of serving his full five-year sentence. He was too well connected politically for that. On Governor Small's desk there already lay letters urging his pardon from six state senators, five state representatives and a criminal court judge. To support themselves while awaiting Spike's release, his brothers hung around the Four Deuces, performing odd jobs for Torrio and Capone and secretly building up resentment against them.

Such were the main Chicago gangs at the outset of Prohibition, and it was a measure of Torrio's statesmanship that despite all their old ethnic, political and commercial rivalries—now intensified by the prospect of fantastic riches—he managed to keep them not only at peace for almost three years but, with few exceptions, cooperative in his own ascendancy.

7

"A. Capone, Antique Dealer"

SO the listing read in the Chicago telephone directory. He had some business cards printed, describing himself less pretentiously as "Alphonse Capone, second hand furniture dealer, 2220 South Wabash Avenue," and he stocked a storefront adjoining the Four Deuces with junk. He never tried to sell any of it. Prospective collectors who made inquiries by phone were told, if anybody answered at all, "We ain't open today." Capone maintained the shop as a cover for illicit dealings. These he handled so expeditiously, he proved so reliable an aide, that Torrio rewarded him with the management of the Four Deuces and a 25 percent share of the profits from all his brothels. In 1920 this came to $25,000. Torrio further promised Capone 50 percent of the bootleg business as soon as it started to produce revenue. They had liked and trusted each other since the early days in New York. They complemented each other, the slight older man, cool, taciturn, reserved, condoning violence only when guile failed; the beefy younger one, gregarious, pleasure-loving, physically fearless, hot-tempered. By the second year they no longer stood in the relationship of boss and hireling; they were partners.

In November, 1920, Capone got bad news from home. For some time his father had been suffering from heart disease, an affliction not improved by the day labor to which he had been reduced after giving up his barbershop. On the evening of the fourteenth he dropped around to the poolroom in Garfield Place, a step from his front door, where Al had once racked up so many victories. While watching a game he collapsed and, carried back to No. 38, died before the doctor came. He was fifty-two. The doctor named as the cause of death myocarditis—inflammation of the cardiac muscle.

"Al's a good boy," Teresa Capone would always insist. When she became a widow, he opened his arms to her and to his brothers and sisters, bringing them one after the other to Chicago as fast as his means allowed—all except Jim, whose fate was still a mystery. He housed them and fed them, found work for the older boys, and generally, in the Italian family tradition, saw to their welfare. He later had his father's remains exhumed, shipped to Chicago and, having bought Plot 48 in Mount Olivet Cemetery, reburied there under a shaft of black marble with a portrait fastened to the base.

The first brother to follow Al to Chicago was Ralph, the second oldest after Jim, who also adopted the *nom de crime* "Brown." At twenty-eight he did not entirely lack underworld experience. He had tended bar in a Brooklyn speakeasy during the first year of Prohibition. He was twice arrested and fined. On the other hand, he had held down more lawful jobs for longer periods than any of his brothers: Western Union messenger at eleven, the year he quit public school; a paper and cloth cutter in the same bindery as Al; streetcar conductor; salesman; longshoreman. When America declared war against Germany, Ralph joined the Marines but got no farther than boot camp on Parris Island, where he was discharged because of flat feet. In Chicago he reverted to bartending in one of the Torrio-Capone resorts. He then replaced Al as manager of the Four Deuces. For a time he shared an apartment on South Wabash Avenue with Al and his wife. Charlie and Rocco Fischetti, first cousins of the Capone boys, who had also come to Chicago at Al's urging, lived in the same building. Like Ralph, they rose to the command level of the Torrio-Capone forces.

In anticipation of his mother's coming to Chicago Al chose a quiet, tree-shaded section of South Prairie Avenue, near St. Columbanas Church, and there built a two-story, fifteen-room red-brick house. The upstairs parlor of No. 7244 had floor-to-ceiling mirrors and gilded cornices. The bathroom accouterments were imported from Germany and included a seven-foot bathtub. A steel gate led from an alley at the rear into the basement. Here the walls were impervious to bullets, having been constructed of reinforced concrete a foot thick, and the windows had steel bars set too close together to admit a bomb.

Al moved into the seven ground-floor rooms with his mother, two sisters, wife and son, while Ralph, who married a girl named Velma Pheasant and had a son and daughter, occupied the eight rooms above. Al enrolled Mafalda in a private girls' school near home, the Richards School, to which he played Santa Claus every Christmas thereafter, driving a Cadillac to the entrance heaped with boxes of candy, baskets of fruit, turkeys and a gift for every student and teacher. The two youngest brothers, John "Mimi" and Matt, also made their home for some years at 7244 South Prairie. Mitzi, a bibulous, girl-chasing youth of eighteen, had barely reached Chicago in 1922 when he was arrested for disorderly conduct and fined $5. Matt, four years younger, had an exemplary record as an adolescent. Al sent him to the Marmion Military School in Aurora, Illinois, then to Pennsylvania's Villanova University. Twenty-seven-year-old Frank Capone completed the family circle. The brothers resembled each other. All had thick, heavy bodies and blunt features, and when assembled in family council, they suggested a small herd of ruminating bison.

Though by 1922 Capone was known to both the underworld and the police of Chicago, he meant so little to newspaper reporters that the first time they had occasion to mention him they got his Christian name wrong and inadvertently gave the original version of the family name, calling him "Alfred Caponi." One of his own best customers, Al drank, gambled and whored. Early one August morning, after a night of carousal, he was racing his car along North Wabash Avenue with a girl beside him and three men in the rear seat. Rounding the corner of East Randolph Street, he crashed into a parked taxi, injuring the driver, one Fred Krause. Jumping to the sidewalk in a drunken rage, Capone flashed a deputy sheriff's badge (evidence of the political patronage he already enjoyed), brandished a revolver, and threatened to shoot Krause. From a passing streetcar the conductor yelled at him to put up his weapon. Capone threatened to shoot him, too. His four companions fled. The police arrived before any further violence occurred, and an ambulance intern bandaged the bleeding cabdriver. "Alfred Caponi" was booked on three charges —assault with an automobile, driving while intoxicated, and carrying a concealed weapon—any one of which would have sufficed to put an ordinary offender behind bars. But like almost every case that was to be filed against "Deputy Sheriff" Capone during the next seven years, it did not even come to trial. He never set foot in court. The charges were not only dropped, but expunged from the record.

The options open to beer brewers when Prohibition came were, in the main, threefold. They could convert to the manufacture of legal near beer, first brewing the standard product with its alcoholic content of 3 percent or 4 percent, then dealcoholizing it to $\frac{1}{2}$ percent. At considerable financial sacrifice they could lease their breweries or sell them outright. Or they could secretly retain part ownership through affiliation with gangsters. Under this last arrangement the brewers furnished the capital, the technical skills and the administrative experience; the gangsters, fronting as officers and company directors, bought police and political protection, fought hijackers and territorial invaders, took the "fall"—the legal liability—when trouble threatened.

One of Chicago's leading brewers was Joseph Stenson, scion of a rich and respectable Gold Coast family. He chose the third course. To the dismay of his three older brothers, he took on Terry Druggan and Frankie Lake as partners in the operation of five breweries: the Gambrinus, the Standard, the George Hoffman, the Pfeiffer and the Stege. Early in 1920 Torrio became a fourth partner and with Stenson's backing obtained control of four more breweries—the West Hammond, the Manhattan, the Best and the Sieben—as well as a few distilleries.

While establishing his lines of supply, Torrio approached the commanders of the top gangs with an argument at once simple and irresistible. Most of them were already involved in one phase or another of bootlegging, though not to the exclusion of burglary, safecracking, bank robbery and sundry crimes of violence. The returns from these traditional practices, Torrio contended, did not justify the risks. Bootlegging, on the other hand, promised to make them all millionaires at negligible risk, and he urged them to concentrate their resources on it. As he saw it, the main prerequisite of success was citywide organization based on the principle of territorial inviolability. No speakeasy, no cabaret, no whorehouse in that territory would be allowed to buy from any alien source. In the event of encroachment by outsiders, of hijacking, the injured party could call on the other treaty members to join in punitive action against the offender. If a gang chose to operate its own brewery or distillery, as some did, it should remain free to do so. Otherwise, Torrio was prepared to supply all the beer needed at $50 a barrel. He also stood ready to supervise interterritory transactions and to arbitrate any disputes arising out of them. This would give him control of almost 1,000 combat-hardened hoodlums.

The gang leaders accepted Torrio's plan. With some of them he reached subagreements. O'Banion's specialty in the liquor traffic, for example, was running whiskey from Canada and cutting it for local distribution, but he felt he must provide beer, too, when his customers demanded it lest they turn to a competitor. Conversely, Torrio preferred to handle beer. Beer was the workingman's drink. Beer was Chicago. The enormous volume consumed left a good margin for profit at a relatively small price per glass. But Torrio had to have hard liquor as well for his city dives and suburban roadhouses. So the Irishman and the Italian submerged their mutual antipathy and agreed to exchange commodities. Beer did not interest the Gennas at all. Their paramount concern was to control Little Italy's alky-cooking industry and the liquor market it supplied. Torrio had little difficulty obtaining from them, in return for recognition of their supremacy in Little Italy, safe passage through Genna territory for his beer trucks.

Peace settled over gangland. Everybody prospered. Torrio and his partners, with a physical plant worth $5,000,000 and working capital of $25,000,000, grossed $12,000,000 a year. Then, during the summer of 1923, Spike O'Donnell came home from Joliet.

With their leader restored to them, the South Side O'Donnells, who had been smarting for years under Torrio's contemptuous treatment, revolted. Reinforced by thugs imported from New York, notably a dauntless savage named Harry Hasmiller, they began hijacking Torrio's beer trucks and running beer into both his territory and the territory claimed by the Saltis-McErlane gang. Their best beer drummers were George "Sport" Bucher and George Meeghan, who applied a system of salesmanship believed to have been invented by Spike O'Donnell and soon adopted by every gang. It consisted of walking into a speakeasy, fixing the owner with a baleful eye, and informing him that henceforth he must buy his beer from the O'Donnells. The alternative would be horrible damage to the premises and to himself. "Or else" was the standard phrase, and in the mouths of Bucher and Meeghan it usually compelled submission.

By September the O'Donnell gang had penetrated deep into the South and Southwest sides when the Saltis-McErlane gang, now Torrio allies, struck the opening blow in the "beer war." On the rainy night of the seventh Bucher and Meeghan, accompanied by Steve, Walter and Tommy O'Donnell and Jerry O'Connor, a paroled Joliet lifer, paid a second visit to Jacob Geis' speakeasy at 2154 West Fifty-first Street. The first time Geis had not only defied the two drummers, but with the aid of his bartender, Nick Gorysko, bounced them out of the place. Steve O'Donnell told him they were giving him a last chance. Geis still refused to do business with them. He was standing behind the bar, helping Gorysko serve half a dozen customers. The invaders dragged him headfirst across to the other side and blackjacked him, fracturing his skull. When Gorysko showed fight, they knocked him unconscious. Their blood up, they went on to storm five other speakeasies that were getting beer from Torrio, smashed the furniture, and beat up anybody who crossed their path. Their last stop was a friendly saloon, Joe Klepka's on South Lincoln Street, where Spike O'Donnell joined them.

All this time three McErlane gorillas, led by Danny McFall, a Ragen-trained gunman, had been stalking them. As they slouched against Klepka's bar, slaking their thirst and devouring sandwiches, the avengers burst through the swinging doors, guns drawn. According to the testimony of one of the six customers present, McFall said "Stick 'em up!" and fired a shot over Steve O'Donnell's head. The four brothers and their companions dived through the exits, all except Jerry O'Connor, a slow mover. McFall held him captive at revolver point. McErlane himself then appeared, fat and red-faced, carrying a sawed-off double-barreled shotgun under his gray raincoat. At a whispered word from McFall he withdrew to wait just beyond the swinging doors. Waving his revolver toward the doors, McFall ordered O'Connor to walk out ahead of him. The instant they reached the sidewalk McErlane put the shotgun to O'Connor's head and blew it off.

Ten nights later, on a stretch of highway a few miles south of Chicago, Bucher and Meeghan were driving two truckloads of beer in tandem. Two men armed with shotguns sprang to the center of the road, halted them, and made them climb down. A car approaching from the opposite direction caught the scene in its headlights. The holdup men shouted to the driver to stop, but he sped on, terrified, as they fired a fusillade of buckshot after him. From the descriptions he later gave the police suspected Frankie McErlane and Danny McFall. The following morning the drummers' bodies were found in a roadside ditch, their arms lashed behind their backs, their heads almost severed by the force of shotgun blasts.

In December, on the same highway, McErlane and a companion whom the police believed to have been Walter Stevens, bagged two more O'Donnell truckers as they were hauling beer to Chicago, William "Shorty" Egan and Morrie Keane, trussed them up and bundled them into the back seat of their car. Egan, one of the few men ever taken for a one-way ride who lived to tell of it, recalled:

"Pretty soon the driver asks the guy with the shotgun, 'Where you gonna get rid of these guys?' The fat fellow laughs and says, 'I'll take care of that in a minute.' He was monkeying with his shotgun all the time. Pretty soon he turns around and points the gun at Keane. He didn't say a word but just let go straight at him. Keane got it square on the left side. It kind of turned him over and the fat guy give him the second barrel in the other side. The guy loads up his gun and gives it to Keane again. Then he turns around to me and says, 'I guess you might as well get yours, too.' With that he shoots me in the side. It hurt like hell so when I seen him loading up again, I twist around so it won't hit me in the same place. This time he got me in the leg. Then he gimme the other barrel right on the puss. I slide off the seat. But I guess the fat guy wasn't sure we was through. He let Morrie have it twice more and then he let me have it again in the other side. The fat guy scrambled into the rear seat and grabbed Keane. He opens the door and kicks Morrie out into the road. We was doing about 50 from the sound. I figure I'm next so when he drags me over to the door I set myself to jump. He shoves and I light in the ditch by the road. I hit the ground on my shoulders and I thought I would never stop rolling. I lost consciousness. When my senses came back, I was lying in a pool of water and ice had formed around me. The sky was red and it was breaking day. I staggered along the road until I saw a light in a farmhouse. . . ."

The O'Donnells were no match for the coalition Torrio had created. The next member of the gang to fall was another beer runner,

Phil Corrigan, shotgunned to death at the wheel of his truck. Walter O'Donnell and the New York bravo, Harry Hasmiller, perished together in a running gunfight with a Saltis-McErlane detachment. It was against Spike O'Donnell, on the evening of September 25, 1925, that McErlane first used his newly acquired tommy gun. Driving past the corner of Sixty-third and Western Avenue, where Spike was loitering, he fired a round at him. Lacking practice, he sent every bullet wild. The tommy gun was still a weapon so unfamiliar to the police that they ascribed the multiple bullet holes in the storefront behind Spike to shotguns or some sort of automatic rifle.

A month later, near the same spot, McErlane machine-gunned Spike's car and wounded his brother Tommy, sitting beside him. Spike finally abandoned the field of combat. Ten times the enemy had tried to kill him, and they had wounded him twice. "Life with me is just one bullet after another," he said with a flash of his old jauntiness. "I've been shot at and missed so often I've a notion to hire out as a professional target." He left Chicago and stayed away for two years.

The victors defeated the law as well. McErlane, who personally accounted for five deaths in the O'Donnell ranks, was charged with the murder of Morrie Keane. Held briefly under a kind of house arrest at the Hotel Sherman by order of State's Attorney Robert E. Crowe, he was unconditionally released. The pressure of public opinion then forced Crowe to seek a grand jury indictment. After months of legal manipulations, an assistant state's attorney nolle prossed the case. Crowe also obtained indictments against McErlane and Danny McFall for the double slaying of Bucher and Meeghan. Those, too, were nolle prossed. A third indictment named McFall as the murderer of Jerry O'Connor. Released on bail, he vanished.

In several of the beer war massacres Al Capone was placed at the scene by eyewitnesses, none of whom, however, would so testify under oath. "I'm only a secondhand furniture dealer," Capone told the police. When the surviving O'Donnell brothers were brought face-to-face with him at police headquarters and asked if they could connect him with any of the killings, they observed the underworld code of silence, but during later questioning Spike O'Donnell, boiling over with frustration, betrayed his belief in Capone's guilt. "I can whip this bird Capone with bare fists any time he wants to step out in the open and fight like a man," said he.

8

Cicero

THE conquest of Cicero, begun by Torrio and com-
pleted by Capone, exemplified in its initial stage the older man's mas-
terly diplomacy, for it was accomplished without a drop of bloodshed.
They first had to reckon with the West Side O'Donnells, Klondike,
Myles and Bernard, who were entrenched not only in the Chicago
Avenue-Madison Street sector, but also in Cicero under the aegis of
its political panjandrum, Eddie Vogel. The town's docile president
(a title equivalent to mayor), Joseph Z. Klenha, took orders from
Vogel, the O'Donnells and Eddie Tancl, a broken-nosed, cauliflower-
eared ex-lightweight fighter, who retired from the ring after killing
a contender called Young Greenberg with a single blow to the jaw
and opened a saloon in Cicero, the Hawthorne Park Café. But though
politically corrupt, Cicero had been relatively free of vice and crime.
It was a dormitory town with a population of about 60,000, the majority first- and second-generation Bohemians, employed in the nearby
factories of Southwest Chicago, an industrious, law-abiding people.
After the day's toil they liked to empty a seidel or two of beer in
their neighborhood saloon, and when the same saloon, with its familiar swinging doors, brass footrails and spittoons, went right on
serving beer during Prohibition, the idea that they were committing
an offense by continuing to patronize it struck them as preposterous.
There were no brothels in Cicero, and gambling was restricted to
slot machines whose operators shared their profits with Vogel.

In October, 1923, Torrio set in motion a long-matured stratagem. To Cicero he moved a score of his prostitutes, installing them in a house he had leased on Roosevelt Road. As he expected, the local police promptly raided the place and locked up the girls. Torrio opened another brothel at Ogden and Fifty-second avenues with the same result. Meekly, he withdrew. But if he had no clout in Cicero, elsewhere in Cook County there were officials who danced to his tune. Such was Sheriff Peter B. Hoffman. Two days after the Ogden Avenue raid he dispatched a squad of deputy sheriffs to Cicero with orders to impound every slot machine they could find. Vogel got the point: If Torrio couldn't have a whorehouse in Cicero, then nobody could have slot machines there.

The upshot was a tripartite treaty. Vogel recovered the slot machines along with the assurance that the sheriff's office would not hamper their operation. The O'Donnells won an exclusive beer franchise in several sections of Cicero, and Torrio reaffirmed their authority on Chicago's West Side. What Torrio really wanted for himself did not, contrary to Vogel's belief, involve prostitution. His existing string of urban and suburban whorehouses produced such wealth that it was no great sacrifice to forgo a Cicero addition. He had bigger stakes in view. Upon his agreeing to import no more whores he was granted permission to sell beer anywhere in Cicero outside the territory allocated to the O'Donnells, to run gambling houses there and to establish a base for all his enterprises save the bordellos.

The treaty infuriated Eddie Tancl, who detested Torrio. He had refused to take part in the negotiations leading up to it. He now proclaimed his intention of buying his beer wherever he chose. His friendship with the O'Donnells, who had been provisioning his saloon, cooled. When they tried to fob off some barrels of needle beer—that is, near beer to which raw alcohol had been added—he broke off all business relations with them. Klondike O'Donnell and Torrio ordered him to get out of town. He laughed in their faces.

In Chicago, meanwhile, the specter of reform confronted Torrio. The abuses of the Thompson regime had become so flagrant as to preclude Big Bill's chances of reelection. His campaign manager, the ex-medicine man Fred Lundin, was indicted with twenty-three co-conspirators for misappropriating more than $1,000,000 of school funds. According to a trial witness, a member of the Board of Edu-

cation, who had protested in behalf of the public against gross over-
payments for school textbooks, Lundin replied: "To hell with the
public! We're at the trough now and we're going to feed." The legal
team of Darrow and Erbstein kept the accused out of jail, but the
stench lingered. Thompson, knowing he was defeated in advance,
withdrew his candidacy from the 1923 primary.

The mayoralty went to a Democrat, Judge William E. Dever, who
chose as his Chief of Police, Morgan A. Collins. An hour after the
bodies of Bucher and Meeghan had been found, Dever summoned
his appointee to a press conference and told him: "Collins, there's
a dry law on the nation's books. This town will immediately become
dry. Tell your captains I will break every police official in whose district I hear of a drop of liquor being sold." Collins tried hard to de-
hydrate Chicago. With his encouragement the police went so far as
to invade private homes and arrest people for possession of as much
as a single bottle of liquor, a crusade that turned the public against
them. Dever also issued a proclamation as well meant as it was over-
optimistic:

> Until the murderers [of O'Connor, Bucher and Meeghan] have
> been apprehended and punished and the illegal traffic for control
> of which they battle has been suppressed, the dignity of the law
> and the average man's respect for it is imperiled and every officer
> of the law and every enforcing agency should lay aside other duties
> and join in the common cause—a restoration of law and order.
> The police will follow this case to a finish as they do all others
> [sic]. This guerrilla war between hijackers, rum runners and il-
> licit beer peddlers will be crushed. I am just as sure that this mis-
> erable traffic with its toll of human life and morals can be stamped
> out as I am mayor that I am not going to flinch for a minute.

How radically the new administration differed from the old Torrio
discovered when he attempted to subvert Collins. Through an inter-
mediary he offered him $100,000 a month not to interfere with his
Chicago activities. For answer Collins padlocked the Four Deuces.
Torrio later offered him $1,000 a day merely to overlook the move-
ment of 250 barrels of beer a day. Collins kept up his attack. In addition to harassing Torrio's Chicago breweries, brothels and gambling
dens, his men arrested about 100 gangsters. They closed 200 of Mont
Tennes' handbook parlors, forcing him to retire from racetrack gambling. By the end of the year gambling had temporarily ceased to be

an important source of the Chicago underworld's revenue. As for vice, the director of the Juvenile Protective Association, Miss Jessie Binford, reported:

> There is no doubt that a sincere, energetic effort has been made to minimize commercialized vice in Chicago. Nightly raids inaugurated by Chief Collins have played havoc with the vice ring and broken a majority of the more notorious resorts and driven others to cover. The Collins drive was at first thought to be a temporary purity move for political purposes. In the underworld the appointment of Collins was lauded, but as time passed and his apparent desire to clean the town and keep it clean had reached the underworld, their ranks have been badly shattered. . . . The administration has stopped the vice ring for the time being. . . .

It occurred to Torrio and Capone that as long as Dever occupied City Hall, they would need a haven beyond his reach. They chose Cicero, and while most of their Chicago establishments continued to thrive—for no reformer could ever completely purge the law enforcement agencies of Chicago—while they maintained homes in the city and spent most of their leisure hours there, Cicero remained their center of operations throughout Dever's tenure. Those who accompanied them or followed them there, charter members of a rapidly growing syndicate, included Ralph and Frank Capone and their cousins the Fischettis; the Guziks; the La Cava brothers, Louis and Joseph; Pete Penovich, Jimmy Mondi, Tony "Mops" Volpi, Peter Payette, Louis Consentino, Frank "the Enforcer" Nitti and Frankie Pope, who had peddled newspapers before he made a killing as a gambler and was hence known as "the millionaire newsboy." Dion O'Banion became an associate in the syndicate's gambling enterprises, as well as in its breweries.

In the fall of 1923 Torrio decided to rest awhile from his labors, and with his wife and mother he set sail for a sightseeing tour of Europe, leaving Capone to consolidate their gains. He carried abroad more than $1,000,000 in cash, negotiable securities and letters of credit with which he opened accounts in various Continental banks. By the seaside near his native Naples he bought his mother an imposing villa, staffed it with servants, settled a small fortune on her, and left her to end her days in regal pomp.

It was this munificence, typical of gang leaders, munificence not only to family but to friends and community, that John Landesco, the scholarly chief investigator of the Illinois Association for Criminal Justice, cited when explaining the admiration men like Torrio aroused among poor immigrants. "Why should they be outcasts in the opinions of the ignorant, humble, needy, hard-working people around them?" he said. "They are the successes of the neighborhood. The struggling, foreign-born peasant woman sees them in their expensive cars and their fur-trimmed overcoats. She hears they are sending their children to private schools, as Joe Saltis does. She hears them called 'beer barons' and if she can read the headlines in the English language newspapers, she sees them described as 'beer barons' and 'booze kings' in print. The word 'booze' has no criminal significance to her, but the words 'king' and 'baron' have a most lofty significance. About all she knows is that these richly dressed young men are making or selling something that the Americans want to buy.

"Incidentally, she hears in gossip with another toilworn neighbor that Johnny Torrio, 'king' of them all, gave his old mother back home in *Italia* a villa with 15 servants to run it.

"If the robber, labor thug and racketeer, the late Tim Murphy, who was the co-criminal of the gangsters of boozedom, spoke at a 13th Ward meeting in behalf of one of gangdom's political henchmen, that did the candidate no harm. For was not a priest sitting next to Murphy on the platform? If some tactless soul asked, 'Is he the Tim Murphy that they said robbed the mails?' the response was deeply resentful. The attitude of the ignorant foreign-born who judged gangdom in the terms of its success would be, first, that it was doubtful whether Murphy did rob the mails and, second, 'What harm did that do us?' Hence the support of Big Tim never hurt Dingbat Oberta, the political henchman of Joe Saltis' gang of beer runners. Oberta gave a stand of colors to the Nellis post of the Veterans of Foreign Wars. Some of the money of racketeer banquets where Murphy acclaimed Oberta would be given to the same organization.

"Thus, and in a hundred other ways, the whole issue between good and bad government and good and bad men is befuddled and the sole conviction of the ignorant is that these 'successes of the neighborhood' seem to take vastly more interest in neighborhood matters than men not in the booze racket do."

In Torrio's absence Capone chose as his Cicero headquarters the centrally located Hawthorne Inn at 4833 Twenty-second Street, a two-story structure of brown brick with white tiles set in the upper façade. He had bulletproof steel shutters affixed to every window, and at every entrance he stationed an armed lookout. Four plaster columns painted green supported the lobby ceiling. On the walls hung stuffed big-game heads. Red-carpeted stairs rose to the second-floor bedrooms, where Capone and his associates often spent the night.

Torrio got back from Europe at a critical juncture in Cicero politics. It was the spring of 1924, election time. The Klenha faction, backed by a bipartisan machine, had ruled the town for three terms, but now the Democrats were putting up a separate slate. Boss Vogel, worried lest the fever of reform raging in Chicago under Mayor Dever should infect Cicero, went to Torrio and Capone with a proposition they found attractive: Let them ensure a Klenha victory and they could count on immunity from the law in any enterprise they undertook in Cicero, whoremongering excepted. Here was a challenge calling for combat rather than diplomacy, work for Capone and his brother Frank, whose quiet, bankerlike demeanor masked considerable savagery. With Torrio agreeing to what he considered a necessary evil, Capone borrowed from their Chicago allies shock troops totaling about 200, including a contingent of Ragen's Colts. The opposition did not reject gangster support either, and to their cause rallied the bootleg beer wholesalers eager to arrogate the Torrio-Capone territory to themselves.

The first casualty was the Democratic candidate for town clerk, William K. Pflaum. Besieging his office on the eve of elections, March 31, the Capone thugs roughed him up and wrecked the place. When the polls opened, a fleet of black, seven-passenger limousines, carrying heavily armed Caponeites, cruised the town, sowing terror wherever they halted. They so far outnumbered the opposition hoodlums that there was never any real contest. They slugged Ciceronians known to favor the Democrats. As a voter waited in line to cast his ballot, a menacing, slouch-hatted figure would sidle up to him and ask how he intended to vote. If the reply was unsatisfactory, the hooligan would snatch the ballot from him, mark it himself, hand it back, and stand by, fingering the revolver in his coat pocket, until the voter had dropped the ballot into the box. Defiant voters were slugged, honest poll watchers and election officials kidnapped and held captive until the polls closed. A Democratic campaign worker named Michael Gavin was shot through both legs and dumped into the basement of a gangster-owned Chicago hotel along with eight other recalcitrant Democrats. Ragen's Colts kidnapped an election clerk, Joseph Price, beat him and kept him gagged and trussed at Harry Madigan's Pony Inn. A policeman was blackjacked. Two men were shot dead on Twenty-second Street near the Hawthorne Inn. A third man had his throat slashed and a fourth was killed in Eddie Tancl's saloon.

A group of horrified Cicero citizens appealed for help to Cook County Judge Edward K. Jarecki. He deputized seventy Chicago patrolmen, five squads of detectives and nine squads of motorized police and rushed them to the beleaguered town. All afternoon gangsters and police fought pitched battles. The climax came toward dusk. A squad car carrying Detective Sergeant Cusick and Patrolmen Mc-Glynn, Grogan, Cassin and Campion pulled up opposite a polling place at the corner of Twenty-second Street and Cicero Avenue. There, intimidating the voters with drawn automatics, stood Al and Frank Capone and their cousin, Charlie Fischetti. Piling out of their car, armed with shotguns and rifles, the police started across the street. When word of what followed reached Dion O'Banion, he immediately called his wholesaler and ordered some $20,000 worth of flowers. . . .

During the early twenties the Chicago flivver police used the same type of long black limousine as the gangsters. Since they were no more eager than the gangsters to proclaim their presence, their cars bore no identifying signs, with the result that the hunted were sometimes confused with the hunters. Thus, the trio at the Cicero Avenue polls may have mistaken Cusick and his men for rival gangsters because the moment the squad moved toward them they began shooting. Frank Capone took point-blank aim at Patrolman McGlynn, but the trigger of his automatic clicked against an empty chamber. Before he could pull the trigger again, McGlynn and Grogan gave him both barrels of their shotguns and he fell dead on the sidewalk. Al Capone, fleeing down the avenue, ran into another squad, held them at bay with a revolver in both hands and finally escaped under cover of night. The police never arrested him. They captured Fischetti but speedily released him.

The obsequies for Frank Capone, attended by such grandees of the underworld as the labor union boss "Dago Mike" Carozzo, the deluxe fence Julian "Potatoes" Kaufman and Hymie Weiss, eclipsed the splendor of even Big Jim Colosimo's funeral. The coffin was satin-lined and silver-plated, and O'Banion surpassed himself in the magnificence of his floral compositions. There was a heart six feet high fashioned of red carnations "from the boys in Chicago Heights" and a monumental lyre of lilies and orchids "from the boys in Hammond." The Chicago *Tribune*, pronouncing the pomp fit for a "distinguished statesman," reported:

> Before noon the entire interior of the [Capone] house was banked with a profusion of blossoms. When every nook and cranny from the kitchen to the attic had been fairly choked with these delicate tributes, they were heaped up on the front porch and hung from the balcony. In only a few minutes more attachés were obliged to park the floral pieces on the lawn.
>
> By nightfall the entire terrace was covered with brilliant blossoms.
>
> Finally the lack of space made it necessary to festoon the trees and lamp posts in front of the house with wreaths, immortelles and hanging baskets.

In Cicero, as a mark of respect for the slain man, nearly every saloonkeeper kept his blinds drawn and his doors locked for two hours.

Riding behind the hearse with his family on the way to Mount Olivet Cemetery, his jowls dark with the ritual growth of stubble. Capone could take comfort from the knowledge that his brother had not died for nothing. The Klenha slate won the election by an enormous plurality.

At the inquest on Frank both Al and Charlie Fischetti declared that they could furnish no relevant information. A year earlier the state's attorney, inquiring into how gangsters obtained permits to carry guns, learned that the Capones got theirs from a Chicago justice of the peace, George Miller. The permits were revoked. Now, in the course of the inquest, it developed that Justice Emil Fisher of Cicero had reissued gun permits to the Capones for "self-protection."

Eddie Vogel kept his side of the bargain. On May 1, one month after the elections, Torrio and Capone launched, without interference, their first Cicero gambling house. the Hawthorne Smoke Shop, next to the Hawthorne Inn. Managed for them by Frankie Pope, it was primarily a floating handbook operating at different addresses under different names—the Subway, the Ship. the Radio. From time to time the police felt constrained for the sake of appearances to stage a raid. They always gave ample advance notice, whereupon the action would shift to one of the alternative addresses. At the original Hawthorne Smoke Shop an average of $50,000 a day was bet on horse races, and during the first years the house netted more than $400,000. The number of gambling establishments in Cicero grew to 161. With cappers drumming up trade at the entrance, with whiskey sold inside at 75 cents a shot, wine at 30 cents a glass and beer at 25 cents a stein, they ran full blast twenty-four hours a day every day. Many of them Torrio and Capone owned outright or controlled. In the latter case they kept a lieutenant on the premises both to protect the proprietor against interlopers and to collect their cut, which ranged from 25 percent to 50 percent of the gross. One of these independents, Lauderback's, at Forty-eighth Avenue and Twelfth Street, catered to some of the country's wildest plungers, with as much as $100,000 riding on a single spin of the roulette wheel. The majority of the gambling dives, as well as of Cicero's 123 saloons, bought their beer, willingly or unwillingly, from the Torrio breweries.

The only influential Ciceronian who continued to defy Torrio and the O'Donnells was Eddie Tancl. He went on buying his beer whereever he wished. Early one Sunday morning, after an all-night spree, Myles O'Donnell and a drinking companion, Jim Doherty, staggered into Tancl's saloon and ordered breakfast. At a table across the room sat Tancl, his wife, his head bartender, Leo Klimas, and his star entertainer, Mayme McClain. Only one waiter, Martin Simet, was still on duty. The bill he brought O'Donnell and Doherty when they finished breakfast furnished the pretext they were looking for. They loudly complained that he had overcharged them.

Tancl came over to their table just as O'Donnell threw a punch at the waiter. The ex-prizefighter stepped between them. O'Donnell gave him a shove. At this the enmity that had been building up for months between the two men exploded. They both drew guns, fired simultaneously, and wounded each other in the chest. Doherty joined the combat, firing wildly. Simet and Klimas rushed him and tried to disarm him. A bullet from O'Donnell's gun sent Klimas crashing back against the bar, dead.

O'Donnell and Tancl, still shooting at each other, fell, bleeding from several wounds, got up, resumed firing until their guns were empty. O'Donnell, pierced by four bullets, lurched out into the street, followed by Doherty. They ran off in opposite directions. Tancl, though mortally wounded, took another revolver from behind the bar and stumbled after O'Donnell, shooting as he went. His gun was empty when he overtook him two blocks from the saloon, and he hurled it at his head. The effort exhausted his last reserves of energy, and he fell to the street. So did O'Donnell. There they lay within reach of each other, but no longer able to move, the one dying, the other unconscious, when Simet arrived. "Get him," Tancl gasped. "He got me." They were his last words. Simet jumped up and down on the senseless O'Donnell, kicked him in the head, and left him for dead.

Jim Doherty, who had also been gravely wounded, dragged himself to a hospital. There the police brought the mangled O'Donnell, and after weeks of treatment both men recovered. Assistant State's Attorney William McSwiggin prosecuted them without success.

Such savagery earned Cicero a unique reputation. Mayor Klenha, injured in his civic pride, claimed it was grossly exaggerated. Cicero, he insisted, was no worse than Chicago; who could tell when one left Chicago and entered Cicero? A Chicago wag observed: "If you smell gunpowder, you're in Cicero."

A week after the Hawthorne Smoke Shop opened its doors, Capone went underground, having committed murder in full view of at least three witnesses. Friendship partly motivated the deed, friendship for Jake "Greasy Thumb" Guzik, the oldest of the three Guzik brothers. Capone used to call him "the only friend I can really trust." Their friendship blossomed during the early days of the Four Deuces, when Guzik, an old hand at brothelkeeping, joined the Torrio outfit. Thirteen years older than Capone, a short, penguin-shaped man, wattled, dewlapped and pouchy-eyed, he wore a perpetually plaintive air. Regarding the significance of his nickname, there were two versions. According to the first, "Greasy Thumb" alluded to Guzik's beginnings as a clumsy waiter whose thumb constantly slipped into the soup. The second version has it that his thumb was always greasy from counting greenbacks.*

* Probably nobody ever walked up to Guzik and said, "Hi, Greasy Thumb." Nor did gangsters address each other as "Schemer," "Enforcer," "Potatoes," etc., except in movies and fiction. Such nomenclature was chiefly a game played by newspapermen. Legend ascribes many of the more picturesque sobriquets to James Doherty, a Chicago *Tribune* crime reporter, and Clem Lane, a Chicago *Daily News* rewrite man, who supposedly amused themselves on slow nights by coining them.

"I don't know why they call me a hoodlum," Guzik once complained. "I never carried a gun in my life." He never did, or indulged in any violent deeds or language. His forte was accountancy, which he applied with brilliant results first to the brothel, then to the bootlegging business. As business manager of the Torrio-Capone syndicate and its No. 3 member, he reorganized it along the lines of a holding company. When Mayor Dever's police closed the Four Deuces, new headquarters were quietly set up two blocks away at 2146 South Michigan Avenue, a doctor's shingle—"A. Brown, MD" —nailed to the door and the front office furnished to resemble a doctor's waiting room. On shelves in the adjoining room stood row upon row of sample liquor bottles. Retailers prepared to place a large order could take a sample and have it analyzed by a chemist. In this way the syndicate built up a reputation as purveyors of quality merchandise.

The rest of Dr. A. Brown's office accommodated Guzik, his clerical staff and records of all the syndicate's transactions in six different areas. One group of ledgers listed wealthy individuals, hundreds of them, as well as the hotels and restaurants buying wholesale quantities of the syndicate's liquor; a second group of ledgers gave all the speakeasies in Chicago and vicinity that it supplied; a third, the channels through which it obtained liquor smuggled into the country by truck from Canada and by boat from the Caribbean; a fourth, the corporate structure of the breweries it owned or controlled; a fifth, the assets and income of its bordellos; a sixth, the police and Prohibition agents receiving regular payoffs.

The syndicate faced catastrophe in the spring of 1924, when, during a raid on 2146 South Michigan ordered by Dever and led by Detective Sergeant Edward Birmingham, these ledgers were seized. Guzik dangled $5,000 in cash under Birmingham's nose as the price of his silence. The detective reported the offer to his superiors. "We've got the goods now," Mayor Dever announced. But the rejoicing proved premature. Before either the state's attorney or any federal agency could inspect the incriminating ledgers, a municipal judge, Howard Hayes, impounded them and restored them to Torrio. Not a scrap of evidence remained on which to base a case.

On the evening of May 8, 1924, during a barroom argument, a free-lance hijacker named Joe Howard slapped and kicked Jake Guzik. Incapable of physical retaliation, the globular little man waddled off, wailing, to Capone. The outrage to his friend gave Capone additional cause to hunt down Howard, for the hijacker had also been overheard to boast how easy it was to waylay beer runners, including Torrio's. Capone found him half a block from the Four Deuces in Heinie Jacobs' saloon on South Wabash Avenue, chatting with the owner. At the bar two regular customers, George Bilton, a garage mechanic, and David Runelsbeck, a carpenter, were guzzling beer. As Capone swung through the doors, Howard turned with outstretched hand and called to him, "Hello, Al." Capone grabbed him by the shoulders, shook him, and asked him why he had struck Guzik. "Go back to your girls, you dago pimp!" said Howard. Capone emptied a six-shooter into his head.

After questioning Jacobs, Bilton and Runelsbeck, whose accounts of the slaying substantially agreed, Chief of Detectives Michael Hughes told reporters: "I am certain it was Capone," and he issued a general order for his arrest. The next day readers of the Chicago *Tribune* beheld for the first time a photograph of the face that would become as familiar to them as that of Calvin Coolidge, Mussolini or a Hollywood star. The newspaper, however, still hadn't got the name quite right. "Tony (Scarface) Capone," ran the caption, "also known as Al Brown, who killed Joe Howard. . . ."

During the hours between the murder and the inquest two of the main witnesses underwent a change of memory. Heinie Jacobs now testified that he never saw the shooting, having gone into the back room to take a phone call when it occurred, and Runelsbeck claimed he would not be able to identify the killer. Bilton was missing.

The police held Jacobs and Runelsbeck as accessories after the fact and the inquest was adjourned for two weeks. With Capone still lying low, it was adjourned again. Then, on June 11, he sauntered into a Chicago police station, saying he understood he was wanted and wondered why. They took him to the Criminal Courts Building, where he was told why by the eager young assistant state's attorney, William H. McSwiggin, sometimes referred to, because of the numerous capital sentences he had obtained, as "the Hanging Prosecutor." For hours McSwiggin questioned Capone, who said he knew no gangsters and had never even heard of such people as Torrio, Guzik or Howard. He was, he insisted, a reputable businessman, a dealer in antiques.

The third and final session of the inquest took place on July 22. Jacobs and Runelsbeck, visibly terrified, added nothing to their previous testimony. The jurors' verdict: Joe Howard was killed by "one or more unknown, white male persons."

Torrio and Capone, faithful to their preelection promises, brought no more prostitutes to Cicero, but in the contiguous communities of Stickney, Berwyn, Oak Park and Forest View they instituted several brothels which, together with those they had established earlier, brought the total to twenty-two and the combined annual gross eventually to $10,000,000. The economics of these brothels were later revealed by records confiscated during a raid on the Harlem Inn in Stickney. They included day-by-day entries for each girl during a period of three weeks. The page reproduced on the next page covers twelve of the girls who were working on April 21, 1926.

When the customer had indicated his choice, a downstairs madam handed him a towel. The girl got another towel from an upstairs madam, who also assigned her a bedroom. The customer was charged $2 for every five minutes, or any fraction thereof, he spent with the girl. After the first five minutes the upstairs madam would knock and demand additional payment. If the customer was too absorbed to respond, she would sometimes walk in and thump him on the back.

Capone-led mobsters so thoroughly infiltrated one village on the Cicero border that it became known as Caponeville. Forest View was originally a farming community with a population of about 300. The idea of incorporating it as a village occurred to a Chicago attorney, Joseph W. Nosek, after he had spent several pleasant days there conferring with a farmer client over an impending lawsuit. A World War veteran and an official of the American Legion, Nosek described the bucolic charms of the place to a number of his fellow Legionnaires with a fervor that made them want to live there, and they agreed to support his project. Papers of incorporation were issued in 1924. A preamble to the village constitution dedicated Forest View "to the memory of our soldier dead so as to perpetuate their deeds of heroism and sacrifice." At the first village meeting Nosek was elected police magistrate and his brother John, president of the village board. For chief of police they chose one William "Porky" Dillon, who claimed to be an ex-serviceman. From the Cook County board the enthusiastic new villagers obtained enough free materials to pave their streets.

Soon after, Chief Dillon informed Magistrate Nosek that Al and

MOND- APR 4 - 12 - 26 -

NAME	BED			HALF			" 90			BAL			BEER			TOTAL		
	24	0	0	12	0	0	1	2	0	10	8	0		3	5	11	1	5
	26	0	0	13	0	0	1	3	0	11	7	0	1	2	5	12	9	5
	26	0	0	13	0	0	1	3	5	11	7	5		1	0	11	8	0
	40	0	0	20	0	0	2	1	0	18	0	0		4	0	18	4	0
	14	0	5	7	0	5		7	0	6	3	0		2	0	6	5	0
	25	0	0	12	5	0	1	2	5	11	2	5		7	0	11	9	5
	36	0	0	18	0	0	1	8	0	16	2	0	2	1	0	18	3	0
	24	0	0	12	0	0	1	2	0	10	8	0	3	0	5	13	8	5
	13	0	0	6	5	0		6	5	5	8	5		3	5	6	2	0
	14	0	0	7	0	0		7	0	6	3	0				6	3	0
	55	0	0	27	5	0	2	7	5	24	7	5		8	0	25	5	5
	43	0	0	21	5	0	2	1	5	19	3	5	1	4	0	20	7	5
Total	34	0	0	1 70	0	0	1 7	0	0		X		10	7	0		X	
				17	0	0												
				1 87	0	0												
					1 0	7	0											
					1 7	4	3	0										
				1 7														

Column 1 lists the girls' names; column 2, their gross earnings; column 3, earnings after the 50 percent house deduction; column 4, the 10 percent charge for towel service; column 5, the balance; column 6, the girls' commissions on liquor sales; column 7, net earnings.

Ralph Capone wanted to build a hotel and social club in Forest View. "I saw no harm," Nosek recalled later, "because I didn't know just who the Capones were. It looked like a good chance to improve our village."

Nosek was appalled when the Capones appeared with their retinue of thugs and harlots. He ordered Dillon to get rid of them. The following day Nosek ran into Ralph Capone, who said that if he ever uttered another word against him or his brother, they would throw him into the village drainage canal. Nosek, thinking Ralph was joking, replied: "If I go into the canal, you'll go with me."

At four o'clock the next morning, two armed thugs called at Nosek's house and marched him to the village hall. Seven other men were waiting there. "They told me they were going to kill me. They beat me over the head with the butts of their guns and though I was streaming with blood and dazed from pain they kicked me over the floor. I'm not ashamed to admit that I got down on my knees and prayed that they let me keep my life."

They agreed on condition that he immediately leave Forest View. "I moved. Others were forced to move. There was our village clerk, for instance, Thomas Logan, who had bought a little place for himself and his widowed mother. Eighteen or twenty of the respectable men in our village were slugged and beaten and driven away. . . ."

At the next election all the successful candidates for president of the village board, trustees and police magistrate were Capone's cat's-paws. Porky Dillon continued in office as chief of police. He turned out to be an ex-convict whom Governor Small had pardoned. The Torrio-Capone syndicate then proceeded to erect its biggest brothel, the sixty-girl Maple Inn, popularly known as the Stockade, which yielded average gross weekly profits of $5,000 and also served Capone as an arsenal and a hideout. An immense old stone-and-wood structure on a country back road, it contained a maze of secret chambers installed behind walls, under floors, above ceilings. The largest, innermost chamber served as a hiding place for the girls when a raid threatened. For a fugitive gangster there was a room beneath the eaves soundproofed with cork lining. The inhabitant could communicate his needs through a speaking tube. A dumbwaiter brought him food and drink. Holes pierced in the eyes of figures painted on the ceiling of the room below afforded a view of the customers crowding the bar and the gambling tables. Throughout the house sliding panels concealed compartments full of guns, cartridges and explosives.

"All the beautiful ideals that my associates in the Legion and I had have been swept away," Nosek lamented. "The streets that we built with so much arduous effort but with such happiness and hope are now little more than thoroughfares for the automobiles of gunmen, booze runners and disorderly women."

9

"Tell them Sicilians to go to hell"

IT was perhaps the most unfortunate outburst ever to escape a gang leader's lips. By "Sicilians" O'Banion meant all his Italian confreres, but when it reached the Gennas' ears, they took it as a mortal affront for which only blood could atone. The wounding words capped a series of offenses O'Banion had committed not only against the Gennas, but against other gangsters with whom he was supposedly friendly. As a result, the alliances cemented through Torrio's carefully wrought treaty began to crumble and, crumbling, foreshadowed warfare that would rage for years and cost hundreds of lives.

Aside from his ethnic antipathies, O'Banion had been nursing a number of specific grievances. During the Cicero elections he had lent Capone several of his most practiced terrorists without receiving any compensation. Torrio later appeased him by ceding the beer distribution rights, worth about $20,000 a month, to a sizable section of Cicero. O'Banion increased these profits to $100,000 by underselling the Sheldon, Saltis-McErlane and Druggan-Lake gangs. He persuaded fifty Chicago saloonkeepers who had been buying beer from those gangs to move to Cicero, where he provisioned them at lower cost. Thus, they presented severe competition to the Cicero saloons operating under Torrio-Capone auspices. Torrio demanded a percentage of this new revenue. O'Banion refused to give him any. Though inwardly seething, the prudent, patient Torrio would risk no breach of the underworld peace. He did not press the point, and he kept Capone from attacking the Irishman.

O'Banion's relations with the Gennas deteriorated when they began to flood his North Side territory with their rotgut whiskey at $3 a gallon. For his own whiskey he charged two to three times as much, but the quality was superior. He warned Torrio and Capone that if they couldn't hold the Gennas to their treaty obligations, he would use more persuasive means. Torrio smiled and nodded and promised to remonstrate with the Sicilian brothers. He may even have tried, but the cut-rate liquor continued to flow through the North Side.

As hijackers, O'Banion and his gang had brought off the two boldest coups since Prohibition became law. One night, early in 1924, they invaded a West Side railroad yard and transferred $100,000 worth of Canadian whiskey from a freight car to their trucks. Not many nights later, they broke into the Sibley Warehouse, trucked out 1,750 barrels of bonded liquor and, to conceal the robbery as long as possible, left in their place an equal number of barrels full of water. Lieutenant Michael Grady of the detective bureau and four detective sergeants in O'Banion's pay convoyed the trucks to his storage depot. They were later indicted. No trial followed, and after a brief suspension they were restored to the force.

O'Banion now determined upon an exploit that would both teach the Gennas a lesson and show his scorn for Torrio. He hijacked a $30,000 shipment of Genna whiskey.

In family council the Gennas voted to kill him. Their hand was temporarily stayed by the president of the Unione Siciliane, Mike Merlo, whom not even the Gennas dared disobey. Like Torrio, Merlo was an underworld strategist who abhorred violence and advocated peaceful negotiation as the surest road to riches. He also happened to like O'Banion, and O'Banion looked upon him as his only Sicilian friend. Thus, as long as Merlo reigned, nobody under his control was likely to attempt O'Banion's life. Yet the Irishman's murderous impetuosity was a constant threat to the general welfare.

Chief of Police Collins maintained a tap on O'Banion's telephone, and one night an extraordinary conversation was recorded. Two West Side policemen had intercepted an O'Banion beer truck and were demanding $300 to let it proceed. The driver called O'Banion. "Three hundred dollars!" the Irishman exclaimed. "To them bums? Why, I can get them knocked off for half that much." Collins, never doubting him capable of it, dispatched a squad of detectives to prevent the slaughter. The beer runner had meanwhile consulted Torrio and was next heard over the tapped wire telling O'Banion: "I just been talking to Johnny and he says to let the cops have the three hundred. He says he don't want no trouble." Reluctantly, O'Banion obeyed. By the time Collins' rescue squad reached the spot the two policemen had vanished with their payoff.

In May, 1924, O'Banion approached Torrio and Capone with a proposition that astonished and delighted them. The three gangsters (with Joseph Stenson, a silent partner) ran the Sieben Brewery on the North Side, one of the biggest in Chicago. For three years it had been producing quality beer under the protection of the precinct police. Now O'Banion wanted to sell out. He was, he explained, quitting the bootleg business and retiring with his wife to Louis Alterie's Colorado ranch. He admitted to fear. If he didn't clear out, he said, the Gennas would surely get him in the end. He asked half a million for his share. His partners were happy to pay it. Upon receipt of the money O'Banion offered, as a parting gesture of goodwill, to assist in the delivery of one last shipment. He specified May 19 as the date most convenient for him.

On the night of the nineteenth thirteen trucks stood in the Sieben Brewery yard, taking on capacity loads of beer barrels. The operation, which involved twenty-two drivers and beer runners, took place under the supervision of two precinct policemen, Torrio, O'Banion, Hymie Weiss and Louis Alterie. Capone, who had killed Joe Howard ten days before, was in hiding. None of the trucks got as far as the street. The brewery was suddenly swarming with police. Led by Chief Collins, they confiscated the beer and herded everybody into patrol wagons, including the two North Side policemen, whose badges Collins ripped off then and there.

At sight of the raiders Torrio had smelled treachery. He was soon certain of it. From a police officer on his payroll, he found out, O'Banion had obtained advance knowledge of the raid and used it to swindle the despised Italians. By offering to help expedite the May 19 shipment he had hoped to allay suspicion of his betrayal. He knew that he, too, risked a heavy fine and possibly jail, but this seemed a paltry price to pay for such a double triumph.

Chief Collins delivered the gangsters, not to police headquarters, but to the Federal Building because, as he announced next day, the federal authorities had promised their full cooperation. From a roll of bills Torrio peeled off $12,500 bail money for himself and half a dozen gang members. For O'Banion, Weiss and Alterie, who lacked the cash, he declined to advance a cent. Without a word, he left them to await their own bondsmen.

Torrio continued for a while to swallow O'Banion's outrages in silence, but the offense to his self-respect was intolerable when O'Banion began bragging about how he had outwitted Torrio in the Sieben Brewery affair. He was reported to Torrio as saying, "I guess I rubbed that pimp's nose in the mud all right." Torrio and Capone now made common cause with the Gennas.

O'Banion's relations with Angelo Genna hardly improved either. On November 3 the Irishman, accompanied by Hymie Weiss and Schemer Drucci, repaired to the Ship, in which Torrio had sold him a small share, for the weekly conference and division of spoils. On Torrio's side of the table sat Capone; Frank Diamond (born Maritote) , captain of Capone's bodyguards and husband of his sister Rose; and two of the syndicate's crack triggermen, Frank Rio and Frank Nitti. As Torrio handed O'Banion his cut, Capone remarked that Angelo Genna had lost heavily at roulette during the week, leaving IOU's for $30,000, and he suggested, in the interests of general amity, that they cancel the debt. O'Banion's response was to spring to the telephone, call Genna, and give him one week to pay up.

When they got back to the North Side, Weiss remonstrated with O'Banion. He deplored such needlessly offensive acts. He urged him to make peace with Torrio and the Gennas. O'Banion shrugged off the advice with the inflammatory words, the last straw, overheard and repeated throughout gangland: "Tell them Sicilians to go to hell."

When next the Genna clan convened, they invited Torrio and Capone to sit in with them. Opinion on what to do about O'Banion was now unanimous. Torrio cautiously reminded the Gennas of Mike Merlo's injunction, but Angelo reassured him. Merlo was in no condition to enforce his will. He was dying of cancer and not expected to last the week. He died on November 8, a Saturday. Frankie Yale, the national head of the Unione Siciliane, who came to Chicago for the funeral, approved Angelo Genna as successor to president Merlo.

O'Banion, the florist, was never busier. He and his partner Scho-field spent all day Sunday and most of Sunday night weaving chrysan-themums, lilies, carnations, orchids and roses into wreaths, lyres, hearts and blankets. Capone placed an order for $8,000 worth of red roses, Torrio for $10,000 worth of assorted flowers. The Unione Si-ciliane had commissioned a sculptor to fashion a life-size wax effigy of the departed which was to precede the hearse, sitting bolt upright in an open limousine massed with flowers. Toward the evening of the ninth Jim Genna and Carmen Vacco, the city sealer, a title equiv-alent to commissioner of weights and measures, who owed his ap-pointment to Merlo's political influence, visited the shop ostensibly to buy a wreath. They asked O'Banion to keep the shop open later than usual since many more of Merlo's friends would be dropping by with orders. Soon after they left, Angelo Genna telephoned and spoke to Schofield about another wreath. He said he would have it picked up in the morning.

At about noon of November 10 O'Banion was in the rear of the shop, clipping the stems of some chrysanthemums. A swinging wicker door divided the main room and on the other side his Negro porter, William Crutchfield, was sweeping up the floral debris from the day before. Neither O'Banion's partner nor any of their assistants had come to work yet, having been up half the night filling orders. Pres-ently, on the opposite side of State Street, directly in front of Holy Name Cathedral, a dark-blue nickel-trimmed Jewett sedan slid to a halt. The driver kept his seat, letting the motor idle. Three men got out. As they crossed the street and entered the flower shop, they were observed from a short distance by an eleven-year-old boy, Gregory Summers, a junior traffic officer, who was guiding some children through the intersection of State Street and East Chicago Avenue. He recalled: "Two of them were dark and they looked like foreigners. The other man had a light complexion."

Inside the shop Crutchfield had just finished sweeping up and was moving to the rear through the wicker door. Over the top of the door he caught a glimpse of the visitors. The man in the middle, he said later, was "tall, well-built, well-dressed, smooth-shaven, wore a brown overcoat and a brown Fedora hat. He might have been a Jew or a Greek." His companions were "Italians . . . short, stocky and rather rough looking."

O'Banion walked toward them, his left hand gripping the flower shears, his right extended in greeting. Though Crutchfield did not know them, it was obvious that his employer did, for O'Banion would never have offered his hand to a stranger. "Hello, boys," he said. "You want Merlo's flowers?"

"Yes," replied the tall man, smiling, and took his hand. He held onto it tightly.

That was all Crutchfield saw. "Mr. O'Banion called for me to close the back room door and I did. I didn't recognize any of the three men; never saw them before, so far as I recall. I shut the door between the back and front rooms of the shop, figuring that Mr. O'Banion had private business with the men." He flung it open again a few seconds later when he heard shooting and rushed out.

O'Banion lay dead amid a chaos of torn and crushed flowers. In his fall he had knocked over several containers of carnations and lilies. His blood was dyeing a blanket of white peonies red. From his post at State and East Chicago the boy Summers, who had also heard the shooting, saw the three men streak across the street, pile into the blue Jewett and head west.

As Chief of Detectives William Schoemaker reconstructed the murder, the tall man shaking O'Banion's hand jerked him forward and pinioned his arms. Before O'Banion could wriggle free, the other men fired six bullets. Two passed through his chest, the third through his right cheek, the fourth and fifth through his larynx. The sixth, the *coup de grâce*, was fired into his brain, after he fell, at such close range that the powder scorched his skin. In short, a textbook gangster killing: the immobilization of the victim's arms, each shot aimed at a vital spot, the bullets through the larynx so that if he failed to die immediately, he would not be able to speak. . . .

"It was," wrote Judge Lyle, recalling the funeral, "one of the most nauseating things I've ever seen happen in Chicago." For three days the body "lay in state"—the newspapers' phrase—in the Sbarbaro funeral chapel, the powder burns and bullet holes disguised by the embalmer's art, a rosary clasped in the folded hands, "the soft tapered hands which could finger an automatic so effectively," as a sob sister pictured them. On the marble slab beneath the casket was the inscription "Suffer little children to come unto me."

The press wallowed in bathos. Describing the casket, which had been bought from a Philadelphia firm and rushed to Chicago in a special express freight car carrying no other cargo, the *Tribune* drooled:

> It was equipped with solid silver and bronze double walls, inner sealed and air tight, with a heavy plate glass above and a couch of white satin below, with tufted cushion extra for his left hand to rest on.
>
> At the corners of the casket are solid silver posts, carved in wonderful designs. Modest is the dignified silver gray of the casket, content with the austere glory of the carved silver post at its corners, and broken only by a scroll across one side which reads, "Dean O'Banion, 1892–1924."
>
> Silver angels stood at the head and feet with their heads bowed in the light of the ten candles that burned in the solid golden candlesticks they held in their hands. . . . And over it all the perfume of flowers.
>
> But vying with that perfume was the fragrance of perfumed women, wrapped in furs from ears to ankles, who tiptoed down the aisle, escorted by soft stepping, tailored gentlemen with black, shining pompadours.
>
> And, softly treading, deftly changing places, were more well formed gentlemen in tailored garments, with square, blue steel jaws and shifting glances. They were the sentinels.
>
> In the soft light of the candles at the head of the $10,000 casket sat Mrs. O'Banion, a picture of patient sorrow.

"Why, oh, why?" the widow sobbed, clinging to her father-in-law's arm. Louis Alterie and Hymie Weiss were reported to have "cried as women might," and "many others had handkerchiefs to their eyes." To the Dead March from *Saul*, Alterie, Weiss, Bugs Moran, Schemer Drucci, Maxie Eisen, labor racketeer and president of the Kosher Meat Peddlers' Association, and Frank Gusenberg, a triggerman, bore the casket to the hearse. Close behind, with solemn tread, seemingly numb with sorrow, followed Torrio, Capone and their principal lieutenants. Once again stubble darkened Capone's jowls. Pious appearances, however, gave the police no sense of security. Lest hostilities erupt during the obsequies, plainclothesmen circulated quietly among the gangsters, confiscating their firearms.

For many blocks in every direction, from the street, the windows of office buildings, the rooftops, thousands watched the cortege forming. A mile long, it included twenty-six cars and trucks to carry the flowers, three bands and a police escort. Chief Collins had forbidden any police under his command to join the mourners, but the authorities of Stickney were less finicky and furnished an honor guard of uniformed officers.

As the cortege started for Mount Carmel Cemetery, about 10,000 people fell in before and behind it. Mounted police had to clear a path through the mob so the motorcade could advance. Every trolley car to the Mount Carmel area was packed. At the cemetery about 5,000 more people waited.

In accordance with Cardinal Mundelein's strictures, no requiem mass was celebrated at Holy Name Cathedral, and the grave was dug in unconsecrated ground. A spokesman for the archdiocese explained: "One who refuses the ministrations of the Church in life need not expect them in death. O'Banion was a notorious criminal. The Church did not recognize him in his days of lawlessness and when he died unrepentant in his iniquities, he had no claims to the last rites for the dead."

A section of Mount Carmel was reserved for lapsed or excommunicated Catholics whose Catholic friends and relatives wanted them buried as near as possible to consecrated ground. O'Banion had bought a plot there for members of his gang, and he was now the second to occupy it. Before the gravediggers threw on the last clod of earth, Father Malloy, formerly of Holy Name Cathedral where O'Banion had sung as a choirboy, who could believe no evil of him, defied the cardinal to the extent of kneeling at the graveside and reciting a litany, three Hail Marys and the Lord's Prayer.

Five months later Anna O'Banion managed to have the remains disinterred and reburied in consecrated ground under a granite shaft inscribed "My Sweetheart." When the cardinal heard of it, he ordered the monument removed. He did not, however, order the eviction of the remains. A simple marker replaced the shaft. It stood within a few feet of a mausoleum containing the bones of a bishop and two archbishops, a proximity which led Police Captain John Stege to remark to Judge Lyle: "Strange, isn't it? A murderer and he's buried side by side with good men of the church."

The day after the funeral Two-Gun Louis Alterie threw down the gantlet to O'Banion's murderers. "I have no idea who killed Deany," he said in a newspaper interview, "but I would die smiling if only I had a chance to meet the guys who did, any time, any place they mention and I would get at least two or three of them before they got me. If I knew who killed Deany, I'd shoot it out with the gang of killers before the sun rose in the morning and some of us, maybe all of us, would be lying on slabs in the undertaker's place." As a dueling ground, he proposed the corner of State and Madison streets, but no gangster cared to advertise his guilt by accepting the challenge.

Alterie's braggadocio enraged Mayor Dever. "Are we still abiding by the code of the Dark Ages?" he asked, addressing himself to the community at large. "Or is this Chicago a unit of an American commonwealth? One day we have this O'Banion slain as a result of a perfectly executed plot of assassination. It is followed by this amazing demonstration. In the meanwhile his followers and their rivals openly boast of what they will do in retaliation. They seek to fight it out in the street. There is no thought of the law or the people who support the law."

With naïveté he concluded: "The gangsters are to be disarmed and jailed or driven out of town. Every one of the six thousand policemen is to be thrown into the fight and public opinion is counted upon to spur municipal and state court judges into co-operation."

The police investigation of the murder shed no light. Capone, however, had a good deal to say to the press about motive. "Deany was all right," he set forth, "and he was getting along to begin with better than he had any right to expect. But like everyone else his head got away from his hat. Johnny Torrio had taught O'Banion all he knew and then O'Banion grabbed some of the best guys we had and decided to be the boss of the booze racket in Chicago. What a chance! O'Banion had a swell route to make it tough for us and he did. His job had been to smooth the coppers and we gave him a lot of authority with the booze and beer buyers. When he broke away, for a while it wasn't so good. He knew the ropes and got running us ragged. It was his funeral."

Following the inquest, the Cook County coroner noted in the margin of the court record: "Slayers not apprehended. John Scalise and Albert Anselmi and Frank Yale suspected, but never brought to trial." Again, as in the Colosimo case, the police had questioned Yale, who was still in the city at the time of O'Banion's death, but both they and the O'Banion gang accepted his plausible explanation for being there. "I came for Mike Merlo's funeral," he told the detectives who stopped him in the La Salle Street railway station a few minutes before the departure time of his train back to New York. "I stayed over for a fine dinner that my friend Diamond Joe Esposito gave for me." With the rest of the coroner's comment, the O'Banion-ites, who conducted their own investigation, agreed. Torrio, Capone and the Gennas, they were convinced, planned the murder. Angelo Genna drove the getaway car. Mike Genna was the one who shook O'Banion's hand. The actual shooting was done by the two recently immigrated Sicilian killers with their garlic-anointed bullets.

Officially, the murder of Dion O'Banion entered the bulging file marked UNSOLVED.

Hymie Weiss, assuming leadership of the O'Banion gang, swore an oath of vengeance.

10

Garlic and Gangrene

WITH the better part of valor Torrio fled Chicago. He and his wife, Ann, embarked upon an extensive tour of American and Caribbean playgrounds. They visited Hot Springs, New Orleans, Havana, the Bahamas, Palm Beach, St. Petersburg. . . . Wherever they went they were trailed by Weiss' gunmen, who never quite caught up with them, missing them usually by a day or two, sometimes by only hours.

Torrio's absence prevented him from attending *the* underworld social event of the season. On January 10, 1925, Angelo Genna married Henry Spingola's sister, Lucille. A blanket invitation to the wedding reception, published in the newspapers—COME ONE, COME ALL —brought 3,000 people to the Ashland Auditorium. They goggled at the wedding cake which its creator, a sculptor named Ferrara, claimed to have based upon a recipe he brought over from Italy thirty years before. Four days in the making, rising in tiers to a height of 12 feet and weighing 1 ton, it consisted of 400 pounds of sugar, 400 pounds of flour, 2,520 eggs and several buckets of miscellaneous flavorings. Multicolored arabesques of frosting decorated the masterpiece, and to crown it, a balcony on which stood a miniature bride and groom. HOME SWEET HOME, read an inscription in icing. It took six men to carry the cake into the auditorium and six to cut and serve it.

Capone stayed in Chicago and soon felt the sting of Weiss' vengeance. On January 12 Capone's chauffeur, Sylvester Barton, drove him and two bodyguards to a restaurant at State and Fifty-fifth streets. Leaving the bodyguards in the car, Capone stepped into the restaurant. The door was closing behind him when a black limousine cruised slowly by. Inside were Hymie Weiss, Schemer Drucci and Bugs Moran, clutching automatics and shotguns. Abreast of Capone's car, they raked it with fire from taillights to radiator cap. "They let it have everything but the kitchen stove," a policeman said later. The bodyguards dropped to the floor in time, but a bullet hit Barton in the back.

The close call led Capone to order from General Motors, at a cost of $30,000, a custom-built Cadillac limousine. Weighing seven tons, it had a steel armor-plated body, a steel-hooded gas tank, bulletproof window glass half an inch thick, a gun compartment behind the rear seat and a movable window enabling passengers to fire at pursuers. Capone seldom traveled in it without a small scout car ahead and a touring car full of sharpshooters behind. For even short distances of a few blocks he rode the Cadillac lest on foot he offer the enemy an easy target. When he had to walk to cross a sidewalk or hotel lobby, a covey of bodyguards moved with him, two or three deep on all sides. In the nightclubs he patronized no strangers were permitted to occupy the adjacent tables. At the opera, bodyguards filled the seats to his right and left, behind and in front. In his headquarters, as a defense against an assassin who might sneak past the bodyguards and shoot him from the rear, he used a swivel chair with a high, armor-plated back. He rarely kept an appointment at the agreed time and place but would send a messenger at the last minute to change them. (Despite these precautions no life insurance company would sell him a policy, as he discovered when he applied for one early in 1925.)

While Sylvester Barton was recovering from his wound in the hospital, Capone replaced him with one Tommy Cuiringione, alias Rossi. He proved to be a chauffeur-bodyguard of exceptional loyalty. Not long after he assumed his new duties, the O'Banionites kidnapped him, hoping to force him to tell where and when they might ambush Capone. One morning a month later, two boys leading a horse through a wood in southwest Chicago stopped at a cistern to water him. The horse backed away, refusing to drink. That afternoon the boys mentioned this odd behavior to a patrolman they knew. He accompanied them to the cistern, leaned over, sniffed. With the boys' help he hauled up what remained of Tommy Cuiringione. The body was mottled with cigarette burns. He had been bent forward across a slab of concrete and his wrists and ankles pulled together with wire that cut deep into his flesh. His torturer had finally put five bullets into his head.

The Torrios returned to Chicago in mid-January. After seven months at liberty on bail, Torrio and eleven co-defendants were to stand trial in the Sieben Brewery case. With Weiss' executioners still in pursuit, shaken by their attempt to kill Capone, he cast about for some sort of sanctuary. The approaching trial suggested one. When, on January 23, Torrio came before Federal Judge Adam Cliffe, he pleaded guilty, confident that no avenging hand could reach him in prison and that by the time he got out Capone would have dealt with Hymie Weiss.

Before passing sentence Judge Cliffe granted Torrio five days in which to settle his affairs. With his wife he spent the afternoon of the twenty-fourth shopping on Michigan Avenue. Their car was laid up for repairs, and they had borrowed Jake Guzik's Lincoln sedan, as well as his chauffeur, Robert Barton, Sylvester's brother. It was almost dusk when the sedan, laden with parcels, swung into Clyde Avenue and stopped at No. 7011, where the Torrios occupied a third-floor apartment. Neither Barton nor his passengers noticed the Cadillac limousine parked at the corner of Clyde and Seventieth Street. It bore no license plates, and the window curtains were drawn.

Barton opened the rear door of the sedan and helped husband and wife gather up their parcels. Ann Torrio went ahead along the short cement walk to the entrance of the apartment house. The Cadillac began to move. As she pushed against the glass door with her back, her hands being full of parcels, the Cadillac stopped across the street, parallel with the sedan. She now saw dimly through its curtained windows the outlines of four men, each holding an automatic, a sawed-off shotgun or both. Torrio had just stepped to the sidewalk. Petrified, she watched helplessly as two men leaped from the car with automatics and charged him. The first man fired two shots, tumbling him to the ground, his jaws broken, a bullet in his chest. As he lay squirming on the sidewalk, the second man shot him in the right arm and the groin. At the same time the two men who had stayed in the Cadillac started blasting away, peppering the sedan with buckshot and bullets. A bullet hit Barton in the right leg below the knee. The first killer bent over Torrio and held the automatic against his temple for the *coup de grâce,* but the chambers were empty. Before he could reload, the driver sounded a warning blast of his horn. The two men ran back to the Cadillac, and it whisked them away.

Still conscious, Torrio crawled a few feet toward his wife, who managed to drag him inside the building. The gunfire had brought the neighbors to their windows, and a Mrs. James Putnam, who had witnessed the onslaught from the beginning, called the nearby Woodlawn police station. An ambulance was summoned. As it sped Torrio to the Jackson Park Hospital, the thought of garlic and gangrene flashed through his mind and he cried out: "Cauterize it! Cauterize it!"

Barton, ignoring his leg wound, had hobbled back into the sedan and gone tearing off toward 71st Street. He passed a car driven by a retired detective sergeant, Thomas Conley, who, spotting the bullet holes in the sedan, his man-hunting instincts aroused, gave chase. He confronted the fugitive in a drugstore as he was emerging from a telephone booth, limping and bleeding. Barton refused to satisfy the old sleuth's curiosity. He broke away from him and drove off again. After a flight across half the city, he was finally forced to the curb by a police patrol car, taken to a station house and thence to a hospital. The person Barton had telephoned, the police concluded, was Capone.

At the Jackson Park Hospital, speaking with difficulty because of his damaged jaw, Torrio muttered in answer to a reporter's question: "Sure, I know all four men, but I'll never tell their names." He never did.

Among the neighborhood witnesses was the seventeen-year-old son of an apartment building janitor, Peter Veesaert. He had been standing in the doorway of the building at the time of the attack. Shown a photograph of O'Banion's pallbearers, he pointed to Bugs Moran as the first man who shot Torrio. He persisted in his identification when the police brought him face to face with Moran, saying: "You're the man." The police wanted to hold Moran until they could establish some evidence in support of the boy's testimony, but Judge William Lindsay released him under $5,000 bail. He was never indicted.

Capone reached the Jackson Park Hospital soon after the ambulance to learn that Torrio's condition was critical. In tears, he refused to leave his bedside. As a security measure, he insisted upon Torrio's removal to an inner room on the top floor, and though two policemen stood guard before the door, he posted four of his own bodyguards in the corridor. These precautions were not idle. During the night the superintendent noticed three carloads of armed men circling the building. She called the police, and at their approach the motorcade dispersed.

Torrio made a swift recovery. In less than three weeks he left the hospital via a fire escape, surrounded by bodyguards. The same day, February 9, with his jaw still bandaged, he appeared again before Judge Cliffe. He was content to pay a $5,000 fine, and without a murmur of protest he accepted a sentence of nine months in Lake County Jail at Waukegan.

The warden fitted the windows of Torrio's cell with bulletproof steel-mesh blinds, assigned two deputy wardens to patrol the corridor outside, and added such touches of comfort and luxury as throw rugs, easy chairs, pictures and a downy mattress.

This was not unheard-of treatment for rich and politically well-connected convicts. In June, 1924, U.S. District Court Judge James Wilkerson issued a permanent injunction against the Standard Beverage Corporation, a property belonging to Terry Druggan and Frankie Lake. They defied it, and on July 11 the judge sentenced them to a year's imprisonment for contempt of court. The day they entered Cook County Jail, Morris Eller, boss of the Twentieth Ward, told Sheriff Peter Hoffman, "Treat the boys right." The boys themselves paid Warden Wesley Westbrook, a former police captain, and other officials bribes totaling $20,000.

One day a reporter from the *American* called to interview Druggan. "Mr. Druggan isn't in today," the jailer told him. The reporter said he would interview Lake instead. "Mr. Lake also had an appointment downtown," the jailer explained. "They'll be back after dinner."

When the stunned reporter repeated this dialogue to his city desk, the editor assigned him to a full-scale investigation. From disgruntled jail personnel, who were not sharing in the Druggan-Lake bounty, the reporter learned that the gangsters came and went as they pleased. Conveyed to and from jail in his chauffeur-driven limousine, Druggan spent most of his evenings with his wife in their $12,000-a-year duplex apartment on the Gold Coast, whose distinctive appurtenances included a solid silver toilet seat engraved with his name, while Lake enjoyed the company of his mistress in her North State Parkway bower. At other times the partners visited their doctor or dentist, shopped, dined in the best Loop restaurants, played golf, attended theaters and cabarets.

As a result of the *American* exposé, Sheriff Hoffman was fined $2,500 and sentenced to thirty days in jail and Warden Westbrook to four months, neither term to be served in their own cozy lockup.

The warden of Lake County Jail allowed Torrio to hold business conferences on the premises. In March, a month after his incarceration, Torrio, Capone and their lawyers held a momentous one. The intergang treaties that Torrio had forged and struggled so hard to implement were now wrecked beyond recovery, all hope of underworld peace gone. Inevitably, Torrio foresaw, the gangs would revert to warfare, and for this he lacked the gumption. Never a physically brave man, he had been cowed by the feel of lead in his body.

Torrio was a criminal far ahead of his time. He anticipated by at least two decades the organization gangster who would forgo personal vendettas, stooping to murder only as a practical necessity and then leaving the execution to remote sublieutenants with whom nobody could associate him, who, guided by corporation counsel, would funnel unlawful profits into lawful channels until, a multimillionaire, his financial stance was indistinguishable from those of reputable businessmen.

To Capone and his lawyers, Torrio announced his retirement from the Chicago scene. He proposed to divest himself of all his interests there. Demanding no payment and stipulating no conditions, he formally transferred everything to Capone—the breweries, brothels, speakeasies and gambling houses which together were producing an annual revenue in the tens of millions of dollars. But with the Torrio coalition disintegrating, it had become a slippery possession. To secure it again, Capone knew he must win back, subjugate or destroy every major gang in the city. He was equipped for the challenge with qualities which made him, by the special standards of the underworld, a paragon, a leader of leaders.

"I would have killed for Al." It is Max Motel Friedman, alias Morris Rudensky, speaking * at a remove of half a century. Red Rudensky, or Rusty, as Capone called him, was twenty when he came to

* To the author.

Chicago, a wiry, flame-haired Jew of German-Polish parentage, born on New York's Lower East Side, already noted in the underworld for his talent as a lock picker, safecracker and escape artist. A former locksmith's apprentice, he claimed he could make a master key to any hotel in the country in ten minutes. From a friendly chemist he had learned enough about explosives to blow a safe neatly with nitroglycerine. He was a fugitive from a New York reformatory, an Illinois state prison and a federal penitentiary. He belonged to no gang but operated on the fringes of gangdom as a free-lance "mechanic." He grew adept at cracking open government warehouses full of bonded liquor. Though he never worked directly for Capone, they occasionally ran into each other at the Four Deuces. The youth's gall and swagger tickled Capone, who treated him as a kind of mascot, and Rudensky hero-worshiped the gang boss. "He was big-hearted, loyal, dynamic. . . ."

Rudensky was not alone in his admiration. To Francis Albin Karpaviecz, the youngest member of Ma Barker's Ozark gang of bank robbers, kidnappers and killers, who Americanized his Lithuanian name to Al Karpis, Capone was "a wonderful person . . . a real man." Karpis formed this judgment years before he met Capone, when he was seeking a refuge between holdups in Cicero. The presence of a fugitive bank robber could cause the local gangsters acute embarrassment by stirring up police activity, and to relieve the stress, some of them had been known to betray such fugitives. "That just wasn't in Al's nature," Karpis recalled.* "He always knew when we hit town and where we stayed, but he never tipped off the cops."

Toward the members of his gang, their family and friends, Capone was paternalistic, protective, a lavish giver in the tradition of the Mafia dons, though he never belonged to the Mafia. On occasion his sense of loyalty transcended his self-interest. An opportunity arose in 1926 to end the enervating feud with Hymie Weiss. The implacable Pole offered to make peace if Capone would betray Scalise and Anselmi into his hands. "I wouldn't do that to a yellow dog," said Capone.

He demanded prime physical fitness in his henchmen and urged them to follow a regular athletic training program. In 1925, when it had become apparent that the well-meaning Mayor Dever was helpless against Chicago's politico-criminal cabal, Capone reestablished

* In an interview with the author.

city headquarters in the seven-story Hotel Metropole at 2300 South Michigan Avenue, around the corner from the Four Deuces. He took a fourth-floor corner suite of eight rooms for himself and half a dozen rooms on the two top floors for his entourage. Two of the seventh-floor rooms he converted into a gymnasium with punching bags, rowing machines, horizontal bars, a trapeze and other body-building equipment. Jack McGurn, the sometime prizefighter, kept in shape by skipping rope.

It was Capone's notion that, in his own words, "When a guy don't fall for a broad, he's through," and from time to time he would test his bodyguards by exposing them to eager, voluptuous women. If they failed to respond enthusiastically enough, he would assign them to a less exacting post or dismiss them altogether.

The Caponeites had a discipline and cohesiveness, a team spirit, equaled only by the O'Banion gang under Dion O'Banion, and like the O'Banionites' *esprit de corps*, it stemmed from the personal power their chieftain had built up through the subversion of public officials. No documentation exists to support two of the most widely circulated anecdotes concerning Capone's power, but his men firmly believed and gloried in them. According to the first, a hoodlum escaped from the Criminal Courts Building. In the search for him a squad of police rookies, acting on an informer's tip, raided the hangout of a South Side gang affiliated with Capone. They failed to find the fugitive; but the gangsters present were heavily armed, and the zealous rookies confiscated several automatics and shotguns. When they delivered the weapons to their commanding officer and told him where they came from, he was consternated. "Who gave you such orders?" he demanded. "Take the stuff back." The raided gangsters, meanwhile, had complained to Capone, who in turn reproved the commanding officer. The latter thereupon advised the rookies to placate the gang leader lest they be banished to some remote beat. They called on Capone at his Hotel Metropole headquarters. "I understand your captain wasn't to blame," he said affably, "that you boys just made a mistake. All right, I'm going to give you a break. But don't pull another boner."

According to the second apocryphal story, a Capone lieutenant was arrested and held without bail. Capone telephoned the judge. "I thought I told you to discharge him," he said. The judge explained that he was not on the bench the day the police brought in the prisoner, but he had given his bailiff a memo for the alternative judge. The bailiff forgot to deliver it. "Forgot!" Capone roared. "Don't let him forget again."

The attempted murder of Torrio marked the beginning of the longest hottest gang war ever fought in Chicago. The *casus belli* went beyond Weiss' lust for vengeance. At stake was nothing less than the control of commercialized crime and vice throughout the area.

The gangs realigned themselves mainly, though not entirely, according to ethnic ties. The Irish, Polish and Jewish gangsters tended to rally behind O'Banion's successor. The West Side O'Donnells, for example, and later the Saltis-McErlane gangs, once allies of Torrio, went over to Weiss. The Sicilians, notably the Gennas, and most of the Italians stuck to Capone. So did Druggan and Lake. Some of the lesser gangs like Ralph Sheldon's and a few independent hoodlums shifted back and forth with the changing fortunes of war.

Applying the lessons Torrio taught him, Capone forged a large, heterogeneous, yet disciplined criminal organization. On the top echelon, at his right hand, stood Jake Guzik, business manager; Frank Nitti, risen from triggerman to treasurer, Capone's chief link with the Unione Siciliane and later with the Mafia; and brother Ralph Capone, director of liquor sales. Ralph acquired the nickname Bottles because of his persuasiveness with saloonkeepers who were reluctant to stock Capone merchandise. Though all the brothers except the college-educated Matt and the vanished James worked for the organization at one time or other, only Ralph achieved a position of major responsibility.

On the managerial level, supervising the distribution of liquor, there were Charlie Fischetti and Lawrence "Dago" Mangano. Frank Pope, who managed the Hawthorne Smoke Shop, paid particular attention to the off-track horse race betting and retained 18 percent of the net from all the gambling games, while Peter Penovich, in charge of roulette, craps, blackjack, etc., got 5 percent. From the gambling houses that Capone did not own outright he exacted a share of the profits as payment for political and physical protection. His chief collector was Hymie "Loud Mouth" Levine. Mike de Pike Heitler and Harry Guzik oversaw the whorehouses. For advice on every phase of his operations Capone often turned to Tony Lombardo, an urbane, cool-headed Sicilian seven years his senior, who had prospered as a wholesale grocer in Little Italy.

Next came the specialists and technicians. Every member of the organization carried a card with a name and phone number to call in case of arrest. The number was that of a pay booth in a Cicero drugstore at Twenty-fifth Street and Fifty-second Avenue; the name, Louis Cowan. When anyone phoned for Cowan, the druggist would go to the door and beckon to a small, frail man sitting inside a newsstand. A green limousine was parked at the curb nearby. The newsdealer, who stood barely 5 feet tall and weighed less than 100 pounds, would dash to the phone, listen intently, dash out again and, after finding somebody to mind his kiosk, hop into the limousine and drive hell for leather to whatever police station his caller had indicated. Cowan was the organization's chief bondsman, a status sufficiently rewarding to have obviated a pursuit as humble as selling papers; but having sold them on the same corner since boyhood, he chose sentimentally to keep the newsstand, and it now doubled as his office. Capone trusted Cowan to such a degree that he placed in his name several apartment buildings he owned worth about half a million dollars. Whenever Cowan went to the aid of an arrested Caponeite, he would take with him documentary proof of these real estate holdings, which he then put up as security for bail.

On the lower echelons there was a choice assortment of bodyguards, sharpshooters and all-purpose muscle men. James Belcastro, a veteran Black Hander, directed a bombing squad. If competitors attempted to open a still or a brewery in territory the organization considered its own, Belcastro would issue a warning. If the interlopers ignored it, his men would obliterate the property. Speakeasy operators who refused to buy the liquor the organization offered them likewise risked a bombing.

Phil D'Andrea, who became Capone's favorite bodyguard, was a rifleman who could split a quarter in midair. William "Three-Fingered" Jack White was an equally good shot with his left hand, his right having been smashed in boyhood by a brick falling from a building under construction. As sensitive about the loss as Capone was about his facial scars, White always wore gloves in public, the empty fingers stuffed with cotton. Another expert torpedo, Samuel McPherson "Golf Bag" Hunt, tracked his prey with a shotgun concealed in a golf bag. To a detective who once opened the bag, Hunt explained: "I'm going to shoot some pheasants." The first man he ever shotgunned failed to die and was known in gangland thereafter as "Hunt's hole in one."

Antonino Leonardo Accardo, alias Joe Batters, a Sicilian shoemaker's son, committed his maiden offense, a traffic violation, at age fifteen. He was arrested twenty-seven times thereafter on charges that included extortion, kidnapping and murder, none resulting in any penalty more serious than a small fine. Felice De Lucia, alias Paul "the Waiter" Ricca, killed two men in his native Naples before his twenty-second year when he immigrated with false identification papers to Chicago. Both Accardo and Ricca joined the Torrio-Capone gang in its formative stage. So did Sam "Mooney" Giancana, who was rejected for military service as a psychopath. Murray Llewellyn "the Camel" Humphreys, who sported a camel's hair overcoat, also made an underworld name for himself early in life by bringing off a long series of robberies for which he never served a day in jail.

Capone valued none of his young recruits more highly than Jack McGurn—"Machine Gun" Jack McGurn, as he was called after the tommy gun became his preferred weapon. He was born Vincenzo De Mora in Little Italy to one of the Gennas' alky cookers, who died full of buckshot following his sale of some alcohol to the competition. The son, according to legend, determined to avenge the murder, began practicing marksmanship by shooting the sparrows off telephone wires with a Daisy repeating rifle. A promising amateur welterweight prizefighter, he received his alias, McGurn, from Emil Thiery, a well-known trainer who agreed to take him on. The relationship was short-lived. Under pressure in the ring McGurn tended to wilt, and Thiery dropped him.

McGurn was the complete jazz age sheik, a ukulele strummer, cabaret habitué and snaky dancer. An insatiable collector of women, preferably blondes, he parted his curly black hair in the middle and slicked it down with pomade until it lay as flat and sleek as Rudolph Valentino's. He wore wide-checked suits heavily padded in the shoulders, flower-figured neckties and pointed patent-leather shoes. The police ascribed twenty-two murders to McGurn, five of them supposedly committed in reprisal for his father's death. As a gesture of contempt after mowing down a victim, he would sometimes press a nickel into his hand.

In the fall of 1927 Danny Cohen, the owner of a thriving North Side cabaret, the Green Mill, offered McGurn a 25 percent interest. All he had to do was persuade the star attraction, a young comic named Joe E. Lewis, to renew his contract. For a solid year Lewis had been packing the place nightly, and Cohen had raised his pay to $650 a week. But a rival establishment, the New Rendezvous Café, promised Lewis $1,000, plus a percentage of the cover charge, and he notified Cohen that he would accept.

The next morning McGurn was waiting for Lewis outside his hotel, the Commonwealth. Lewis repeated his decision. He was opening at the Rendezvous on November 2. "You'll never live to open," said McGurn. Years later Capone, a Lewis devotee from the start, asked him, "Why the hell didn't you come to me when you had your trouble? I'd have straightened things out." Lewis often asked himself the same question.

No harm befell him opening night, but the morning of November 10, a week later, there was a knock at his bedroom door. He let in three men. Two of them carried pistols, and they fractured his skull with the butts. The third had a knife. He drove it into Lewis' jaw, drew it up the left of his face to his ear. Twelve times he struck, gashing his throat and tongue.

Incredibly, Lewis lived. But for months he could barely articulate, and the damage to his brain by the pistol butts left him unable to recognize words. He had to learn again to talk, read and write. He was performing within a year, but a decade passed before he recovered his early success. During his darkest days Capone gave him $10,000.

While retaining their identity, several of the smaller gangs became virtual subsidiaries of the Capone syndicate. The most important were the Guilfoyle gang and the Circus gang. Martin Guilfoyle, whose disciples included Matt Kolb, a Republican politician, and Al Winge, an ex-police lieutenant, controlled the liquor and gambling concessions along West North Avenue. The Circus gang, composed chiefly of gunmen and labor racketeers, took its name from its meeting place, the Circus Café, at 1857 West North Avenue. The founder was John Edward "Screwy" Moore, better known as Claude Maddox, a Missourian with a criminal record dating from his seventeenth year. These two Northwest Side gangs together served as a counterforce to the North Side Weiss gang.

In addition, the organization had occasional recourse to various independent technicians and specialists—"boxmen" (safe blowers), cracksmen like Red Rudensky for breaking into government bonded liquor warehouses, arms merchants. Among the last was Peter von Frantzius, an alumnus of Northwestern University Law School, a member of the National Rifle Association and the owner of a sporting goods store, Sports, Inc., at 608 Diversey Parkway. Capone had been following with passionate interest the reports of Frank McErlane's tommy gun exploits. After his initial failure to remove Spike O'Donnell, McErlane had turned his tommy gun upon other foes with more impressive results. Firing a burst from his car as it sped past the Ragen Athletic Club, Ralph Sheldon's hangout, he had demolished Charles Kelly, who chanced to be standing in front of the building, and maimed a Sheldonite inside. In an attempt to eradicate two beer runners for a rival gang he had sprayed a South Side saloon with about fifty missiles, wounding, though not killing his quarry. Amazed by McErlane's new weaponry, if not his aim, Capone hastened to equip his own arsenal with tommy guns. His brother John and Charlie Fischetti bought the first three for him from a dealer named Alex Korocek. It was Von Frantzius, however, a timid, myopic man with a pencil-line mustache, who became his regular armorer. Sports, Inc., furnished machine guns and other firearms that would figure in some of the most spectacular gang killings of the decade.*

The organization's greatest power derived from those close associates who held political office like Johnny Patton, the mayor of Burnham. Patton was so close an associate as to be a virtual member of the gang. He continued to keep Burnham safe for vice. His chief of police tended bar at the Arrowhead Inn, in which Capone had a controlling interest, and several town officials worked there as waiters. During periods when Prohibition agents maintained too tight a surveillance on the organization's Chicago breweries for them to produce anything except near beer the Arrowhead Inn became an important source of needle beer. Capone's trucks would haul barrels of the legal beverage from the Chicago plants to the roadhouse, with his eighteen-year-old brother Mimi bringing up the rear in a Ford coupe, accompanied by a triggerman, tommy gun at the ready, eyes peeled for hijackers. On their arrival all hands would pitch in. Mezz Mezzrow, who led the Arrowhead jazz band, described the process in his autobiography:

* Sports, Inc. still exists in Chicago. Although the founder died in 1968, the company's letterhead continues to list "P. von Frantzius, Pres. & Gen. Mgr."

One day along about noon Frank Hitchcock [a part owner] yanked us all out of our pads and took us downstairs. . . . We were called out to the backyard, where we saw some men putting up a large circus tent. . . . When we went inside the tent we saw barrels of beer being lined up in long rows and a large ice-box being built off to one side . . . a man named Jack, one of Capone's lieutenants, came along. He gave us a brace and bit, a box of sticks like the butcher uses to peg meat with, and some galvanized pails. Then he yelled, "One of you guys drill holes in these barrel plugs and let three-quarters of a pail run out of each barrel. Then another guy plugs up each hole with these here wooden sticks, to stop the beer from running out." . . .

After we let out the right amount from a barrel, another guy came along with a large pail that had a pump and gauge attached to it. In this pail was a concoction of ginger ale and alcohol, just enough to equal the amount of beer that was drawn off. This mixture was pumped into each barrel, plus thirty pounds of air, and you had a barrel of real suds. I think they got as high as seventy-five bucks for this spiked stuff.

Jack showed up for the next maneuver. That cat was stronger than Samson after a raw steak dinner. He would roll a barrel over so the plug was facing up, then break off the meat stick and place a new plug over the old one. With one mighty swing of a big wooden sledgehammer he would drive the new plug all the way in, forcing the old one clean into the barrel. In all the time I understudied at this spiking routine, I never saw Jack take a second swing at a plug.

Capone, who had assumed the role of father to his younger brothers and sisters, was disturbed when Mimi became attached to a singer in the band. "Get her out of here," he ordered Mezzrow. "If I hear of any more stuff about her and Mimi, you're booked to go too."

"I won't fire her," said Mezzrow, frightened by his own temerity. "She's one of the best entertainers we got around here. Why don't you keep Mimi out of here, if that's the way you feel about it?"

"She can't sing anyway."

"Can't sing. Why, you couldn't even tell good whiskey if you smelled it and that's your racket, so how do you figure to tell me about music?"

Capone turned, laughing, to a group of his henchmen. "Listen to the Pro-fes-sor! The kid's got plenty of guts." He turned back to

Mezzrow, the laughter fading. "But if I ever catch Mimi fooling around here it won't be good for the both of you."

Under the presidency of Joseph Klenha Cicero's round-the-clock illicit resorts grew to number more than 100 gambling dens, many hundreds of beer flats, saloons and speakeasies and brothels by the score. Here Capone was the law. The real seat of municipal administration was the Hawthorne Inn. The gang sometimes stored its liquor in the basement of the Town Hall. Once when Klenha neglected to carry out an order, Capone knocked him down the Town Hall steps and kicked him as he struggled to rise. A policeman patrolling the block calmly watched, shrugged, and moved on. Another time, as the town council was about to ratify an ordinance displeasing to Capone, a squad of his toughs marched into the council chamber, dragged the chairman outside, and blackjacked him. The objectionable ordinance was rescinded.

Yet there remained a thorn in Capone's side. This was a young newspaper editor, the youngest, in fact, in the country. Robert St. John was barely twenty-one when an older friend, an advertising man, Jack Carmichael, proposed that they start a weekly newspaper in Cicero. The town already had one paper, the Cicero *Life,* but St. John agreed with Carmichael that it was growing fast enough to support two. They formed a publishing corporation. Under Illinois law every corporation required at least three directors and so they took in a friend of St. John's, Tom Foss.* St. John and Carmichael each held 49 percent of the stock, Foss 2 percent. The Cicero *Life* confined itself to reporting social trivia, but from its first issue in 1922, the *Tribune* devoted its front page to the activities of the Capone organization and the editorial page to attacking the alliance between the gangsters and the local politicians. At about the same time, in the adjoining town of Berwyn, St. John's brother Archer founded the Berwyn *Beacon* with a policy identical to the *Tribune*'s.

Capone first tried to starve out the crusaders. Emissaries from both the Hawthorne Inn and the Town Hall roamed Cicero, warning its merchants against advertising in the *Tribune.* The defiant were subjected to official harassment. The tax assessor would increase the valuation of their property. NO PARKING signs would suddenly appear at the curb in front of their door. Fire and health inspectors would find them guilty of various violations. In exceptionally stubborn

---

* In deference to St. John's wishes I have disguised the names of his co-directors.

cases Capone's strong arm men might intervene with a slugging or bombing. The *Tribune* managed nevertheless to sell enough space to survive.

Capone tried a new tack. At his instructions Louis Cowan, whose newsstand the *Tribune* overlooked, felt out St. John about the possibility of selling the paper. He failed to arouse a flicker of interest.

In 1925 the Capone syndicate opened a new brothel on the southern boundary of Cicero, near the Hawthorne Race Track. St. John assigned a reporter to investigate it. Two weeks later the reporter resigned by registered letter. He never revisited the *Tribune* office, not even to collect the salary due him. St. John took over the investigation himself. The brothel, he discovered, also contained a death chamber. Recalling his experience years later, he wrote:

> One night I put on shabby clothes, emptied my pockets of all identification and set out.
>
> The place was a square, unpainted frame building two stories high and the size of a small armory. . . . It was entered through a room large enough for one table and a miniature bar. . . . This was not a drinking establishment. What was served at the bar was near beer, obviously designed to discourage any interest in lingering longer than necessary in this antechamber. . . .
>
> To pass from the bar into the main building, it was necessary to go through a series of three doors only a foot or two apart. The first and third were hinged on the right; the middle one on the left. The bartender was the establishment's "spotter." He controlled all three doors with electric buttons. It was possible for him to allow a client to get through the first door and then lock all three electrically, thus imprisoning the visitor. The establishment's "bouncer" sat at a small table just inside the main building. The barman could communicate with him by house telephone. If a man marked for extermination were to be locked in the small corridor with the three doors, it was simple for the bouncer to fire a few bullets through the door on his side. Although the place had been open for business only about two weeks, the doors already looked like pieces of Swiss cheese and there were black stains on the floor and walls of the corridor.
>
> The ground floor of the main building was a single large room, its four walls lined with wooden benches. A client coming from the bar took a seat on a bench just to the left or right of the bar door.
>
> The procedure from then on was obvious at a glance. A girl

wearing only the two most essential feminine garments would come down from upstairs, enter the large waiting room through a door in the far wall, make a slow circuit of the room, greeting anyone she already knew, and then would go back upstairs, accompanied by the man who occupied the spot on the bench just to the left or right of the far door. The man next to the place now vacated would move into it. This was a signal for all the other bench warmers to move a foot or two closer, ultimately leaving a vacancy by the bar door. The bouncer would then communicate by phone with the barman, who would press his electric buttons and allow another client to enter.

Little conversation was taking place. Traffic moved rapidly. It took about half an hour to get from entrance to exit. In that time nearly one hundred different girls would each have made two appearances. When a man had worked his way to a place by the exit door, he had the privilege of leaving with the next girl going upstairs or, if he had taken a fancy to some particular female employee during the half hour, he could wait for her. . . .

The closer I got to the exit door, the more frightened I became. I was still not yet a man, although I shaved regularly. . . . I had undertaken to try, almost singlehanded, to crush or at least to drive out of town one of the most powerful underworld organizations America had ever known, but that night I was afraid for many reasons.

During the half hour of waiting I studied the faces of hundreds of girls. I finally found one whom I thought perhaps I could trust. She was older than the others and looked intelligent. I waited for her.

One paid the five-dollar fee just before going upstairs, where there were at least one hundred small rooms.

The girl's name was Helen. I had brought ten ten-dollar bills with me, and handed her one as soon as she had locked the door. Stumblingly I explained that I was a "writer." I had come here only to get "material." Would she be willing just to talk to me for the next fifteen minutes?

I was lucky in the choice I made. . . . She answered every question I asked with what seemed like honesty. . . .

As the night advanced, Helen passed him along to other talkative girls until he had amassed "enough material for a modern Moll Flanders." At about 4 A.M. word reached the upper regions of the bordello that Ralph Capone had arrived to check the night's receipts. St. John left by a fire escape.

The story that filled the entire next issue of the *Tribune,* one of the longest, most detailed exposés of a whorehouse ever published by a newspaper, sold thousands of extra copies, scandalized respectable Ciceronians and infuriated Capone. A result particularly gratifying to the author was a meeting of clergymen from Cicero and the surrounding Capone-infested communities. It was organized by the Reverend Henry C. Hoover of Berwyn, a tall, bony young man not much older than St. John, whose studious expression was enhanced by a pince-nez. Out of that meeting grew the West Suburban Citizens' Association dedicated to combating gangsterism. As an initial step, a delegation called on local officials like President Klenha and Cicero's chief of police, Theodore Svoboda, on County Sheriff Hoffman and State's Attorney Crowe. Everywhere they were courteously received and promised swift action. No action followed. So the Citizens' Association took the law into its own hands. It appointed an action committee budgeted at $1,000, with no questions asked and no explanations wanted. The committee handed over the money to a member of the Weiss gang. Early one morning, after the last customer had left, the new whorehouse burned to the ground.

The day after the fire Cowan called on St. John. "Capone's sore," he said. "Tell him I'm sore, too," the editor replied. He was sore, he added recklessly, because the gang wouldn't clear out and leave the town alone.

When St. John approached his office two mornings later at about eight thirty, Cowan was already at his newsstand. On the northeast corner of Fifty-second Avenue a policeman was standing in front of a cigar store, reading a newspaper. On the opposite corner another policeman was leaning against a mailbox. As St. John reached the middle of the avenue, he saw a big black car heading toward him at top speed. It screeched to a halt a few feet away. Of the four men who jumped out he recognized Ralph Capone and a hoodlum named Pete Pizak. The two others were unknown to him. Capone stood aside, barking commands. Pizak advanced, holding a pistol by the barrel. The second man had a blackjack, and the third swung a woolen sock with a cake of soap in the toe. Wielded by a skilled hand, this last weapon, striking the base of the victim's brain, could kill without leaving a noticeable mark. Neither of the policemen stirred. St. John flung himself to the ground, curled up into a ball, and covered his head with his hands. After the first few blows he lost consciousness.

In Berwyn the same morning a mayoral election was beginning. Archer St. John, who ran his newspaper all by himself, had announced a special edition that would expose Capone's political alliances. Before he could start the press run, he was hustled into a car at gunpoint, handcuffed, blindfolded, and held prisoner until the balloting ended.

Robert St. John spent a week in the hospital. When he stopped at the cashier's office to pay his bill, he was told that somebody had already paid it. The cashier described this benefactor as dark and husky with a long scar across his cheek.

Before returning to his desk, the young editor went to the Town Hall to see Chief of Police Svoboda. He demanded warrants for the arrest of Ralph Capone and Pete Pizak on charges of assault and battery and "John Doe" warrants against his two other assailants. Svoboda was aghast. He could not, he explained, issue warrants against members of the Capone gang. He implored St. John not to embarrass him. If St. John had to swear out warrants, let him apply to the police of another town. But even if he succeeded, what cop would have the nerve to serve them? St. John stood his ground. At length Svoboda seemed to give in. If St. John came back next day, he promised, the warrants would be ready.

In the morning Svoboda directed him to a room on the second floor. He found it empty. Presently, a bulky figure lumbered through the door, closed it behind him, and turned toward St. John, smiling and holding out his hand. He was impeccably dressed—blue serge suit, blue pocket handkerchief, blue necktie with a diamond stickpin, black homburg and shoes shined to a high gloss. The scar barely showed through the heavy coating of powder. Though they had never spoken, St. John knew Capone by sight.

The gang leader was all conciliation and flattery. He had heard a lot about St. John and was delighted to meet him at last. He hastened to correct any bad impressions St. John might have. "I'm an all right guy," he said. "Sure I got a racket. So's everybody. Most guys hurt people. I don't hurt nobody. Only them that get in my way." Never would he harm a hair of a newspaperman's head. Newspapermen were too valuable to him. They gave his business the kind of advertising no amount of money could buy. He apologized for the beating. He swore that he had forbidden his men to lay a finger on St. John. Unhappily, Ralph and his companions were homeward bound from an all-night party when they spotted the editor, and anger, stoked by alcohol, had got the better of them. As he talked, Capone produced a wad of greenbacks. It was he himself, he disclosed, fingering the cash, who had paid the hospital bill, but, of course, that hardly compensated St. John for the loss of his time. How much was it worth—five hundred? Seven hundred? A thousand? St. John walked out, slamming the door.

Soon after, his partner, Carmichael, left for Florida, pleading frayed nerves. The same day Louis Cowan turned up at the *Tribune* office, swollen with self-importance. His friends, he announced, did not like the story about Ralph in the current issue. The editor gave him a short answer. Maybe, said the little man, St. John didn't realize who owned the *Tribune* now. Capone owned it. While the editor was in the hospital, Carmichael had sold his 49 percent interest. This St. John could believe, for he had come to mistrust Carmichael, but that his friend, Tom Foss, would have sold his 2 percent, giving Capone control of the paper, he found hard to accept. In Cowan's presence he phoned the third director. Flabbergasted, Foss quoted a note he had received during St. John's absence: "Please make over your shares to Louis Cowan." It was signed "Bob St. John." A forgery, the editor assured Foss, and he entreated him not to let the note out of his sight until they could prove it so in court. Foss groaned. In all innocence he had handed the note, along with his stock certificates, to Cowan.

When St. John disconsolately hung up, Cowan, whom Capone had named publisher of the *Tribune,* took a friendlier tone. He reminded St. John that he still had a 49 percent interest in the paper, and Capone wanted him to go on running it. Nobody would interfere. He could keep every penny the *Tribune* earned. All they asked was a little discretion when reporting the activities of the organization.

"Well, Mr. Publisher," said St. John, "I guess you and your scar-faced friend have won. Say goodbye to him for me." He left Cicero that day, never to set foot in it again.*

Among the employees later hired by publisher Cowan was Capone's nineteen-year-old brother, Albert John Capone, who went to work in the circulation department.

Though St. John was defeated, Al Capone had still to contend with the Reverend Hoover and his West Suburban Citizens' Association. On May 16, 1925 (Derby Day), having badgered a reluctant Sheriff Hoffman into taking action against the Hawthorne Smoke Shop, the minister accompanied—in effect, led—a token force of deputy sheriffs, reinforced by the association's most militant members. While they scattered through the building, armed with search warrants, Chester Bragg, a Berwyn real estate broker, stood guard at the front entrance. Thousands of people gathered in the street, hooting and cheering. Presently, Capone, who had spent the night at the Hawthorne Inn next door, elbowed his way through the crowd. It was noon and he had not yet shaved. He wore silk pajamas under his coat. Bragg, who had never seen the burly gangster before, refused to let him pass. "What do you think this is, a party?" he said, as Capone tried to force an entrance.

"It ought to be my party!" Capone shouted, and he added four words whose ultimate disastrous consequences nobody could have foreseen. "I own the place."

Bragg stepped aside with a mocking flourish. "Come on in, Al. We've been looking for you."

David Morgan, a machinist from Western Springs, went upstairs with Capone to the main room where about 150 customers had been gambling. Under the direction of the Reverend Hoover and a police lieutenant attached to the sheriff's staff, the raiders were dismantling roulette wheels, chuck-a-luck cages and crap tables, preparatory to loading them onto three trucks that had been backed up to the entrance. "This is the last raid you'll ever pull!" Capone yelled at Hoover.

"Who is this man?" the young minister asked, peering at Capone through his pince-nez.

* After editorial jobs on newspapers in Vermont, Pennsylvania and New Jersey, St. John joined the Associated Press in New York as city editor. During World War II he was its Balkan correspondent. Since then he has been a radio news commentator, lecturer and author of a dozen books.

"I'm Al Brown," Capone answered, reverting to his favorite alias, "if that's good enough for you."

"I thought it was someone like that, more powerful than the President of the United States."

Capone stepped into a back room, took the money and IOU's out of a cash box, and stuffed them into his pajama pockets. He ordered his bookkeeper, Leslie Shumway, to remove the contents of the safe downstairs, but the raiders had already emptied it. One of them happened to be a magistrate, and he filled out warrants charging Capone and eight of his employees with violations of the antigambling laws. Capone returned to the Hawthorne Inn. He reappeared shortly, shaved, powdered, effulgently attired from the crown of his pearl-gray fedora to his white-spatted shoes, and in a pleasanter frame of mind. He drew Hoover aside. "Reverend," he said, "can't you and I get together—come to some understanding?" The minister asked what he meant. "If you'll let up on me in Cicero," Capone explained, "I'll withdraw from Stickney."

"Mr. Capone," said Hoover, "the only understanding you and I can have is that you must obey the law or get out of the western suburbs."

The raiders did not leave the scene unscathed. Capone's thugs, who had been mingling with the crowd outside, broke Bragg's nose with a blackjack. They threw Morgan to the ground and kicked him in the face. Between then and the trial before a Judge Dreher, they and their fellow vigilantes were continually threatened. One night four gangsters waited for Morgan in his garage, shot him, and left him for dead. He was a month recovering in the hospital.

Rather than expose its members to further reprisals, the Citizens' Association decided to participate in no more raids. None of them testified at the trial, and though there was documentary evidence enough to convict the defendants, Judge Dreher dismissed the case. Bragg wrote him a scorching letter of condemnation. The judge turned it over to friends of his in the Cicero Town Hall, suggesting that they muzzle troublemakers like Bragg.

The Hawthorne Smoke Shop underwent no radical change. Half an hour after the raid new gambling equipment and cash reserves had been moved in, and by nightfall it was operating again at full tilt.

11

The Fall of the House of Genna

AFTER the honeymoon, while they went house hunting, Angelo Genna and his bride occupied a suite in the fashionable Hotel Belmont, near the lakeshore. Ex-Mayor Thompson lived opposite, and the neighborhood glittered with the domed and turreted mansions of the city's social elite. Like his brother Tony and like Al Capone, Angelo loved bel canto and loved to play host to its exponents from the Chicago Civic Opera such as Tito Schipa, Titta Ruffo, Luisa Tetrazzini, few of whom were too fastidious not to accept his princely hospitality.

In May, 1925, the newlyweds found a suburban bungalow they liked. The price was $15,000, and on the morning of the twenty-fifth Angelo set out in his rakish roadster with the cash to pay it. As he drove south on Ogden Avenue, six blocks from the hotel, a touring car darted out of a side street. In the rear seat (so the police concluded later) sat Weiss, Moran and Drucci; Frank Gusenberg probably drove. Genna tried to outdistance them. Turning the corner of Hudson Avenue too fast, the roadster skidded and crashed into a lamppost. The pursuit car slowed to a stop, the trio in back aimed sawed-off shotguns at their trapped quarry. . . .

With a stubble-faced Capone among the mourners, Angelo was buried in an unconsecrated plot at Mount Carmel Cemetery, a step from Dion O'Banion's grave.

On the morning of June 13, less than three weeks later, a double

double cross of Byzantine intricacy was played out in South Chicago. The principals were four members of the Genna gang—Mike Genna, Samoots Amatuna, John Scalise and Albert Anselmi—plus the same three men whom the police suspected of having mowed down Angelo Genna. A few days earlier the O'Banionites had approached Amatuna with a promise of rich reward if he would deliver Scalise and Anselmi into their hands. They wanted him to lure the pair to the corner of Sangamon and Congress streets, where they would pick them off from a waiting car. The time was 9 A.M. of the thirteenth. Amatuna, who hated the North Side gang as fiercely as the Gennas did, pretended to accept the offer, then divulged it to the intended victims. In the counterplot that Mike Genna contrived, the hunters became the prey, the snipers became the target. At the appointed time and place Moran and Drucci were waiting confidently in their car (Weiss had business elsewhere) when a limousine streaked by, spewing buckshot. Moran and Drucci, both wounded, managed to fire an answering volley and drive a few blocks in pursuit, but neither they nor their bullet-riddled car were in any condition for further combat. They abandoned the car on Congress Street, stumbled across the sidewalk, spattering it with their blood, and ended up in a hospital where they were weeks recuperating.

The enemy were bowling south down Western Avenue. At Forty-seventh Street they passed a northbound detective squad car. Its occupants—Michael Conway in command, Harold Olson at the wheel, William Sweeney and Charles Walsh—were in vengeful mood, three of their mates having been slain by gangsters the week before. Recognizing Genna at the wheel, Conway ordered Olson to overtake the speeding limousine. With its gong clanging, the squad car spun around and picked up a speed of 70 miles an hour. At Fifty-ninth Street a truck lumbered out into the avenue, forcing Genna to swerve. He hit a telephone pole. Unhurt, the three men leaped to the road with their shotguns. The squad car screeched to a halt a few feet from them, and the detectives scrambled out, their revolvers drawn. "Why didn't you stop?" Conway shouted. "Didn't you hear our gong?"

The shotguns answered him. He went down, wounded in the chest. Walsh and Olson were killed. Sweeney, the youngest officer, barricaded himself behind the squad car and fired at the gangsters over the hood. South Western Avenue was an industrial district, and hundreds of factory workers piled into the streets. Factory whistles blew a warning. Riot calls flooded the switchboard of the precinct police stations. The gangsters fled. With Sweeney close behind, a revolver in each fist, they raced across a vacant lot. Scalise and Anselmi ducked into an alley. Alone, Genna turned to face the advancing detective and raised his shotgun. Both chambers were empty. Flinging the gun aside, he ran toward a house beyond the lot. A revolver bullet hit him in the upper leg, cutting the femoral artery. He fell, dragged himself to a basement window, smashed it, and wriggled through. When Sweeney and two policemen found him, he was sitting on the basement floor, blood gushing from the severed artery. In the ambulance carrying him to Bridewell Hospital a guard leaned over him to adjust the stretcher. Genna kicked him in the face, crying, "Take that, you son of a bitch." He bled to death before the ambulance reached the hospital.

Having lost their hats in their flight, Scalise and Anselmi dashed into a dry goods store on Fifty-ninth Street to buy new ones. The owner, Edward Issigson, his ears still ringing with the din of battle, was suspicious of the bedraggled pair, babbling in a foreign tongue, and he refused to sell them anything. Just then a streetcar rattled to a stop near the corner. The fugitives ran for it. At the same time another police flivver came roaring down Western Avenue. Issigson hailed it and pointed to the two escaping Sicilians. As the streetcar started to move, the police pulled them off the rear platform.

After Chief of Detectives William Schoemaker had questioned Scalise and Anselmi through an interpreter at the central detective bureau, they were charged with first-degree murder. In a radio broadcast State's Attorney Crowe proclaimed: "These men will go straight to the gallows." He assigned Assistant State's Attorney McSwiggin to the prosecution.

Capone shed no tears over the deaths of Angelo and Mike. Though the Gennas' participation had been indispensable to Torrio's master plan, their blind greed, treachery and lunatic spasms of savagery made them allies to be handled as cautiously as scorpions. Moreover, they blocked Capone's path to the control of Little Italy and its booming alky industry. For that the minimal requirement was the prestige of high office in the Unione Siciliane, which the Gennas had held ever since Mike Merlo's death. As a non-Sicilian Capone could not qualify for even rank-and-file membership. He proposed to dominate the fraternity through those of its officers whom he could make beholden to him. This precluded the intractable Gennas. In the president's chair, to which Angelo had succeeded, Capone longed to see his own *consigliere*, Tony Lombardo. It was without regret, therefore, that he watched the dissolution of the clan. In fact, he contributed to it.

If what an informer from Little Italy told the police can be credited, Mike Genna was doomed that day regardless of how the two skirmishes ended. According to this source, Scalise and Anselmi had secretly defected to Capone and accepted a contract to eliminate Genna. Thus, as Mike drove with them along Western Avenue, after the attempt to kill Moran and Drucci, he was himself being "taken for a ride."

Bloody Angelo, killed May 25.

Mike the Devil, killed June 13.

July 8, Giuseppe Nerone, *Il Cavaliere,* the disaffected member of the Genna gang who felt that the brothers failed to appreciate his talents, telephones Tony. He has important information for him. Could they meet in front of the Cutillas' grocery store on Grand Avenue? There, at 10:30 A.M., the murder of Dion O'Banion is imitated. As Nerone firmly grasps Tony's hand in greeting, a figure steps out of a doorway, presses an automatic against Tony's back and pulls the trigger five times. Dying in the County Hospital, Tony murmurs to his mistress, Gladys Bagwell, what sounds like "Cavallaro." The police look for a nonexistent Sicilian by that name instead of Nerone the Cavalier. By the the time they realize their mistake Nerone has been shot to death while being shaved in a North Side barbershop. As for the identity of the man who shot Tony Genna, the police are divided, some suspecting Schemer Drucci, others, one of Capone's executioners.

As Tony was buried next to Angelo in Mount Carmel Cemetery, one of the mourners, noting the proximity of Dion O'Banion's grave, remarked, "When Judgment Day comes and them three graves are open, there'll be hell to pay in this cemetery."

The surviving Gennas fled in panic, Jim to his native Sicily, Sam and Pete to hiding places outside Chicago. In Palermo Jim Genna was arrested for stealing the jewels adorning the statue of the Madonna di Trapani and went to prison for two years. All three brothers eventually returned to Chicago; but their power had been broken, and they lived out their days in comparative obscurity, importing cheese and olive oil.

To Capone's extreme annoyance, his man, Tony Lombardo, failed to capture the presidency of the Unione Siciliane. In the Gennas' absence Samoots Amatuna rallied the remnants of their gang behind him and flanked by two armed protégés, Abraham "Bummy" Goldstein and Eddie Zion, strode into union headquarters and claimed the coveted office for himself.

The road to the gallows promised for Scalise and Anselmi took a circuitous course. Three months elapsed without trial. Meanwhile, Capone, the Unione Siciliane and what remained of the Genna gang (who never suspected that the defendants had intended to kill Mike Genna) jointly sponsored a campaign to raise a defense fund. Under the personal direction of President Amatuna, collectors solicited contributions among the immigrant families of Little Italy with the plea that the colony's good name was at stake. But the gang leaders had a different reason to be concerned. They knew that their power rested partly on their ability to protect those who served them. To loosen tight purse strings, the collectors used blackmail and blackjacks.

The most effective squad of collectors operated under the command of Tropea the Scourge, and consisted of Baldelli the Eagle, Vito Bascone, *et al.* Within a few weeks they had raised more than $50,000.

Scalise and Anselmi finally went to trial for the murder of Detective Olson on October 5. On the eleventh, during the selection of a jury, the home of Detective Sweeney, the state's star witness, who, like other witnesses, had been receiving threats through the mail all summer, was demolished by a bomb. So many veniremen were threatened that it took three weeks to complete the jury. Two of the jurors finally selected had to be guarded by police day and night.

Seldom had clearer-cut proof of guilt been presented in a criminal court. Numerous eyewitnesses to the shooting on Western Avenue identified Scalise and Anselmi. Their tall and elegant young chief counsel, Michael J. Ahern, whose clientele included Capone and other top-ranking gang lords, never attempted to refute the evidence, but enunciated a curious principle in vindication of killing policemen. "If a policeman detains you, even for a moment, against your will," he argued, "you are not guilty of murder, but only manslaughter. If the policeman uses force of arms, you may kill him in self-defense and emerge from the law unscathed."

The defendants broke into broad grins as the jury found them guilty of manslaughter only and fixed their penalty at fourteen years in the penitentiary. The mother of the slain detective, an aged deaf mute, had been present throughout the trial. When a companion explained the verdict to her in sign language, Mrs. Olson's fluttering fingers spelled out: "I cannot understand why they did not send the murderers of my son to death on the gallows. The verdict is a blow to justice."

The cry of outrage from both police and public moved the presiding Judge William V. Brothers to announce that the defendants would be returned to his court without delay to face trial for the murder of Detective Walsh. Three months passed.

In late October Torrio was released from Lake County Jail. Three automobiles full of bodyguards, provided by Capone, waited for him at the gates and convoyed him nonstop through Chicago to Gary, Indiana. In Gary he boarded a train to New York where his wife met him and a few days later they sailed for Italy. From there, every year, Torrio continued to send Capone's son a $5,000 birthday bond.

In preparation for the second Scalise-Anselmi trial the fund raisers of Little Italy redoubled their efforts, though Samoots Amatuna was no longer there to spur them on. A few weeks earlier the North Siders and the West Side O'Donnells had joined forces with the main object of preventing what Amatuna was struggling to achieve—the reconstruction of the disintegrated Genna gang under his leadership. On the evening of November 13, before accompanying his betrothed, Rose Pecorara, to a performance of *Aida*, Amatuna dropped into a Cicero barbershop for a shave and manicure. Two men entered after him, walked up to his chair, and drew revolvers. Amatuna leaped to his feet and crouched behind the chair. The first man fired four shots, all misses. Then the second man fired, and each of his bullets found its mark. On his deathbed in Jefferson Park Hospital Amatuna asked a priest to marry him and Rose Pecorara, but he died before the ceremony began. (This second shooting in a barbershop prompted the proprietor of a Michigan Avenue barbershop, patronized by gangsters, to keep the chairs facing the door at all times and never to cover a client's face with a towel.)

Though the police could make no arrests for want of witnesses willing to talk, the identity of Amatuna's assailants was common knowledge in the underworld. Schemer Drucci fired the first volley, and Jim Doherty, who abetted Myles O'Donnell in the killing of Eddie Tancl, fired the second. Three days later, returning from

Amatuna's funeral, Eddie Zion was ambushed and killed. Two weeks after that Bummy Goldstein was murdered in a drugstore. Having no weapon of his own at the time, the assassin filched a shotgun from a police car parked nearby.

These deaths suited Capone because they cleared the way for Tony Lombardo's accession to the presidency of the Unione Siciliane. Upon taking office, Lombardo composed a paean to his fellow immigrants and to himself:

> Chicago owes much of its progress and its hope of future greatness to the intelligence and industry of its 200,000 Italians, whose rise in prestige and importance is one of the modern miracles of a great city.
>
> No people have achieved so much from such small beginnings, or given so much for what they received in the land of promise to which many of them came penniless. Each life story is a romance, an epic of human accomplishment.
>
> Antonio Lombardo is one of the most outstanding of these modern conquerors. . . . He was one of hundreds who cheered joyously, when, from the deck of the steamer, they saw the Statue of Liberty, and the skyline of New York, their first sight of the fabled land, America. With his fellow countrymen he suffered the hardships and indignities to which the United States subjects its prospective citizens at Ellis Island without complaint, for in his heart was a great hope and a great ambition.
>
> Mr. Lombardo . . . accepted the hardships as part of the game, and with confidence in his own ability and assurance of unlimited opportunities, began his career. . . .

The year 1925 ended for Capone with some extramural carnage.

Nostalgia occasionally drew various members of the Capone family back to Brooklyn. Capone's mother especially loved to revisit her old neighborhood and when she did, Frankie Yale, Lucky Luciano or another of her son's New York colleagues would provide a bulletproof Cadillac, chauffeur and bodyguard.

What brought Al and Mae Capone to Brooklyn in late December was the illness of their only child. At the age of seven Sonny Capone had developed a deep mastoid infection, necessitating radical surgery. The parents preferred to have New York surgeons perform it. They consulted three of them, who agreed that the risks were high, but unavoidable. "I'll give you a hundred thousand dollars if you pull him through," Capone said. The operation took place the day before Christmas. The boy survived it, but was left partially deaf and had to wear a hearing aid.

"It was Christmas Eve," Capone recalled, "when my wife and I were sent home to get some sleep. We found her folks trimming the Christmas tree for her little nieces and nephews and it broke her up."

The following night, according to Capone's version of events, "a friend of mine dropped in and asked me to go around the corner to his place to have a glass of beer. My wife told me to go: it'd do me good. And we were no sooner there than the door opens and six fellows come in and start shooting. My friend had put me on the spot. In the excitement two of them were killed and one of my fellows was shot in the leg. And I spent the Christmas holidays in jail."

It is probable, however, that Capone himself planned the killings well in advance as a service to old associates and a defense of local Italian gang interests. His friend's place was none other than the tawdry haunt of his youth, the Adonis Social Club, where he once practiced marksmanship in the cellar, shooting at beer bottles. Orange bunting festooned the main room, and crude lettering pinned to it spelled out MERRY CHRISTMAS AND HAPPY NEW YEAR. Ragtime rhythms drifted from a tinny piano in the back barroom. There, hell-roaring drunk, his one good leg firmly planted on the bar rail, stood the red-headed chieftain of Brooklyn's Irish "White Hand" gang, Richard "Peg-Leg" Lonergan, author of at least twenty murders and the terror of the borough's Italian colony. Guzzling with him were such lesser White Handers as his best friend, Aaron Harms; Cornelius "Needles" Ferry, a drug addict; James Hart; "Ragtime Joe" Howard; and Patrick "Happy" Maloney.

Ever since Capone could remember, Irish gangsters had controlled Brooklyn dock labor. First "Wild Bill" Lovett, then after he was mysteriously murdered in 1923, Lonergan, his brother-in-law, had held the stevedores in thrall, squeezing a few pennies out of every pay envelope. But lately Italian gangsters had been challenging the Irish monopoly, and the White Handers had responded by killing a few of them.

Lonergan's presence in the Adonis Social Club, traditionally an Italian dive, was an added provocation, and he aggravated it by loudly referring to both the regular customers and the management as "dagos" and "ginzos." He chased away some Irish girls who walked in on the arms of Italian escorts, shouting after them, "Come back with white men!"

Capone arrived at about 2 A.M. of the twenty-sixth with several companions, including his local bodyguard, Frank Galluccio, the forgiven assailant who inflicted his facial scars years before. Besides the White Handers there were about ten other roisterers in the place, the majority Italians like the owners, "Fury" Agoglia and Jack Stabile, alias Stickum; the bartender, Tony Desso; and the waiters and bouncers, George Carozza, Frank Piazza and Ralph Damato. The instant Capone and his party sat down at a table in the back room somebody turned out the lights and bullets began to fly. Chairs and tables toppled over; glassware shattered; screams rent the air as the customers piled hatless and coatless into the street.

Shortly after, when Patrolman Richard Morano of the Fifth Avenue Police Station passed the place on his early-morning rounds, it was dark and silent. In the gutter, near the entrance, he came upon the body of Aaron Harms, the back of his head shot off. With his flashlight Morano followed a trail of blood through the club door into the back room. Lonergan and Needles Ferry, both shot through the head, lay in front of the piano. The sheet music on the rack was open to "She's My Baby."

Another patrolman found James Hart a few blocks away, crawling along the sidewalk. He had been shot in the thigh and legs and was taken to the Cumberland Street Hospital.

After rounding up everybody thought to have visited the Adonis Social Club that night and obtaining only vague and contradictory information, the police arrested the owners, their four employees and Capone, who was still so little known outside Chicago that the Brooklyn *Daily Eagle* mistook him for a "club doorman."

Lonergan's sister Anna, the widow of Wild Bill Lovett, attributed the slaughter to "foreigners." "You can bet it was no Irish American like ourselves who would stage a mean murder like this on Christmas Day," she said.

The seven suspects were arraigned in Homicide Court and held without bail pending Hart's recovery, for on his testimony rested the only hope of a conviction. Hart not only refused to testify, but denied having set foot in the Adonis Social Club the night of the shooting. He was wounded in the street, he insisted, by stray bullets from a passing car. The court released the prisoners on bail bonds of $5,000 to $10,000 and later dismissed the case.

Capone got back to Chicago as Tropea and his crew were stepping up their money-raising campaign in behalf of Scalise and Anselmi. Contributors to the first fund were proving reluctant to give more, and Tropea decided upon stern measures. When the late Angelo Genna's brother-in-law, the lawyer Henry Spingola, who had already subscribed $10,000, rejected another demand for the same amount, Tropea invited him to dinner. He chose Amato's Restaurant on South Halsted Street, a favorite resort of local celebrities, and, in fact, the opera stars Désiré Defrère and Giacomo Spagony were there that evening, January 10. After an elaborate meal, Spingola started for home at about nine o'clock. Two men, waiting across the street in a car driven by Baldelli, cut him to pieces with shotgun fire.

The brothers Agostino and Antonio Morici, macaroni manufacturers and purveyors of yeast and sugar to Little Italy's whiskey distillers, had also contributed handsomely to the first defense fund. Declaring their generosity at an end, they hired bodyguards to protect them against Tropea's wrath. Unfortunately, the bodyguards did not accompany them on the snowy night of January 27, when they drove north toward the Lakeside Place house they had recently bought from the fugitive Jim Genna. With Baldelli at the wheel, the collectors overtook them and filled them with buckshot, sending their car hurtling into a signboard.

The friends and family of the murdered men were quick to retaliate. In the case of Tropea his fellow gangsters intervened when they discovered that he had been pocketing part of the defense funds. On February 15 two shotgun blasts, delivered as the Scourge was strolling along Halsted Street, ended his career. Nine days later Vito Bascone's body was found in a ditch in Stickney, a bullet hole between his eyes and the index finger of each hand shot off, presumably when he lifted them in last-minute supplication. At the bottom of a stone quarry nearby lay the ruins of Baldelli's car which had been rolled into it from the road above. The body of Baldelli himself turned up the same night on an ash heap in a North Chicago alley. He had been beaten, kicked, hacked, and finally shot.

Tony Finalli died of shotgun wounds on March 7. Felipe Gnolfo survived three attempts against his life but succumbed to a fourth in

1930, bringing the number of killings attributable to the Scalise-Anselmi fund-raising drive to eight.

In the second trial, begun on February 7, the same difficulties were encountered completing a jury. Of the first 246 veniremen called, all but 4 managed to disqualify themselves. One of them, Orval W. Payne, told Judge Brothers why: "It wouldn't be healthy to bring in a verdict of guilty. Pressure is brought to bear on our families. I'd have to carry a gun for the rest of my life."

The defendants won an acquittal thanks mainly to two defense witnesses who swore that Mike Genna fired at the detectives before they fired at him. In May Scalise and Anselmi went to Joliet to begin the fourteen-year sentence imposed by Judge Brothers after the first trial. But Chicago had not heard the last of them.

The day Bascone and Baldelli were killed the Vice President of the United States, Charles G. Dawes, presented to Congress, at the request of the Better Government Association of Chicago and Cook County, a petition demanding a federal investigation of outlawry in the area:

> There has been growing up in this community [the petition read] a reign of lawlessness and terror, openly defying not only the Constitution and laws of the State of Illinois, but the Constitution and laws of the United States.
>
> There has been for a long time in this city of Chicago a colony of unnaturalized persons, hostile to our institutions and laws, who have formed a supergovernment of their own—feudists, black handers, members of the Mafia—who levy tribute upon citizens and enforce collections by terrorizing, kidnapping and assassinations.
>
> There are other gangs, such as the O'Donnells, the McErlanes, Ragens Colts, Torrio and others, some of whom are citizens of the United States.
>
> Many of these aliens have become fabulously rich as rum-runners and bootleggers, working in collusion with police and other officials, building up a monopoly in this unlawful business and dividing the territory of the county among themselves under penalty of death to all intruding competitors.
>
> Evidence multiplies daily that many public officials are in secret alliance with underworld assassins, gunmen, rum-runners, bootleggers, thugs, ballot box stuffers and repeaters, that a ring of politicians and public officials operating through criminals and with dummy directors are conducting a number of breweries and

are selling beer under police protection, police officials, working out of the principal law enforcement office of the city, having been convoying liquor—namely alcohol, whisky and beer—and that one such police officer who is under Federal indictment is still acting as a police officer. . . .

The petition went on to list breweries so operated. It concluded with a tabulation of Chicago bombings perpetrated during 1925, more than 100 of them, only a few of which led to prosecution and none to any serious penalties. Congress referred the petition to the Immigration Committee.

The petitioners hurled their harshest accusations at the state's attorney. Few officeholders had ever promised so much and delivered so little. When first elected in 1921 with Big Bill Thompson's Republican slate, Crowe manfully told the Cook County police, "You bring 'em in and I'll prosecute 'em." The cases he actually prosecuted were vastly outnumbered by the hundreds of indictments he failed to follow up. Though he successfully prosecuted Fred Lundin, mainly to wreck the Thompson clique with whom he had broken, he never acted upon the true bills returned against thirty-nine other peculating members of the Board of Education.

During Crowe's first two terms the number of murders in Cook County almost doubled, an increase he attributed, logically enough, to Prohibition. Of the 349 victims, 215 were gangsters killed in the beer wars. Yet despite the size of Crowe's staff—70 assistant state's attorneys and 50 police, the largest in the history of the office—it obtained only 128 convictions for murder, none involving gangsters, and only 8 murderers went to the gallows. Bombings during the same period totaled 369 without a single conviction. While the rise of gangsterism accounted for a good deal of these statistics, only its partnership with police and politicians could explain the low percentage of convictions. There were 2,309 convictions for major crimes of every kind in 1921; in 1923 there were 1,344. Of the felony charges brought before the Municipal Court in 1923, 23,862 were either reduced to lesser offenses or dropped altogether.

The state's attorney was a man of professorial mien, heavy-browed, with a small, sharp nose, small eyes obscured by thick tortoiseshell-rimmed lenses, and a thin mouth frequently arched in an expression of lofty scorn. He craved power and in pursuit of it drew upon a gift for oratory. Crime inspired some of his loftiest flights. "Give me plenty of judges," he once declaimed, "so I can try the killer while the blood of his victim is still warm!"

Robert Emmett Crowe was of Irish extraction, born in Peoria in 1879. For three years after graduating from Yale Law School he practiced privately with the Chicago firm of Moran, Mayer & Meyer. He married Candida Cuneo, the daughter of an Italian merchant who founded Chicago's oldest wholesale produce firm. At thirty he entered politics as an assistant state's attorney on the staff of John E. W. Wayman, the Republican politician, tolerant of the Levee's vice and gambling overlords until reform groups obliged him to close the red-light district. Under the Democratic administration of Mayor Carter H. Harrison, Jr., begun in 1914, Crowe served a year as an assistant city corporation counsel and a year as a Cook County circuit court judge. In 1919 he was named chief justice of the Criminal Court, the youngest man, at thirty-eight, ever to have sat on that bench. By then he had joined the Thompson faction, which two years later carried him to the post of state's attorney. It was in the same elections that Thompson won the mayoralty for the second time and Len Small, the governorship.

Crowe's tenure was not without merit. He transformed the office of state's attorney, expanding its scope of operations and recruiting vigorous, ambitious young law school alumni. The normal quota of judges available to the state's attorney was six. Crowe's oratory in appeals to administrative and civic committees brought about an increase of twenty. His eloquence further obtained for his budget an extra $100,000 a year with which to retain special assistants, and at his urging 1,000 policemen were added to the city force.

Crowe recognized the folly of Prohibition and the unenforceability of the Volstead Act, and he repeatedly inveighed against them. Eighty percent of the Cook County population, he contended, was wet, and this included most judges and jurors. "A specimen of the idiocy to which the dry law reduces otherwise sane men," he said in a notable speech, "is the recent wordy war between Mayor Dever and the United States District Attorney [Edwin A.] Olson in Washington. Dever says the town is dry because he dried it up and because he threatened to report Olson to President Coolidge, which made Olson get busy. Olson testified that in spite of all his efforts, which eventually dried the town, it again became wet because the mayor's police are corrupt. In other words, each of these officials says the town is dry because he dried it and wet because the other fellow hasn't dried it. That is, it is both wet and dry!

"I'll tell you something: the town is wet and the county is wet, and nobody can dry them up. They holler about Sheriff Hoffman permitting the county to run wide open. Well, it is wide open. But for every dive in the county there are two in the city, and everybody in Chicago knows it except Dever.

"Why don't I get busy and stop it? For the simple reason that I am running a law office, not a police station. If Chicago wants things cleaned up, let somebody bring the law violators in here and I'll send them to the penitentiary. But I will not be both arresting officer and prosecutor."

Among Crowe's major court victories (as he never tired of reminding the public) was the breakup of a statewide auto-theft ring. He also assigned one of his crack assistants, Charles Gorman, to the prosecution of Fred "Frenchy" Mader, president of the Building Trades Council. With bombs and threats of strikes Mader had been extorting from Chicago construction firms 10 percent of the costs whenever they put up a new building. Despite the bribery of jurors and the intimidation of witnesses, Mader and forty-nine members of his gang were convicted. They served no prison sentence. Governor Small pardoned them all.

"Probably the worst handicap this office confronts is Len Small's parole and pardon system," said Crowe. "He lets them out as fast as we put them in. It takes us two weeks to get the guilty man convicted and it takes the Governor two seconds to sign his name on a pardon blank. In 1923, for example, I put 59 burglars and 97 robbers in Joliet, and Small released 88 burglars and 97 robbers!"

But first and last Crowe was the total politician, a magisterial player of the power game. A running mate of Thompson and Small in the 1921 elections, he broke with their machine over the control of Chicago's richest single source of patronage and graft—the Police Department. Thompson had chosen for police chief Charles C. Fitzmorris, a former city editor on William Randolph Hearst's Chicago *American* and no admirer of Crowe. The state's attorney formed his own anti-Thompson, anti-Small cabal within the party fold.

The co-drafters of the petition to Congress, Dean Edward T. Lee of Chicago's John Marshall Law School, and Dr. Elmer T. Williams, director of law enforcement for the Better Government Association, accused Crowe of consorting with criminals. He once attended a banquet given by the Gennas, they charged. "Liars!" retorted Crowe and dismissed the whole petition as a publicity stunt, part of a political campaign to "put over Diamond Joe Esposito and others like him" in the coming primary. Diamond Joe thereupon revealed that during the previous elections, when he refused to support Crowe's candidacy, Crowe sent Jim Genna to him with threatening messages. Throughout his first term, Diamond Joe maintained, the state's attorney kept vengefully persecuting him; again and again his detectives raided the Bella Napoli Café.

The recriminations were still echoing when there occurred a murder that would lead to the fullest disclosure yet of the complicity between public officials and outlaws. As the Illinois Crime Survey summarized it, the *cause célèbre* involved "most of the aspects of organized crime."

12

"I paid him plenty and I got what I was paying for"

THE questions tantalized Chicagoans all that spring and summer: What had an assistant state's attorney been doing, driving around Cicero with four notorious hoodlums? What had he been doing, drinking bootleg beer with them, when only a few months earlier he had tried hard (or so it seemed at the time) to send two of them to the gallows?

At twenty-six William H. McSwiggin was one of the smartest, toughest prosecutors on Crowe's staff. The previous year he had won convictions in nine capital cases. Short but powerfully built, handsome, dapper and witty, "Little Mac" had grown up in Chicago's West Side Irish colony, a comrade of future gangsters like the O'Donnells, Jim Doherty and Tom "Red" Duffy. Like Doherty and Duffy, he was a policeman's son, the only boy among five children born to Sergeant Anthony McSwiggin, who joined the Chicago force in 1881. He attended De Paul Academy, a Roman Catholic institution, then De Paul University and finally the university law school, earning his tuition as a department store salesman, movie usher, dance hall bouncer, trucker and special agent for the American Railway Express Company. He graduated with such high honors that Crowe immediately offered him a place on his staff. Academic distinction, however, was not what originally impressed Crowe. As a popular Thirteenth Ward Republican, young McSwiggin had garnered votes for the state's attorney in 1920 and again in 1924. So had the O'Donnell gang.

This political labor also brought him into contact with Capone, who often spoke of him as "my friend, Bill McSwiggin." A bachelor, Mc-Swiggin lived with his parents and four sisters at 4946 West Washington Boulevard. His father was continually begging him to break with the disreputable companions of his youth.

The sequence of events that so agitated Chicago (as the police, a succession of grand juries and various special investigating committees pieced them together over a period of months) began on April 17 in the Hawthorne Inn. McSwiggin went there to confer with Capone. Though Capone later confirmed rumors of the meeting, he never disclosed its purpose. Police Sergeant McSwiggin, who claimed he knew what took place between his son and the gang leader, also refused to discuss it. "If I told," he said, "I'd blow the lid off Chicago. This case is loaded with dynamite. It's dangerous to talk about it."

At 6 P.M. on the evening of the twenty-seventh McSwiggin was eating supper at home when Red Duffy dropped in. Leaving his meal unfinished, McSwiggin followed him out to the street, saying he was going to play cards in Berwyn. They got into Jim Doherty's car. Doherty, whom McSwiggin had unsuccessfully prosecuted for the murder of Eddie Tancl, sat behind the wheel. Doherty's co-defendant, Myles O'Donnell, was in the rear seat with his brother Klondike. They had had a busy day. In the recent Republican county primaries the Crowe slate had defeated the ticket endorsed by Senator Deneen, who thereupon demanded a recount. The O'Donnells, Doherty and Duffy had spent the day in the County Building in Chicago, wearing the badges of ballot watchers for the Crowe machine. The recount confirmed the Crowe victory (and later investigations of election frauds by four special grand juries failed to upset it). As Klondike O'Donnell left the County Building, he boisterously remarked to his companions, "We'll adjourn to Cicero and brace up on some good beer. I know it's good because I delivered it myself." A Capone spy happened to overhear the boast and at once reported it to Capone by telephone at the Hawthorne Inn. Before proceeding to Cicero, the four gangsters stopped for McSwiggin.

The numerous explanations advanced later to explain McSwiggin's actions were as disparate as their sources. The Crowe office acclaimed him as a valiant, dogged prosecutor who accompanied the gangsters only to gather material information for several pending cases, among them the second Scalise-Anselmi trial. According to the O'Donnells, simple kindness motivated McSwiggin; he had sought their help in recovering some bulletproof vests that had been stolen from a friend, a salesman named Albert Dunlap. The anti-Crowe faction imputed corrupt motives to the assistant state's attorney. He was an underworld tool, they said; his conduct of the first Scalise-Anselmi trial had been cunningly manipulated so as to spare the killers the extreme penalty. To others, it seemed possible that McSwiggin had committed no offense more serious than an impropriety. Clan loyalties among Chicago's Irish were as durable as those of the Italians and in many instances accounted for the friendships of Irish gangsters and politicians raised in the same neighborhood.

Jim Doherty had driven only a few blocks when his engine began to sputter. He left his car for repairs in a West Side garage, and the five men changed to Klondike O'Donnell's new Lincoln sedan. A sixth man joined the party, Edward Hanley, a former police officer. He drove. They roamed Cicero for about two hours, drinking beer in several saloons. Their last stop was Harry Madigan's Pony Inn at 5613 West Roosevelt Road. A two-story, white brick building with a big weedy lot behind, it stood a mile north of Capone's Hawthorne Inn stronghold.

Relations between Capone and the O'Donnells had deteriorated to the brink of open combat. The Irishmen grew daily bolder in their encroachments upon Capone's Cicero territory. Harry Madigan later explained to Chief of Detectives Schoemaker how matters had stood: "When I wanted to start a saloon in Cicero more than a year ago, Capone wouldn't let me. I finally obtained strong political pressure and was able to open. Then Capone came to me and said I would have to buy his beer, so I did. A few months ago Doherty and Myles O'Donnell came to me and said they could sell me better beer than Capone beer, which was then needled. They did and it cost fifty dollars a barrel, where Capone charged me sixty. I changed, and upon my recommendation so did several other Cicero saloonkeepers."

As soon as Klondike O'Donnell's boast in the County Building was reported to Capone, he took from behind a sliding panel a tommy gun, one of the three supplied by Alex Korocek, and an extra 100-cartridge magazine. Assembling a crew of his triggermen, he instructed them to fetch five cars which were to be deployed as follows:

A lead car to ram any police flivvers the motorcade might encounter during the getaway.

Two cars to move close behind the lead car, but hugging the curb so that they could block traffic at the street intersections until the car carrying Capone and three other armed men got past.

Capone's driver to keep 50 feet behind the first three cars.

The fifth car to cover the rear and in case of pursuit, to stage an accident, paralyzing traffic.

There remained to discover where the prey would alight. Shortly after eight o'clock a Capone lookout recognized Klondike O'Donnell's Lincoln parked in front of the Pony Inn. Within fifteen minutes the Capone cars were lined up half a block away. When, at about eight-thirty, the merrymakers emerged, sodden with beer, and crossed the sidewalk to the Lincoln, the motorcade started toward them. An eyewitness, a Mrs. Bach, who lived above the saloon, testified later: "I saw a closed car speeding away with what looked like a telephone receiver sticking out the rear window and spitting fire. . . ."

Duffy, Doherty and McSwiggin all suffered terrible injuries, but Hanley and the O'Donnells saved themselves by pitching headlong to the pavement behind the sedan. The brothers panicked. Daunted by the prospect of the awkward questions they would face if they took their wounded companions to a hospital, they decided to take them to Klondike's house nearby on Parkside Avenue and call a doctor. McSwiggin, with slugs in his back and neck, lay twisting on the sidewalk. Both of Doherty's legs had been shattered and his chest ripped open. The survivors bundled them into the sedan. Duffy, who looked beyond help, they left propped up against a tree.

Before they reached the O'Donnell house both wounded men died. Leaving Doherty's body in the car, the brothers carried McSwiggin into the house. They emptied his pockets, cut all identifying marks from his clothes and carried him back to the car. With one brother following in a smaller car, the other drove to Berwyn, and halting beside a lonely stretch of prairie, they dumped the bodies of their boyhood comrades. They continued north to Oak Park where they abandoned the sedan. They then vanished, not to be seen or heard from again for a month. Capone, too, vanished that night and hid for three months.

Duffy was found first. He was still alive when a motorist picked him up and drove him to a hospital. "Pretty cold-blooded to leave me lying there," he said. He died the next morning. In his pockets the police found a list of sixty Cicero saloons and speakeasies, many of them checked off with a pencil mark. The list mysteriously disappeared. When it finally turned up again in the coroner's office, the check marks had been obliterated.

A passerby chanced upon the bodies of McSwiggin and Doherty at about 10 P.M., and the Berwyn police delivered them to the morgue; but it was midnight before a Chicago newspaper reporter identified State's Attorney Crowe's star aide.

The morning headlines defied belief. Chicagoans had come to view with complacency the gang wars that had claimed more than 200 lives in four years, 29 of them since the beginning of 1926. "They only kill each other"—so ran the stereotype—"good riddance." But the murder of an assistant state's attorney startled Chicago and the nation.

The threat to Crowe's political security moved him to fiery rhetoric. "It will be a war to the hilt against these gangsters," he promised. He ordered his detectives to arrest every known hoodlum on sight. He had Sheriff Hoffman deputize 100 city detectives for county duty and sent them into the suburbs under the command of Chief Schoemaker and Deputy Chief Stege to raid saloons, speakeasies, gambling houses and brothels. He headed the Cicero raiding party himself. For information leading to the arrest of McSwiggin's murderers he offered a reward of $5,000 out of his own pocket.

Yet many prominent Chicagoans, among them clubwomen, clergy and captains of commerce, were skeptical. The president of the august Union League Club, Harry Eugene Kelly, contending that politics would prevent Crowe from disinterested action, demanded a special grand jury, financially independent of both the state's attorney's office and the County Board, to investigate the murders. "I have nothing against Mr. Crowe personally," Kelly said, "but obviously he is unfit to go into the 'beer racket' because it is mixed up all down the line with politics. He is not only a capable politician but is the head and front of a powerful faction known as the 'Crowe wing.' He is the directing head of a faction organized for politics and politics only. Therefore, the citizens cannot expect Mr. Crowe to prosecute the kind of investigation this city requires."

Crowe counterattacked with the accusation that his critics were hampering justice. "Under the law," he said, "the people of Cook County select their State's Attorney. They do not delegate his powers to self-appointed investigators. I am engaged in the investigation of the most brazen and dastardly murder ever committed in Chicago. Selfish notoriety seekers, who are called by some newspapers 'civic leaders,' have started a backfire on the State's Attorney of this county, while he is engaged in this arduous and not entirely safe duty. I appeal to the law-abiding men and women of this county for their moral support and sympathy in this crisis; and I appeal to these officious meddlers, that if they have any information, to present it to me; if they can be of any assistance, to cooperate with me, and cease giving aid and comfort to gangsters by attempting to divert my attention from the task in hand."

Crowe then outmaneuvered the opposition by petitioning Judge William V. Brothers to create a special grand jury. Brothers, who belonged to the same political wing as Crowe, complied. Crowe, however, had no intention of relinquishing control of the inquiry and permitting any jury to delve into the connection between Cook County politics and Cook County crime. Seeming to disqualify himself, he called on Attorney General Oscar Carlstrom, another reliable party hack, to direct the grand jury. In reality he dictated the moves from behind the scenes.

Thanks to a broad mandate from Judge Brothers to examine the roots of all crime in the county, Carlstrom was free to pursue diversionary tactics. Instead of focusing the jury's attention on the McSwiggin murder, he attacked as the chief cause of crime the parole abuses at Joliet from which convicts had been buying their way out. None of the evidence Carlstrom presented led to an indictment.

The Cook County coroner, Oscar Wolff, an official as notorious for his ineptitude as he was for his association with gangsters, also set up a special jury to sit on the McSwiggin inquest. As the hearings bumbled along irrelevantly, he conceived a gesture designed to show that he meant business. In Terre Haute, Indiana, a prosecutor named Joseph Roach had recently distinguished himself by sending scores of malfeasant officials and their underworld allies to jail. Coroner Wolff now proposed that Roach be appointed a special Illinois state's attorney so that he could take part in the inquest. Roach arrived amid great fanfare but got no opportunity to demonstrate his investigative skill. Almost immediately Wolff adjourned the inquest. It was reconvened twice during the next two years without reaching a verdict.

About all that Wolff achieved was to assemble dossiers on thirty-odd gangsters whom he accused of various murders and refer them to Carlstrom. The attorney general ignored most of them. His jury did vote a few indictments, none remotely related to the McSwiggin case and none that went to trial. When he finally got around to the McSwiggin case, the witnesses included more than 200 Cicero saloon-keepers, and while they shed no light on the murder itself, they told the jury a good deal about the sources of their liquor. This information could have been helpful to the federal grand jurors then investigating bootlegging in Cicero, but Carlstrom did not transmit it to them.

A week after the McSwiggin murder the Chicago *Tribune* reported: "The police have no more actual evidence as to the motives of the shooting and the identity of the killer than they did when it happened." The Carlstrom grand jury reaffirmed this. According to a review of its investigation, "A conspiracy of silence among gangsters and intimidation of other witnesses after a murder has been committed, immediately operates and there is an element of fear involved because anyone who does aid the public officials by giving facts is very likely to be 'taken for a ride.' . . . Notwithstanding every effort has been made to solve the murder of William H. McSwiggin, it has been impossible for the jury to determine guilt or to ascertain the guilty parties in that case. Silence and sealed lips of gangsters make the solution of that crime, like many others, thus far impossible."

But on the day the *Tribune* ran its story Crowe, who seldom hesitated to prosecute a case in the newspapers, issued the following statement to reporters: "It has been established to the satisfaction of the state's attorney's office and the detective bureau that Capone in person led the slayers of McSwiggin. . . . It has also been found that Capone handled the machine gun, being compelled to this act in order to set an example of fearlessness to his less eager companions."

The dead man's father, Sergeant McSwiggin, told reporters, "I thought my life work was over, but it's only begun. I'll never rest until I've killed my boy's slayers or seen them hanged. That's all I have to live for now."

He undertook a private investigation of his own. When an auto thief, Theodore Thiel, was extradited from Detroit on suspicion of complicity in the triple killing, the old policeman went to the jail and pleaded with him, tears in his eyes, "Tell me who killed my boy."

"I wish I could help you," said the prisoner.

"You can't help me," said the policeman. "They killed me, too, when they killed my boy. But you can help yourself by talking. You may not have known my boy was in that automobile when you tipped it off to Capone. But we know you did tip it off and we want you to tell."

Thiel appeared to weigh the consequences of telling whatever it was he knew.

"Think it over tonight," the policeman urged him. "We can do you some good in those automobile cases. Capone can do you no harm. We'll talk again tomorrow."

The plea failed.

Sergeant McSwiggin eventually named as the four killers of his son Capone, Frank Rio, Frank Diamond and a Cicero bootlegger, Bob McCullough, and as the accomplices who directed them to the victims, Eddie Moore and Willie Heeney. An oath of secrecy, he added, prevented him from revealing the source of his information.

Crowe's deputy raiders, meanwhile, inflicted costly damage upon Capone's suburban empire. It was a low point in his fortunes. He owned or controlled twenty-five of the thirty-three resorts that the raiders overran, smashing slot machines, roulette wheels and crap tables, beer barrels, cases of liquor and drums of alcohol by the hundreds, arresting the girls, and hauling away safes full of cash and ledgers. They partially wrecked Capone's biggest brothel, the Stockade. The next night three carloads of Forest View vigilantes completed the destruction. Emboldened by the West Suburban Citizens' Association, they set fire to the place. The local fire brigade arrived, but only to make sure the flames didn't endanger any neighboring homes. They didn't, and the brigade stood around idly watching the brothel burn to the ground. "Why don't you do something?" a Caponeite asked. "Can't spare the water," replied a fireman. Deputy Chief Stege laughed when he heard of it. "Investigate?" he said. "I should say not. No doubt the flames were started by some good people of the community." Said the Reverend William H. Tuttle of the Citizens' Association: "I appreciate the wonderful news. I am sure no decent person will be sorry."

The most interesting seizures made by Stege and his men were the ledgers. In addition to the weekly earnings of each whorehouse employee, they showed the yield of every installation from the quarter-in-the-slot player pianos to the chuck-a-luck tables as well as the amount (usually 10 percent) paid for protection. For example, the page of a ledger found at the Barracks, a small Burnham dive, covering the week beginning September 6, 1925, read as follows:

Slot machines	$ 906.00
Piano	55.25
Rooms [*i.e.*, prostitution]	5,891.00
Bar	2,677.10
Tables [gambling]	1,800.00
GROSS	$ 11,329.35
Paid out 10% [protection]	1,133.00
	$ 10,196.35
EXPENSES	8,450.00
NET	$ 1,746.35

The Stockade netted almost three times as much, and the total weekly average of all twenty-five Capone resorts came to about $75,-000 or close to $4,000,000 a year.

The Hawthorne Smoke Shop, too, was raided and the books found there taken to the state's attorney's office, where they remained un-examined, gathering dust for four years.

The federal grand jury sitting in Cicero began to uncover evidence with a possible bearing on the McSwiggin case. Immediately after the murder, federal agents learned, Cicero policemen visited every saloon in town, appropriated a few bottles of beer, and warned the saloon-keepers (in the words of one of them): "There's going to be a big investigation. Don't tell anybody anything. If you open your face, these samples go to the prohibition office and your prosecution under federal statutes is certain."

On May 27 the federal jury indicted members of both the Capone and O'Donnell gangs, specifically Al and Ralph Capone, Charlie Fischetti and Peter Payette, the three O'Donnells and Harry Madigan. The charge was conspiracy to violate the Volstead Act.

The search for the fugitive Capone took the Chicago detectives to New York, to the woods of northernmost Michigan and to Couderay, Wisconsin, where he had recently acquired a country estate for $250,000 and raised a lookout tower near the main house with em-placements for machine guns. They found no trace of him.

The O'Donnells were captured in Chicago or surrendered—the

point was never cleared up—the same day the federal jury indicted them, and Chief Schoemaker took them directly to the state's attorney's office instead of to police headquarters. This breach of normal procedure gave rise to the suspicion that the brothers had been arrested according to a prearranged plan and given ample time to fabricate their stories. They refused to testify before the grand jury until threatened with jail for contempt of court. They then set forth their version of the events of the night of April 27. For the first time they mentioned bulletproof vests as the reason McSwiggin went to Cicero. They were not with him at the fatal moment, they swore. He was carried afterward to Klondike's house, by whom they would not say. Nor did they have any explanation to offer of how the bodies of McSwiggin and Doherty came to end up in a Berwyn prairie.

The state authorities took no further action against the O'Donnells, and the federal charges for liquor law violations, after pending two years, were dropped.

The Illinois law limited the life of a special grand jury to one month. If the investigation were to continue, another jury had to be empaneled. The Carlstrom jury disbanded on June 4. In its concluding report it absolved McSwiggin of any wrongdoing and accepted the story of the bulletproof vests. (Crowe described his assistant's evening with gangsters as a "social ride.") The jurors surmised, probably correctly, that "the murderers had no knowledge of the identity or position of the young man. . . ." The report acclaimed the state's attorney for his vigorous prosecution of the case and denounced his detractors: "Baseness and pernicious criticism by groups of persons or newspapers when actuated by malice or political motives only result in aiding and encouraging crime and criminals. And it is deplorable that prominent citizens in public life make criticisms which are published in the press, as in the cases of Mr. Harry Eugene Kelly and Coroner Oscar Wolff, which statements when called before the grand jury they failed in any manner to substantiate."

As for the basic causes of crime in Cook County, the alliance of politicians and gangsters was not among those the jury enumerated. Overstating the obvious, the report named as the main causes the profit to be made from bootlegging and the ease of obtaining firearms. The report ended on a complacent note:

> On the whole, a review of the years gives no special occasion for alarm at the present moment. Crime, in volume and type,

wheels and rotates in cycles. In the last thirty or forty years there
have been periodical outbursts of gang activities in the criminal
groups. The one through which we are now passing has been pe-
culiarly vicious and has produced many murders by gangsters because the stakes played for have been great. Gang after gang has
been wiped out by internecine warfare. Remnants of gangs have
fled the city and the situation is well enough in hand to encourage the hope that there will be no outbreak on any such scale as
in the recent past.

To still the clamor that greeted the jury's feeble performance,
Crowe petitioned Chief Justice Thomas J. Lynch of the Criminal
Court to empanel a second special grand jury. It was needed, he said,
to investigate vote frauds during the recent primaries, as well as the
McSwiggin case. Thus, Crowe again confused and sidetracked the
central issue by diffusing the new jury's duties. Under the direction
of Charles A. McDonald, a former judge, it made no more progress
than the first. A third special grand jury followed. On July 28, toward
the end of its equally futile existence, Capone, for whose arrest secret
warrants had been issued, reappeared. From Indiana he notified
Crowe that he was ready to surrender. As he waited for Crowe's chief
investigator, Pat Roche, to pick him up at the Illinois state line, he
spoke to reporters. "Some time in the forenoon," he said, "I will go
with Mr. Roche to the Federal Building. We have been talking by
long distance phone and I think the time is ripe for me to prove my
innocence of the charges that have been made against me.

"It's a bad time to say anything. I've been convicted without a hearing of all the crimes on the calendar. But I'm innocent and it won't
take long to prove it. I trust my attorneys to see that I'm treated like
a human being and not pushed around by a lot of coppers with axes
to grind."

To a suburban reporter whose paper had speculated that Capone
killed McSwiggin by mistake, thinking he was Hymie Weiss, he said:
"Of course, I didn't kill him. Why should I? I liked the kid. Only the
day before he was up to my place and when he went home I gave
him a bottle of Scotch for his old man."

Why, then, did Capone flee Chicago after the murder? Because he
feared the police would shoot him on sight. "The police have told a
lot of stories. They shoved a lot of murders over on me. They did it
because they couldn't find the men who did the jobs and I looked like
an easy goat. They said I was sore at McSwiggin because he prose-

cuted Anselmi and Scalise for killing two policemen. But that made no difference. He told me he was going to give them the rope if he could and that was all right with me."

In his volubility Capone committed an indiscretion horribly embarrassing to Crowe. "I paid McSwiggin," he informed reporters. "I paid him plenty and I got what I was paying for."

Arriving at the Federal Building, Capone announced: "I'm no squawker, but I'll tell what I know about this case. All I ask is a chance to prove that I had nothing to do with the killing of my friend, Bill McSwiggin. Just ten days before he was killed I talked with him. There were friends of mine with me. If we had wanted to kill him, we could have done it then. But we didn't want to. We never wanted to. I liked him. He was a fine young fellow.

"Doherty and Duffy were my friends, too. I wasn't out to get them. Why, I used to lend Doherty money. Big-hearted Al I was, just helping out a friend. I wasn't in the beer racket and didn't care where they sold. Just a few days before that shooting, my brother Ralph and Doherty and the O'Donnells were at a party together."

The day after Capone's return to Chicago he appeared before Justice Lynch with Michael Ahern's law partner, Thomas D. Nash. An assistant state's attorney, George E. Gorman, withdrew the murder charge. "This complaint," he said, "was made by Chief of Detectives Schoemaker on cursory information. Subsequent investigation could not legally substantiate the information." Justice Lynch thereupon dismissed the case.

As Capone sauntered out of the courtroom, beaming, Sergeant McSwiggin, who had followed him there, remarked, "They pinned a medal on him and turned him loose." The old man never recovered from his grief. He was often heard to murmur, "They killed me, too, when they killed my boy."

No sooner had a fourth special grand jury been empaneled at Judge McDonald's request—again, to investigate both vote frauds and the McSwiggin case—than it was distracted by still another issue. On August 6, as two eyewitnesses later testified, Joe Saltis and his chauffeur, Frank "Lefty" Koncil, shot to death a member of the Sheldon gang, John "Mitters" Foley, who had been selling beer in Saltis-McErlane territory. The jurors interrupted their original inquiries to indict the pair.

The only other accomplishment of the fourth special grand jury was to return indictments against forty election officials of the Forty-second Ward. The State Supreme Court later quashed them all. Concerning the murder of McSwiggin, Crowe took the witness stand to testify—on what evidence he did not indicate—that his blameless young assistant had been killed by gunmen imported from either Detroit or New York.

"I know who killed McSwiggin," said Judge McDonald in asking Justice Lynch to empanel a fifth grand jury, "but I want to know it legally and be able to present it conclusively. Neither Sergeant McSwiggin nor anyone else has at any time given me or my assistants the name of any one witness who would appear before the grand jury and identify Al Capone or any other person as the murderer."

Two new clues and two new witnesses had been found, he claimed. "It is necessary to keep the names of the witnesses secret. The moment any of the witnesses learn that they are wanted they disappear, or are even killed." Justice Lynch granted the request on condition that the jury confine itself to the McSwiggin case. It adjourned the first day, pending the presentation of the promised evidence. Neither new clues nor new witnesses ever materialized.

A sixth special grand jury brought the investigation to a fumbling close in October. Long before, the question of who killed McSwiggin and why had assumed less importance than the panorama of civic corruption that had been unveiled.

> . . . the McSwiggin case [said the Illinois Crime Survey] marks the beginning of intense public interest in organized crime. . . . The killing of McSwiggin dramatized to the public the relation between criminal gangs and the political machine. It is true that the coroner's jury and six grand juries were of no avail in solving the murder of an assistant state's attorney and his two gangster companions, but their findings did convince the public of the existence and power of organized crime—a power due in large part to its unholy alliance with politics. The very failure of the grand juries in solving the mystery of McSwiggin's death raised many puzzling and disturbing questions in the minds of intelligent citizens about the reasons for the breakdown of constituted government in Chicago and Cook County and its seeming helplessness when pitted against the forces of organized crime.

13

War

August 10, 1926—The First Battle of the Standard Oil Building

SO far the Weiss forces had kept the initiative and struck the hardest blows. They had wounded Torrio and put him to flight, attacked Capone twice and his men a dozen times, killed Tommy Cuiringione. . . .

Hymie Weiss and Schemer Drucci had an appointment in the offices of the Metropolitan Sanitary District of Greater Chicago at 910 South Michigan Avenue, the new nineteen-story Standard Oil Building. They were to meet with Morris Eller, political boss of the Twentieth Ward, who had recently been elected a trustee of the department, and John Sbarbaro, gangland's favorite funeral director, as well as an assistant state's attorney. Drucci was then living in the Congress Hotel, four blocks north of the rendezvous, and Weiss joined him there at about 9 A.M. After breakfasting in Drucci's eighth-floor suite, they set out on foot for the Standard Oil Building.

The exact nature of their business remained a secret among the parties involved. It called for a payment of $13,500, which Drucci brought with him in cash. He later referred vaguely to a "real estate deal." Whatever the transaction, it was not consummated that morning. As Weiss and Drucci approached the bronze, neo-Italian Renaissance doors of the building, four men bolted out of a car on the opposite side of the avenue and ran toward them with drawn automatics. Weiss and Drucci, shielding themselves behind a car parked in front of the entrance, pulled their guns out of their shoulder holsters. At that hour of the day the block teemed with people hurrying to work. A bullet nicked an office clerk in the thigh.

The street emptied as people dived for cover into doorways. The shooting went on, chipping hunks of concrete from buildings and smashing windows, until both sides ran out of ammunition. A police flivver then reached the scene. The attackers raced back to their car. One of them fell behind and the others drove off without him. The police recognized the Capone gunman, Louis Barko. Weiss fled into the Standard Oil lobby. Drucci leaped onto the running board of a passing car, held his revolver to the driver's temple and ordered him to keep going. But before the car could pick up speed, the police had dragged Drucci backward to the pavement.

At the stationhouse both Barko and Drucci gave false names and addresses. Drucci denied ever having set eyes on Barko. There had been no gang fight, he insisted. "It was a stickup, that's all. They were after my roll."

August 15—The Second Battle of the Standard Oil Building

Toward midmorning Weiss and Drucci were traveling south on Michigan Avenue in a sedan. As they came abreast of the Standard Oil Building, a car that had been trailing them close behind suddenly shot ahead, swerved to the right, and rammed them. Bullets from the car smashed all their windows. They jumped out and scampered into the building, firing over their shoulders as they ran. ("A real goddam crazy place!" said Capone's Brooklyn schoolmate Lucky Luciano after a visit to Chicago. "Nobody's safe in the streets.")

September 20—The Siege of the Hawthorne Inn

Frankie Rio saw through the ruse first. He and Capone were finishing lunch in the rear of the restaurant, facing the windows and Twenty-second Street. The place was packed, every table taken, this being the day of the big autumn meet at the nearby Hawthorne Race Track. Capone and his lieutenant were sipping coffee when they heard the roar of a speeding car mingled with the clatter of machinegun fire. In the silence after the car passed they rushed to the door with the other startled diners. There were no bullet marks, for the gunner had been firing blanks. Rio understood—a decoy to draw Capone out into the open. He flung himself to the floor, pulling Capone down on top of him, as bullets streaked over their heads, splintering the woodwork, smashing glassware and crockery. There were ten cars in the motorcade that had been moving single file behind the decoy car, and gun barrels stuck out of every window like the quills on a porcupine. The attackers took their time. As each car came abreast of the hotel, it stopped while they systematically sprayed the façade left to right, right to left, up and down. Louis Barko, entering the restaurant during the first burst, fell, a bullet through his shoulder. The cars standing at the curb, scores of them belonging to race fans, were perforated by the hail of lead. Clyde Freeman had driven all the way from Louisiana with his wife and five-year-old son. They were still in the car when the gunners opened fire. A bullet ripped through Freeman's hat. Another gashed his boy's knee. Flying shards of glass from the windshield cut Mrs. Freeman's arm and pierced her right eye. When the last carload of attackers stopped before the hotel, a man in a khaki shirt and overalls got out, carrying a tommy gun. He walked calmly up to the entrance, knelt, thrust the gun barrel through the doorway and, setting the mechanism at rapid fire, emptied a 100-cartridge drum in about ten seconds. The driver of the lead car sounded his klaxon three times. The man in khaki returned to the rear car, and the motorcade continued in orderly formation along Twenty-second Street toward Chicago.

The attack had left the restaurant, the hotel lobby and the neighboring storefronts in ruins, but the only human casualties were Barko and the Freemans. As Capone stood up, he showed no fear. His reaction was rather one of awed fascination with the power of tommy guns. He later told his reporter friend Edward Dean Sullivan: "That's the gun! It's got it over a sawed-off shotgun like the shotgun has it over an automatic. Put on a bigger drum and it will shoot well over a thousand. The trouble is they're hard to get."

When he learned that Mrs. Freeman's injured eye would require major surgery and a long hospitalization, he insisted on paying the entire bill. It came to $10,000. He also paid for repairs to the damaged stores adjoining the Hawthorne Inn.

Chief of Detectives Schoemaker, who felt sure he knew the identity of at least five of the attackers, summoned Louis Barko to a lineup and in it put Weiss, Drucci, Bugs Moran, Frank Gusenberg and his brothers, Pete and Henry. Barko, observing the gangster code as scrupulously as Drucci had done after the first battle of the Standard Oil Building, swore they all were strangers to him.

October 4—Truce

Torrio would have applauded Capone's next move. It reflected his mentor's policy of shared spoils ("There's plenty for everybody"). Repressing his natural urge to kill Weiss, he proposed a peace talk. Weiss agreed to a meeting at the Morrison Hotel. Capone prudently refrained from attending himself. He sent Tony Lombardo as his surrogate and, to placate the enemy, authorized him to offer Weiss exclusive sales rights to all the beer territory in Chicago north of Madison Street, a handsome concession. But the minimum price Weiss would accept for peace was the removal of Scalise and Anselmi. Lombardo phoned for instructions. When he transmitted Capone's answer—"I wouldn't do that to a yellow dog"—Weiss stalked out of the hotel in a fury.

October 11—The State Street Ambush

The three-story rooming house at 740 North State Street, kept by a Mrs. Anna Rotariu, had a curious literary association. The property belonged to the prolific crime writer, Harry Stephen Keeler (*The Spectacles of Mr. Cagliostro, Sing Sing Nights* and fifty-three others). He was born and reared in the house and wrote some of his thrillers there, moving away after his marriage in 1919. Next door, at 738, stood the old Dion O'Banion flower shop. William Schofield now ran it, and Hymie Weiss used the rooms above as his headquarters.

Early in October, a young man calling himself Oscar Lundin, or Langdon, rented lodgings from Mrs. Rotariu. He wanted a room on the second floor, facing State Street, but all the front rooms were occupied. So he agreed to take a back room until one should fall vacant, as it did on October 8. It was a dismal, musty room, small and meanly equipped with a pair of straight-backed wooden chairs, an old oak dresser, a tarnished brass bedframe, a tin food box, a gas ring, a shelf holding a few cracked plates and stained cutlery. But Lundin appeared delighted.

The same day that he came to Mrs. Rotariu's house a pretty blond woman, giving her name as Mrs. Theodore Schultz and her address as Mitchell, South Dakota, rented a front room on the third floor of an apartment building at 1 Superior Street, which ran at a right angle to State Street, south of the flower shop. Lundin's windows commanded an unobstructed view of the east side of State Street from Holy Name Cathedral to the corner, while Mrs. Schultz's windows overlooked both front and rear entrances of the flower shop. Anybody approaching or leaving the immediate neighborhood in any direction had to pass within close visual range of one or the other rooms.

Lundin occupied his quarters for only one day. After paying a week's rent in advance, he vanished. Two men, who had been visiting him during his stay, then moved into the room. As Mrs. Rotariu described them, one was about thirty-five years old, wearing a gray overcoat and gray fedora; the other, considerably younger, wore a dark suit and light cap. Mrs. Schultz also vanished after paying a week's rent, and two men, believed to be Italians, took possession of her room.

Hymie Weiss spent a large part of October 11 in the Criminal Court Building, four blocks from his headquarters, watching the selection of a jury in the trial of Joe Saltis and Lefty Koncil for the murder of Mitters Foley. The trial held a special interest for Weiss, as evidenced by the list of veniremen in his pocket and the list of state's witnesses in a safe back at his headquarters, documents whose later discovery would give substance to the rumor that he had disbursed $100,000 to ensure an acquittal.

When the court recessed for the day, Weiss left the building with four companions. There was his driver and factotum, Sam Peller; Paddy Murray, his bodyguard and a part-time beer runner; Benny Jacobs, a Twentieth Ward politician and private investigator for lawyers; and William W. O'Brien, one of Chicago's leading criminal lawyers, who headed the Saltis-Koncil defense staff. Four years earlier O'Brien had defeated a move to disbar him for having tried to suborn two assistant state's attorneys. His reputation was further blemished when he refused to name the gangster who shot him in a South Side saloon.

At about 4 P.M. Peller parked Weiss' Cadillac coupe in front of Holy Name Cathedral, opposite the flower shop, and the five men started across State Street. The swarthy pair in Mrs. Rotariu's rooming house had been waiting for two days, their chairs drawn up to the windows, tommy guns and shotguns at hand. A hundred cigarette stubs littered the floor. The coverlet of the bed on which they had taken turns napping was splotched with black shoe polish. The two men in the side-street apartment had also been keeping vigil since October 9, chain-smoking and drinking wine, but now they saw they were no longer needed. In their hasty retreat they left behind an automatic shotgun and two bottles of wine.

The date of the construction of Holy Name Cathedral and the Vulgate version of St. Paul's Epistle to the Philippians (2:10), were carved on the cornerstone—A.D. 1874 AT THE NAME OF JESUS EVERY KNEE SHOULD BOW IN HEAVEN AND ON EARTH. The bullets that poured from the windows of No. 740, as the five men reached the center of the street, chipped off the date and all but six words of the text, leaving EVERY KNEE SHOULD HEAVEN AND EARTH.* Ten bullets hit Weiss, killing him almost instantly. Murray, pierced through by fifteen bullets, fell dead beside him. O'Brien, with bullets in his arm, thigh and abdomen, dragged himself to the curb. The first policeman on the scene found Peller, shot in the groin, begging people in the swelling crowd to take him to a doctor. Jacobs, bleeding from a leg wound, was supporting himself against a mailbox.

The killers ran down a back staircase, climbed through a ground-floor window into an alley, and made a clean getaway. The only clue to their escape route was a tommy gun dropped on top of a dog kennel, a block south of Superior Street. Detectives searching the ambush counted thirty-five empty tommy-gun shells and three fired shotgun cartridges. On the bed they found a gray fedora bearing the label of a Cicero haberdashery near the Hawthorne Inn. They also found in Weiss' pockets, along with the list of veniremen, $5,300 and in Paddy Murray's pockets, $1,500. O'Brien was carrying $1,500.

O'Brien, Peller and Jacobs all eventually recovered, but none had any helpful information to offer the coroner's jury. No trace of the killers was ever uncovered. Nor were the accomplices who rented the rooms for them ever identified.

While the Sbarbaro embalmers were preparing Weiss' body for burial, Capone in slippered, shirt-sleeved ease, puffing on a rich cigar,

---

* Chicago taxi drivers still point out the cornerstone to strangers. The cathedral had largely been restored when I last visited the city, but a bullet scar was still visible.

received the press at the Hawthorne Inn. "That was butchery," he said in the course of several interviews, as he dispensed cigars and drinks to the reporters. "Hymie was a good kid. He could have got out long ago and taken his and been alive today. When we were in business together in the old days, I got to know him well and used to go often to his room for a friendly visit. Torrio and me made Weiss and O'Banion. When they broke away and went into business for themselves, that was all right with us. We let 'em go and forgot about 'em. But they began to get nasty. We sent 'em word to stay in their own backyard. But they had the swell head and thought they were bigger than we were. Then O'Banion got killed. Right after Torrio was shot—and Torrio knew who shot him—I had a talk with Weiss. 'What do you want to do, get yourself killed before you're thirty?' I said to him. [Weiss died at the age of twenty-eight; he was a year older than Capone.] 'You'd better get some sense while a few of us are left alive.' He could still have got along with me. But he wouldn't listen to me. Forty times I've tried to arrange things so we'd have peace and life would be worth living. Who wants to be tagged around night and day by guards? I don't, for one. There was, and there is, plenty of business for us all and competition needn't be a matter of murder, anyway. But Weiss couldn't be told anything. I suppose you couldn't have told him a week ago that he'd be dead today. There are some reasonable fellows in his outfit, and if they want peace I'm for it now, as I have always been.

"I'm sorry Hymie was killed, but I didn't have anything to do with it. I phoned the detective bureau that I'd come in if they wanted me, but they told me they didn't want me. I knew I'd be blamed for it. There's enough business for all of us without killing each other like animals in the street. I don't want to end up in the gutter punctured by machine gun slugs, so why should I kill Weiss?"

The rhetorical question brought a growl of disgust from Chief of Detectives Schoemaker. "He knows why," he told the reporters, "and so does everyone else. He had them killed." Chief of Police Collins agreed. It was his contention that when Capone went to New York at Christmastime, he hired more bodyguards, bringing the total to eighteen, and picked four of them to kill Weiss. Asked why, then, Capone remained at liberty, Collins replied: "It's a waste of time to arrest him. He's been in before on other murder charges. He has his alibi."

A group of Hymie Weiss' boyhood classmates at St. Malachy's School bore his bronze casket with silver fittings to the Sbarbaro hearse. The last rites of the church having been denied him, he was buried in unconsecrated ground at Mount Carmel Cemetery. The floral tributes and general display fell considerably below gangster standards. The only underworld figures of any stature to attend were Schemer Drucci and Bugs Moran, who now jointly ruled the O'Banionites, and Maxie Eisen, the fish and meat market racketeer.

No important politicians attended Weiss' funeral, but placards fastened to the mourners' automobiles advertised a number of political candidates—JOHN SBARBARO FOR MUNICIPAL JUDGE . . . JOE SAVAGE FOR COUNTY JUDGE . . . KING-ELLER-GRAYDON FOR SANITARY DISTRICT TRUSTEES. . . .

October 21—The Hotel Sherman Treaty

The revelations that followed Weiss' death held a disagreeable surprise for Capone. He still assumed Joe Saltis and Frankie McErlane to be his allies. The 200-odd saloons they operated with Dingbat O'Berta had been a major outlet for his beer and whiskey. But it now appeared from the lists of veniremen and state's witnesses found in Weiss' possession that a shift of allegiance had occurred; these supposed allies must have secretly entered into a pact with his enemies. Further investigation by Capone indicated that Saltis had been about to throw his saloon business Weiss' way. Such perfidy would normally have demanded a crushing reprisal, but Capone, in his eagerness to reestablish peace among the gangs and restore territorial boundaries as they existed in Torrio's prime, decided to overlook it for the moment.

The initial impetus toward peace came this time from Saltis. Terrified of what Capone might do to him, he turned for advice to Dingbat O'Berta, who was awaiting a separate trial for the murder of Mitters Foley. Dingbat consulted Maxie Eisen, whom the underworld respected as a man of rare wisdom and experience. It was Eisen's opinion that Saltis' safety, once he regained his freedom, lay in a general armistice, and he offered to try to arrange it. He went first to Tony Lombardo and asked him to sound out his patron. Lombardo reported back to Eisen the next day: Capone desired nothing so much as peace. After two *pourparlers* in the office of Billy Skidmore, the ward heeler, court fixer and gambling magnate, the gang leaders and their chief adjutants, thirty men in all, convened at the Hotel Sherman, which stood within the shadows of both City Hall and police headquarters. They came, as agreed, without arms or bodyguards. The Capone delegates numbered, besides Al Capone, his brother Ralph, Tony Lombardo, Jake Guzik and Ed Vogel of Cicero. From the North Side there were Drucci; Bugs Moran; Potatoes Kaufman; Frank Foster, alias Citro, an importer of Canadian whiskey; Jack Zuta, whoremaster and director of the O'Banionites' vice operations; and, from the O'Donnell gang, the brothers Myles and Klondike. Billy Skidmore and Christian P. "Barney" Bertche, another prominent figure in the gambling world, formerly a safecracker, were present. While loosely affiliated with the North Siders, Skidmore and Bertche each ran his own independent gambling houses. Ralph Sheldon was the only member of his gang on hand, and Maxie Eisen represented the Saltis-McErlane-O'Berta interests.

Little effort was made to keep the meeting secret. A detective from across the street sat in as an observer. Reporters, though excluded from the meeting room itself, waited in the corridor outside and were apprized of every development. Eisen opened the meeting with an appeal to common sense. "Let's give each other a break," he said. "We're a bunch of saps, killing each other this way and giving the cops a laugh." Capone, who dominated the proceedings as much by the force of his personality as by the size and power of his organization, then submitted a five-point treaty:

1. All standing grievances and feuds to be buried—a general amnesty.
2. The renunciation of violence as a means of settling inter-gang disputes; arbitration instead.
3. An end to "ribbing" (a common weapon of psychological warfare among gangsters, involving malicious gossip. If A wished to destroy B without risking an open attack, he might tell C that A was plotting against him, thus inciting C to strike first. Or he might feed the press a story about A sure to enrage C).
4. No more stealing another gang's customers; no encroachments upon their established territories.
5. The head of each gang to punish violations committed by any member.

According to the reapportionment of territory, the O'Banionites were to withdraw from all the sectors they had invaded since O'Banion's death and confine their activities to the Forty-second and Forty-third wards. There and there only they could enjoy exclusive franchises to the sale of beer and liquor, to prostitution and gambling. This limitation imposed no great hardship, for the two wards constituted a densely populous business and residential area almost five miles square, stretching east to west from Lake Michigan to the Chicago River and north to south from Belden Avenue to Wacker Drive. The Saltis-McErlane gang was to divide equally with the Sheldon gang a portion of southwest Chicago, roughly three miles square, lying between the lake and the river. Skidmore and Bertche could operate their gambling houses as before, but under Capone's jurisdiction. For the smaller gangs, like Marty Guilfoyle's, Capone made provision out of his holdings. The determination of the O'Donnells' territory he reserved to a later meeting, and in view of their grievous offenses against him it would depend on how scrupulously they observed the terms of the treaty. This left to Capone nearly all Chicago below Madison Street and most of the suburbs, a domain embracing about 20,000 speakeasies and only he and his top executives knew how many roadhouses, gambling dens and brothels.

"I told them we're making a shooting gallery out of a great business," Capone recalled later, "and nobody's profiting by it. It's hard and dangerous work and when a fellow works hard at any line of business, he wants to go home and forget it. He don't want to be afraid to sit near a window or open a door. Why not put up our guns and treat our business like any other man treats his, as something to work at in the daytime and forget when he goes home at night? There's plenty of beer business for everybody—why kill each other over it?"

He added reasons of paternal sentiment. "I wanted to stop all that because I couldn't stand hearing my little kid ask why I didn't stay home. I had been living at the Hawthorne Inn for 14 months. He's been sick for three years—mastoid infection and operations—and I've got to take care of him and his mother. If it wasn't for him, I'd have said: 'To hell with you fellows! We'll shoot it out.' But I couldn't say that, knowing it might mean they'd bring me home some night punctured with machine gun fire. And I couldn't see why those fellows would want to die that way either."

The conferees accepted the treaty with little argument. "We shook hands and made peace and we promised each other that if anything ever came up between us that made us mad, we'd get together and talk it over peaceably and straighten it out."

The meeting adjourned to Diamond Joe Esposito's Bella Napoli Café for a peace celebration. It was a night of ghastly gaiety. "A feast of ghouls," a reporter whom Capone allowed to join the revels called it. Arm in arm, back-slapping, howling with laughter, former enemies recalled how they had tried to kill one another, merrily described the tortures they had inflicted on their captives, boasted of old murders to the victims' friends.

"Remember that night when your car was chased by two of ours," one hoodlum asked another, playfully prodding him.

"I sure do."

"Well [roguish chuckle], we were going to kill you, but you had a woman with you."

They doubled up with glee.

In the deepening vinous haze the atmosphere grew cloying with expressions of remorse, entreaties for forgiveness, sentimental tears, oaths of eternal friendship. Each gang leader made a speech. "You know," said one of them, "I'd never have had my boys shoot any of yours if it hadn't been for the newspapers. Every time there'd be a little shooting affair the papers would print the names of the gang who did it. Well, when any of my boys were shot up and the papers came out with the right hunch as to who did it, I just naturally decided that in honor I'd have to have a few guys bumped myself."

On November 7 Hymie Weiss' last complot bore posthumous fruit. The jury acquitted Joe Saltis and Lefty Koncil, and the separate pending trial of Dingbat O'Berta was removed from the court calendar. "I expected a different verdict on the evidence presented," said Judge Harry B. Miller in a wistful understatement. "I think the evidence warranted a verdict of guilty." Special Prosecutor McDonald, whose grand jury had indicted the trio, was blunter. "A number of unusual and significant circumstances arose both prior to and during the prosecution of the trial," he said. "Prior to the trial two of the state's important witnesses disappeared, the immediate members of their families either refusing or being unable to give any information or clue as to their whereabouts. . . . ." He spoke of the discovery in Hymie Weiss' safe of "the identical copy of the list of the state's witnesses that had been furnished counsel for the defendants by order of the court," and he concluded: "In addition to these significant facts, certain of the state's witnesses testified to having been threatened with violence in the event they testified against the defendants, and of having been approached with offers of bribery for either withholding their testimony or testifying falsely."

The day before Christmas the Illinois Supreme Court granted Scalise and Anselmi, who had served seven months of their fourteen-year sentence in Joliet, a new trial on their lawyer's plea that if they were guilty of murder, the sentence was "but a mockery of justice" and if guilty of only manslaughter, "an injustice." They were released on bail of $25,000 to await the third trial.

They returned to an underworld where all was peaceful. "Just like the old days," as Capone remarked to a reporter. "They [the O'Banion gang] stay on the North Side and I stay in Cicero and if we meet on the street, we say 'hello' and shake hands. Better, ain't it?"

14

Big Bill Rides Again

HE did not abide long in limbo after his 1923 defeat by the reform candidate Judge Dever. That summer he recaptured the public's fancy with a typically Thompsonian antic. He proposed to organize a yachting expedition to the South Seas to take motion pictures of mudskippers, the fish that can live on land for long periods, jump as high as three feet in pursuit of insects, and climb trees. The idea of hunting them had been suggested to Thompson by a press agent for the cypress wood industry. The latter's clients were happy to supply the material to construct a yawl for the expedition. Christened the *Big Bill,* it bore a cypress figurehead carved in the likeness of the corpulent ex-mayor. Thompson obtained the additional support of the Fish Fans Club, which he had founded the year before "to urge and encourage the propagation of fish in American waters." In early July the *Big Bill,* carrying an assortment of politicians, businessmen and beer-swilling sports, sailed down the Chicago River into Lake Michigan, cheered on its way by thousands lining the shores. It never left continental waters. The expedition having served its purpose as a publicity stunt, Thompson abandoned it midway to New Orleans.

Hurrying home, he began to rebuild his political strength, heartened by the realization that, as a case-hardened old politician jubilantly cried three decades later when Richard Daley became mayor,

"Chicago ain't ready for reform yet." He campaigned for Governor Small's reelection, and he made peace overtures to State's Attorney Crowe, who accepted them despite his earlier declaration that "any man interested in protecting gambling and vice I refuse to travel along with, politically or otherwise."

He entered the Republican mayoral primary in the fall of 1926, against Edward R. Litsinger, a member of Senator Deneen's faction, and Dr. John Dill Robertson, a former health commissioner and a defector from the Thompson ranks. They inspired him to some of the crassest rhetoric ever to flow from a politician's mouth. Reacting to their cry of "Who killed McSwiggin?" and their accusations of collusion with criminals, Thompson ranted: "Litsinger is dry and Robertson is so dry he never even takes a bath. The Doc used to boast he hadn't taken a bath in years. . . . The Doc is slinging mud. I'm not descending to personalities, but you should watch Doc Robertson eating in a restaurant—eggs in his whiskers, soup on his vest. It's enough to turn your stomach. . . . Imagine anyone thinking of electing a man for mayor with a name like John Dill Pickle Robertson! . . . I'm not a mud-slinger, but the papers have been saying things about me that I can't let pass. And Ed Litsinger's been making statements about me. I've told you and I tell you again that he's the biggest liar that ever was a candidate for mayor. And you know what else? He plays handball in the semi-nude! That's right, with only a little pair of pants on. I know one thing. You won't find Bill Thompson having his picture taken in the semi-nude. . . ."

The Republican majority loved it. They chose Thompson by the biggest margin of votes, 180,000, yet recorded in a Chicago Republican primary—to the disgust of the *Tribune,* which commented editorially: "Thompson is a buffoon in a tommyrot factory, but when his crowd gets loose in the City Hall, Chicago has more need of Marines than any Nicaraguan town."

At the subsequent campaign rallies the crowds chanted an anthem written by an ex-vaudevillian, Milton Weil, celebrating one of the two major planks in the Thompson platform:

America first and last and always!
Our hearts are loyal, our faith is strong.
America first and last and always!
Our shrine and homeland, tho' right or wrong.

> United we stand for God and country,
> At no one's command we'll ever be.
> America first and last and always!
> Sweet land of freedom and liberty.

Hugging an American flag to his breast, Thompson shouted: "This is the issue! What was good enough for George Washington is good enough for Bill Thompson. . . . I want to make the King of England keep his snoot out of America! America first, and last, and always! . . . If you want to keep that old American flag from bowing down before King George of England, I'm your man. If you want to invite King George and help his friends, I'm not. . . . America First! The American who says 'America second' speaks the tongue of Benedict Arnold and Aaron Burr. . . . There never was an Englishman who was the equal of an American and if there was, he could make a million dollars in an hour and a half by beating that brave Gene Tunney, our world champion fighter. . . ."

Claiming that the history books used in Chicago's public schools were partial to the English, he attacked Dever's school superintendent, William McAndrew, and promised, if elected, to fire him. "Read these histories for yourselves. The ideals you were taught to revere, the great Americans you were taught to cherish as examples of self-sacrificing devotion to human liberty, are subtly sneered at and placed in a false light, so that your children may blush with shame when studying the history of their country. These men and others falsified and distorted facts to glorify England and vilify America. . . . When I went out of office, Washington fell out and the King of England fell in. This King George! If King George had his way, there'd be a million American boys in China today to fight the battle for the dirty Englishmen and help the King make a billion dollars in the opium trade. And McAndrew is his lackey. Didn't he refuse to let our schoolchildren contribute their pennies to preserve Old Ironsides? You know why? Because Old Ironsides kicked hell out of every British ship she met and the King of England wouldn't like to have us preserve that ship. So he gave orders to his stooge, this McAndrew, and our children were not permitted to solicit pennies to preserve a priceless heritage. It's up to us, the red-blooded men and women of Chicago, to stand fast until the city is rid of pro-British rats who are poisoning the wells of historical truth."

The issue could not have mattered less to Al Capone, but the second plank in Thompson's platform enlisted his wholehearted enthusiasm. It was unabashedly, wholeheartedly antireform. "I'm wetter than the middle of the Atlantic Ocean," Thompson brayed. "When I'm elected, we'll not only re-open places these people [the Dever administration] have closed, but we'll open 10,000 new ones." The prospect was so attractive to Capone that he contributed $260,-000 to Thompson's campaign chest and applied every technique of bribery and terrorism in his behalf. He was credited with the slogan "Vote early and vote often."

At the turn of the year Capone was momentarily diverted from the political conflict by a resumption of gang warfare. Hilary Clements, a beer runner for Ralph Sheldon, had been selling his brew to saloons inside the Saltis-McErlane territory. Instead of referring this breach of the Hotel Sherman treaty to arbitration, as stipulated, Saltis ordered Clements' death. A shotgun blast killed the beer runner on December 30, shattering a peace that had lasted seventy days. Sheldon protested to Capone, who reluctantly acknowledged the necessity for stringent disciplinary measures if the treaty was to be saved. As a result, Lefty Koncil and another Saltis henchman, Charlie "Big Hayes" Hubacek, were executed on March 11. The O'Banionites, meanwhile, restive under the restraints imposed by the treaty and unable to reconcile themselves to Capone's supremacy, renewed their attack against him. They struck first at a man he cherished.

Theodore "the Greek" Anton ran a popular restaurant above the Hawthorne Smoke Shop. His feelings for Capone verged on idolatry. He never tired of extolling his virtues. As an instance of the gang leader's tenderheartedness, he liked to recount the incident of the newsboy who wandered into the restaurant one winter night, blue with cold. "How many papers you got left, kid?" Capone asked him. "Abouty fifty," the boy replied. "Throw them on the floor and run along home to your mother," said Capone and slipped him $20.

On the night of January 6 Capone was eating a late snack in Anton's restaurant. Anton got up from the booth where they were chatting and went to the entrance to greet some customers. He never returned. The O'Banionites, lurking outside, pulled him into their car. When Capone understood what had happened, he burst into tears and for the rest of the night sat in the booth, weeping inconsolably. Anton's body was found encased in quicklime. Like Tony Cuiringione, he had been tortured, then shot.

In March Capone took a short pleasure jaunt to Hot Springs, Arkansas. Drucci, who somehow got wind of it, followed him there, fired a shotgun at him, but missed.

As April 5—election day—drew near, Capone's Hotel Metropole suite became a covert annex to the Thompson campaign headquarters on the sixteenth floor of the Hotel Sherman. To and fro between them, carrying messages and money, scurried such middlemen as Daniel Serritella, ex-newsboy, founder of the Chicago Newsboys' Union and First Ward politician, a particular Capone friend; Morris Eller, the Twentieth Ward boss; Jack Zuta, the whoremaster, a member of the William Hale Thompson Republican Club, who contributed $50,000 to the campaign chest and bragged: "I'm for Big Bill hook, line and sinker and Bill's for me hook, line and sinker." Capone, hunched over a mahogany conference table behind a battery of nine telephones, a cigar in his mouth, issued orders to his forces scattered through the city, to triggermen, sluggers, kidnappers, bombers. . . .

The first act of violence had not been planned by Capone, but the end result could scarcely have gratified him more. The O'Banionites, too, like most Chicago gangs, were cheering Thompson and his wide-open town policy. The day before the election a band of them, led by Schemer Drucci, broke into the offices of the Forty-second Ward's Alderman Dorsey R. Crowe, a Dever champion, bent upon mayhem. Finding no sign of Crowe, they beat up his secretary, toppled over filing cabinets, and smashed windows. The police picked up Drucci that afternoon. One of his captors, Detective Dan Healy, enraged him by laying rough hands on him. In the squad car taking him to the stationhouse, Drucci yelled: "I'll get you for this!" and tried to grab the detective's gun. Healy pulled back, freeing the gun, and holding it close to Drucci's body, killed him with four shots. "Murder?" said Chief of Detectives Schoemaker when a lawyer retained by the gangster's widow demanded an investigation. "We're having a medal struck for Healy." The police had thus rid Capone of one of his deadliest foes.

Drucci was buried in unconsecrated ground at Mount Carmel Cemetery under a blanket of 3,500 flowers. Though denied the last rites of his church, he was accorded military honors by the Harold A. Taylor Post of the American Legion, to which he belonged, having served in the World War. A squad of uniformed Legionnaires fired a salute over the flag-draped casket, and a bugler blew taps. Capone, who had sent one of the showiest floral offerings, stood unshaven at the graveside.

Mayor Dever's chief of police reduced the likelihood of further violence by assigning more than 5,000 men to special election day duties. A police detail guarded every polling place, while detectives in squad cars, carrying machine guns and canisters of tear gas, patrolled the adjoining streets. The day was exceptionally peaceful for a Chicago election. Only two bombs were thrown, both of them at Forty-second Ward Democratic clubs, only two election officials beaten and kidnapped, and about a dozen Dever supporters prevented from voting by hoodlums with guns. Only one polling booth and one private home were shot at.

In the Hotel Sherman's Louis XIV Ballroom that evening Thompson leaped up on a chair, brandishing a ten-gallon hat, and in a voice furry with bourbon bellowed: "The lead is now 52,000! I thank you one and all, I thank you. Tell 'em, cowboys, tell 'em! I told you I'd ride 'em high and wide!" The final count gave him a plurality of 83,072 votes.

Thompson's return to City Hall for a third term heralded an era of bloodshed, racketeering and civic corruption which made the earlier Chicago seem a model of law and order. His first appointments set the tone of his administration. For chief of police he brought Michael Hughes back from obscurity in the Highway Patrol Department. A cousin of State's Attorney Crowe, Hughes had resigned as chief of detectives during Mayor Dever's term when censured for attending the testimonial banquet to Dion O'Banion. For city controller Thompson chose his former chief of police, Charles Fitzmorris, who once publicly admitted: "Sixty percent of my police are in the bootleg business," and for city sealer, Daniel Serritella, who proceeded to pervert the function of his office by conspiring with merchants to short-weight the consumer. Serritella served as Capone's agent in the City Council. For corporation counsel of Chicago the mayor appointed his old friend Samuel Ettelson, who also represented the financial pirate Samuel Insull. Morris Eller's pay as sanitary trustee was augmented by the pay of city collector. Dr. Arnold Kebel, the Thompson family physician, became the new health commissioner.

Not long after the election a *Daily News* reporter asked a deputy commissioner of police, William P. Russell, how it happened that policy numbers racketeers were operating openly in his district. "Mayor Thompson was elected on the open town platform," Russell replied. "I assume the people knew what they wanted when they voted for him. . . . I haven't had any order from downtown to interfere in the policy racket and until I do get such orders you can bet I'm going to keep my hands off. . . . Personally, I don't propose to get mixed up in any jam that will send me to the sticks. . . . If the downtown authorities want this part of the city closed up, the downtown authorities will have to issue an order. I'm certainly not going to attempt it on my own."

No such order ever came. But Russell's discretion was remembered in his favor. He eventually succeeded Hughes as chief of police.

Within a month of the election Capone had enlarged his Hotel Metropole headquarters to fifty rooms, reserving the Hawthorne Inn as a secondary base for suburban operations. The Metropole was convenient to both City Hall and the Police Department. From the former came a steady stream of purchasable magistrates, administrators and politicians. From the latter—in effect, a garrison of mercenaries at the disposal of the highest-paying *condottiere*—came police officers to collect their reward for such services as escorting consignments of liquor to their destination, warning of raids about to be staged to pacify the reform element, furnishing Capone's triggermen with officially stamped cards, reading: "To the Police Department— You will extend the courtesies of this department to the bearer." Phil D'Andrea wore the star of a Municipal Court bailiff and drew a salary of $200 a month from the city. Usually, the police either ignored the crimes committed by D'Andrea and his brethren or entered them in the records as "unsolved." Capone estimated the total payoff to police from all sources at $30,000,000 a year. His own payroll listed roughly half the entire Chicago police force.

Sunday morning after church was the time for conferences and money changing hands. Then the Metropole teemed with police, politicians and gangsters. But their activities were not confined to business. They could slake their thirst at a blind pig operated in the lobby by a ward boss. Capone and his lieutenants had their own upper-story service bars. The management gave them storage space in the basement for their private stock of wines and liquor, more than $100,000 worth. Accessible women freely roamed the hotel. Nearly every top Caponeite had a favorite whom he set up in one of the suites. Several rooms were given over to gambling. Capone was a compulsive gambler and an unlucky one, who seldom staked less than $1,000 on a throw of dice and as much as $100,000 on the spin of a roulette wheel or a horse race. At the horse or dog track he never backed his choice to place, only to win. Because he lost so heavily and lived so extravagantly, Capone could accumulate no great fortune. He told the *Tribune* police reporter, Jake Lingle, his favorite newspaperman and the best informed on underworld activities, that he had dropped almost $10,000,000 on horse races alone since coming to Chicago.

The Hotel Metropole was a landmark in the First Ward where Bathhouse John Coughlin and Hinky Dink Kenna had long reigned. Capone reduced them to the status of satellites. Summoning them to his suite, he warned them that their continued prosperity would depend on their usefulness to the gang; without the gang's backing, they could not hope to win reelection and enjoy their old privileges. "We don't want no trouble," Capone said, using a favorite expression. The aldermen put up no resistance. "My God, what could I say?" Kenna told his followers after the meeting. "Suppose he said he was going to take over the organization. What could we do then? We're lucky to get as good a break as we did."

How high Capone's stock rose under the new Thompson administration was patent on May 15, when the Italian flier Commander Francesco de Pinedo, circling the globe as Mussolini's goodwill ambassador in his hydroplane the *Santa Maria II,* landed on Lake Michigan off Chicago's Grant Park. The welcoming committee consisted of the Italian consul, Italo Canini; the president of the city's *Fascisti,* Ugo Galli; the collector of customs, Anthony Czarnecki; officers of the Sixth Air Corps; Mayor Thompson's personal representative, Judge Bernard Barasa; and Al Capone. Capone was among the first to shake De Pinedo's hand as he stepped ashore. Some Chicagoans questioned the propriety of including Capone. This drew a sorry admission from the police. An anti-Fascist demonstration was expected, they claimed, and they were not sure of being able to prevent a riot. So they had asked Capone to serve on the committee, believing that he could quell any riotous anti-*Fascisti.* As it happened, the need never arose. The demonstrators were few and orderly.

The month of June brought Capone a satisfaction of another kind.

The third trial of Scalise and Anselmi, to whom he had been rendering moral and material aid ever since they had killed Detectives Walsh and Olson two years before, began on the ninth. The familiar problem of completing a jury—100 veniremen got themselves excused—delayed the proceedings a week. Taking the witness stand on June 22, Scalise admitted he fired a bullet—only one—at the detectives. The burden of Counselor Nash's summation was that his clients had acted in self-defense against "unwarranted police aggression." The jury voted "Not guilty." "There's nothing more to be done," said Detective Walsh's widow. "My husband and his friend were killed by these men who now have a crowd waiting to shake their hand. I give up."

Capone gave a banquet to celebrate the acquittal. Champagne was the principal beverage, vintage champagne imported from Canada at $20 a bottle, and it flowed abundantly as toast after toast was drunk to the jury that set the guests of honor free. More than 100 celebrants jammed the dining room, among them the elite of the Little Italy underworld. The life of the party was a flip, strutting, bandboxical Sicilian gunman, a crony of Scalise and Anselmi, Giuseppe Giunta, called Hop Toad because of his nimbleness on a dance floor. The festivities reached a climax in a sham battle with popping champagne corks for missiles. Surveying the merry, drenched and drunken scene, Capone could hardly have imagined that three of his guests would soon join a conspiracy to destroy him. They were Hop Toad Giunta, Scalise and Anselmi.

"The War of the Sicilian Succession," as one crime reporter called it, became inevitable when Tony Lombardo, with Capone's backing, attained the coveted presidency of the Unione Siciliane. The runner-up was Joseph Aiello, who with his eight brothers and countless cousins had replaced the Gennas as the kingpins of Little Italy's alky industry. He was a squat, black-browed figure, who lived regally in a three-story mansion. What appeared to be leather-bound volumes covered the living room walls from floor to ceiling. They were imitations, masking a store of arms and explosives. For years Aiello and Lombardo had been profitably associated both as powers in the Unione Siciliane and in the cheese import, bakery, brokerage commission, alky cooking and other businesses. Political contention within the Unione damaged the relationship, and it broke up altogether after Lombardo won the presidential election. Bent upon eliminating his opponent as well as the gang chieftain behind him, Aiello formed an alliance on the North Side with the O'Banionites, now captained by Bugs Moran, and on the West Side with Billy Skidmore, Barney Bertsche and Jack Zuta.

The word spread through gangland that the Aiellos would pay $50,-000 to anybody who killed Capone. Between the spring and fall of 1927 four free-lance out-of-town torpedoes came to Chicago—Tony Torchio from New York, Tony Russo and Vincent Spicuzza from St. Louis and Sam Valente from Cleveland. Capone's intelligence network must have been functioning at top efficiency because none of the mercenaries lasted more than a few days after they got to Chicago. Each was found tommy-gunned to death, a nickel clutched in his hand—Jack McGurn's signature. During the same period four local Aiello adherents fell before the fire of a gunner, or gunners, never identified. A fifth victim, a barman named Cinderella, was trussed up after death, stuffed into a sack, and left in a ditch. For this killing the police arrested McGurn and a fellow Capone bodyguard, Orchell De Grazio, who had been seen near the ditch, but lacking any other evidence, they let them go.

The Aiellos tried poison. Knowing Capone to be a frequenter of Diamond Joe Esposito's Bella Napoli Café, they offered the chef $35,000 if he would lace his minestrone with prussic acid. The chef agreed, then developed qualms, and betrayed the plot to the intended victim.

Faced with eleven unsolved gang killings in less than six months, the new chief of detectives, William O'Connor, felt he should make some sort of reassuring public gesture. Accordingly, he announced he was organizing a special armored car force to wipe out gangsters. He said he wanted volunteers from the police ranks who had fought overseas in World War I and knew how to handle a machine gun. To the squad thus formed, he then issued an order of stupendous irresponsibility. "Men," said he, "the war is on. We've got to show that society and the police department, and not a bunch of dirty rats, are running this town. It is the wish of the people of Chicago that you hunt these criminals down and kill them without mercy. Your cars are equipped with machine guns and you will meet the enemies of society on equal terms. See to it that they don't have you pushing up daisies. Make them push up daisies. Shoot first and shoot to kill. If you kill a notorious feudist, you will get a handsome reward and win promotion. If you meet a car containing bandits, pursue them and fire. When I arrive on the scene, my hopes will be fulfilled if you have shot off the top of their car and killed every criminal inside it." Chief O'Connor did not say what he would do if they mowed down innocent bystanders.

Tony Lombardo lived with his wife and two small children in a spacious suburban villa at 442 West Washington Boulevard, north of Cicero. Directly opposite stood an apartment building with flats renting by the week. On November 22 a stool pigeon's tip led O'Connor's detectives to one of the flats. They found an array of machine guns trained on the Lombardos' front door. The gunners were not around. The stool pigeon then suggested they raid a certain flat 10 miles away at 7002 North Western Avenue. There the detectives uncovered a cache of dynamite. The absent tenant had left behind a key to a room in the Rex Hotel, still farther north on Ashland Avenue. Making their third call of the day, the detectives burst in upon Angelo Lo Mantio, a young gunman from Milwaukee, Joseph Aiello and two of his cousins. They whisked the lot off to the detective bureau. Lo Mantio proved a frail reed who quickly broke under questioning and confessed that the Aiellos had brought him to Chicago to kill Capone and Lombardo. A second ambush, he added, had been set up for Capone on South Clark Street. Hinky Dink Kenna owned a cigar store at 311 South Clark, which he used as his political headquarters. Capone often stopped by for a chat. Across the street was the Hotel Atlantic. The windows of Room 302 framed the cigar-store entrance, and to the sills Lo Mantio had clamped high-powered rifles.

It was probably some official on Capone's payroll who notified him that Lo Mantio and Aiello had been taken to the detective bureau lockup. Within an hour of their arrival, a fleet of taxis drew up before the thirteen-story building and disgorged a score of men. A policeman, glancing casually out of an upper-story window, took them at first to be detectives bringing suspects to the bureau for questioning. But none entered the building. They scattered, some to the street corners and down side streets, others into doorways and alleys. Presently, three men started toward the bureau's main entrance. One of them reached inside his overcoat to shift an automatic from holster to side pocket. As the policeman recognized Louis "Little New York" Campagna, a stubby, hook-nosed ex-Five Pointer, whom Capone had recently added to his corps of bodyguards, the incredible truth burst upon him: Capone gangsters, out to kill Aiello, had surrounded the detective bureau and were about to lay siege to it. His startled cry sent dozens of detectives flocking to the street. They seized the trio, disarmed and handcuffed them and hustled them to the lockup. They were lodged in a cell adjoining Aiello's, and a detective who understood Sicilian dialect, posing as a prisoner, listened from a cell nearby. This is what he heard:

Campagna: "You're dead, friend, you're dead. You won't get up to the end of the street still walking."

Aiello (terrified) : "Can't we settle this? Give me fourteen days and I'll sell my stores, my house and everything and quit Chicago for good. Can't we settle it? Think of my wife and baby."

Campagna: "You dirty rat! You've broken faith with us twice now. You started this. We'll finish it."

When his lawyer obtained his release on a writ of habeas corpus, Aiello did not venture into the street. He ran, quaking, to Chief O'Connor and begged him to provide police protection. Conscious of the newspaperman within earshot, O'Connor replied: "Sure, I'll give you police protection—all the way to New York and onto a boat. The sooner you go the better. You can't bring your feud ideas here and get away with it, so you'd better start back. You'll get no police protection around Chicago from me." Upon seeing Aiello's wife and small son, whom the lawyer had brought to the bureau, he relented and let a pair of policemen escort them all to a taxi.

With his brothers Tony and Dominic, Aiello left Chicago that night. They went to Trenton, New Jersey, and, except for a surreptitious return visit or two, stayed there almost two years. But they never wavered in their resolve to exterminate Capone.

After the Aiellos' departure Capone spoke expansively to reporters. With an air of kingly magnanimity, he said: "When I was told that Joey Aiello wanted to make peace, but that he wanted 14 days to settle his affairs, I was ready to agree. I'm willing to talk to anybody any place to bring about a settlement. I don't want no trouble. I don't want bloodshed. But I'm going to protect myself. When someone strikes at me, I will strike back."

He reminded his interviewers: "I'm the boss. I'm going to continue to run things. They've been putting the roscoe [revolver] on me now for a good many years and I'm still healthy and happy. Don't let anybody kid you into thinking I can be run out of town. I haven't run yet and I'm not going to. When we get through with this mob, there won't be any opposition and I'll still be doing business."

What he failed to reckon with was Mayor Thompson's soaring ambition.

"I do not choose to run for President in 1928," said Calvin Coolidge, and the Republican candidacy was up for grabs. Thompson, emboldened by his phenomenal political resurgence, saw no reason why it should not carry him into the White House. With a noisy retinue of press agents, advisers and drinking companions, he set out in the fall of 1927 on a cross-country train tour ostensibly to enlist support for flood control through the Mississippi Valley, actually to test the national reaction to himself. At each station stop the press agents touted him as the founder of the America First movement and distributed chauvinist leaflets and buttons, while a quartet sang "America First and Last and Always." William Randolph Hearst welcomed Thompson at his California ranch. When the mayor got back to Chicago, State's Attorney Crowe, now firmly reestablished in the Thompson camp, delivered an encomium: "He is a great American. He has done more for Chicago than anything that has happened in my lifetime. And he has, by this trip, reduced the prejudice that has existed in some localities, created by unfair critics of Chicago."

As a Presidential aspirant, Thompson needed no adviser to tell him what a liability Capone's conspicuous, unfettered presence in Chicago would be. He passed the word to Chief of Police Hughes, and the treatment of the gang leader swiftly changed from indulgence to harassment. His henchmen were arrested on tenuous charges, his breweries, brothels and gambling houses were repeatedly raided, and he himself was kept under continuous surveillance.

On December 5 Capone held a press conference at the Hotel Metropole to announce his departure for St. Petersburg, Florida. Ensconced in his armor-backed chair, his massive head wreathed by cigar smoke, he said: "Let the worthy citizens of Chicago get their liquor the best way they can. I'm sick of the job. It's a thankless one and full of grief."

Misunderstanding and injustice, he complained, were forcing him into exile. "I'm known all over the world as a millionaire gorilla. The other day a man came in here and said that he had to have $3,000.

If I'd give it to him, he said, he would make me a beneficiary in a $15,000 insurance policy he'd taken out and then kill himself. I had to have him pushed out. Today I got a letter from a woman in England. Even over there I'm known as a gorilla. She offered to pay my passage to London if I'd kill some neighbors she's been having a quarrel with. . . . That's what I have to put up with, just because I give the public what the public wants. I never had to send out high pressure salesmen. I could never meet the demand.

"I violate the prohibition law, sure. Who doesn't? The only difference is I take more chances than the man who drinks a cocktail before dinner and a flock of highballs after it. But he's just as much a violator as I am."

He digressed to express his contempt for dishonest politicians. "There's one thing worse than a crook and that's a crooked man in a big political job. A man who pretends he's enforcing the law and is really making dough out of somebody breaking it, a self-respecting hoodlum hasn't any use for that kind of fellow—he buys them like he'd buy any other article necessary to his trade, but he hates them in his heart.

"I could bear it all if it weren't for the hurt it brings to my mother and my family. They hear so much about what a terrible criminal I am. It's getting too much for them and I'm just sick of it all myself."

Concerning his police record, he said: "I have never been convicted of a crime nor have I ever directed anyone else to commit a crime. I have never had anything to do with a vice resort. I don't pose as a plaster saint, but I never killed anyone. I never stuck up a man in my life. Neither did any of my agents ever rob anybody or burglarize any homes while they worked for me. They might have pulled plenty of jobs before they came with me or after they left me, but not while they were in my outfit." He upheld Cicero as a model of civic virtue. "The cleanest burg in the U.S.A. There's only one gambling house in the whole town and not a single so-called vice den."

His own business, he claimed—and he undoubtedly believed it—was a boon to his fellow Chicagoans. "I've been spending the best years of my life as a public benefactor. I've given people the light pleasures, shown them a good time. And all I get is abuse—the existence of a hunted man. I'm called a killer. Ninety percent of the people of Cook County drink and gamble and my offense has been to furnish them with those amusements. Whatever else they may say, my booze has been good and my games have been on the square. Public service is my motto. I've always regarded it as a public benefaction if people were given decent liquor and square games."

Asked what a gangster thought about when he killed another in a gang war, he replied: "Well, maybe he thinks that the law of self-defense, the way God looks at it, is a little broader than the lawbooks have it. Maybe it means killing a man who'd kill you if he saw you first. Maybe it means killing a man in defense of your business—the way you make the money to take care of your wife and child. I think it does. You can't blame me for thinking there's worse fellows in the world than me."

He said he did not know when he would return to Chicago, if ever, and he added with heavy sarcasm: "I guess murder will stop now. There won't be any more booze. You won't be able to find a crap game even, let alone a roulette wheel or a faro game. I guess Mike Hughes won't need his 3,000 extra cops, after all. Say, the coppers won't have to lay all the gang murders on me now. Maybe they'll find a new hero for the headlines. It would be a shame, wouldn't it, if while I was away they'd forget about me and find a new gangland chief? . . .

"I leave with gratitude to my friends who have stood by me through this unjust ordeal and forgiveness for my enemies. I wish them all a Merry Christmas and a Happy New Year."

At the last minute he changed his itinerary. Instead of St. Petersburg, he took his wife, his son and two bodyguards to Los Angeles. Their reception was unfriendly. Though he registered at the Hotel Biltmore under his favorite alias, Al Brown, he was recognized and his visit blazoned in the newspapers, rousing a storm of public protest. Barely twenty-four hours after the Capones arrived, the Biltmore manager ordered them to leave. "We're tourists," Capone objected and refused to budge. "I thought you people liked tourists. We have a lot of money to spend that I made in Chicago. Whoever heard of anybody being run out of Los Angeles that had money?"

The Los Angeles chief of police personally confirmed the eviction and allowed Capone twelve hours to leave the city. In Chicago Chief Hughes had told the press: "The police drove Capone out of town. He cannot come back." Shortly before taking the eastbound Santa Fe Chief on December 13, Capone defiantly proclaimed: "I'm a property owner and a tax payer in Chicago. I can certainly return to my own home."

At Chillicothe, Illinois, a *Herald-Examiner* reporter boarded the train and rode in Capone's drawing room as far as Joliet. (The only other reporter so privileged was the ubiquitous Jake Lingle.) The gang boss was in melancholy mood. "It's pretty tough," he said, "when a citizen with an unblemished record must be hounded from his home by the very policemen whose salaries are paid, at least in part, from the victim's pocket. You might say that every policeman in Chicago gets some of his bread and butter from the taxes I pay. And yet they want to throw me in jail for nothing when I seek to visit my own home to see my wife and my little son. I am feeling very bad, very bad. I don't know what all this fuss is about. How would you feel if the police, paid to protect you, acted towards you like they do towards me? I'm going back to Chicago. Nobody can stop me. I've got a right to be there. I have property there and a family. They can't throw me out of Chicago unless they shoot me through the head. I've never done anything wrong. Nobody can say I ever did anything wrong. They arrest me. They search me. They lock me up. They charge me with all the crimes there are, when they get me into court. The only charge they can book against me is disorderly conduct, and the judge dismisses even that because there isn't any evidence to support it. The police know they haven't got one black mark against my name and yet they publicly announce that they won't let me live in my own home. What kind of justice is that? Well, I've been the goat for a long time. It's got to stop some time and it might as well be now. I've got my back to the wall. I'm going to fight."

Knowing the police would be waiting for him at the Chicago terminal, he had telephoned ahead to his brother Ralph to meet him in a car at Joliet. But the Joliet police were also waiting. Ralph and the three gunmen with him had been incautious. Reaching Joliet on the morning of the sixteenth, an hour before the Santa Fe Chief pulled in, they hung around the depot until a patrolman noticed the bulges in their pockets. He ran them into the station house, where they were charged with carrying concealed weapons. When Ralph's brother and his two bodyguards stepped off the train, Joliet's Chief of Police John Corcoran was on hand to greet them. "You're Al Capone," he said. "Pleased to meet you," said Capone, as Corcoran relieved him of two revolvers. "You may want some ammunition, too. These are no good to me now." And he handed him two cartridge clips. Mae Capone and Sonny were allowed to go on to Chicago.

Capone was lodged in a cell with two tattered derelicts. "Pay their

fines and take them away," he told the warden. "They bother me."
He authorized the warden to deduct the fines from the wad of cash,
totaling almost $3,000, he had in his pocket when arrested.

The lawyers, Nash and Ahern, accompanied by about twenty-five
Caponeites, arrived from Chicago in the afternoon and posted a bail
bond of $2,400 for each prisoner. That evening Capone slipped
quietly into Chicago, dined with Jake Guzik in a restaurant, and retired early to his Prairie Avenue home even as Chief Hughes was
betting a reporter the price of a new hat that the gang leader would
not dare show his face in the city. "My orders still stand," he said.
"He's to be taken to jail every time he shows himself."

But the period of repression was just about over. The political con-
siderations that had prompted it no longer obtained. Thompson saw
that his Presidential chances were nil. "I don't want to be President,"
he declared in a face-saving speech. "I'm a peace-loving man and I'm
afraid if I were President I'd plunge this country into war, for I'd
say 'Go to Hell!' to any foreign nation which attempted to dictate
the number of ships we could build or which tried to flood in propaganda as is being done now."

He reverted to his former lenity toward lawbreakers, and Capone
emerged from disfavor stronger than ever. By the time he and his
fellow defendants stood trial in Joliet, on December 22, he had fully
recovered his customary brio. When Circuit Court Judge Fred A.
Adams remarked, after imposing fines and costs aggregating $1,580.80,
"I hope this will be a lesson to you not to carry deadly weapons,"
Capone retorted: "Yes, judge, it will teach me not to carry deadly
weapons—in Joliet." Blithely, he waved aside the $10.20 change the
court clerk tendered him. "Keep it," he said, "or give it to the Salvation Army Santa Claus on the corner and tell him it's a Christmas
present from Al Capone."

Capone's humiliating experience on the West Coast had left him
determined to establish a second home to which he could retreat
whenever a change in the Chicago political climate might so require.
What he wanted was both a sanctuary and a recreational winter haven
in the sun. Feelers sent out to several resort communities produced no
offers of hospitality. To set foot in St. Petersburg, New Orleans, the
Bahamas or Cuba, he gathered, was to risk immediate arrest and ex-
pulsion. During the last days of 1927 he headed incognito for Miami.

15

"...the sunny Italy of the new world"

JOINED shortly by his wife and son, he spent his first Miami winter in a furnished bungalow on the beach, renting at $2,500 for the season. The absent owner, a Mrs. Sterns, had listed the property with a real estate agent and was appalled to learn that her tenant, "Al Brown," was Al Capone. She passed anxious weeks, wondering how much damage her home would suffer. It suffered none. The Capones left the place not only in impeccable condition, but enhanced by extra sets of china and silverware they had bought for large parties. A letter from Mae Capone urged the owner to accept them as gifts. In the cellar Mrs. Sterns found several unopened cases of wine, to which she was also invited to help herself. The only disagreeable surprise was a telephone bill for $780 in calls to Chicago. Soon after Mrs. Sterns received it, a Cunningham 16-cylinder Cadillac pulled into her drive, and out stepped a slender young woman, quietly dressed, her blond hair falling below her shoulders, her pearly skin lightly tinted by the Florida sun. "I'm Mrs. Capone," she said in a soft, low voice. The telephone bill had slipped her mind, she apologized, and she wanted to pay it without further delay. When Mrs. Sterns mentioned the charges, she handed her a $1,000 note. "Never mind the difference," she said. "We may have broken a few little things, but this should cover it."

In addition to the beach bungalow, Capone retained a suite on the top floor of the nine-story Hotel Ponce de Leon in downtown Miami to use for both business and pleasure. A close rapport developed between him and the lessee, a rolypoly young rip of twenty-four named Parker Henderson, Jr., whose late father had been mayor of Miami. Henderson, Jr.'s tastes ran to prizefights, horse races, dog races and the company of celebrities, no matter what their title to fame. To slap a Capone familiarly on the back, call him Snorky, shoot craps and drink with him, perhaps to share some dark, professional secret, was deeply satisfying to the mayor's son. He could not do enough for his top-floor tenant, and Capone rewarded him, as he did many people who pleased him, with a diamond-studded belt buckle.

When Capone needed cash, Henderson would happily lend himself to a scheme devised to confuse any officials interested in the gang lord's finances. From Chicago one of the Capone associates would send a Western Union money transfer to "Albert Costa," an alias adopted for the purpose. Henderson would then trot down to the Miami Western Union office, sign for the transfer, disguising his handwriting, cash it, and deliver the money to Capone. Between January and April, 1928, he collected $31,000 for him.

Miami was in two minds about the prospect of Capone as a resident. Publicly, nearly everybody viewed it with alarm. Privately, many businessmen hated to see all that money spent elsewhere. The economy of southern Florida was still reeling from the collapse of its postwar land boom. Mortgages so heavily encumbered real estate that foreclosure proceedings could cost more than they yielded. In the Miami-Palm Beach sector, moreover, the hurricane of September, 1926, had destroyed $100,000,000 worth of property and left 50,000 people homeless. For Miami's mayor, John Newton Lummus, Jr., the conflict of interests created by Capone was acutely painful. In his official capacity he could hardly ignore the protests of his own City Council, not to mention the Miami *Daily News*, which kept clamoring for Capone's expulsion. At the same time, as vice-president of Lummus & Young, realtors, he hoped to sell him a house.

Capone, shrewdly counting on the profit motive to prevail, made a public show of candor. He requested a meeting with Miami's chief of police, Leslie Quigg, to be followed by a press conference. "Let's lay the cards on the table," he said. "You know who I am and where I come from. I just want to ask a question. Do I stay or must I get out?" He had, he hastened to add, no intention of operating a gambling house or any other illicit business.

"You can stay as long as you behave yourself," said Quigg.

"I'll stay as long as I'm treated like a human being," said Capone.

He turned to the newspapermen. "Gentlemen, I'm at your service. I've been hounded and pushed around for days. It began when somebody heard I was in town. All I have to say is that I'm orderly. Talk about Chicago gang stuff is just bunk."

He launched into a eulogy of Miami calculated to enrapture its Chamber of Commerce. ". . . the garden of America, the sunny Italy of the new world, where life is good and abundant, where happiness is to be had even by the poorest. I am going to build or buy a home here and I believe many of my friends will also join me. Furthermore, if I am permitted, I will open a restaurant and if I am invited, I will join the Rotary Club."

Two days later, under the combined pressure of the City Council and the *Daily News,* the mayor and the city manager, C. A. Henshaw, enacted a little comedy. After a talk with Capone at City Hall, Lummus told the press: "Mr. Capone was one of the fairest men I have ever been in conference with. He was not ordered to leave Miami Beach, but he decided it would be to the best interests of all concerned if he left. It was a mutual agreement."

The city manager chimed in: "There was no argument or threat. Our conference was made up simply of statements of fact on both sides and Mr. Capone announced he was leaving immediately."

Capone stayed, continuing to divide his time between the Sterns bungalow and the Ponce de Leon, between the racetrack at Hialeah and the nightclubs. He took up golfing and tennis. A duffer at both games, he hated to lose and occasionally, in a temper tantrum, would smash his club or racket.

Henderson testified later: "Some real estate agents wanted me to get in touch with Mr. Capone in regard to selling him some property. I was closely connected with Mr. Newton Lummus and I asked him what he thought about it. Lummus said that if anybody sold Capone any property, he and I should try. So I asked Al if he was interested in buying any property and he said he was, in buying a winter home. So we made an appointment with him and carried him out and showed him several places. This place on Palm Island he seemed to like very much. . . ."

Palm Island, a man-made sausage-shaped sliver of residential real estate, lies in Biscayne Bay about midway between the mainland and the beach. The house at 93 Palm Avenue was built in 1922 by the St. Louis brewer Clarence M. Busch. At the time of Capone's initial inspection it belonged to a Miamian named James Popham. Legend has endowed it with the magnificence of a doge's palace, but as Miami pleasances went, it was only middling splendid. A two-story neo-Spanish structure of white stucco with a flat green-tiled roof, shaded by twelve royal palm trees, it stood in the center of a plot 300 by 100 feet. There were fourteen rooms and a long, wide, glass-enclosed sun porch. A gatehouse spanning the graveled driveway contained three rooms. Mosaic patios and walks rimmed both buildings. A dock on the north side could accommodate three or four sizable craft.

The price was $40,000. Capone gave Henderson $2,000 to put down as a binder, and not long after, he added $8,000, making up the first of four annual payments, exclusive of 8 percent interest. Henderson took title to the property in his own name, then deeded it to Mae Capone. When the *Daily News* exposed the transaction, both Capone and Lummus came under heavy attack. A citizens' indignation meeting demanded the mayor's resignation. At the insistence of the City Council a five-man police detail followed Capone wherever he went.

Yet Capone did not wholly lack influential connections. It was an election year. A Republican campaign worker, James Sewell, later recalled in a talk with a federal investigator: "I don't believe there was a politician in town who didn't solicit Capone's aid, his financial aid."

"Did you ever hear Capone say that he gave any of these local politicians money?" the investigator asked.

"Yes."

"Do you think Capone was financially interested in any candidate for the office of Solicitor?"

"I think he was interested in all of them."

"Were you in Capone's hotel when any of the local politicians who were running for office came in and asked for him or went to his room?"

"I've seen a lot of them around the hotel. . . . There were all kinds of people up there, Catholic priests on down, all of them. . . ."

Capone had not yet taken possession of the Palm Island estate when political developments in Chicago urgently required his presence.

* * *

In a violent prelude to the Republican primary elections for state and county offices—the Pineapple Primary—the first victims were Thompsonites. On the evening of January 27, ten weeks before the elections, the homes of the Thompson-appointed city controller, Charles C. Fitzmorris, and of Dr. William H. Reid, the commissioner of public service, were bombed within half an hour of each other. "This is a direct challenge from the lawless," declared His Honor. "When the fight is over, the challengers will be sorry." The warning passed unheeded. On February 11 another bomb damaged the home of State's Attorney Crowe's brother-in-law and secretary, Lawrence Cuneo. A week later a fourth bomb exploded in the Sbarbaro funeral parlor, where the bullet-torn remains of so many gangsters had been prepared for the last journey. Thanks largely to Thompson's endorsement, Sbarbaro himself now sat on the Municipal Court.

Senator Deneen's choice to replace Crowe as state's attorney was Circuit Judge John A. Swanson, and the senator's great admirer, Joe Esposito, had promised to help by running again for Republican ward committeeman. On the morning of March 21, with the primary three weeks away, Diamond Joe received a threat by telephone: "Get out of town or get killed." Later in the morning two Capone lieutenants dropped into the Bella Napoli Café and repeated the message. Diamond Joe's associates begged him to yield, but he told them he must keep his word to the senator. Late that evening he left the Esposito National Republican Club and started for home, a short stroll, flanked by his bodyguards, the Varchetti brothers, Ralph and Joe. His wife, Carmela, and their three children were watching for him at a window. As he came within sight, an automobile carrying three men approached him from behind. Moving slowly abreast of their prey, they opened fire with two double-barreled shotguns and a revolver, tossed the weapons out of the car and, picking up speed, vanished around the corner. The Varchettis had dropped to the sidewalk in time, but Diamond Joe lay dying, blood gushing from many bullet holes. Carmela rushed to his side, shrieking, "Is it you, Giuseppe?" She turned to her horror-stricken neighbors. "I'll kill them for this!"

Despite their vows of vengeance, neither widow nor bodyguards identified any of the killers. They failed to furnish a single clue. Nobody was ever arrested for the murder of Diamond Joe Esposito.

The funeral was attended by a constellation of political nabobs, foremost among them Senator Deneen. The next day violence flared up anew. A charge of dynamite wrecked the front of the senator's three-story Chicago residence, and Judge Swanson, turning his car into his drive late that night, narrowly escaped the full blast of a bomb hurled from a passing car.

A black-humored columnist lapsed into parody:

> The rockets' red glare, the bombs bursting in air
> Gave proof through the night that Chicago's still there

Deneen mouthed the obvious: "The criminal element is trying to dominate Chicago by setting up a dictatorship in politics." Said Judge Swanson: "The pineapple industry grew up under his administration." Fearing more bombings at the primary polls, a federal marshal asked the U.S. Attorney General to commission 500 more marshals for special guard duty. Senator George W. Norris of Nebraska urged President Coolidge to withdraw marines from Nicaragua, where they were fighting anti-American guerrillas, and transfer them to Chicago. Both requests were rejected.

Mayor Thompson seconded an accusation by Crowe so cynical as to alienate many of their own supporters. "I am satisfied," Crowe said, "that the bombings were done by leaders in the Deneen forces . . . to discredit Mayor Thompson and myself. They realize they are hopelessly defeated and in a desperate attempt to overcome their tide of defeat they are resorting to these dangerous tactics." The Chicago Crime Commission, until then partial to Crowe, issued an open letter to voters, denouncing him as "inefficient and unworthy of his great responsibility to maintain law and order in Cook County" and demanding his ouster.

As the primary drew nearer, it became national, then international news. European editors assigned correspondents to Chicago as to a war. Their expectations were not dashed. Thompson met his match as a master of vituperation in Edward R. Litsinger, who was contending for the County Board of Review against the mayoral favorite, Judge Barasa. Truckling to the laborers in the enemy's native district, Thompson bellowed during a meeting there a week before the primary: "Litsinger was brought up back of the gashouse, but it wasn't good enough for him, so he moved up to the North Side and left his poor old mother behind. . . ." The meeting broke up in chaos when Litsinger's sister jumped to her feet, shouting: "You're a liar! My mother died long before my brother moved."

The next night Litsinger returned the attack from the stage of the Olympic Theater. Thompson, he said, was a "low-down hound," a "befuddled beast" who "should be tarred and feathered and ridden out of town." He was a "man with the carcass of a rhinoceros and the brain of a baboon." Holding an envelope aloft, Litsinger resorted to an old trick. "I have affidavits here relating to the life of the big baboon. Shall I read them?" His listeners licked their chops. "Yes, yes!" "No," said Litsinger piously, "that old German mother of mine this man has struck at through me is looking down on me from above and may God strike me speechless if I ever descend to Thompson's level." He then descended. "You know the Three Musketeers. They are Big Bill, Len Small and Frank L. Smith [the Thompson senatorial candidate]. The right way to pronounce it is three-must-get-theirs . . ."

On Easter Sunday, two days before the primary, the clergy of Chicago—Catholic, Protestant and Jewish—spoke out as one voice against the Small-Thompson machine: "We have a governor who ought to be in the penitentiary. . . . Ours is a government of bombs and bums. . . . O Lord! May there be an awakening of public spirit and consciousness. Grant that we may be awakened to a sense of public shame. . . ."

April 10, the primary. The party hacks on both sides, with the entrenched Thompson forces in the vast majority, now employed the stratagems that had been perfected through generations of Cook County electoral chicanery. Those who had managed to get themselves appointed election officials padded the registration lists with fictitious names under which fraudulent voters could vote. They inserted the names of unregistered voters friendly to their slate, submitted by the ward bosses, who had verified them from preelection pledge cards. They registered vagrants whose votes the bosses had bought for a few dollars, assigning them false names and addresses. Before the polling booths opened, they stuffed the ballot boxes with bundles of ballots premarked in favor of their faction. They let the bosses' hirelings remove additional bundles for marking and mixing with the legitimate ballots during the final tally. They diverted ballots intended for bedridden voters into other hands.

As the voting got under way, Capone's henchmen, packing bombs and guns and far outnumbering the thugs enlisted under the Deneen banner, cruised the polling areas in cars bearing America First stickers. Capone himself directed his battle troops. With threats of mayhem they drove off voters thought favorable to the opposition. Now and then they ran into a contingent of pro-Deneen hoodlums and a skirmish ensued. But the Capone camp had the numerical supremacy, and it remained in control of the field. The Caponeites terrorized scrupulous election officials into keeping away from their posts. If intimidation failed, they dragged them away and held them captive until the polls closed. This obliged the polling judges to appoint a substitute at the last minute, and the gangsters saw to it that the only choices at hand were all Thompsonites.

The paid fraudulent voters ran to five main types. There was the stringer, who voted according to a relay system. The first man in a string entered the polling booth with two ballots, the usual blank one furnished by the clerk and a premarked ballot. After dropping the latter into the ballot box, he slipped the blank to the next man in the string who repeated the process and so on to the end of the string. The floater, recruited from among the city's transient tramps, voted frequently during the day, as gangsters whisked him by car from precinct to precinct. The stinger was an armed floater prepared to shoot any poll watcher who might try to expose him. The ward bosses had gone so far as to house some vagrants in their ward during the thirty-day preprimary period required by the residency law. They were called mattress voters. The repeater voted as many as a hundred times in the same precinct, but under different aliases and addresses. One repeater gave the same address sixteen times. In a postprimary grand jury investigation this turned out to be a riding stable, which prompted the gibe, "Every horse voted."

With the counting of the ballots, a miscellany of other dodges came into play. Corrupt officials disqualified hostile ballots by surreptitiously double marking them—that is, inserting an X in the boxes left empty opposite the adversaries' names. They transferred the totals on the tally sheets to the credit of their candidates, substituted bogus tally sheets, fabricated totals. Thousands of anti-Crowe votes were destroyed altogether. To discourage protests from honest officials, gangsters menacingly paced the rooms where the counting took place.

None of these ploys could have succeeded without the connivance of the police. They helped by their absence. The precinct captains, obeying orders from the ward boss, and in many cases directly from Capone, under pain of demotion or promise of reward, assigned their subordinates to duties remote from the polls. Morris Eller, who was Thompson's choice for Republican committeeman of the Twentieth Ward, put it tersely: "The police are with us."

Murder capped the Pineapple Primary. A Negro attorney, Octavius Granady, had dared challenge Boss Eller's candidacy. Never before had a Negro demanded political equality in the Twentieth Ward. But how many votes he may have won became academic. Shortly after the polls closed, Granady was standing outside, chatting with friends, when a shot from a passing car barely missed him. He jumped into his car and fled. The assassin's car turned and followed, shotguns blazing away. Granady's car crashed into a tree. An easy target in the head-lights of his pursuers, he was torn apart by a dozen slugs. Eventually, four policemen and three gangsters, including James Belcastro, stood trial for the murder. All were acquitted.

The political seers had been forecasting a victory for the Small-Thompson-Crowe axis. The best organized, most powerful party machine in Chicago's history, it had never lost a primary. Through patronage it controlled practically every state, county and city office. In addition to its militant gangster arm, it could muster 100,000 campaign workers. The prophets predicted a primary turnout of about 430,000, with the great majority voting for the incumbent faction.

What they failed to foresee was the boomerang effect of violence. Chicagoans who had seldom bestirred themselves for a primary before were jolted out of their lethargy by the bombs, the gunplay and Thompson's cynicism. "Sure, we have crime here," the mayor had nonchalantly conceded after the bombings of the Deneen and Swanson homes. "We always will have crime. Chicago is just like any other big city. You can get a man's arm broken for so much, a leg for so much, or beaten up for so much. Just like New York, excepting we print our crime and they don't. . . . There'll always be bombings just as long as there is prohibition." The paramount electoral issue, transcending all others—America Firstism, the United States and the League of Nations, the Draft-Coolidge-for-President movement—became Al Capone. Was the gangster overlord to go on unchallenged as the dominant influence behind the government of Chicago?

The answer was a resounding no. The turnout on April 10 exceeded by nearly 100 percent the most optimistic estimates. Close to

800,000 voted, and not all the fraud and terrorism could save a single Thompson candidate. Governor Small and State's Attorney Crowe sank under a tidal wave of revulsion. Although Thompson himself had three more years to serve as mayor, his political career had been shattered beyond repair. The rebuff, together with a judicial inquiry into his conduct and the whiplashes of a hostile press, left him with little zest for further combat as his party prepared to confront the Democrats in the fall elections. Physically and mentally deteriorated, drinking heavily, he retreated for the summer to a country hideaway, abandoning City Hall to Acting Mayor Samuel Ettelson. The Chicago *Tribune* jubilantly attributed his defeat to "the work of an outraged citizenship resolved to end corruption, the machine gunning, the pineappling, and the plundering which have made the state and the city a reproach throughout the civilized world."

The election over, Capone hurried back to Miami to fortify and embellish his newly acquired Elysium. Dade County's best architects, landscape artists, masons and carpenters, recommended to Capone by Parker Henderson, were kept busy for months. A wall of concrete blocks went up all around the estate. Heavy oaken portals were hung behind the already-existing spiked iron entrance gate, completely shutting off the view of the interior. A house phone by the gate enabled callers to announce themselves. None was admitted until an armed bodyguard, stationed behind the portals, had inspected them through a Judas hole. Between the house and the bay was installed the biggest swimming pool in the area, 60 by 40 feet, with one of the first filter systems adaptable to both fresh and salt water, and on the bay side, a two-story bathhouse in the style of a Venetian loggia. A rock pool, its borders lushly planted, contained rare tropical fish to which Capone and his son would toss bread crumbs. For fishing and cruising Capone maintained a variety of craft, among them a Baby Gar speedboat, which he named the *Sonny and Ralphie,* and a 32-foot cabin cruiser, the *Arrow.* When his cronies visited him, he liked to pack a picnic of salami sandwiches and beer and charter a seaplane (at $60 an hour plus $100 an hour for the pilot) to fly them to Bimini.

In the living room, stuffed with massive, overupholstered furniture, the central adornment was a life-size oil painting of the Capones, father and son.

The master bedroom at the rear of the main house afforded a

sweeping view of pool, loggia and bay. Capone slept in an immense four-poster, at the foot of which stood a wooden chest full of cash. ("Don't keep your money in a bank," he would say. "Keep it like I do.") When showering, Capone liked the feel of hard needle spray everywhere on his body, and he had a stall shower built with seven extra shower heads jutting from the sides. The cost of all these improvements came close to $100,000.

Regretfully, Capone reached the decision that his old friend and early patron, the Brooklynite who had once employed him as a barroom bouncer, Frank Yale, must be exterminated. The reasons were twofold. The first bore upon the Unione Siciliane, or the Italo-American National Union, as it was now called. When the killing of Angelo Genna vacated the presidency of the Chicago chapter, Yale, as national president, had temporized. Wanting to retain the goodwill of both Capone and the North Siders, he had refrained from coming out flatly in favor of either contender for the succession—Capone's Tony Lombardo or the North Siders' Joe Aiello. Upon Capone's insistence he did not oppose Lombardo, but at the same time he quietly encouraged Aiello in his hopes of later capturing the presidency. Actually, it mattered little to Yale who ran the Chicago chapter as long as he continued to receive a substantial share of its profits from alky cooking and various rackets. Under Lombardo's rule that share dwindled to mere token payments. Lombardo, in effect, revolted against the national leadership. And now, according to Capone's sources of intelligence, Aiello was in New York, aided and comforted by Yale, having sworn to restore the customary tribute if Yale would help him overthrow Lombardo.

The Brooklyn boss' second grave offense involved liquor. Since 1926 Capone had been expanding his bootleg operations on a national scale. Through a network of interstate alliances—among others, Abe Bernstein's all-Jewish Purple Gang in Detroit, Egan's Rats in St. Louis, Max "Boo Boo" Hoff in Philadelphia—Capone was obtaining liquor of the highest quality, landed at lake and coastal points by rum-runners from Canada, Cuba and the Bahamas, and marketing it all over the Midwest. Yale, who supervised landings on Long Island, had undertaken to ship regular consignments to Chicago by truck. Beginning in the spring of 1927, a good many of the trucks were hijacked before they ever left Brooklyn. To sell liquor, then hijack it was a common enough form of double cross, and Capone wondered whether Yale might not be practicing it. He sent a henchman named James Finesy de Amato to Brooklyn as a spy. Evidently De Amato gave himself away because within a month he was shot down in the street—not, however, before he had transmitted enough information to confirm Capone's suspicion. Yale received an anonymous warning: "Someday you'll get an answer to De Amato."

During the last week in June Capone conferred at the Ponce de Leon with several associates from Chicago, among them Charlie Fischetti, Jake Guzik and Dan Serritella. A few days earlier he had asked the ever-obliging Henderson to procure some firearms for him, and Henderson had bought a dozen assorted pieces from a Miami pawnshop. They included two .45-caliber revolvers. On June 28 six of the visiting Caponeites boarded the Southland Express for Chicago. At Knoxville, Tennessee, four of them got off the train, bought from the local Nash agency a used black sedan for $1,050, and proceeded in it to New York. There they were met by an affiliate of the Capone gang.

Toward midafternoon on July 1, a Sunday, Frank Yale, his jet-black hair and dark skin set off by a Panama hat and light-gray summer suit, was drinking in a Borough Park speakeasy when the bartender called him to the phone. What he heard sent him hurrying out to his car parked nearby. A few minutes later on Forty-fourth Street a black sedan crowded him to the curb; bullets from a variety of weapons—revolvers, sawed-off shotguns, a tommy gun—nailed him to the seat. The tommy gun was the first ever used to kill a New York gangster.

The killers abandoned the Nash along with their weapons on Thirty-sixth Street between Second and Third avenues. The serial numbers on two .45-caliber revolvers led detectives to Parker Henderson, who was then brought to New York. He had, he admitted before a grand jury, bought the revolvers for Capone, but he insisted that, after he delivered them, he never saw them again. The tommy gun, meanwhile, was traced to Peter von Frantzius' Chicago sporting goods store. "In my opinion," said New York's Police Commissioner Grover Whalen when the grand jury had disbanded without indicting anybody, "there was enough evidence not only to get an indictment but a conviction as well."

A white ribbon fluttering from a wreath of roses and orchids at the

Yale funeral, the most spectacular New York had ever witnessed, bore an ominous promise spelled out in gold letters—WE'LL SEE THEM, KID.

The Yale murder reopened the War of the Sicilian Succession. Two months later the Aiello forces, restored to full strength in their Little Sicily bastion, staged yet another of those daylight street shootings for which the city had become world-famed. The Chicago address of the Italo-American National Union was 8 South Dearborn Street, the Hartford Building. There, in an eleventh-floor office, Tony Lombardo normally spent the afternoon attending to his presidential duties. On the afternoon of September 7, just as he finished work, a phone call came from Peter Rizzito, a North Side merchant, and it kept him at his desk for almost fifteen minutes. According to the rumors that circulated later, Rizzito was a false friend and secret Aiello ally, whose real purpose had been to detain Lombardo while the enemy gang set a trap in the street below. Lombardo left the office at about four thirty with two bodyguards, Joseph Ferraro and Joseph Lolordo, whose older brother, Pasquale, was a Unione politician. They turned into Madison Street, moving with effort through the dense crowd of shoppers and office workers. As they passed a restaurant midway down the block, Lolordo heard a man's voice behind him saying, "Here he is," then four shots. Lombardo pitched forward, half his head torn away by dumdum bullets. Ferraro fell beside him, two bullets in his back. Lolordo saw two men running in opposite directions, one wearing a dark suit, the other dressed in gray. Drawing his revolver, he started after the man in gray. A patrolman stopped him and wrested the revolver from him. The killers escaped.

At Ferraro's hospital bedside Assistant State's Attorney Samuel Hoffman asked him to name his murderers. Ferraro gave no answer. "You're going to die," Hoffman told him. Ferraro remained silent to the end, which came two days later. Though Lolordo had seen both killers clearly, had begged the patrolman who disarmed him to let him pursue them, he insisted at the coroner's inquest that he could remember nothing.

Lombardo was the fourth Unione president to die by an assassin's hand since political terrorists shot Anthony D'Andrea in 1921. He was not the last. During the next three years the presidency proved lethal to every incumbent, as well as to several candidates. But the emoluments, if one lived long enough to enjoy them, were too tempting to resist. Under Unione control the alky-cooking cottage industry had grown to embrace the majority of Chicago's immigrant Italian households. There were about 2,500 home stills constantly bubbling away, producing the raw material for a multimillion-dollar bootleg market.

In the race to succeed Lombardo as Unione president Pasquale Lolordo outstripped Peter Rizzito and took office on September 14. Rizzito died soon after, shot down in front of his Milton Street store near Death Corner, whether by order of Capone or of Joe Aiello was never disclosed. The same week the Caponeites launched a machine-gun attack against Aiello headquarters, wounding Tony Aiello and an aide. In various subsequent skirmishes they killed four Aiello gunmen and lost two of their own.

Lolordo lasted less than five months. Under the delusion that the Aiellos were friends he invited three of them to his North Avenue apartment for a drink. They shot him as he was proposing a toast. His wife, Aleina, hearing the gunfire from the next room, rushed in to see them finish him off with a second volley. In her grief she identified Joe Aiello as one of the killers from a photograph the police showed her, but once mistress of herself again, she fell silent like a good Sicilian widow.

Thus, Joe Aiello finally won the presidency of the Unione Siciliane. He held it almost a year. Then, on the evening of October 23, 1930, as he left a friend's house at 15 North Kolmar Avenue, he was caught in a crossfire from two machine-gun nests that had been set up in nearby flats rented ten days earlier, a well-tested Capone tactic. The hour of Joe Aiello's death was commemorated by the floral *pièce de résistance* at his funeral—a clock face made of roses with the hands pointing to eight thirty.

Aiello's Capone-supported successor, a macaroni manufacturer named Agostino Loverdo, also reigned for a year before he was killed in a Cicero dive.

One of the rare few Unione presidents to survive his tenure was the Capone bodyguard Phil D'Andrea.

16

"I've got a heart in me"

DURING the summer of 1928 Capone shifted his Chicago headquarters from the Metropole to the Lexington, diagonally across the street. The Lexington had formerly ranked among the city's most select and imposing hotels. President Cleveland once addressed Chicagoans from the balcony opening off its colonnaded grand ballroom. If no longer select, it was still imposing with its bay windows and turreted corners, the sweep of its lofty public rooms from the main entrance on South Michigan Avenue through to Wabash, its lobby rising a full story to a circumambient shopping gallery.

Of the Lexington's ten floors Capone and his entourage occupied the entire fourth, most of the third, and rooms scattered throughout the hotel where they put up their women. When Capone wished to dine in his six-room suite, for which he paid $18,000 a year, the food and wine were brought to him on rolling tables from a fourth-floor kitchen the management had installed for his exclusive use. His private chef, who lived next to the kitchen, partook of each dish and bottle before they were served, a precaution in force ever since the Aiellos tried to have Capone poisoned. At night little Louis Campagna slept on a cot in front of Capone's bedroom door.

To conceal his comings and goings, Capone devised an escape hatch that necessitated the cooperation of both the Lexington management and the owners of the adjacent office building. Convoyed by half a dozen bodyguards, he would ride the freight elevator to the second floor and slip into a maids' changing room. There a full-length mirror, hinged at one side to the wall, masked a door that had been cut to Capone's specifications. Swinging aside the mirror, he would step through to the office building and walk down two flights to a side entrance where his car and driver would be waiting.*

On rare occasions Mae Capone shared her husband's hotel suite, but hardly ever did she accompany him to a theater, nightclub or racetrack. Few members of the gang and still fewer outsiders came to know her. In the tradition of the old-country Italian dons Capone confined the women of his family to a kind of purdah in either his Prairie Avenue or Palm Island house.

At the time he moved to the Lexington his mistress was a plump, blond, teen-age Greek whom he had salvaged from one of his suburban brothels. He installed her in a two-room suite on the floor above him. When Capone, his family or a member of his gang needed medical attention, they consulted a Dr. David V. Omens, who was also an investor in the Hawthorne Kennel Club, drawing dividends of as much as $36,000 a year. The Greek girl went to him one day, complaining of a genital sore. Owens diagnosed syphilis and began a series of arsphenamine injections. He then urged Capone to take a Wassermann test, but the thought of a needle penetrating his vein and withdrawing blood horrified the gang leader. Neither the doctor's assurance that the pain would be negligible nor his graphic description of the slow devastation inflicted by untreated syphilis could persuade him to it. There was nothing the matter with him, Capone insisted.

He had been established at the Lexington for three months when Frank Loesch went to him with his plea in behalf of the Chicago voter. Whether Republicans or Democrats won, an honest election was bound to fill the county offices with anti-Thompsonites sworn to crush Capone. It seems at first blush that in acceding to Loesch he acted against his own interests. No doubt vanity played a part. It must have deeply gratified him, this hat-in-hand appeal from the illustrious president of the Chicago Crime Commission. Capone craved admiration and gratitude and continually sought to win them with a

* The secret door was discovered by the present owner of the Lexington (renamed the New Michigan). He spotted it from the street, a door to nowhere, after the office building had been torn down. An aged porter, who had worked at the Lexington ever since Capone's day, explained its use.

show of civic spirit or the distribution of largesse. His munificent gifts to his followers, his ostentatious gratuities of $5 to newsboys, $20 to hatcheck girls, $100 to waiters, his donations of food, fuel and clothing to the destitute—he saw to it that they all were publicized.

Capone once thought seriously of trying to retain Ivy Lee, the public relations genius who so successfully gilded the public image of John D. Rockefeller. "There's a lot of people in Chicago that have got me pegged for one of those bloodthirsty mobsters you read about in storybooks," Capone complained, "the kind that tortures his victims, cuts off their ears, puts out their eyes with a red-hot poker and grins while he's doing it. Now get me right. I'm not posing as a model for youth. I've had to do a lot of things I don't like to do. But I'm not as black as I'm painted. I'm human. I've got a heart in me. I'll go as deep in my pocket as any man to help any guy that needs help. I can't stand to see anybody hungry or cold or helpless. Many a poor family in Chicago thinks I'm Santa Claus. If I've given a cent to the poor in this man's town, I'll bet I've given a million dollars. Yes, a million. I don't take any credit to myself for being charitable and I'm just saying this to show that I'm not the worst man in the world." *

But his vanity was not so blind as to betray him into any real peril. The Thompson machine was doomed in any event. Moreover, though Capone might wish it to prevail, he had reason to feel secure no matter how the majority voted. Two administrations had risen and fallen since he came to Chicago. Neither had seriously hampered his operations. Under both he had weathered reform crusades, raids, police shake-ups, grand jury investigations. Officeholders had come and gone; the system remained intact. What had he to fear from a new administration? Capone could afford to grant Loesch's flattering petition, and so there took place what Loesch remembered as "the squarest and the most successful election day in 40 years"—a Republican victory, but a repudiation of Big Bill Thompson.

In the national elections Herbert Hoover defeated Al Smith. The Chicago vote was 650,000 for Hoover, 629,000 for Smith. Soon after his victory, the President-elect visited Miami as the guest of the

---

* There are survivors of the era who agree, like the aged waitress in a South Side pizzeria who told me: "I think Al was a wonderful person. He took from the rich and gave to the poor, didn't he?" or the former Negro doorman, found by a local feature writer still living near the site of the Four Deuces, who remembered: "They was swell guys, all of them. These folks 'round here never knowed who paid the rent, but it was Al. . . . They was all fine boys and they was real good to me."

Southern chain store magnate J. C. Penney. The Penney estate on Belle Isle was not far from Palm Island, a circumstance that gave currency to several indestructible fictions. According to one of these fictions, the sounds of revelry at night from No. 93, of shooting, shouting and females screeching, disturbed Hoover's sleep, and he vowed then and there to crush Capone. According to another persistent version, Hoover was miffed because the newsmen paid more attention to Capone than to him, on one occasion turning away from him in a Miami hotel lobby and flocking to the gang chieftain. It is a fact that early in his Presidential career Hoover ordered an all-out attack against Capone, but personal pique had nothing to do with it.

Liquor continued to produce the bulk of Capone's profits. The necessity for diversification, however, was a lesson learned early from Johnny Torrio, who saw that Prohibition could not last forever, and he applied it so astutely that even had Repeal come much sooner than it did, he could have recouped a good deal of his loss through other sources. Some were entirely legitimate. The New Orleans pinball machine company, for one, in which he invested as a partner of Phil Kastel. He also acquired a 25 percent interest in his favorite Levee nightclub, the Midnight Frolics, where, sealed off from the ordinary customers by bodyguards, he would turn up two or three nights a week to hear Joe E. Lewis sing "Sam, You Made the Pants Too Long," stamp his feet to the rhythms of Austin Mack and his Century Serenaders, and drink whiskey out of a teacup. He seldom brought women with him, and he never danced.

But Capone's most profitable alternative to bootlegging was racketeering.

A "racketeer" [as the Chicago *Journal of Commerce* described him in its issue of December 17, 1927] may be the boss of a supposedly legitimate business association; he may be a labor union organizer; he may pretend to be one, or the other, or both; or he may be just a journeyman thug.

Whether he is a gunman who has imposed himself upon some union as its leader, or whether he is a business association organizer, his methods are the same; by throwing a few bricks into a few windows, an incidental and perhaps accidental murder, he succeeds in organizing a group of small businessmen into what he calls a protective association. He then proceeds to collect what fees and dues he likes, to impose what fines suit him, regulates prices and hours of work, and in various ways undertakes to boss the outfit to his own profit.

Any merchant who doesn't come in or who comes in and doesn't stay in and continue to pay tribute, is bombed, slugged or otherwise intimidated.

Chicago racketeering involved most consumer goods and services with a consequent rise in prices. The Employers' Association of Chicago estimated the annual cost to consumers at $136,000,000 or about $45 per inhabitant. For example, until Maxie Eisen terrorized 380 West Side kosher butcher shops into joining his Master Jewish Butchers' Association their customers paid 90 to 95 cents per pound for corned beef. To raise the protection money Eisen demanded, the butchers had to increase the price to $1.25.

Concerning Eisen's depredations in the fish market, a victim named David Walkoff mustered the courage to tell the state's attorney's office: "In 1925 Eisen came to a store I had on Taylor Street. He had four sluggers with him. He made me close my store because it was within four blocks of another association store. A month later he told me I could return to the fish business by buying an association store at 1016 South Pauline Street. I paid the store owner and had to pay Eisen $300 to return to the association. Two years later I sold the store for $650 and had to pay Eisen 10 per cent commission. I have bought and sold two other stores since then. Each time I bought it was $300 to Eisen for the association and each time I sold it was 10 per cent to Eisen for the commission." Another courageous victim, Mrs. Mamie Oberlander, a fifty-two-year-old widow with five children, complained to the Chicago Crime Commission: "I went to Eisen and pleaded with him to let me open a fish store and he agreed on condition that I gave him $300. I have no money as I am a poor woman. I threatened to tell my trouble to some public officials, but this brought a hearty laugh from Eisen. He said he is the boss and is not afraid of any official or anybody in the city or county, that nobody can make him do what he doesn't want to do."

So prevalent did the rackets become that a special Rackets Court was established with jurisdiction over the following frequently committed offenses: destruction of property and injury of persons by explosives (in 1928 racketeering hoodlums exploded approximately fifty bombs); making or selling explosives, throwing stench bombs, malicious mischief to houses, collecting penalty payments; entering premises to intimidate, kidnapping for ransom, mayhem, intimidation of workmen.

During the twenties more than 200 different rackets flourished in Chicago under such brimming titles as the Concrete Road, Concrete Block, Sewer and Water Pipe Makers' and Layers' Union, Local No. 381; the Soda Dispensers and Table Girl Brotherhood; the Bread, Cracker, Yeast and Pie Wagon Drivers' Union. The 10,000 members of the Midwest Garage Owners' Association each paid its organizer, David Albin, alias Cockeye Mulligan, $1 a month for every car handled. In one month Albin's bully boys slashed 50,000 tires on cars belonging to the customers of nonassociation garages.

Simon J. Gorman, a veteran of Ragen's Colts, who started his racketeering career as business agent of the Cook County Horseshoers' Union, became the czar of Chicago's laundry rackets. With his partner, Johnnie Hand, he organized the Chicago Wet and Dry Laundry Owners' Association, which netted them $1,000 a week. Gorman had powerful City Hall connections, and he used them to discipline holdouts. At his behest a safety inspector would visit the recalcitrant laundryman and condemn his boilers. Hand ended full of machinegun bullets in a lot behind the Hawthorne Inn, but Gorman went on to dominate the Laundry Owners, Linen Supply, Hand Laundry and Laundry Service associations, imposing levies as high as 10 percent of the gross business.

Poison was the persuader adopted by the Kosher Meat Peddlers' Association. They hurled bottles of it into delicatessens that bought their sausages from unaffiliated wholesalers. The Beauty Parlors' Protective Association approached unwilling prospects in two stages—first, a little black powder ignited on the ledge of a rear window; then, if that failed to break down resistance, a stick of dynamite tossed into the middle of the shop. For a time few sporting events could be held in Chicago without casualties unless the promoters hired their help from the Theater Ticket Takers' and Ushers' Union at $5 a head. Since the union's labor pool consisted largely of small boys happy to take tickets or usher for nothing if they could watch the game, its margin of profit was exceptionally big.

The Electric Sign Club found it relatively easy to extort protection payments of $1,500 to $2,000 from theater owners after its thugs flooded one theater with gasoline and set it afire. The Janitors' Union operated in tandem with the Milk Drivers' Union to victimize apartment-building owners. The milk drivers would deliver no milk to apartments that did not employ extra janitors, while the janitors would not stay on the job unless the tenants bought their dairy products from designated suppliers. The Elevator Operators obtained an assessment of $1,000 from each of twenty-five Loop skyscrapers on pain of suspending service without warning, leaving hundreds of people stranded on the top stories. Not even the lowly bootblacks escaped exploitative unionization. They had to pay an initiation fee of $15 plus monthly dues of $2.

Toward the end of 1928 the state's attorney's office compiled a list of ninety-one Chicago unions and associations that had fallen under racketeer rule. Affecting nearly every small business and a good many big ones, they included the Retail Food and Fruit Dealers (initiation fee: $25; monthly dues: $5), the Master Photo Finishers, the Junk Dealers and Peddlers, the Candy Jobbers (still another Gorman enterprise, it was said to gross $7,000,000 a year), the Commission Wagon Owners, the Newspaper Wagon Drivers and Chauffeurs, the Building Trade Council, the City Hall Clerks, the Steamfitters and Plumbers, the Marble Setters, the Theater Treasurers and Box Office Men, the Glaziers, the Bakers, the Excavating Contractors, the Window Shade Manufacturers, the Barbers, the Soda Pop Peddlers, the Ice Cream Dealers, the Garbage Haulers, the Window Cleaners, the Street Sweepers, the Banquet Organizers, the Golf Club Organizers, the Automobile Mechanics, the Distilled Water Dealers, the Electrical Workers, the Clothing Workers, the Musicians, the Dentists' Technicians, the Safe Movers, the Florists, the Structural Iron Workers, the Motion Picture Operators, the Painters and Decorators, the Vulcanizers, the Carpet Layers, the Undertakers, the Coal Teamsters, the Jewish Chicken Killers, the Poultry Dealers, the Master Bakers of the Northwest Side, the Wholesale and Retail Fish Dealers —the last four associations organized by the sharklike Maxie Eisen.

Gradually, Capone or one of his affiliates came to control the majority of the Chicago rackets. Some investigators put it as high as 70 percent. Of the estimated $105,000,000 the Capone syndicate grossed in 1928, about $10,000,000 flowed from the rackets. That year, as a result of his dominant position among the racketeers, Capone found himself a partner in a legitimate business. How this came to pass demonstrated more forcibly than any event in his career the scope of his power and the impotence of the police.

The most omnivorous Chicago racket was the Master Cleaners' and Dyers' Association. It not only skimmed 2 percent from the gross annual earnings of every member wholesale plant, but exacted dues and fees totaling $220 a year from every retail shop that collected clothing for the plants and every trucker that delivered it to them. A favorite device of its terrorists for forcing independents into the fold was the exploding suit. Into the seams of a suit they would sow inflammable chemicals, then send it for cleaning to the defiant plant. When detectives from the state's attorney's office asked the association's business agent, Sam Rubin, who had never worked as a cleaner or dyer, how he qualified for his position, he replied: "I'm a good convincer."

In the spring of 1928 the association decreed a citywide increase in the price of pressing from $1 to $1.75 for men's suits and from $2 to $2.75 for women's dresses. Morris Becker, an independent who operated a chain of retail stores as well as a wholesale plant, defied the order. Shortly, his foreman introduced him to Rubin. "Oh, you are the Mr. Rubin I hear so much about," said Becker (as he had the pluck to testify later before a grand jury).

"Yes," said Rubin, "and you will hear a great deal more. I want to tell you something—you are going to raise prices."

"The Constitution guarantees me the right to life, liberty and full pursuit of happiness," said Becker.

"To hell with the Constitution. I am a damned sight bigger than the Constitution."

Three days later a blast of dynamite partly wrecked Becker's main plant. This was followed by a visit from another association officer named Abrams. "I want you to know," Becker told him, "that these are our prices and we will stick by them."

"If you do, Becker, you're going to be bumped off," said Abrams.

Becker filed a complaint with the state's attorney's office. Fifteen officers, among them Sam Rubin, were indicted. Clarence Darrow defended them. The only prosecution witnesses to show up for the trial were Becker and his son, Theodore. When they asked the assistant state's attorney trying the case what had become of the others, he replied: "Go out and get your own witnesses. I'm a prosecutor, not a process server." The racketeers were acquitted.

Since the law could not protect him, Becker turned to Capone. The result was a newly incorporated chain, the Sanitary Cleaning Shops, with Capone, Jake Guzik and Louis Cowan sharing a $25,000 equity. The first Sanitary Cleaning Shop opened near Capone's Prairie Avenue home. "I have no need of the police or the Employers' Association now," said Becker in a public statement infuriating to both. "I now have the best protection in the world."

CAPONE WARS ON RACKETEERS was the headline over a Chicago *Daily Journal* story that poured scorn on the authorities; INDEPENDENT CLEANERS BOAST GANGSTERS WILL PROTECT WHERE POLICE FAILED. The temporary beneficiary was the consumer. The Sanitary Cleaning Shops maintained the old price scale, and the association had no choice but to do the same. When Capone was asked thereafter to give his occupation, he liked to say, "I'm in the cleaning business."

If Dan Serritella's word can be credited, at about the time Capone succored Morris Becker he performed an equally valuable service for the autocratic publisher of the Chicago *Tribune,* Colonel Robert R. McCormick. As Serritella recounted the story two years later in a letter to Mayor Thompson:

> . . . Max Annenberg, director of circulation, told me the *Tribune* was having some trouble with their chauffeurs and drivers . . . they were going to call a strike for the following Saturday, and he wanted me to get someone to talk to the executive committee. . . . He said that Dullo, business agent of the union . . . demanded $25,000 to straighten out the strike. Annenberg said he wanted to treat the boys right and that he wanted to reach someone who could get the executive committee to fix the strike up.
>
> I told him that as president of the newsboys' union there was nothing I could do. Then Max Annenberg said he would call up Capone and see if he could do anything in the matter, which he did and made an appointment with Capone to meet him in the *Tribune*'s office. I attended this meeting, at which Capone agreed to use his influence to stop the strike, which prevented same. Max Annenberg then . . . introduced McCormick to Capone. McCormick thanked Capone for calling off the strike and said, "You know, you are famous, like Babe Ruth. We can't help printing things about you, but I will see that the *Tribune* gives you a square deal."

The letter, published by Thompson in a campaign booklet entitled *The Tribune Shadow—Chicago's Greatest Curse*, drew a different version from McCormick: "I arrived late at a publishers' meeting. Capone walked in with some of his hoodlums. I threw him out and after that I traveled around in an armored car with one or two bodyguards. Capone didn't settle anything. And he didn't take over the newspapers as he wanted to do."

Yet a news delivery strike had been threatened and averted. Forever after, when Capone, in self-appraisal, would enumerate what he considered to have been his major public benefactions, the abortive strike figured high on the list. "People don't understand that I settled it," he would say in an aggrieved tone. "McCormick wanted to pay me afterward, but I told him to give the money to a hospital."

The inventor of the mechanical rabbit for dog racing was a St. Louis promoter and greyhound fancier named Oliver P. Smith. He first tested the device in 1909 and spent the next decade developing it. After filing patent application papers, he formed a partnership with a sharp-witted young St. Louis lawyer, Edward J. O'Hare. For the right to install a mechanical rabbit dog track owners paid them a percentage of the gate. Smith died in 1927, considerably enriched by a sport that had caught on in both America and Europe, and under an arrangement with his widow O'Hare obtained control of the patent rights.

Dog racing was then illegal throughout the country (Florida became the first state, in 1931, to legalize it), and the track owners to whom O'Hare leased the rabbit ran mainly to mobsters. Capone's initial venture into the field, undertaken jointly with Johnny Patton, was the Hawthorne Kennel Club on the outskirts of Cicero. Unlike the later closely supervised legal sport, the dog racing of the twenties was fraught with traps for the innocent bettor. Nothing was easier than to rig a pari-mutuel race. Given eight entrants, for example, overfeeding seven of them by a couple of pounds of meat or running them a mile before the race would guarantee victory to the eighth dog. O'Hare despised the men he had to deal with as much as he enjoyed the riches they showered on him. "You can make money through business associations with gangsters," he once said, "and you will run no risk if you don't associate personally with them. Keep it on a business basis and there's nothing to fear."

O'Hare's own record was not without blemish. At the outset of Prohibition the enforcement authorities permitted a liquor whole-saler, George Remus, to store about $200,000 worth of whiskey in the same building where O'Hare had his law office, after Remus had put up a $100,000 bond as surety that he would not remove a single bottle without government sanction. Nevertheless, by 1923 all of it had found its way into the bootleg markets of Chicago, New York and other cities, not a drop of it to Remus' profit. In his fury he brought charges that caused the indictment for theft of twenty-two men, among them O'Hare. The lawyer was sentenced to a year in jail and fined $500 but won a reversal on appeal when Remus withdrew his original testimony. O'Hare, it developed years later, had secretly agreed to indemnify Remus.

"Artful Eddie," as some of his colleagues referred to him after that, was a well-mannered, cultivated, attractive man. A crack ath-lete, he rode, boxed, swam and played golf, preserving a youthful body into middle age. He never smoked and drank no hard liquor. Married young, he fathered two girls and a boy. The boy, Edward H. O'Hare, nicknamed Butch, who was twelve at the time his father first met Capone, he idolized. "My son, Butch" were words frequently on his tongue, and more than anything he wanted for himself he wanted a distinguished career for his son.

A dog track produced profits so much greater than the mere leas-ing of Oliver Smith's brainchild that O'Hare decided to operate a track of his own. In Madison, Illinois, across the river from St. Louis, he started the Madison Kennel Club. The money poured in until a series of police raids forced him to shut down. A Cook County judge, Harry Fisher, meanwhile, had come to the aid of the Capone outfit by declaring dog racing tracks legal and enjoining the police from raiding them. The judge's brother, Louis Fisher, a lawyer, repre-sented the dog track owners. The Illinois Supreme Court eventually overruled him, but for a time the Hawthorne Kennel Club pros-pered. O'Hare leased land nearby and opened the Lawndale Kennel Club. This was a bold intrusion, but he felt safe enough. He let it be known that should anybody attempt to harm him or to put him out of business, he would withhold the rights to the mechanical rabbit in Cook County. If he couldn't operate there, nobody could. Capone proposed they merge their tracks, and O'Hare agreed.

The public had gone mad about dog racing. The syndicate could not build grandstands and parimutuel booths fast enough to keep up with the increasing crowds. The weekly net ran as high as $50,000. O'Hare acted as counsel and manager, a double function he executed with such skill that the syndicate later entrusted him with other dog tracks in Florida and Massachusetts. O'Hare might continue to hold himself socially aloof from the Caponeites, but he became inextricably entangled in their affairs.

As Capone expanded into ever more diversified fields, he repeatedly found the same challengers blocking his advance. The North Siders under Bugs Moran were foes as relentless as ever they had been under O'Banion, Weiss or Drucci. On the Detroit-Chicago highway they hijacked truck after truck of liquor consigned to Capone by the Purple Gang, and from a Canadian ship moored off the lakeshore they once lifted an entire cargo of whiskey meant for Capone. They bombed six saloons that were buying his beer. They abetted the Aiellos in their struggle to recapture the alky-cooking monopoly. There were growing indications that Bugs Moran had helped plan, if he did not take a direct hand in, the murder of Pasquale Lolordo. His North Siders twice attempted to kill Jack McGurn. The second time the Gusenberg brothers caught him in a telephone booth at the Hotel McCormick and fired a tommy-gun burst through the glass. Major surgery and a long hospital confinement saved his life. The rivalry spread to dog racing. Moran started a track in southern Illinois, while his business manager, Adam Heyer, alias John Snyder, opened the Fairview Kennel Club in Cicero itself. North Side guerrillas went so far as to set fire to the Hawthorne Kennel Club track. Moran's latest incursion took him into the cleaning and dyeing business. Seizing control of an independent plant, the Central Cleaning Company, he installed two of his followers, Willie Marks and Alfred Weinshank, as vice-presidents.

He missed no chance to taunt Capone, calling him the Beast and the Behemoth. "The Beast uses his muscle men to peddle rot-gut alcohol and green beer," he said in an interview with the Reverend Elmer Williams, a Methodist minister who published a monthly magazine, *Lightnin'*, devoted to exposés of gangsterism and crooked politicians. "I'm a legitimate salesman of good beer and pure whiskey. He trusts nobody and suspects everybody. He always has guards. I travel around with a couple of pals. The Behemoth can't sleep nights. If you ask me, he's on the dope. Me, I don't even need an aspirin."

Capone left again for Miami in late December. McGurn visited him there in early February. From 93 Palm Island (as telephone company records would show) Capone talked at length every day with Jake Guzik, living in Chicago's Congress Hotel. The calls stopped on February 11. Three days later was St. Valentine's Day.

17

Against the Wall

CAPONE rose earlier than usual, having been summoned to the office of Dade County solicitor Robert Taylor. He took a dip in his swimming pool, a black one-piece bathing suit stretched tight over his barrel of a torso. After a copious breakfast he dressed carefully in gray flannel slacks, white shoes and a camel's hair sports jacket. His chauffeur, driving a Packard with a three-tone electric horn, then took him across the causeway into downtown Miami. It was shortly after nine when he walked into the county solicitor's office, unruffled and cheerful.

A light snow was powdering North Clark Street when the big black Cadillac touring car edged toward it from Webster Avenue. There was a police gong on the running board and, fastened to the back of the driver's seat, a gun rack such as police squad cars carried. The driver, who had on horn-rimmed glasses, wore a policeman's uniform, complete to blue cap and brass star. So did the man beside him. The three men in the rear seat wore civilian clothes.

County Solicitor Taylor's questions reflected the curiosity of two other agencies besides his own. His concern was confined mainly to Capone's local activities, current and prospective, but he had undertaken a further inquiry in behalf of both the New York City police, who were trying to solve the Yale murder, and the Bureau of Internal

Revenue's Intelligence Unit, which had begun to look into Capone's income. A stenographer, Ruth Gaskin, recorded the dialogue.

"Do you remember when you first met Parker Henderson?" Taylor asked.

"About two years ago," Capone replied.

"That was when he was running the Ponce de Leon Hotel?"

"Yes."

"Can you remember who was staying there with you that winter?"

"I don't like to disclose their names unless you tell me what this is all about."

Taylor persisted.

"I don't remember," Capone said finally.

"Under what name did you register?"

"My own name."

"You didn't register under the name of A. Costa?"

"No."

The night before, the hijacker had telephoned Bugs Moran to offer him a truckload of whiskey from Detroit at the bargain price of $57 a case. Moran had told him to deliver it around ten thirty in the morning to his warehouse at 2122 North Clark Street, where his men would help unload it. Seven North Siders were waiting there now, but Moran had started late. With Ted Newberry, a gambling concessionaire, he left his Parkway Hotel apartment, close by the warehouse, a little after ten thirty. The temperature had dropped to fifteen degrees below freezing, and a bone-chilling wind was blowing from the west. Pulling up their coat collars, Moran and Newberry took a shortcut though an alley toward the rear of the warehouse. Willie Marks, one of the gang's specialists in business racketeering, was also tardy. He arrived from the Clark Street side by trolley car at almost the same instant.

"You left money with Henderson, $1,000 to $5,000 at a time, didn't you?"

"I don't remember."

"You didn't receive any money by Western Union from Chicago?"

"I don't remember. I'll try to find out."

"Then you keep a record of your money transactions?"

"Absolutely."

As the Cadillac turned the corner of North Clark Street, twenty blocks west of its starting point, a truck sideswiped it, forcing it to a stop. The truckman, Elmer Lewis, horrified at having hit what he took to be a police car, scrambled down from his seat and, full of remorse, hurried toward the Cadillac. The blue-uniformed figure behind the wheel smiled and waved him back reassuringly as if nothing had happened. Baffled but relieved, Lewis watched the car go on for half a block, then stop again in front of No. 2122. . . .

"How long has Dan Serritella been living with you?"
"He's not living with me. He's just a friend of mine."
"How much did you give Parker Henderson to buy your home?"
"$50,000."
"Was that in cash?"
"Yes."

The warehouse was a one-story red-brick building, 60 feet wide and 120 feet long, dwarfed by the four-story buildings on either side. Both the plate-glass front window and the glass-paneled door to the right of it had been painted black. A white placard with black lettering filled the lower half of the window:

S–M–C CARTAGE–CO
Shipping   Packing
Phone Diversey 1471
Long Distance   Hauling

Behind the sign, running the width of the building, was a narrow office separated from the warehouse proper by a wooden partition. Formerly a garage, the warehouse had concrete flooring and brick walls, the original whitewash a grimy yellow with age. Tall, wide doors at the rear opened on the loading area in the alley.

On the morning of February 14 three empty trucks stood against the side walls. A fourth had been jacked up in the center of the floor, and lying on his back under it, wearing oil-smeared overalls, Johnny May was repairing a wheel. A forty-year-old ex-safecracker, whom Moran had hired as an auto mechanic at $50 a week, May shared a nearby slum flat with a wife, six children and a German shepherd named Highball. The dog was tied by his leash to the axle of the truck. May had brought some scraps of meat for him in a paper bag.

A coffeepot percolated on an electric plate, and the six other men sat around it with their hats and overcoats on, for the warehouse was unheated. A naked 200-watt bulb overhead shed a fierce white light on them. There were the Gusenberg brothers, Frank and Pete; James Clark, alias Kashellek, Moran's brother-in-law; Adam Heyer; Al Weinshank; and Reinhardt H. Schwimmer. The Gusenbergs had a long day ahead of them. As soon as the hijacked liquor had been delivered, they were to drive two of the empty trucks to Detroit to pick up some smuggled Canadian whiskey. Heyer, a business college graduate and expert accountant before he went to prison for embezzlement, handled all of the gang's financial transactions, as well as the management of the Fairview Kennel Club. Weinshank, the newest gang member, had helped Moran muscle into the cleaning and dyeing business. Heavyset and round-faced, he looked a little like Moran from a distance. The resemblance was enhanced on this particular morning by the similarity of their dress: Both happened to wear tan fedoras and gray overcoats. All six were heavily armed, and to pay for the expected delivery, they carried cash in their pockets, totaling almost $5,000. Schwimmer was an anomaly. In the gang but not of it, enjoying the company of criminals but not himself inclined to criminality, he had met Moran at the Parkway Hotel, where he, too, resided, and become his beglamored friend. He was an optometrist by profession, aged thirty. Like Parker Henderson, he derived an excitement, a vicarious feeling of power from intimacy with gangsters. He had dropped into the warehouse, as he frequently did on his way to work, to see what the North Siders were up to, and he had stayed to chat.

"Besides gambling you're a bootlegger, aren't you?"
"No, I never was a bootlegger."
"Do you know Jake Guzik?"
"Yes."
"What does he do?"
(Jokingly) : "He fights."

Elmer Lewis was not the only person to see the Cadillac stop at the warehouse and four of the men go inside, those in uniform leading the way. On the second floor of her rooming house next door, as she was ironing a shirt, the noise of the truck scraping the Cadillac

drew Mrs. Max Landesman to the window. Surprised that no alterca-
tion took place, she watched until the quartet had entered the warehouse.

When Moran and Newberry saw the car, they assumed a police
raid or a shakedown was taking place, and they swiftly retraced their
steps back to the Parkway. A third Gusenberg brother, Henry, who
also lived there, had been about to join them at the warehouse, but
they warned him not to go near it. Willie Marks, approaching from
south of the warehouse, reached the same conclusion. Shrinking into
a doorway, he jotted down the car's license number.

"And you don't know anybody who sent you money under the
name of A. Costa?"

"No."

"But you did receive it from Chicago?"

"That is correct. All of it comes from Chicago, from my gambling
business."

"Are you going to buy Cat Cay?"

"I don't know. I don't think I will get it."

"How much do they want for it?"

"Half a million."

"Who is Mitchell of Oak Park, Illinois? He called your home three
times on January 20th?"

"He commissions money on racetracks for me."

"Did you get any money from Charlie Fischetti while you were
staying at the Ponce de Leon? Henderson said you received various
sums from $1,000 to $5,000."

"What has money got to do with it?"

With that indignant question left unanswered the interview ended.
For Capone it had been a welcome confrontation in at least one respect: Miss Gaskin's stenographic transcript would establish beyond
the slightest doubt where he had spent the morning of February 14,
1929.

It sounded like the chatter of a pneumatic drill. Or drumbeats,
furiously fast. It started a few moments after the five men entered
the warehouse and lasted a minute or two. Then, two single blasts
like a car backfiring. A dog began to howl. Vaguely disturbed,
Mrs. Landesman moved back to the window and glanced down at the

snowy, windy street. Her friend across the way, Mrs. Alphonse Morin, looked out of her third-floor window at the same time, and they both saw the men reappear. The first two came out with their hands raised. The two men behind them, wearing the uniforms, held pistols to their backs and prodded them toward the car. A police raid and an arrest, the women concluded; the fifth man must have been a plainclothes detective. The car continued south on Clark Street to Ogden Avenue and there turned right. . . .

As the dog kept up its howling, Mrs. Landesman's uneasiness grew. Finally, she asked one of her lodgers, a man named McAllister, to see what ailed the animal. He went into the warehouse. He did not stay long. He came running out, pale and sick. "They're all dead," he said.

He was mistaken. Frank Gusenberg still breathed. Though fourteen machine-gun bullets had hit him, some passing through his body, he had managed to crawl about twenty feet away from the rear wall. The others lay dead where they had fallen at the foot of the wall, Kashellek on his face, Weinshank, Heyer, May and Schwimmer on their backs. Pete Gusenberg had died kneeling, his upper body slumped against a chair. The hapless optometrist, Schwimmer, still wore his hat, and Weinshank's tan fedora rested on his chest. Where the seven had stood before the bullets flew, blood slopped down the yellowish bricks, and blood from the bodies snaked across the oily stone floor. Highball, howling and snapping, tore at his leash. The executioners had been systematic, swinging their machine guns back and forth three times, first at the level of the victims' heads, then chests, then stomachs. Some of the corpses were held together in one piece only by shreds of flesh and bone. Yet evidently life had still flickered in Kashellek and May after the machine-gun volleys, for they had also been blasted with shotguns at such close range as to all but obliterate their faces.*

Capone returned to a busy household. A big party was in preparation. With the Miami winter season at its peak and boxing enthusi-

---

* In 1945 a couple named Werner, who knew nothing about the building's lurid history, converted the front office into an antique shop. They were soon besieged by crime buffs. "They come here from all over the world—England, France, even New Zealand," Mrs. Werner complained. "If I had known, I never would have come here." The building was torn down in 1967. I know several Chicagoans who treasure a brick from it as a souvenir.

asts already converging on the resort for the approaching world championship fight between Jack Sharkey and "Young" Stribling, Capone had invited more than 100 guests to Palm Island—sports-writers, gamblers, show folk, racketeers, politicians. A boxing enthusiast himself, who favored Sharkey to win the title, he frequently visited his training camp and was photographed by news cameramen standing between Sharkey and Bill Cunningham, sportscaster and former All-American center.

As Detective Sweeney bent over the still-breathing gangster, he recognized a boyhood companion. Clarence Sweeney and Frank Gusenberg had gone to the same public school not six blocks from the warehouse. "Frank," said the detective, "in God's name what happened? Who shot you?"

But Gusenberg was unconscious. He revived a little in the Alexian Brothers Hospital, and Sweeney, at his bedside, repeated the question.

"Nobody shot me," said Gusenberg.

He did not have long to live, the detective told him. His brother Pete was dead. Let him speak. The law would avenge them.

"I ain't no copper." They were his last words.

When Bugs Moran learned of the massacre that he had escaped by only minutes, he said: "Only Capone kills like that."

The guests feasted on an elaborate buffet and drank champagne served by half a dozen of Capone's bodyguards. The night was hot, and the bodyguards had been allowed to remove their jackets and pistol holsters. They were otherwise impeccably attired, young, most of them, and muscular. ("Capone hires nothing but gentlemen," attested a thug named Harry Dore, who once worked for him, bursting with professional pride in the association. "They must be well-dressed at all times; they must have cultured accents; must always say, 'Yes, sir' and 'No, sir' when he addresses them. He hires men with great care and takes pains that they are his own type in dress and conduct.")

Mae Capone hovered quietly in the background, seeing to everybody's wants. At Sonny's bedtime his father took him by the hand and led him from group to group to say good-night. The small boy with the hearing aid, a shy, withdrawn little figure, his big eyes opened wide in bewilderment, made a pathetic contrast in that strident gathering.

Jack Kofoed, the New York *Post*'s sports editor, brought his wife, Marie. As the steamy night wore on, she decided to cool off in the swimming pool. Retiring to the Venetian loggia with her swimsuit, she saw, in a corner of the ladies' dressing room, what appeared to be a chest covered by a tarpaulin. She sat on it to remove her shoes and quickly got up again with a cry of pain. Lifting the tarpaulin, she uncovered a tangle of machine guns, shotguns and revolvers.

Tact restrained the guests from discussing too loudly the Chicago massacre that was reported in the evening papers and radio broadcasts. The next morning, when additional details had been published, among them Moran's comment, Jack Kofoed called again on his host. "Al, I feel silly asking you this," he said, "but my boss wants me to. Al, did you have anything to do with it?"

"Jack," Capone replied, "the only man who kills like that is Bugs Moran."

Mortified by this latest gory blot on the city's reputation, the Chicago Association of Commerce posted a reward of $50,000 for the arrest and conviction of the killers. An aroused public subscribed $10,000 more. The City Council and the state's attorney's office each added $20,000, bringing the total to $100,000, the biggest price ever put on the heads of gangsters.

No agency wanted a swift solution more eagerly than the police, for some people believed what the killers meant them to believe: that policemen had done the deed. Such was the disrepute into which the Chicago Police Department had fallen. The newspapers quoted the local Prohibition administrator, Frederick D. Silloway, as saying: "The murderers were not gangsters. They were Chicago policemen. I believe the killing was the aftermath to the hijacking of 500 cases of whiskey belonging to the Moran gang by five policemen six weeks ago on Indianapolis Boulevard. I expect to have the names of these five policemen in a short time. It is my theory that in trying to recover the liquor the Moran gang threatened to expose the policemen and the massacre was to prevent the exposure."

To which Chief of Police Russell rejoined: "If it is true that coppers did this, I'd just as soon convict coppers as anybody else," and Chief of Detectives John Egan added: "I'll arrest them myself, toss them by the throat into a cell and do my best to send them to the gallows."

The next day Silloway retracted his accusation, claiming he had been misquoted. To mollify the Police Department, his superiors in Washington transferred him to another district. But the damage was done. The suspicion lingered.

The investigation proceeded with Chief Egan, the state's attorney's staff and the Cook County coroner, Dr. Herman N. Bundesen, each grappling with different aspects of the case. Scouring the warehouse, Egan and his men recovered seventy empty .45-caliber machine-gun cartridges and fourteen spent bullets of the same caliber. Across the street, at Nos. 2119 and 2125, were rooming houses run, respectively, by Mrs. Michael Doody and Mrs. Frank Orvidson. As Assistant State's Attorney Walker Butler was canvassing the neighborhood for information, they came forward with corroborating stories. Ten days before the massacre three young men appeared, looking for rooms to rent. Mrs. Doody was able to accommodate two of them, and Mrs. Orvidson took in a third. They said they were cabdrivers, working a night shift, and they insisted on front rooms overlooking Clark Street. None of them hardly ever left his room. When either landlady went in to clean, she usually found him sitting by the window, watching. The three men vanished on the morning of the massacre. Having suspected from the start that the Purple Gang was involved, Butler showed the landladies photographs of sixteen members. They identified three of them as the mysterious lodgers. But when questioned, at Butler's request, by the Detroit police, all three produced unshakable proof that they had been nowhere near Chicago.

On February 22 chance aided the investigators. A fire broke out in the garage behind the house at 1723 North Wood Street, about three miles west of the warehouse. The firemen who extinguished it found a black Cadillac touring car which had been partly demolished by an acetylene torch, axes and hacksaws. The torch, they surmised, had accidentally started the blaze, putting the wreckers to flight. In a corner lay a Luger pistol and the charred wooden handles of two other small arms. Notified by the Fire Department, Egan examined the remains of the Cadillac. The still decipherable engine number enabled him to trace the car to a Michigan Avenue dealer, who said he had sold it in December to a man identifying himself as "James

Morton of Los Angeles." From the owner of the Wood Street property, a neighborhood grocer, Egan learned that a "Frank Rogers" rented the garage on February 7. He gave 1859 West North Avenue, around the corner, as his address. That house was now deserted, but, significantly, it adjoined the Circus Café, headquarters of Claude Maddox, whose ties to Capone, the Purple Gang and Egan's Rats were well-known. Tony Accardo was then a member of the Circus gang and, according to a police theory developed later, helped plan the massacre. Soon after, he became a Capone bodyguard and was sometimes seen in the lobby of the Hotel Lexington with a tommy gun across his knees.

The police could uncover no trace of either "James Morton" or "Frank Rogers," and they had no legal grounds on which to detain Maddox. As for Bugs Moran, he refused to disclose anything about the hijacker who had phoned him on the eve of the massacre except that he had long known and trusted him. ("Moran raves when he talks about him," one detective reported. "He threatens all the tortures of the Spanish Inquisition.") But on the basis of the clues gathered thus far, combined with their knowledge of intergang relationships, the investigators reconstructed the events of February 14 as follows:

The plot that Capone conceived to exterminate the North Siders called for two men who could persuade the victims to surrender their arms without a fight. Hence, the police disguise. The masqueraders, of course, had to be total strangers to the victim. Probably, Maddox imported them for Capone from either Detroit or his native St. Louis, kept them under cover until needed, and provided them with the spurious police car.

The function of the three Clark Street lodgers was to watch for Moran—echoes of past Caponian ambushes!—informing the killers by phone the moment he entered the warehouse. What saved Moran's life was his resemblance to Weinshank. The business racketeer chanced to arrive first, and the watchers phoned too soon.

The collision on Clark Street suggested the route the killers took —north along Wood Street for a mile to Webster Avenue, then east for two miles on Webster to Clark, a fifteen-minute drive at most. The three men wearing civilian clothes probably waited in the warehouse office while their uniformed accomplices relieved each victim of his weapons. They then emerged with their tommy guns adjusted to rapid fire and ordered the seven North Siders to face the wall. Though the killers must have realized by then that Moran was not present, they dared not let the others live. It was to confuse any witnesses to their getaway that they staged the final scene, reappearing on the street posing as policemen after a raid with their prisoners.

On February 27 the police obtained a warrant for the arrest of Jack McGurn. It was based on the testimony of a youth named George Brichet. He was passing the warehouse on the morning of the fourteenth, he said, when five men entered it. He heard one of them say, "Come on, Mac," and he identified McGurn from a rogues' gallery photograph as the man so addressed.

The arresting officer found McGurn living at the Hotel Stevens with a young blonde named Louise Rolfe. Following his indictment for seven murders, bail was set at $50,000. He raised the amount by putting up as surety a hotel he owned valued at more than $1,000,000.

Coroner Bundesen, meanwhile, had summoned before his blue-ribbon jury every gun dealer in the county. Among them was Peter von Frantzius, the reputed armorer of gangland. Could he tell the jury anything about recent sales of tommy guns? Yes, Von Frantzius admitted, he had sold six to a Frank H. Thompson. He understood that the buyer was acting for the Mexican consul general, whose government wanted them to put down revolutionaries. The police knew Thompson as an ex-convict, safecracker, hijacker, rum-runner and, lately, middleman in arms deals. He was then wanted for attempting to machine-gun his wife and her lover in his hometown of Kirkland, Illinois.

Thompson surrendered to Bundesen. He confirmed his purchase of the tommy guns but mentioned a different consignee—James "Bozo" Shupe, subsequently killed. Shupe, the police knew, was a close associate of Scalise, Anselmi and Joseph Giunta, the current, Capone-backed president of the Unione Siciliane. On these thin grounds they arrested the three Sicilians. Giunta they were obliged to release almost immediately for lack of evidence, but new witnesses placed Scalise and Anselmi in the fake police car. They, too, were indicted and freed on bail of $50,000 each.

Two days later Assistant State's Attorney Stansbury added three more names to the list of alleged assassins, making the total six instead of five. The first was Joseph Lolordo, a natural suspect, being the brother of the Unione Siciliane president whose murder Moran possibly engineered. During the World War Lolordo served with a detachment of machine gunners, and Stansbury ascribed most of the St. Valentine's Day gunnery to him. He had since disappeared.

The disclosure of the second and third names followed a piece of information furnished by a prominent Chicagoan. The collision on Clark Street had also been witnessed by H. Wallace Caldwell, president of the Board of Education. Passing close to the Cadillac, he had noticed that the driver in police uniform lacked an upper front tooth. That distinguishing mark fitted one of Egan's Rats, Fred "Killer" Burke. At the time of the massacre he was a fugitive under indictment in Ohio for bank robbery and murder. So was his constant companion, James Ray. Their *modus operandi,* when robbing banks, was to wear police uniforms.

McGurn's alibi before the grand jury—his "Blonde Alibi," as the press called her—was Louise Rolfe. He never left her side at the Hotel Stevens, he swore, from 9 P.M. of February 13 to 3 P.M. of February 14. The state's attorney thereupon had him indicted for perjury, but before McGurn could be tried on that charge, he married Louise. A wife cannot be obliged to testify against her husband.

As for the murder charge, under an Illinois statute if the accused demanded trial at four separate terms of court and the state was not prepared to prosecute him, then the state must discontinue the case. Between the spring and winter of 1929 McGurn made four demands for trial. None was met, and on December 2 he walked out of the courtroom a free man. By then the authorities had revised their version of his role in the St. Valentine's Day massacre. They concluded that though McGurn may not have accompanied the firing squad, he served as its logistician. To prove this, however, they had still less evidence.

During the early stages of Coroner Bundesen's inquest a detective giving testimony referred to the cartridges and shells collected from the Clark Street warehouse. Asked by the foreman of the blue-ribbon jury, Burt A. Massee, what purpose was served by preserving them, he explained the principles underlying the relatively new science of forensic ballistics. Every firearm, he said, leaves its own characteristic marks on the bullets passing through it. The bore of a rifle, for example, imprints distinctive ridges on the sides of the bullet. The firing pin makes an indentation on the primer; the tooling of the breech imparts concentric circles to the base of the shell when the

shell recoils against it. Each part of the mechanism coming into contact with shell or bullet writes its signature, and like fingerprints, no
two markings are identical. Thus, with a microscope and various
measuring instruments, the expert could match a bullet with the
weapon that fired it.

Unfortunately, the detective added, the Chicago Police Department lacked the equipment for such analyses. This struck foreman
Massee and a juror named Walter E. Olson, both prosperous and
civic-spirited businessmen, as an inexcusable deficiency. With a group
of other wealthy Chicagoans, whose interest they enlisted, they put
up the money for a scientific crime detection laboratory to be installed at Northwestern University. Completed by 1930, it was the
first of its kind, the model for many others, including the FBI Laboratory. To direct it, Major Calvin H. Goddard, the country's foremost authority on forensic ballistics, was brought from New York.
The first case to absorb his attention was the St. Valentine's Day massacre and his findings dispelled once for all the still-lurking suspicion
that real policemen took part in it.

> Complying with the request of the coroner [Goddard reported],
> I have tested out various Thompson machine guns in the hands of
> the police of the City of Chicago. I examined altogether some eight
> Thompson machine guns, five in the hands of the Chicago police,
> one at Melrose Park Police Headquarters and two in the possession
> of the Cook County Highway police. I fired a number of rounds of
> ammunition of the same caliber, type, make, and vintage as used in
> the murder, through each of these. The bullets were recovered un-
> deformed from a receptacle of cotton waste into which they were
> fired and each bullet and empty shell was numbered with the num-
> ber of the gun from which it had issued. The bullets and shells so
> recovered were carefully compared with specimens of the fatal bul-
> lets and shells. In no instance did I find a duplication of markings
> to indicate that any of the police weapons had been employed in
> the killings.

Without the weapons, Goddard could reach no positive conclu-
sions. Almost a year elapsed. Then, on the evening of December 14,
1929, in St. Joseph, Michigan, Patrolman Charles Skelly overtook
a hit-and-run driver, forcing him to the curb. As he jumped onto
his running board, the driver shot him three times and continued
his flight. Skelly died in the hospital. The fugitive's car was found

on U.S. Highway 12, near St. Joseph, cracked up against a telephone pole. The registration papers in the glove compartment bore the name Fred Dane and an address on the city outskirts. There, in addition to a Mrs. Fred Dane, who professed to know nothing of either her husband's business affairs or his whereabouts, the police found $319,850 in stolen negotiable bonds and an arsenal that included two tommy guns and men's shirts with the laundry marking FRB. One of the policemen guessed the initials stood for "Fred R. Burke," the long-sought man with the missing front tooth. The St. Joseph authorities immediately notified Chicago, and at the urgent request of Coroner Bundesen the district attorney personally delivered the tommy guns to the Northwestern Crime Laboratory. The drums contained bullets of various makes. Many were of the same make as those gathered in the Clark Street warehouse. Selecting thirty-five of these, Goddard fired twenty through one of the tommy guns into a container of cotton waste and fifteen through the other.

> The result of these studies was to demonstrate conclusively that the two guns found in the Burke home were those that had been used in the St. Valentine's Day massacre. . . . I did not devote unnecessary time to pinning various of the fatal bullets to one particular gun but satisfied myself by determining that the single bullet from the body of Reinhardt Schwimmer had been fired by one of the two guns and that one of the bullets from the body of James Clark had issued from the other.

That was not all. The New York police submitted to Goddard the bullets that had been taken from Frankie Yale's body a year and a half earlier. They, too, proved to have been fired by one of Burke's tommy guns.

The Bundesen jury recommended "that the said Burke, now a fugitive from justice, be apprehended and held to the Grand Jury on the charge of murder as a participant in said murder [*i.e.*, of James Clark]. . . ." Burke was captured the following April, but the Michigan authorities refused to surrender him to Illinois, preferring to try him for the murder of Patrolman Skelly. He was sentenced to life imprisonment in the Michigan State Penitentiary and died there.

Efforts by sundry agencies, both public and private, to discover the identities of the other St. Valentine's Day Killers continued for years and flushed a rich assortment of suspects.* But the only man who can be said with moral certainty to have had a hand in the massacre was Fred Burke.

* The St. Valentine's Day murder team, I was assured in 1969 by the Barker gangster Al Karpis, after he had served thirty-three years in federal penitentiaries, consisted of Burke, Maddox, George Ziegler, Gus Winkler and "Crane Neck" Nugent. These five, according to Karpis, who got his information from Nugent, constituted an execution squad regularly employed by the Capone syndicate and its affiliates. They were paid $2,000 a week plus an occasional bonus and travel expenses. Ziegler, said Karpis, actually planned the massacre, and a sixth hoodlum, not on the regular payroll, Byron Bolton, was one of the Clark Street lookouts.

18

"Nobody's on the legit"

THERE were twenty-seven of them, Sicilians all. White-spatted and velvet-collared, their fingers ablaze with diamonds, carrying shiny new matched leather luggage, they strode into the hotel with a proprietary air and demanded the best accommodations. They came from Chicago, Gary, St. Louis, Buffalo, New York, Newark and Tampa. The first contingent of eleven men arrived at dawn in touring cars, and by midmorning the deliberations were in full swing.

As a non-Sicilian, Capone could not participate, but he had representation. The majority were Chicagoans, among them Pasquale Lolordo, who owed his rise in the Unione Siciliane largely to Capone's helping hand, and Joe Giunta, who had not yet turned traitor to Capone. The next biggest group were the New Yorkers, three of whom, Joe Profaci, Joe Magliocco and Vincent Mangano, would each head a Mafia family. (Thirty years later Profaci figured among the 100-odd delegates to the great gangster conclave on the estate of Joe Barbara in Apalachin, New York.)

Some authorities date the beginning of modern nationally organized crime from that meeting held in a suite at Cleveland's Hotel Statler on December 5, 1928. Certainly, it was the first such meeting of which any record exists. Theretofore the loose links between the scattered Mafia cells, as well as between the branches of the quasi-respectable front organization, the Unione Siciliane, had been maintained chiefly through a national president who would travel from one to another.

A record of the Cleveland meeting exists because a desk clerk disliked the look and manner of the flashy out-of-towners. After assigning them rooms on the seventh floor, he reported their presence to the policeman patrolling the block. The patrolman notified headquarters, and in the course of the morning a squad of detectives interrupted the conference. Arrested on "suspicion," the conferees were taken to police headquarters, fingerprinted, photographed and questioned about their business in Cleveland. The detectives could obtain no very illuminating answers, and lacking any legal cause for further action, they let their captives go.

What the Sicilians talked about remains conjectural. In all probability the agenda included the national presidency of the Unione Siciliane, vacant since Yale's death, and the distribution of corn sugar, vital to whiskey production, of which the local supply was monopolized by a Cleveland Mafioso. But more important than any specific topic was the fact that gangsters from six states had come together to discuss common problems. It indicated a step toward the kind of confederacy that Torrio had always advocated and that Capone had striven to establish among the Chicago gangs.

Coincidentally, Torrio had just returned to America after five years abroad and, his nerve recovered, was resuming his relationships in the New York and Chicago underworlds.

On February 17 a deputy United States marshal served Capone with a subpoena to appear in Chicago the following month before a federal grand jury investigating bootlegging. He had not set foot in the city since December, 1928, and now, with Moran alive and howling for his blood, he was so reluctant to do so that he decided to plead illness. He had undergone a mild bout of bronchitis in January, and the young Miami physician who treated him, Dr. Kenneth Phillips, obligingly furnished an affidavit dated March 5, deposing:

> . . . that since January 13th, 1929, said Alphonse Capone has been suffering with broncho-pneumonia pleurisy with effusion of fluid into the chest cavity and for six weeks was confined to his bed at his home on said Palm Island, and has been out of his bed only for ten days last past, but has not fully recovered from said disease . . . that, in the professional opinion of affiant, the said Capone's

Chicago Tribune.

Jake Lingle.

His murderer (?), Leo Vincent Brothers.

His death in the underpass.

Above left:
Joe Saltis.

Above right:
Tony "Mops" Volpe.

Left:
Frankie Yale at the height of his power as Brooklyn gang lord and Unione Siciliane bigwig.

United Press International.

Below left:
Edward "Spike" O'Donnell.

Below right:
Frank McErlane.

Above left:
Jack Zuta.

Above right:
Frank Lake.

SOME FRIENDS AND FOES

Right:
James "King of the Bombers" Belcastro.

Below left:
William "Klondike" O'Donnell.
Wide World Photos.

Below right:
Mayor William Hale "Big Bill" Thompson.
Chicago Tribune.

United Press International.

At Chicago's Comiskey Park, Capone, surrounded by bodyguards, watches with paternal pride as Gabby Hartnett of the Cubs autographs a baseball for twelve-year-old Sonny Capone.

CAPONE AT PLAY

Capone's winter retreat on Palm Island, Miami.

Wide World Photos.

Brown Brothers.

Fishing from his motor cruiser, moored off Palm Island.

Sports-loving Capone watches the action at a Miami prizefight training camp.

At heavyweight Jack Sharkey's training camp shortly before the Sharkey-Young Stribling world championship fight in 1929. Left to right: Bill Cunningham, ex-football star, Al Capone and Sharkey.

United Press International.

The slaughter of seven O'Banionites on St. Valentine's Day, 1929 (the seventh does not appear in this picture, having crawled to the door of the S-M-C Cartage warehouse before collapsing), left the Caponeites masters of the Chicago underworld.

Wide World Photos.

Peter von Frantzius, "the armorer of gangland," whose Chicago sporting goods store the police suspected of having furnished the tommy guns used in the St. Valentine's Day massacre.

Fred "Killer" Burke, the only man of whom it can be said with moral certainty that he pulled a trigger in the St. Valentine's Day Massacre.

Machine Gun Jack McGurn, who helped plan, if he did not take part in, the St. Valentine's Day massacre, was himself machine-gunned in a Chicago bowling alley on St. Valentine's Day seven years later. Here detectives read the comic valentine that the killers left on his body.

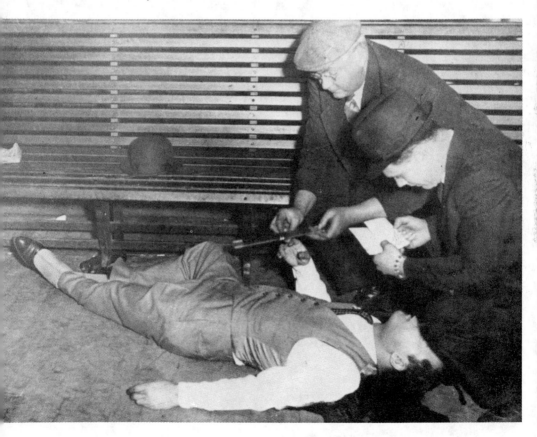

John Scalise.   Albert Anselmi.   Joe "Hop Toad" Giunta.

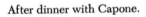

After dinner with Capone.

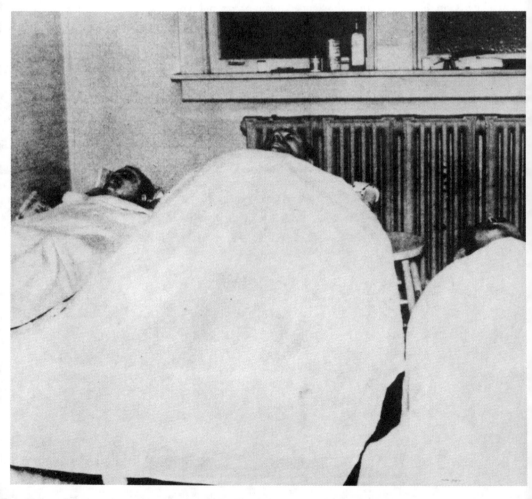

physical condition is such that it would be dangerous for him to
leave the mild climate of southern Florida and go to the City of
Chicago, state of Illinois, and that to do so would, in the professional opinion of affiant, imperil the safety of the said Capone,
and that there would be a very grave risk of a collapse which might
result in his death from a recurrent pneumonia. . . .

Armed with this affidavit, Capone's lawyers requested Federal
Judge James H. Wilkerson to postpone the hearing for forty days.
The judge allowed them only a week. The U.S. attorney had meanwhile discovered that during the time Capone was supposedly in-
capacitated he spent the better part of a morning in the Dade County
solicitor's office, attended the races at Hialeah and the Sharkey-
Stribling fight in Flamingo Park, flew to Bimini, and sailed to Nas-
sau. Charged with contempt of court, he was left at liberty, pending trial, under a $5,000 bond.

The state was as yet no more prepared to try Scalise and Anselmi
for the St. Valentine's Day massacre than they had been to try
McGurn. But the need never arose. According to the account generally accepted,* Capone learned of their disloyalty from Frankie
Rio. With Giunta installed as president of the Unione Siciliane and
Scalise and Anselmi as his vice executives, they were talking and
acting as if they considered Capone superfluous. "I'm the big shot
now," Scalise had been heard to brag. Rumor further attributed to
the trio a move to wrest from Capone control of both bootlegging
and business rackets.

At first Capone would not believe it, not of the men he had refused to sacrifice to Hymie Weiss' vengeance, to whose defense in
the Olson-Walsh murder trials he had contributed so generously. To
convince him, Rio contrived a test.

Early in May Capone invited the Sicilians to dinner at the Hawthorne Inn. During the meal he and Rio pretended to quarrel. Rio
slapped him in the face and stalked out. The Sicilians took the bait.
The next day they approached Rio, full of sympathy. Capone, they
said, deserved a lesson. Rio agreed, cursing and uttering terrible
threats against his leader. At this Scalise disclosed that the Aiellos
had a standing offer of $50,000 for anybody who could get rid of

---

* By the underworld, by stool pigeons, by knowledgeable old cops like John Stege
and by Chicago's top crime reporters like Ray Brennan and Clem Lane.

Capone. Why not combine forces? For three days, at a lakeside hide-away, the four men explored ways and means. Then Rio reported to Capone.

The Sicilians' execution, following a banquet at the Hawthorne Inn, occurred on May 7. Their bodies were loaded into the back seat of their own car, which the driver abandoned near Hammond, Indiana. When the coroner examined the bodies, he found hardly a bone unbroken, hardly an area of flesh without bruises.

And so no one remained to stand trial for the St. Valentine's Day massacre.

Both Capone and Torrio attended the all-important conference held at the President Hotel in Atlantic City five months after the Cleveland meeting. Cutting across all the old ethnic and national divisions, there gathered around the table not only Italians and Sicilians, but also Jews, Irish and Slavs, more than thirty gangsters in all. From Chicago came Frank McErlane and Joe Saltis; the Capone-ites, Jake Guzik, Frank Nitti and Frank Rio; from Philadelphia, Max "Boo Boo" Hoff, Sam Lazar and Charles Schwartz; from New York, Frank Costello, Lucky Luciano and Arthur Flegenheimer, alias Dutch Schultz; from Atlantic City itself, the political boss and numbers racketeer, Enoch J. "Nucky" Johnson. . . .

The conference lasted three days from May 13 through 16, 1929. The main subjects of discussion were disarmament, peace and amalgamation on a nationwide scale. "I told them," Capone disclosed later, "there was business enough to make us all rich and it was time to stop all the killings and look on our business as other men look on theirs, as something to work at and forget when we go home at night. It wasn't an easy matter for men who had been fighting for years to agree on a peaceful business program. But we finally decided to forget the past and begin all over again and we drew up a written agreement and each man signed on the dotted line."

Under this agreement all gangs were to renounce assassination and the use of firearms and to join in a defensive, nonviolent alliance against overzealous police and their informers. The country was divided into spheres of influence. Small gangs were to disband and their individual members to accept the jurisdiction of a single territorial organization; Chicago's North and South Side gangs were to

merge under Capone's leadership; the Unione Siciliane was to re-
organize from top to bottom with a new national president. An
executive committee was formed to arbitrate all disputes and mete
out punishment for violations of the agreement. Torrio served as
chairman.

Bugs Moran did not attend the conference. With remnants of his
gang he was still seeking an opportunity to kill Capone. Also, as
Capone knew, a good many Chicago Sicilians had sworn to avenge
Scalise, Anselmi and Giunta. Thus threatened, physically and ner-
vously depleted, Capone adopted the same course as Torrio when the
North Siders were tracking him. He had himself jailed.

There was a detective on the Philadelphia police force, James
"Shooey" Malone, with whom Capone had been friendly ever since
they had met at the Hialeah racetrack the year before. As soon as
the conference ended on May 16, Capone telephoned a Philadelphia
ally, asking him to deliver a message to Malone. With Rio he then
drove to the city, arriving toward 7 P.M. They went to a movie on
Market Street. When they came out two hours later, Malone and
another detective, John Creedon, were waiting for them.

"You're Al Capone, aren't you?" said Malone for the record.

"My name's Al Brown," Capone replied. "Call me Capone if you
want to. Who are you?" The detectives flashed their badges. "Oh,
bulls, eh? All right, then here's my gun," and he handed over a .38-
caliber revolver, thereby establishing grounds on which to convict
him for carrying a concealed weapon. He prodded Rio, who likewise
surrendered a revolver. What greater loyalty could a bodyguard show
than to follow his master into prison?

The police magistrate before whom they were arraigned shortly
after midnight fixed bail at $35,000 each. They had only a few thou-
sand between them, and the two lawyers Capone had sent for, Bernard L. Lemisch and Cornelius Haggerty, Jr., accused the police of
railroading their clients into jail. But Capone was content.

Philadelphia's director of public safety, Major Lemuel B. Schofield, hailed the arrest as a triumph of police vigilance and proudly
accepted the felicitations that poured into his office. Burning with
curiosity, he had the two prisoners brought to him that very night.
Capone was subdued, polite, responsive, but Rio, who had begun to
chafe under restraint, shouted that he was being robbed of his rights.

"Listen, boy," Capone told him. "You're my friend, and you've been a faithful pal, but I'll do the talking." The bodyguard gave no more trouble.

"Did you know that assistant state's attorney who was knocked off a couple of years ago?" Schofield asked Capone.

"Yes," said Capone. "Little Mac was a fine fellow. He was a great friend of mine, always trying to help everybody. I was talking to him just before he was shot."

The conversation turned to the Atlantic City conference. The major lent an eager ear, and Capone poured bathos into it. "I'm tired of gang murders and gang shootings," he said. "I'm willing to live and let live. I have a wife and eleven-year-old kid, a boy, whom I idolize, and a beautiful home in Florida. If I could go there and forget it all, I'd be the happiest man in the world. It was with the idea of making peace amongst the gangsters that I spent the week in Atlantic City and got the word of each leader that there will be no more shooting."

"What are you doing now?" Schofield asked.

"I'm living on my money. I'm trying to retire."

"You should get out of the racket and forget it."

"I've been trying to, but I can't do it. Once you're in, you're always in. The parasites trail you, begging you for favors and dough. You fear death and worse than death; you fear the rats who would run to the cops, if you didn't constantly satisfy them with money."

"How can you have peace of mind?" Schofield wanted to know.

"Well, I'm like any other man. I've been in the racket long enough to realize that I must take the breaks, the fortunes of war. Three of my friends were killed in Chicago last week [Scalise, Anselmi and Giunta]. That certainly doesn't get you peace of mind. I haven't had peace of mind in years. Every minute I was in danger of death. Even on a peace errand you're taking a chance on the light suddenly going out. I have to hide from the rest of the racketeers, even to the point of concealing my identity under assumed names in hotels and elsewhere when I'm traveling. Why, when I went to Atlantic City, I registered under a fictitious name."

The deluded director of public safety announced afterward: "I had a most interesting discussion with Capone on the racket in the United States. He was in a reminiscent mood and seemed to be at the point where he was anxious to be at peace, not only with gangsters but the law. In a quiet, gentlemanly manner he told me he was on an errand of peace when Detectives Creedon and Malone grabbed him."

In the morning the chief of detectives confronted Capone. "You are charged with being a suspicious character and carrying concealed deadly weapons. What have you to say?"

Capone had nothing to say. He laughed. Had he ever been arrested before? Once, he allowed, in Joliet for the same offense, but he was not held. In fact, he had never seen the inside of a prison. What about New York? Wasn't he arrested in New York? "Yes, eighteen years ago. Pardon me, I'm a little twisted. I guess I'm not fully awake. I was arrested in New York about three or four years ago. I was picked up on suspicion of murder [Pegleg Lonergan], but I was discharged. I was also arrested in Olean, New York, on a disorderly charge. . . ."

In his Prairie Avenue home Capone's mother, an austere figure in black silk, intermingling a few words of broken English with Italian, presided over a living room full of puzzled, overwrought Italians. Her daughter Mafalda, who had just graduated from Lucy Flower High School at the age of eighteen, said: "Of course, Al would carry a gun. Would anyone expect him to walk the streets anywhere without protection?" Her black hair hung loose to her shoulders, and she wore an apple-green silk negligee, having gotten out of bed with a severe cold to help her mother entertain the sympathizers. "Probably the Philadelphia police and the judge, too, wanted some publicity. After it quiets down a little they will let him go, because they could not expect him to go unarmed."

Mama Teresa passed a tray laden with soft drinks and snacks. Mae Capone and Sonny, Mafalda explained, had gone to the Florida house for the winter, Matt was in his second year at Villanova, and Bert (Albert John) in a boys' prep school. "If people only know Al as I know him," she said, "they wouldn't say the things about him they do. I adore him. And he's mother's life. He's so very good, so kind to us. People who only know him from newspaper stories will never realize the real man he is."

With his parting words to Major Schofield Capone had asked him to notify Mae Capone at once "in case I get a bad break." He got a very bad break. Taken before Judge John E. Walsh in the criminal division of the Municipal Court, he pleaded guilty, assuming he would draw a light sentence, perhaps three months, time enough to plan his next moves in safety, while his associates reduced the dangers threatening him on the outside through diplomacy or warfare. Judge Walsh imposed the maximum sentence of one year. As Capone, incredulous, was led off with the hapless Rio to Philadelphia's Holmesburg County Prison, he tore a diamond ring from his finger and handed it to Attorney Lemisch, instructing him to forward it to his brother Ralph. Between arrest and imprisonment barely sixteen hours had elapsed.

Holmesburg, with more than 1,700 prisoners jammed into cell blocks built to hold 600, was one of the country's worst jails. A few weeks before Capone entered it, the prisoners, rioting in protest against the foul food and brutal guards, set fire to their mattresses. The word went out from Chicago that a $50,000 fee awaited any lawyer able to procure Capone's release. None succeeded. Nor did an attempt to bribe the district attorney of Philadelphia, John Monoghan, with an offer of $50,000. But in August Capone was transferred to the city's larger and better-equipped Eastern Penitentiary. There Warden Herbert B. Smith made him more comfortable, giving him a cell to himself and letting him furnish it with rugs, pictures, a chest of drawers, desk, bookshelf, lamps and a $500 radio console. As his work assignment, he drew the untiring one of library file clerk. For ordinary inmates visiting hours were limited to Sundays, but Capone's friends and family could come any day. From the warden's office he was allowed to telephone whomever he chose, and he spoke often to his lawyers, his underworld colleagues and various politicians, including Pennsylvania Congressman Benjamin M. Golder. He continued to direct his organization chiefly through Jake Guzik and Ralph Capone, with whom he remained in constant communication.

The reporters Capone was willing to talk to had little difficulty getting to him either and they filled column after column with the minutiae of his daily existence. CAPONE GAINS ELEVEN POUNDS . . . CAPONE DOESN'T GO TO CHURCH ON SUNDAYS . . . CAPONE PICKS CUBS TO WIN 1930 FLAG . . . CAPONE READS LIFE OF NAPOLEON. . . . Concerning Napoleon, the following sentiments were ascribed to him: "I'll have to hand it to Napoleon as the world's greatest racketeer, but I could have wised him up on some things. The trouble with that guy was he got the swelled head. He overplayed his hand and they made a bum out of him. He should have had sense enough after that Elba jolt to kiss himself out of the game. But he was just like the rest of us. He didn't know when to quit and had to get back in the racket. He simply put himself on the spot. That made it easy for the other gangs to take him and they were no dumbbells. If he had lived in Chicago, it would have been a sawed-off shotgun Waterloo for him. He didn't wind up in a ditch as a coroner's case, but they took him for a one-way ride to St. Helena, which was about as tough a break."

His views on a wide range of weighty issues were accorded equally serious attention. The modern woman, for example. "The trouble with women today is their excitement over too many things outside the home. A woman's home and her children are her real happiness. If she would stay there, the world would have less to worry about the modern woman."

Though he looked forward ardently to his wife's visits, he could not, he told one interviewer, bear to have his son see him in prison. "My boy thinks I'm in Europe. Whenever he sees a picture of a big boat, he asks his mother if it's bringing Daddy home."

He bought $1,000 worth of arts and crafts produced by his fellow prisoners and mailed them to friends as Christmas gifts. He donated $1,200 to a foundering Philadelphia orphanage. Such Samaritan deeds, described at length by the press, aroused a good deal of sympathy for Capone. A civil engineer from Chicago, a total stranger to him, coming to Philadelphia on business, obtained permission to visit him, clasped his hand and told him, "Al, we're with you."

Shortly after entering Eastern Penitentiary, Capone had to have his tonsils out. The surgeon who performed the operation, Dr. Herbert M. Goddard of the Pennsylvania State Board of Prison Inspectors, could scarcely contain the admiration he came to feel for his patient. "In my seven years' experience I have never seen a prisoner so kind, so cheery and accommodating," he declared in a public eulogy delivered toward the end of Capone's term. "He does his work faithfully and with a high degree of intelligence. He has brains. He would have made good anywhere, at anything. He has been an ideal prisoner. I cannot estimate the money he has given away. Of course, we can't inquire where he gets it. He's in the racket. He admits it. But you can't tell me he's all bad after I've seen him many times a week for ten months. . . ."

Good behavior won Capone a reduction of his sentence by two months, and it was announced that he would leave the prison on March 17, 1930. Warden Smith's solicitude followed him into freedom. With the complicity of the Philadelphia police and the governor of the state, John S. Fisher, he fooled the reporters, cameramen and rubberneckers waiting outside the prison, as well as any assassins who might be gunning for him. The police aided the deception by roping off a clearing before the main gate and patrolling all the approaches to the prison. Motorcycle officers stood beside their machines, gripping the handlebars as if to take off at any moment as escorts. On a nearby landing field a small private plane waited to fly Capone north, or so the pilot said. And from Warden Smith's office there issued periodic communiqués: Capone was eating scrambled eggs for breakfast . . . he was restless . . . the commutation papers requiring the governor's signature were expected to arrive momentarily from Harrisburg. . . .

Actually, Capone was long gone. The parole board had received the papers several days before. On the sixteenth Capone had been smuggled in the warden's car to the town of Graterford, about 20 miles northwest of Philadelphia, and lodged there pending the legal hour of release at 4 P.M. of the seventeenth. Some of his own men had driven to Graterford to pick him up. At 8 P.M., when he was 200 miles or so farther along on his way back to Chicago, Warden Smith emerged from the prison, smirking, and announced: "We stuck one in your eye. The big guy's gone."

Nobody was more incensed than the *Tribune*'s Jake Lingle, who could normally see Capone any time he wanted to. He had twice interviewed him during his imprisonment. He considered himself a personal friend. He had been a guest several times at the Palm Island house. He wore one of the diamond belt buckles Capone gave to people he particularly liked. Still fuming when he got back to Chicago, he telephoned Ralph Capone at the Prairie Avenue house. The wire had been tapped by a special Prohibition task force from the Department of Justice and he was heard to inquire: "Where's Al? I've been looking all over for him, and nobody seems to know where he is."

"I don't know where he is either, Jake," Ralph lied. "I haven't heard a word from him since he got out."

"Jesus, Ralph, this makes it very bad for me. I'm supposed to have my finger on these things. It makes it very embarrassing with my paper. Now get this, I want you to call me the minute you hear from him. Tell him I want to see him right away."

Ralph promised. Lingle called again an hour later. Ralph pretended he still had no word. "Listen, you guys ain't giving me the runaround, are you?" Lingle said. "Just remember, I wouldn't do that if I was you."

"Now, Jake, you know I wouldn't do that. It's just that I haven't heard from Al. What else can I tell you?"

"Okay, okay. Just remember to tell him I want to talk to him right away."

The leader of the federal agents, Eliot Ness, wondered what power enabled a lowly legman to order a Capone around.

The thick oak door of the Prairie Avenue house opened a crack to a reporter's ring, and Ralph Capone's nine-year-old son peered out.

"Where's Grandma?" the reporter asked.

"Out," said the boy.

The reporter rattled a paper bag full of candy, and the door opened a little wider. "Is Grandma going to have a special kind of spaghetti for Uncle Al's homecoming?"

"Yeah, walnut-flavored, prob'ly— Say, I won't tell you anything. Another paper sent some people out here to play marbles with me. I won ninety cents, and I didn't tell them a thing." The door closed.

Capone did not venture near South Prairie Avenue for four days. Captain Stege, having proclaimed his determination to arrest him on sight and run him out of town, though he had no legal grounds for doing either, had set a watch of twenty-five policemen around the home. Capone spent his first night holed up in a Cicero hotel, the Western, rampaging drunk. In the early morning of the eighteenth the wiretappers intercepted a call from an unidentifiable member of the gang to Ralph Capone. "Listen, Ralph," said the caller, "we're up in Room 718 in the Western and Al is getting out of hand. He's in terrible shape. Will you come up, please? You're the only one who can handle him when he gets like this. We've sent for a lot of towels."

"I'll be up a little later," Ralph promised. "Just take care of things the best you can right now."

When calm and sober, Capone crossed the street to his old headquarters in the Hawthorne Inn and for the next three days reviewed his financial situation with Jake Guzik. The figures gave them no cause for rejoicing. The Great Depression, now in its fifth month, was sharply reducing their profits. The carefree spenders of the Jazz Age had little money left to spare for booze, gambling and girls. Capone's 1929 income—as much of it as Internal Revenue could trace, which is to say, a minute fraction of the actual total—came to slightly over $100,000, not exactly deprivation, but still down 50 percent from the 1928 IRS figure.

There were other tribulations. The Ness team, driving a 10-ton truck with a flat bed to support scaling ladders and a reinforced steel bumper, had so far battered down the doors of nineteen Capone distilleries and six breweries, seized or destroyed more than $1,000,-000 worth of trucks, equipment, beer and whiskey. The idea for the special task force had originated with the Chicago Association of Commerce Sub-Committee for the Prevention and Punishment of Crime, consisting of six business leaders. When the chairman, Colonel Robert Isham Randolph, declined to name his five colleagues lest he endanger their lives, the press dubbed them "the Secret Six." Along with the Chicago Crime Commission, founded in 1919, it constituted the most tenacious private force combating what Randolph described as "the most corrupt and degenerate municipal administration that ever cursed a city—a politico-criminal alliance formed between a civil administration and a gun-covered underworld for the exploitation of the citizenry." In April, 1923, the Crime Commission published its first list of "persons who are constantly in conflict with the law," twenty-eight of them, to whom Frank Loesch gave the name that caught the popular fancy—"Public Enemies." "Alphonse Capone, alias Scarface Capone, alias Al Brown" headed the list. Another of his bodyguards, Tony "Mops" Volpe, placed second and Ralph Capone third.*

On Capone's fourth day of freedom he breezed into the detective bureau, having been apprized of his rights by his lawyer, Thomas

* The others: (4) Frank Rio, alias Frank Kline, alias Frank Gline (5) Jack "Machine Gun" McGurn (6) James Belcastro (7) Rocco Fanelli (8) Lawrence "Dago Lawrence" Mangano (9) Jack Zuta (10) Jake Guzik (11) Frank Diamond (12) George "Bugs" Moran (13) Joe Aiello (14) Edward "Spike" O'Donnell (15) Joe "Polock Joe" Saltis (16) Frank McErlane (17) Vincent McErlane (18) William Niemoth (19) Danny Stanton (20) Myles O'Donnell (21) Frank Lake (22) Terry Druggan (23) William "Klondike" O'Donnell (24) George "Red" Barker (25) William "Three-Fingered Jack" White (26) Joseph "Peppy" Genero (27) Leo Mongoven (28) James "Fur" Sammons.

Nash, who accompanied him there. "You were looking for me, I believe," he said to Captain Stege.

"You're no better than any other hoodlum," replied Stege, discomposed by the unexpected surrender. "You're not wanted in Chicago, and we don't intend to let you live here. You'll be arrested as often as you show yourself to any of our detectives."

Stege, of course, had no more legal authority to order such arrests than he had to throw a cordon around Capone's home. There were no warrants outstanding against him, no county indictments. But the law in its frustration tended to treat gangsters with scant regard for constitutional guarantees.

Challenged by Nash to specify the complaint, Stege lamely admitted that he held no warrant for Capone. But perhaps the state or the government would wish to press charges. A detective escorted Capone first to U.S. Attorney George Q. Johnson's office in the Federal Building, then to State's Attorney Swanson's office in the Criminal Courts Building. Neither prosecutor was prepared as yet to proceed against him on any grounds and they dismissed him. Assistant State's Attorney Harry Ditchburne, however, followed him back to Stege's office. "Al," he asked, "what do you know about the Valentine Day massacre?"

"I was in Florida then," Capone replied.

"Yes," Stege interposed, "and you were in Florida when Frank Yale was murdered."

"I get blamed for everything that goes on here, but I had nothing to do with any of the things you talk about."

"Perhaps you personally don't commit the murders," said Ditchburne, "but we're not far wrong in assuming your gang is responsible."

"I'm not responsible for what others do."

"You're not a good citizen. If you were walking along the street with your brother and he was killed, you wouldn't come here and tell us who killed him."

"Well, put yourself in my place and see what you'd do."

"There used to be a time when we wouldn't have a hundred murders in ten years, but since you gangsters have been at war, we've had three hundred murders a year." This was an exaggeration. The total number of gang murders since 1920 came to about 500.

Stege: "That's why we're driving you out of town."

"You, Mr. Ditchburne, as a lawyer, know the police can't do that," said Nash.

"I'm not here to tell the police what not to do," the prosecutor retorted. "I'm here to advise them what to do. I'm not interested in protecting Capone. If he feels that he's being arrested wrongfully, he has his remedy. He can sue for false arrest."

"Go as far as you like in suing me," said Stege.

"I don't want to sue anybody," said Capone. "All I want is not to be arrested if I come downtown."

"You're out of luck," Stege told him. "Your day is done. How soon are you getting out of town?"

"I want to go to Florida some time next week. I don't know when I have to go to the federal court for trial on the contempt charge."

"I've given you notice, and you can go because no one wants to put a complaint against you today. But the next time you go into the lockup and you go to court next morning." He turned to Nash. "You'd better advise him to get out of Chicago."

"Lenin and Trotsky rebelled at that kind of treatment," the lawyer observed darkly.

"I hope Capone goes to Russia," was Stege's parting shot.

As Capone passed the press corps waiting outside the detective bureau, he remarked, chuckling, "I guess nobody wants me," and headed for the Lexington.

To the first reporter who interviewed him at the hotel, the *Tribune*'s Genevieve Forbes Herrick, he delivered a tirade of self-justification. Capone probably never considered himself a criminal. His practices were, after all, only slightly rougher than those then prevalent among respectable big businessmen, such as the stock manipulators who bilked the public of millions or the industrialists who hired thugs to beat up labor organizers. . . .

"I never had a number," he told Miss Herrick, "until they picked me up in the City of Brotherly Love for carrying a gun and gave me a year, not for carrying a gun, but because my name was Capone. I'd never been indicted before [glossing over the pending federal indictment for contempt of court]. Why should I be? All I ever did was sell beer and whiskey to our best people. All I ever did was supply a demand that was pretty popular. Why, the very guys that make my trade good are the ones that yell the loudest about me. Some of our best judges use the stuff. They talk about me not being on the legitimate. Why, lady, nobody's on the legit. You know that and so do they. Your brother or your father gets in a jam. What do you do? Do you sit back and let him go over the road, without trying to help him? You'd be a yellow dog if you did. Nobody's really on the legit, when it comes down to cases, you know that. Whatever I did in jail, everybody was watching to see that Al Capone didn't get any favors. When I'd been there six months, I came up for parole. I had a writ of relief, they call it, before the Supreme Court. It's even more important than a writ of habeas corpus. The judge is supposed to allow it or deny it, with reasons for what he does. If I'd been plain John Smith from Oshkosh, he'd have allowed it. All I did, you know, lady, was carry a gun. But because my name was Capone from Chicago, he wouldn't pay any attention to it. Yes, sir, there's a lot of grief attached to this limelight. Say, if I was just plain Izzy Polatsky, living in Chicago, I'd not stand in the gutter trying to get a peep at Al Capone. I'd attend to my business and let him attend to his. No use making a laughing stock of the city. You notice I didn't come in with a brass band. Neither did I come in with all those bodyguards the papers talked about. One man, the driver of my car. I'm not afraid of anybody."

He pressed a buzzer, summoning an aide. "Please ask my wife and sister to come here." Presently, Mae Capone and Mafalda, who were sharing the suite for a few days, entered and chatted awhile with the reporter. When they had retired, Capone asked her: "Did you notice my wife's hair?" Miss Herrick murmured a compliment. "No, I mean the streaks of gray. She's only 28 [she was actually thirty-one, two years older than her husband] and she's got gray hair just worrying over things here in Chicago. . . . I've been blamed for crimes that happened as far back as the Chicago fire. . . ."

"The public has one idea of my husband," Mae Capone said many years later, when rejecting a publisher's offer of $50,000 for the story of her life with Capone, though she sorely needed money at the time. "I have another. I will treasure my memory and I will always love him."

19

Case Jacket SI-7085-F

PRESIDENT Hoover liked to start his day with mild exercise. Before breakfast he would meet with members of his Cabinet on the White House lawn by the magnolia tree Andrew Jackson had planted in memory of his wife and, while discussing affairs of state, toss a medicine ball. Among Hoover's pressing concerns during the early weeks of his administration was Al Capone. "Have you," he would ask his Secretary of the Treasury, Andrew Mellon, as he heaved the 15-pound ball at him, "have you—*thwunk*—got that fellow—*thwunk*—Capone yet?" And as the exercise period ended: "Remember—*thwunk*—I want that man Capone in jail—*thwunk!*"

It was Colonel Frank Knox, publisher of the Chicago *Daily News,* who, despairing of any decisive move against Capone by either city or state authorities, had led a deputation to the White House to ask the President to intervene. The two major aspects of Capone's activities that fell within the federal purview were bootlegging and income-tax evasion. He had never filed a return in his entire life. Following Knox's appeal, a two-pronged attack was launched, the one by Eliot Ness and his Department of Justice raiders to wreck Capone financially, the other by Internal Revenue agents to send him to prison.

Why a special Prohibition detail? Because few civil servants had ever proved more venal than the untrained, ill-paid recruits of the original Prohibition Unit during its first seven years under the Treasury Department. In 1928 the unit was transferred to Justice, and when that department appointed Ness, a twenty-six-year-old University of Chicago graduate, to run the special detail, he searched the personnel records for agents with, as he later put it, "no Achilles' heel in their make-ups." He finally selected nine, all under thirty and variously skilled in marksmanship, truck driving and wiretapping. Many years after, in a book and television series both entitled *The Untouchables,* a sobriquet purportedly bestowed by the underworld because the Ness group could be neither bought nor scared off, their achievements were wildly melodramatized. They did undoubtedly cause Capone considerable financial loss. They did accumulate enough evidence to indict him and many of his aides for conspiracy to violate the Volstead Act. They did not, however, as Ness claimed, either dry up Chicago, with its 20,000-odd places where one could buy a drink, or destroy Capone. Ness loved personal publicity. He kept the press informed of his battle plans and often, when he besieged a Capone brewery, cameramen would arrive to record the scene. This severely limited the raiders' effectiveness. The revenue agents, on the other hand, operated in such secrecy and anonymity that one of them was able to infiltrate the Capone organization in the guise of a gangster.

President Hoover did not actually initiate the investigation of Capone's tax delinquencies, but he expedited it. As early as 1927, Elmer L. Irey, the chief of Internal Revenue's Enforcement Branch, was given a powerful weapon to wield against gangsters. That year the Supreme Court handed down its decision in the case on appeal of a bootlegger named Manley Sullivan, who had filed no tax return on the grounds that income from illegal transactions was not taxable and, moreover, that to declare such income would be self-incriminatory within the meaning of the Fifth Amendment. The Supreme Court ruled against him, finding no reason "why the fact that a business is unlawful should exempt it from paying taxes that if lawful it would have to pay." As for self-incrimination, "It would be an extreme if not extravagant application of the Fifth Amendment to say that it authorized a man to refuse to state the amount of his income because it had been made in crime."

Irey chose the Chicago gang lords against whom to test the new legal weapon. His first quarries were Terry Druggan, Frank Lake and their Standard Beverage Corporation. For unpaid taxes for the years 1922 through 1924 Internal Revenue had already assessed them $615,917.83. They had disregarded demands for payment until the Supreme Court ruling. They then made an offer in compromise totaling $50,000, submitting with it a statement of their assets. The bureau rejected the offer. Instead Irey set a group of his special agents, headed by Frank J. Wilson, to investigating the statement. A former Buffalo realtor, taciturn and poker-faced, chain-smoking nickel cigars, Wilson was said to "sweat ice water." He later became chief of the U.S. Secret Service. In 1927 he married a girl he met in a Washington dancing class, Judith Barbaux, the daughter of a Defense Department employee. Transferred temporarily to Chicago, Wilson and his colleagues uncovered concealed assets of Druggan and Lake that included an apartment house, five racehorses, Cadillacs and Rolls-Royces, a farm and assorted real estate. In March, 1928, they were indicted for failing to file returns and in November, 1929, for falsifying their statement of assets. They pleaded guilty. Legal maneuvering delayed their sentences until 1932, when Federal Judge Wilkerson sent them to Leavenworth, Druggan for two and a half years, Lake for eighteen months. Shortly after the first indictment, Frank Wilson was promoted to agent in charge of the Baltimore tax district.

Irey next turned his attention to Ralph Capone. He viewed the case his special agents developed as a dress rehearsal for the major battle against brother Al. Ralph was less shrewd, less prudent than Al, and through petty greed he made the investigators' task relatively easy. In practice Internal Revenue did not prosecute tax delinquents if they voluntarily paid what they owed before investigation began. There was in the Chicago division a zealous young agent, Eddie Waters, who assigned himself the mission of lecturing gangsters, whenever he could find them, on the folly of holding out against the government. He kept after Ralph Capone for three years until finally, in 1926, Ralph weakened. He still resisted the mental labor of filling out the forms, however. Waters offered to do it for him, if he would furnish the figures. So Ralph ventured a modest estimate of $70,000 grossed between 1922 and 1925. Waters duly filled out the forms in quadruplicate, acknowledging a tax obligation of $4,065.75 and Ralph signed it. That was all Ralph did. Though he had actually made hundreds of thousands, he could not bring himself to part with the trifling sum.

The following January, Internal Revenue obtained warrants of distraint empowering it to seize his property. Guided by cupidity, Ralph hastened to the tax collector and pleaded poverty. But, he added, if the government would accept $1,000 in full settlement, he would borrow the money. "My client," his lawyer explained, "has sustained considerable loss as the result of the sickness and death of his race horses throughout the past year. He has also lost a great deal gambling. All he has left is a half-interest in two race horses and at the present time he is using up practically all his income trying to get them into shape."

Irey had been hoping for some such clumsy lie. He instructed the Chicago agent in charge, Arthur P. Madden, to prove it so. Madden assigned to the task Archie Martin, a deceptively raffish-looking figure who had built up an encyclopedic knowledge of the enterprises the Capone syndicate owned or controlled, and Nels E. Tessem, a wispy little calculating wizard of Swedish descent. When Ralph realized he was under investigation, he raised his offer of settlement to $2,500; then, when the government rejected it, he agreed to pay the full amount. It was too late.

Shortly before the government rebuffed Ralph, the local police had raided the Subway, one of the Capone syndicate's Cicero gambling houses. According to the records they carried away and turned over to the special agents, the apparent owner was one Oliver Ellis. To save himself from an income-tax audit if he persisted in that fiction, Ellis revealed to Martin the existence of an account he kept under an alias in Cicero's Pinkert State Bank. Among the canceled checks in that account, which Tessem then began to analyze, was one for $3,200 drawn to a James Carroll. Carroll, too, Tessem learned, once carried an account in the Pinkert State Bank, but had long since closed it. As for Carroll's identity, Ellis dared not disclose it, and the bank officers insisted they knew nothing about Carroll. Tessem turned the bank inside out. He examined thousands of clearance sheets before he uncovered a clue: Carroll opened his account with a sum identical to that in the account of a James Carter when *it* was closed. The Carter account, furthermore, contained the same sum at the start as did the account of a James Costello the day *it* was closed. Tessem's lynx eyes detected another curious similarity among the different accounts. Many of the amounts deposited were divisible by 55. The current wholesale price of beer was $55 a barrel.

The series of apparently related bank accounts continued with those of a Harry Roberts, a Harry White, back finally to an account closed on October 27, 1925, and the balance transferred to Harry White. The name of that original depositor was Ralph Capone. Carroll, Carter, Costello, Roberts, White—Tessem now knew them all to be aliases under which Ralph concealed his assets. The day he pleaded poverty, for example, the account of "James Carter" totaled more than $25,000. All together, from 1925 to 1929, almost $8,000,-000 had passed through the series of accounts.

According to the bank officers, after Ralph Capone opened the account in his own name in 1925, he never again crossed the threshold. A messenger boy always brought the money for deposit, accompanied by a short, fat, olive-skinned man. The description of the latter sugguested Ralph's bodyguard, Tony Arresso. From rogues' gallery photographs the bank officers confirmed this. Martin and Tessem then showed some of the canceled checks that had been drawn against the five accounts to the payees—a jeweler, various salesmen, saloonkeepers. . . . Enough of them identified Ralph Capone as the man who wrote out the checks to convince the October, 1929, grand jury of his guilt, and it returned seven indictments against him. The seventh invoked a rarely used Lincolnian statute enacted to prosecute Civil War profiteers who "cheat, swindle or defraud the Government." On October 8, as Ralph moved toward a front row seat at a Chicago prizefight, Special Agent Clarence Converse arrested him. He was released the next day in $35,000 bail, and to the syndicate's stable of lawyers fell the task of delaying trial.

It took place six months later before Judge Wilkerson. Ralph was convicted, fined $10,000, and sentenced to three years' imprisonment. "I don't understand this at all," he muttered and looked to his lawyers to save him on appeal.

Neither, at first, did Al Capone understand. It was incomprehensible to him that after a decade of plundering and murdering with impunity, such a penalty could be incurred for merely withholding money owing the government. If his lawyers had ever told him about the Sullivan ruling, the knowledge had evidently failed to penetrate, for at dinner with some cronies one evening he was overheard to say: "The income-tax law is a lot of bunk. The government can't collect legal taxes from illegal money." And if his lawyers had advised him, as surely they must have, to pay up voluntarily before prosecution started, he had thus far chosen to ignore them. Ralph's indictment had shaken him, however, and after he came home from the Philadelphia prison, he retained a Washington tax lawyer, Lawrence P. Mattingly.

The Pinkert State Bank proved to be a mother lode of evidence against other tax-delinquent Caponeites. Between 1927 and 1929 it had issued almost $250,000 worth of cashier's checks to "J. V. Dunbar." The chief teller was evasive when Tessem asked him to describe Dunbar (who, it developed later, used to tip him $15 a week). Tessem found a more helpful witness in a former Pinkert teller. Dunbar's real name, he revealed, was Fred Ries. A former cashier for the Ship and other Capone gambling houses, he would bring the money with which he bought the checks in gunny sacks. The teller added a curious detail. Ries had a horror of insects. Once when a cockroach crawled out of a gunnysack full of bills, he turned ashen.

From one of his informers inside the Capone gang Wilson learned that Ries had moved to St. Louis, and he drove there with Tessem. On the chance that the cashier was receiving mail under his real name, they enlisted the aid of the post office inspectors. Shortly, a special delivery letter arrived for Ries and the agents followed the postman to its destination. Ries was reading the letter when they rang his doorbell. It came from Jake Guzik's brother-in-law, Louis Lipschutz, and it indicated that Guzik had been paying Ries to lie low first in Miami, then in St. Louis. Guzik now wanted him to go to Mexico. As the agents drove him back to Illinois, Ries swore he had never heard of the Pinkert bank or ever gone near Cicero. Remembering what the teller had told him about Ries' entomophobia, Wilson had him committed as a material witness to a scruffy little jail in Danville, 100 miles south of Chicago, likely to be swarming with insect life. Ries held out for four days. "The bedbugs are eating me alive!" he cried when he saw Wilson again. "I'll explain those cashier's checks. But for God's sake get me away from these bugs!"

Largely on the strength of Ries' testimony a grand jury, convening in the dead of night to hear it, indicted Guzik on October 3. It was not that, like Capone, he had filed no tax returns at all, but that the income he did report for the preceding three years fell about $980,000 short of his actual net.

"Who was your boss?" the prosecutor asked Ries at the trial that began on November 12.

"Jack [as some people also called him] Guzik was my immediate boss," he replied.

"Were there others?"

"Al Capone, Ralph Capone and Frank Nitti."

"What was the average net profit of a gambling house?"

"About $25,000 to $30,000, when business was good."

"Did you ever know of the house to lose money?"

"No."

"What did you do with the profits?"

"I bought cashier's checks and gave them to Bobbie Barton, Jack's chauffeur, as I had been told to do."

The prosecutor produced $144,000 worth of those checks, endorsed by Guzik. Convicted on November 18, he drew a fine of $17,500 and a five-year penitentiary sentence.

The next important Caponeite indicted by the federal grand jury was Frank Nitti. On December 20 he pleaded guilty to evading $158,-823 in taxes. His sentence was a $10,000 fine and an eighteen-month prison term.

Wilson's concern was now to keep Ries alive for future use. The government made no provision for protecting witnesses before trial. So the Silent Six intervened. They put up $10,000, enabling Ries to live in South America until needed, guarded by a federal agent.

The first entries under SI (Special Investigation) -7085-F, the case jacket number assigned to Al Capone himself, antedated all these investigations. As early as the fall of 1928 Special Agent Charles W. Clarke of the Miami office was writing to Irey:

> . . . I have completely checked the public records and taken full information therefrom regarding the purchase of [the Palm Island home]. . . .
>
> I have been able to secure from the Miami Beach Bank and Trust Company (from a detailed check of their "remittance sheets") a list of all moneys received by Capone which passed through that bank. . . . This information was obtained through leads furnished by another bank who happened to notice one item which passed the Miami Beach Bank and Trust Company. The informing bank stated that the Beach bank had come to them with a $1,500 Western Union draft payable to and endorsed by Capone and wanted large bills in it. The bank told the other bank to wash their own dirty linen and refused to have anything to do with the draft. With this lead, and after the Beach bank tried to steer me

clear of their books, I was able finally to get the information, which
was a long, tedious job of searching through thousands of clearance
items on out-of-town banks. . . .

It is believed that Parker Henderson will give me detailed information, but I am letting the Chief of Police handle him first
in order to feel out his state of mind and willingness to disclose
what he knows. . . .

Capone while here is a lavish spender.

Thus, by January, 1929, when Secretary of the Treasury Mellon,
fresh from tossing a medicine ball, transmitted to Irey the Presidential directive concerning Capone, the gang leader had been under
investigation for several months. Recalling Frank Wilson from Baltimore, Irey reassigned him to Chicago with a free hand to choose any
agents he wanted as assistants. He asked for Nels Tessem, William
Hodgins, Clarence Converse, James N. Sullivan (of the New Haven
office) and Michael F. Malone. Of Malone—Mysterious Mike Malone, his colleagues called him—Wilson wrote almost four decades
later:

> I thought then, and still think, [he] was the greatest natural
> undercover worker the Service has ever had. Five feet, eight inches
> tall, a barrelchested, powerful two hundred pounds, with jet black
> hair, sharp brown eyes underscored with heavy dark circles and a
> brilliant, friendly smile, Mike could easily pass for Italian, Jew,
> Greek or whomever the occasion demanded. He was actually "black
> Irish" from Jersey City. During World War One he had been in an
> airplane crash, then married the nurse who attended him. They
> had one child, a little girl, who was killed by a truck at the age of
> three. After that, Mike and his wife drifted apart. He went into
> undercover work for the government. And he seemed to lose in-
> terest in everything else. It became his total life.

The challenge confronting Wilson was to find Capone's gross income over $5,000 (the then standard exemption) for years in which
he filed no return, and a formidable challenge it was since Capone,
unlike his brother Ralph, never maintained a bank account or acquired property under his own name, endorsed no checks, signed no
receipts, and paid cash for everything. To trap taxpayers who concealed income, Internal Revenue had developed two methods of in-
direct proof based on circumstantial evidence, the first involving
their "net worth," the second their "net expenditure." According to

the first method, the taxpayer's scale of living and any outward indications of wealth were analyzed. If commensurate with an income of only a few thousand dollars, Internal Revenue assumed that he had increased his net worth by an unreported amount. This gain it then declared taxable. According to the second method, the investigators applied the same yardstick to the taxpayer's running expenses aside from his accumulated assets. In Capone's case they adopted both methods.

Searching Chicago and Miami for shops, real estate agents, hotels, establishments of any kind with which Capone might have dealt, they compiled a partial list of his outlay for goods and services during the years 1926–29, together with evaluations of his fixed possessions. From two Chicago furniture companies they learned that he ordered $26,-000 worth of chairs, sofas, tables, beds and rugs for his Prairie Avenue and Palm Island houses and his Hotel Lexington headquarters. Two Chicago jewelers sold him $20,000 worth of silverware, a gold-plated dinner service and personal ornaments, including thirty diamond belt buckles. His custom-made suits with the extra strong pistol pockets, his silk monogrammed shirts, shorts, undershirts, pajamas and handkerchiefs, his detachable stiff collars and flannel winter underwear—most of it from Marshall Field & Company—came to about $7,000. For Dan Serritella he once bought ten Marshall Field suits at $135 each. His Chicago hotel bills ran between $1,200 and $1,500 a week. The night of the Dempsey-Tunney fight he gave a party that cost $3,000. His telephone bills totaled $39,000. He traded in a 1924 McFarland town car, for which he had paid $5,500, against a new, more expensive model, and he also bought a $5,000 Lincoln limousine. Among the Miami purchases that Special Agent Clarke catalogued were draperies, bedspreads and upholstery ($3,225), linen, glassware and kitchen utensils ($800), meat and poultry ($20 to $50 a day), doctors' bills ($2,000). In addition to $40,000 for the Palm Island house, Capone spent $18,000 for two new docks, a boathouse and a second garage. All told the revenue detectives uncovered about $165,000 of taxable income.

But this did not satisfy Wilson. The sum was trivial in view of the millions that flowed to Capone from illicit sources. Furthermore, the legality of the net worth-net expenditure principles as a basis for criminal conviction had not yet been fully tested. (Nor was it until 1954 that the Supreme Court, reviewing four convictions for income-tax evasion, upheld it.) Ideally, to ensure the kind of prison sentence President Hoover wanted for Capone, Wilson needed evidence directly linking the gang leader to his breweries and distilleries, his gambling houses and brothels, evidence of ownership.

Special Agent Sullivan, borrowed from the New Haven office, undertook a study of the brothels. The local police customarily chose a Saturday night to raid them because it was the busiest night. During Sullivan's first months in Chicago a federal grand jury began investigating different phases of gangsterism, and before releasing the girls after a raid, the police would take them before a grand jury for questioning. None dared testify. It occurred to Sullivan, however, that a show of sympathy combined with payment might persuade some girl to talk to him privately. So on Saturday nights he would haunt the Federal Court Building, sizing up each girl as the police brought her in. Following a raid on the Harlem Inn, he took note of a bedraggled veteran in her fifties, at the end of her professional career, who called herself "Reigh Count" after the 1928 Kentucky Derby winner. He sensed a potential informer, and his intuition proved sound. For $50 a week, a fortune compared to her usual earnings, she went to work for him.

Meanwhile, the Hotel Lexington—the Fort, as it had come to be known—acquired a new guest. A black-haired foreigner with an Italian accent, wearing a white snap-brim hat, a checked overcoat and a purple shirt, he signed the register "Michael Lepito—Philadelphia." He was given Room 724, next to Phil D'Andrea. For hours every day Lepito sat in the lobby behind a newspaper, talking to nobody, looking at nobody. His main interest appeared to be gambling, for which no dearth of opportunity existed in the hotel, and he shot craps a good deal at sizable stakes. Capone's wary sentinels finally ran a check on the stranger. They intercepted his mail. Postmarked Philadelphia, it bristled with cryptic underworld lingo. They searched his room. His noisy wardrobe bore the labels of Wanamaker's department store in Philadelphia. One day a Caponeite named Michael Speringa approached Lepito and bluntly asked him his business. "Keeping quiet," he said, by which Speringa understood him to be a fugitive outlaw. A few days later Speringa stood him a drink, and a few days after that, while returning his hospitality, Lepito confided that the Philadelphia police wanted him for burglary. The gang liked Lepito's style, and they befriended him. They let him join their poker game. He ate with them at the New Florence Restaurant around the corner. Whenever he found himself alone and unobserved, Mike Malone (for it was none other) telephoned Frank Wilson.

Malone and Sullivan between them fed Wilson invaluable background material. When Capone gave a birthday party at the Lexington for Frank Nitti, he invited Lepito-Malone, who was thus afforded a close look at the gang in its most unguarded mood. From Reigh Count, Sullivan obtained a detailed picture of prostitution under Capone management. The two agents also made important contributions to the tax cases against Nitti and Guzik. But hard evidence directly relating Capone to the sources of his income continued to elude them.

Wilson, who throughout the investigation shared a room at the Sheridan Plaza Hotel with his wife and worked out of an office in the Federal Court Building, fared no better. He visited scores of banks and credit agencies, looking for records of any financial transactions involving Capone. Month after month he tramped the South Side and Cicero, eyes and ears open for the faintest sign of Capone ownership, of how money was channeled from speakeasy or gambling dive into his pockets. More than a year passed.

"Unusual difficulties were encountered," he wrote later in a summary memorandum to Irey, "because all important witnesses were either hostile to the government and ready to give perjured testimony in order to protect the leaders of their organization or they were so filled with fear of the Capone organization . . . that they evaded, lied, left town and did all in their power to prevent the Government using them as witnesses. . . . In order to locate them and serve them with subpoenas it was necessary to pick them up on the streets near the Capone headquarters at the Lexington Hotel, at Cicero hotels and at nightclubs, also through various subterfuges. Considerable work in locating witnesses was performed at night in and around the hang-outs of the Capone organization by Special Agents Tessem, Malone, Converse and Sullivan and the agents were facing danger in the event their identity was discovered by the gangsters."

In April Capone's tax lawyer, Mattingly, telephoned Wilson to assure him that his client wished to clear up any indebtedness and would furnish information about his business activities. "Bring him in," said Wilson. "I want to talk to him." They came on the seventeenth, leaving a brace of bodyguards standing outside the building. Capone wore a double-breasted blue serge suit, black shoes tipped with white and his customary complement of bejeweled ring, belt buckle and watch chain. In addition to Wilson, there were present Ralph Herrick, the tax agent in charge of the Chicago enforcement unit, William Hodgins and a stenographer. "Glad to see you, Mr. Capone," said Wilson. Capone held out his hand, but Wilson pretended not to notice it. Lifting a silk handkerchief out of his breast pocket, Capone dabbed at a corner of his mouth, and Wilson caught a whiff of lily of the valley.

Herrick opened the interrogation. "I think it is only fair to say that any statements which are made here, which could be used against you, would probably be used."

"Insofar as Mr. Capone can answer any questions without admitting his liability to criminal action," said Mattingly, "he is here to cooperate with you and work with you."

Herrick turned to Capone. "What records have you of your income, Mr. Capone; do you keep any records?"

"No, I never did." His tone was low and respectful.

"Any checking accounts?"

"No, sir."

"How long, Mr. Capone, have you enjoyed a large income?"

"I never had much of an income."

"I will state it a little differently—an income that might be taxable?"

"I would rather let my lawyer answer that question."

"Well, I tell you," said Mattingly, "prior to 1926, John Torrio, who happens to be a client of mine, was the employer of Mr. Capone and up to that point it is my impression his income wasn't there; he was in the position of an employee, pure and simple. That is the information I get from Mr. Torrio and Mr. Capone."

Wilson took over the questioning. Capone pulled out a fistful of cigars and offered him one. "I don't smoke," said Wilson.

"Did you furnish any money to purchase real estate which was placed in the name of others?" he asked.

But to this and almost every other question that followed—did Capone's wife or relatives keep brokerage accounts? Safe-deposit boxes? What about the money transfers wired to him in Miami? Was he ever connected with the Hawthorne Kennel Club?—the response was the same: "I would rather not answer that question." His voice grew louder and rough-edged. "They're trying to push me around," he growled at one point, "but I'll take care of myself."

At the end he stared fixedly at his tormentor. "How's your wife, Wilson?" he asked, and as he left: "You be sure to take care of your-self."

"Frank," said Hodgins, when they were alone. "Watch your step from now on."

In June Mike Malone told Wilson that Frankie Pope, the manager of the Hawthorne Smoke Shop, had quarreled with Capone over a large sum he felt the organization owed him and might be persuaded to talk. However disaffected, Pope did not, when Wilson approached him, give away much, but he dropped a hint. Jake Lingle, he intimated, not only knew more about gang activities than any reporter in Chicago, but had a relationship with Capone far closer than anybody realized.

Wilson called on Colonel McCormick to ask if he could question Lingle confidentially. The publisher promised his cooperation, and a meeting was arranged in the Tribune Tower for eleven o'clock on the morning of June 10. Lingle did not appear.

20

Mr. and Mrs. Alphonse Capone
Request the Pleasure. . . .

"IT is reported that Al Capone is on his way to Florida," Governor Doyle E. Carlton informed the state's sixty-seven county sheriffs after Capone's release from prison. "Arrest promptly if he comes your way and escort him to the State border. He cannot remain in Florida. If you need additional assistance, call me." He ordered the local court officers to lock Capone out of his Palm Island home, and he appealed to all right-thinking Floridians "to cooperate by all legitimate means towards ejecting a public menace and imposter and to exterminate the growth of organized crime." To Miami's public prosecutor, allowing Capone to inhabit the area would be as great an evil as allowing "a rattlesnake to live in a garden where it could bite children."

Before Capone arrived, the Dade County sheriff raided the Palm Island estate, arrested the five men staying there as guests—the brothers Albert and John Capone, Louis Cowan, Jack McGurn and a Frankie Newton—and charged them with illegal possession of liquor. The cases were dismissed.

Renewed rumors that Capone would seek a retreat elsewhere raised similar cries of alarm from other communities. A curious exception was Rapid City, South Dakota, in which Capone had expressed no interest whatever. The secretary of its Chamber of Commerce, Dan Evans, wrote him an unsolicited letter, extolling the beauties of the Black Hills, which had so enchanted President Coolidge when he vacationed there, and urged him to come live "where the stranger is not judged by reports of his past record." Evans promised him "a glad hand of welcome into a community practically free from crime. We extend this invitation with the sincere belief that with the associates you would meet here you would soon outlive the intimated crimes that have been credited to you without any proof whatever and soon you would be recognized as a law-abiding, upright citizen and a credit to the community."

Governor William J. Bulow overruled Evans. "I'll cast the first stone," he said. "We don't need Capone or any of his kind in South Dakota."

Capone ended the controversy with the announcement: "I have no desire to live in the Black Hills."

In the Miami law firm of Gordon & Giblin Capone found a stalwart defender. Vincent Giblin, an ex-football player of demonic energy, quickly established his client's legal rights of domicile. From a federal court he obtained an injunction restraining Florida's sheriffs from "seizing, arresting, kidnapping and abusing the plaintiff" and served it on all sixty-seven of them. Under pressure from influential winter residents who wanted no gangsters for neighbors— Albert D. Lasker, the advertising magnate, for example, John D. Hertz, founder of the Yellow Cab Company, James M. Cox, former governor of Ohio and publisher of several newspapers, including the Miami *Daily News*—the police continued, extralegally, to harass Capone and his visitors. They interrupted Jack McGurn at his favorite sport of golf, dragged him off the links, and kept him prisoner until Captain Stege, at their request, sent detectives to escort him back to Chicago. During the month of May they arrested Capone four times for "vagrancy." The indomitable Giblin swore out warrants against the city authorities and publisher Cox, charging them with conspiracy to deprive Capone of his liberty. (When his client later balked at a fee of $50,000, the former athlete stormed into his home, grabbed him by the shirtfront and threatened to knock his teeth down his throat. Capone was so startled that he handed over what cash there was in the bedroom chest. Gordon & Giblin had to sue him to collect the full amount.)

As it grew clear that Capone could not be dislodged, the harassment let up. His victory opened the way to Miami for other gangsters. Terry Druggan was among the next to own property there, followed by the Fischettis. It became *de rigueur* for the successful bootlegger or racketeer to spend part of each winter in a waterfront villa or a suite at a Miami Beach hotel.

The Capones acquired a certain social position. Curiosity, daredeviltry or inverted snobbishness brought both year-round Miamians and winter visitors to their parties. Even as Cox's paper was clamoring for Capone's ouster, sixty business and professional men accepted an engraved invitation to a banquet and musicale. As each guest passed through the main gate, a servant pinned a miniature American flag to his lapel. The main dish was an elaborate *pasta*. For beverages the host discreetly offered nothing stronger than mineral water or soda pop. At the table a Miami elder rose, formally introduced Capone as "the new businessman of the community," and presented him with a fountain pen. The entertainment then began with an operatic recital and ended with a Highland fling.

The Capones also gave a big party for Sonny, a pupil at the Gesu Catholic School in Miami Beach. They invited fifty children but with consummate diplomacy stipulated that they must bring a letter of consent from home. Few parents withheld it.

Showfolk were always favored guests on the Palm Island estate. At one time or other he lavished hospitality upon Harry Richman (who many years later was still proudly referring to him as "my very good friend") , Joe E. Lewis, George Jessel, Al Jolson, Eddie Cantor and many other stars who played the Miami nightclubs. Cantor, a naïve and timorous soul, assumed he had been sent for to entertain and was terrified of incurring the gang leader's ire. So he brought along his accompanist, immediately seated him at the living-room piano and, banjo eyes wide, beating his fingertips together, started to sing, "If you knew Susie like I know Susie—" "Hold it!" said Capone. "I didn't ask you here to perform. I just wanted to meet you."

In the late spring of 1930 a nautical mishap nearly ended Capone's career. The detachment with which he faced the prospect of sudden death, he who shrank from the prick of a doctor's hypodermic needle, left an indelible impression upon the young lawyer who shared the experience. Capone wanted to buy another pleasure craft. A Miami rum-runner of his acquaintance, Ralph Senterfit, offered him a 40-foot cabin cruiser, on which he had been bringing in "hams" from Bimini. A ham consisted of six bottles swaddled in straw inside a gunnysack. Attached to each sack was a bag of salt and a red marker.

If chased by the Coast Guard, the rum-runner would race for shallow water and drop the hams overboard. The bags of salt would usually keep them on the bottom until the danger passed. Then, as the salt melted, the markers would rise to the top, enabling the rum-runner to retrieve his sunken treasure. Often, the bottles were still damp when they reached the consumer.

Capone fancied the boat but insisted before buying it that his own captain, one A. H. Caesar, test it. On the trial run he took along the junior member of another Miami law firm handling his affairs, William Parker, and an Argentine bodyguard, a small man lugging a gun almost as big as he was. Captain Caesar put the boat through its paces on Biscayne Bay. He spun the wheel back and forth so vigorously that he probably weakened the steering cable. As he started back toward the dock, two boys in a rowboat with an outboard motor crossed his path. He swung sharply to port to avoid them, and the cable snapped. The cruiser was then speeding straight for a steel oil barge. Parker and the Argentine scrambled into the stern, covering their heads with their arms. Caesar cut the engine, crouched low, and pulled at the wheel. But Capone stood in the prow, coolly eying the barge ahead. At the last instant the cruiser swerved. It struck the barge a glancing blow, knocking Caesar, Parker and the bodyguard flat, then bounced off undamaged and slowed to a stop. Capone had kept his feet without a quiver. Towed to the dock, he stepped ashore unhurriedly, lit a cigar, and nodded to Senterfit. "I'll take her. Have her fixed up and send me the bill."

On June 9 Capone received shocking news from Chicago about his friend Jake Lingle.

21

A Murder a Day

ALFRED "Jake" Lingle was twenty when he went to work at the *Tribune* as a copyboy. His only previous employment had been that of stock clerk and messenger for a surgical supply company. Born to West Siders of moderate means, he grew up in the dingy neighborhood that bred the old Valley gang. His education ended in the Calhoun elementary school on West Jackson Boulevard, some of whose graduates succeeded as businessmen, some as politicians, and some as gangsters. Lingle lost sight of none of them.

Though cynical, self-satisfied and secretive, he could, when it suited him, radiate boyish charm. He was a solidly built man of medium height, with curly black hair, ruddy cheeks and a cleft chin. The extensive acquaintanceship he cultivated served him well when he had persuaded the *Tribune*, after only a few weeks in the office, to let him work on the outside as a police reporter.

Lingle had no aptitude for writing. He could only transmit facts. He was a legman, and a legman he remained for eighteen years, earning, at his top salary, $65 a week. But the *Tribune* considered him a great asset. Crime was almost daily front-page news in the Chicago of the twenties, and every paper relied heavily on its house crime expert, its gangologist. In that category Lingle had few equals and no superior. He frequently scooped the competition, for not only did he enjoy easy access to Capone, among other underworld bosses, but he was on intimate terms with both Police Commissioner

Russell and Deputy Commissioner Stege. The former friendship dated from Russell's nonage as a patrolman pounding a West Side beat. He and Lingle golfed together, attended the theater and sports events together, borrowed money from each other. So close were they that people would later speak of Lingle as "Chicago's unofficial chief of police."

At the age of thirty he married a boyhood sweetheart, Helen Sullivan. They had two children a year apart, Alfred, Jr., and Dolores. In addition to a house on the West Side, where they were both reared, Lingle bought a summer bungalow at Long Beach, Indiana, for $18,000. In the winter he sometimes took his family to Cuba or Florida for a vacation. He owned a Lincoln and employed a chauffeur. During the last half of 1930 he kept a room in the Stevens Hotel on Michigan Avenue. The switchboard operator had instructions never to disturb him unless the caller's name appeared on the lists Lingle gave her from time to time. Otherwise, as the house detective pointed out later, "How could he get any sleep? His telephone would be going all night. He would get in around two or three and he wanted rest."

Whatever kept Lingle out so late, it was not dissipation. He was a faithful husband, and he limited his drinking to a glass or two of beer. He had a stomach ulcer. His one vice was gambling. He frequently risked $1,000 or more on a horse race.

Such extravagance for a $65-a-week legman puzzled Lingle's colleagues until he told them that his father had bequeathed him $50,-000. Also, he said, the value of some stocks he bought during the 1928 bull market had almost tripled.

Since he worked for a morning newspaper, Lingle seldom bestirred himself before noon. On June 9 at that hour he left the Stevens Hotel and strolled a mile and a half north to the Tribune Tower. He talked briefly with the city editor about rumors of another gang upheaval that he was trying to verify, then continued on his way. It was race day at the Washington Park track in Homewood, a day of cloudless sky and brilliant sunshine. Having decided to dispense with his car and chauffeur, Lingle walked south across Wacker Drive toward the suburban station of the Illinois Central Railroad, two blocks distant at Randolph Street and Michigan Avenue. He had almost an hour to spare before the one thirty racetrack special left, and he took a slight detour for a bite of lunch in the coffee shop of the Hotel Sherman, two blocks west of the avenue. Upon entering the lobby, he ran into Police Sergeant Tom Alcock, to whom he made a strange remark. "I'm being tailed," he said without further explanation. He did not appear troubled.

Retracing his steps to Randolph Street, he stopped at the newsstand in front of the Public Library to buy the *Daily Racing Form*. A man he knew called to him from a car parked at the curb: "Play Hy Schneider in the third, Jake." "I've got him," Lingle called back. Lighting a cigar, he hurried down the stairs into the pedestrian tunnel running under Michigan Avenue to the station. He was too absorbed in his paper to notice the old friend walking ahead of him, Dr. Joseph Springer, a former medical examiner. Nor did he pay any attention to the commotion behind him caused by the tall blond young man who, in his haste, was elbowing people aside. As Lingle reached the east ramp, the young man fetched up within a few inches of him, took a gun out of his pocket, and leveled it at his head. The bullet plowed through Lingle's brain, and he fell forward, the *Racing Form* clutched in his hands, the still-burning cigar in his mouth.

At least fourteen people saw the killer in the course of his flight. Dropping his gun, he ran back to the stairway at the opposite end of the tunnel and took the steps two or three at a bound, colliding with a man coming down. He paused at the top, then zigzagged through the traffic across Michigan Avenue. In the tunnel a woman shouted: "Isn't somebody going to stop him!" and her husband dashed up the steps in pursuit. But the killer outdistanced him. From Randolph Street he dashed through a maze of alleys to Wabash and lost himself in the crowd.

Dr. Springer, the first to reach Lingle's body, felt his pulse. He was dead.

It was Chicago's eleventh murder in ten days.

> The meaning of this murder is plain [thus spoke the mighty *Tribune*]. It was committed in reprisal and in an attempt at intimidation. Mr. Lingle was a police reporter and an exceptionally well informed one. His personal friendships included the highest police officials and the contacts of his work made him familiar to most of the big and little fellows of gangland. What made him valuable to his newspaper marked him as dangerous to the killers.
>
> It was very foolish to think that assassination would be confined to the gangs which have fought each other for the profits of crime

in Chicago. The immunity from punishment after gang murders would be assumed to cover the committing of others. Citizens who interfered with the criminals were no better protected than the gangmen who fought each other for the revenue from liquor selling, coercion of labor and trade, brothel house keeping and gambling. . . .

[Murder] has become the accepted course of crime in its natural stride, but to the list of Colosimo, O'Banion, the Gennas, Murphy, Weiss, Lombardo, Esposito, the seven who were killed in the St. Valentine's day massacre, the name is added of a man whose business was to expose the work of the killers.

The *Tribune* accepts this challenge. It is war. There will be casualties, but that is to be expected, it being war. . . . The challenge of crime to the community must be accepted. It has been given with bravado. It is accepted. Justice will make a fight of it or will abdicate.

In a message condoling with the *Tribune,* the president of the American Newspaper Publishers' Association, Harry Chandler of the Los Angeles *Times,* eulogized the slain reporter as a "first line soldier" in their campaign against outlawry, and his fellow press lords the country over joined him in demanding that Lingle's martyrdom be swiftly avenged.

For information leading to the murderer's conviction Colonel McCormick posted a $25,000 reward. Hearst's Chicago *Herald and Examiner* matched it, the *Evening Post* added $5,000, and various civic groups brought the total to $55,725. Convening the Chicago Newspaper Publishers' Association, of which he was president, immediately following Lingle's funeral on June 12, McCormick proposed to set up a special investigative committee under the joint command of Charles F. Rathbun, a *Tribune* lawyer, and Patrick T. Roche, chief investigator for the State's Attorney's office, the *Tribune* to pay all expenses beyond what the county could spend. The publishers concurred, and State's Attorney Swanson raised no objections.

The meeting had barely adjourned before the image of Lingle as martyr began to crumble. One of the earliest intimations of the truth was received by Frank Wilson. Talking to Frankie Pope the morning after the murder, he mentioned the conference that was to have taken place. Pope sneered. "Jake was a fixer," he said, and the facts he recited convinced Wilson. Later that day a reporter whom Wilson once did a good turn phoned to chat about the Lingle case. This was John T. Rogers of the St. Louis *Post-Dispatch*. Wilson had once put him in the way of exposing a corrupt federal judge. The story won a 1927 Pulitzer Prize. Without betraying his informer, Wilson now passed along Pope's disclosures. After making his own investigation, Rogers called McCormick, told him what he had discovered, and announced that the *Post-Dispatch* would shortly print it. The colonel exploded.

The first findings of Rathbun and Roche afforded McCormick no comfort. Street rumors concerning Lingle's extra-journalistic activities had prompted them to look into his financial status. Probate Court records showed that the senior Lingle had left his son not $50,000, but less than $500. As for the reporter's vaunted stock market killing, it was true, the investigators learned from the four brokerage houses in which he kept trading accounts, that had he liquidated his securities at the peak of the bull market in September, 1929, he would have turned a profit of $85,000, but he held them, and on October 24—the Black Thursday that heralded the Depression—the paper profit, plus $75,000 more, evaporated. His friend Russell suffered with him, for in one of the brokerage firms they had opened a joint account.

Yet Lingle did not lower his standard of living; he raised it, if anything. Moreover, between the end of 1928 and the spring of 1930 he deposited in the Lake Shore Savings and Trust Bank a total of $63,900. Where did he get the money? Rathbun established $12,800 of it as "loans" by politicians, police officers and gamblers—loans not repaid—but the question was never fully answered.

The dark rumors multiplied: They pictured Lingle as the liaison between the Capone organization and City Hall, as the protector of bootleggers and gamblers, using his influence with the Police Department in their behalf. While Mayor Thompson was debating whether to dismiss his police commissioner, Russell relieved Deputy Commissioner Stege from his command of the detective bureau, then resigned himself.

The rumors dealt a severe blow to journalistic pride. The corrupting force of gangsterism in league with politicians, spreading like an oil slick, had stained the community in almost every strand of its fabric. But the press held itself to be inviolable. The press accused, the press judged, and the press took for granted the integrity of its reporters and writers. Now, through the dereliction of one of the *Tribune's* most valued reporters, it, too, fell under obloquy. How many other newspapermen, the public was asking, did politicians or gangsters control?

McCormick swallowed the bitter pill, and on June 18 the *Tribune* ran its second major editorial about the Lingle case.

> When Alfred Lingle was murdered the motive seemed to be apparent . . . his newspaper saw no other explanation than that his killers either thought he was close to information dangerous to them or intended the murder as notice given the newspapers that crime was ruler in Chicago. . . .
>
> Alfred Lingle now takes a different character, one in which he was unknown to the management of the *Tribune* when he was alive. He is dead and cannot defend himself, but many facts now revealed must be accepted as eloquent against him. . . . The reasonable appearance against Lingle now is that he was accepted in the world of politics and crime for something undreamed of in his office and that he used this in undertakings which made him money and brought him to his death. . . .

If a trusted employee of the *Tribune* had been capable of such iniquity, might not its rival newspapers also be tainted? The colonel chose to believe so, especially as his competitors were gloating over his discomfiture. The editorial writer added sourly: "There are weak men on other newspapers."

A second St. Louis reporter, Harry T. Brundige of the *Star*, took his cue from this and proceeded to investigate the Chicago press. In a series of ten articles he revealed that:

Julius Rosenheim, a tipster for the *Daily News*, killed by gangsters the preceding February, had blackmailed bootleggers, gamblers and brothelkeepers with threats of exposure in the *News;*

James Murphy, a police reporter, had been discharged by the *Times* upon his admission that he was the partner of a speakeasy owner;

Ted Tod, a criminal court reporter for the *Herald-Examiner*, doubled as press agent for the North Side gang's Fairview Kennel Club dog track;

Matt Foley, assistant circulation manager of the same newspaper, promoted a lottery that swindled thousands (he was later convicted of fraud but only fined $250) ;

Harry Read, city editor of the *Evening American,* had been Capone's guest in Miami half a dozen times and accompanied him on a junket to Havana.

Brundige alleged improprieties or criminal offenses against employees of nearly every newspaper in Chicago except the *Tribune.* The omission, combined with the *Tribune's* publication of his series, gave rise to the suspicion that McCormick had put Brundige up to it. "There's no use beating about the bush," he had told the *Star* reporter. "If the newspapers of Chicago are to maintain a foremost place in the life of this country, we must clean house. The *Tribune* has nothing to conceal. It is bigger than any or all of its personnel and I will not only discharge but prosecute any man on our payroll who has used his employment dishonestly . . . I will personally request the grand jury to make a thorough investigation of all facts and rumors having to do with alliances between newspapermen of Chicago and the underworld."

With no assurance that Capone would talk to him, Brundige stepped off the train in Miami at 8:15 P.M. on July 16, after a two-day trip from St. Louis, and took a taxi to Palm Island. As soon as the bodyguard announced him, Capone appeared, beaming. "This is a surprise," he said. "Come on in." He led him to the sun porch and seated him facing the moon-speckled Biscayne Bay. "You seem to have raised hell in Chicago. What brings you here?"

"I thought I'd ask you who killed Jake Lingle?" said Brundige.

"Why ask me?" Then, after a moment's pause: "The Chicago police know who killed him."

"Was Jake your friend?"

"Yes, up to the very day he died."

"Did you have a row with him?"

"Absolutely not."

"It is said you fell out with him because he failed to split profits from handbooks."

"Bunk, bunk. The handbook racket hasn't been really organized in Chicago for more than two years."

"How many rackets was Lingle engaged in?" Capone shrugged. "What was the matter with Lingle?"

"The horse races."

"How many other Lingles are there in Chicago?"

"In the newspaper racket? Phooey—don't ask."

"How many reporters do you have on your payroll?"

"Plenty."

They talked for almost four hours. "Listen, Harry," Capone said toward the end, throwing an arm around his shoulders, "I like your face. Let me give you a hot tip: Lay off Chicago and the money-hungry reporters. You're right and because you're right, you're wrong. You can't buck it, not even with the backing of your newspaper, because it's too big a proposition. No one will ever realize just how big it is, so lay off. They'll make a monkey out of you before you get through. No matter what dope you give that grand jury, the boys will prove you're a liar and a faker. You'll get a trimming."

"I'm going to quote you as saying that," Brundige forewarned him.

"If you do, I'll deny it."

Both the *Star* and the *Tribune* printed the interview, and as promised, Capone branded it a fabrication.

In its final report the July grand jury declared itself unable to substantiate any of Brundige's allegations against his fellow newspapermen.

The prime physical clue to Lingle's assassin was the revolver he dropped in his flight. It was a snub-nosed .38-caliber Colt, a detective special, also called a belly gun because triggermen commonly carried one stuck inside their trouser waistband. The manufacturer's serial number had been filed off. The die that stamps the number on a gun leaves two impressions. The second, deep in the metal and invisible to the eye, is known as the tattoo. Colonel Goddard had developed a process for raising the tattoo. He would grind down the surface as far as the second impression, polish it, and treat it with an etching solution of alcohol and acids. Coroner Bundesen telephoned the number thus uncovered to the Colt factory in Hartford, Connecticut, and within the hour the revolver was identified as one of six delivered in June, 1928, a year before the Lingle murder, to—who else?—Peter von Frantzius. Though the gunsmith had committed no crime under the still-lax gun laws, Bundesen, a detective and a young *Tribune* reporter, John Boettiger, managed between them to terrify him into revealing the purchaser. He named Frank Foster, a Sicilian, born Citro, a veteran O'Banionite and one of the first bootleggers to import Canadian whiskey. Another North Sider, Ted Newberry, accompanied him when he bought the six revolvers, and it was at Newberry's insistence that Von Frantzius filed off the serial numbers. Both Newberry and Foster had recently defected to the Capone ranks.

Since none of the witnesses to Lingle's murder recognized Foster from the photographs the police showed them, the investigators concluded that he himself did not pull the trigger, though he probably knew who did and was therefore an accessory to the crime. Failing to find him in his accustomed Chicago haunts, they launched a nationwide search. It ended in Los Angeles, to which Foster had fled two days after the murder. He was extradited and indicted as an accomplice of the murderer, but following his lawyers' fourth demand for trial, State's Attorney Swanson conceded the evidence to be insufficient to warrant further prosecution and entered a nolle prosequi.

The case against Foster was one of many to collapse.

A few days before Lingle died, John J. "Boss" McLaughlin, a former state legislator and political fixer for the North Side gang, opened a gambling house at 606 West Madison Street. Commissioner Russell promptly closed it. McLaughlin thereupon telephoned Lingle at the *Tribune,* asking him to intercede. A reporter, whom Lingle signaled to listen in on an extension, later reconstructed the conversation verbatim from his notes.

> McLaughlin—Swanson told me it was all right to go ahead and I don't see why Russell is butting in.
>
> Lingle—I don't believe Swanson told you any such thing, but if it's true, you get Swanson to write a letter to Russell, notifying him that it's all right for you to go ahead.
>
> McLaughlin—Do you think Swanson is crazy? He wouldn't write such a letter.
>
> Lingle—Well, Russell can't let you run. That's final.
>
> McLaughlin—(cursing) I'll catch up with you and it won't be long either.

McLaughlin was picked up within hours of the murder. "Why, I wouldn't hurt a hair of Jake's head," he assured Roche. "I liked Jake. I might have asked him a favor or two, but I certainly never wished him harm." In the absence of any evidence other than a threat uttered in anger, Roche let him go.

*   *   *

At their zenith, before the St. Valentine's Day massacre, Bugs Moran's North Siders extended their protection to one of Chicago's most elegant gambling houses, the oddly named Sheridan Wave Tournament Club on Waveland Avenue, which Julian "Potatoes" Kaufman operated in partnership with Joey Brooks, alias Josephs. Admission was by invitation only. Liveried attendants served food and drink at no charge to the fashionable clientele, who nightly enriched the owners by tens of thousands of dollars. Twenty-five percent of the gross went to Moran, and Lingle was rumored to receive 10 percent. When, in June, 1928, the police under Commissioner Michael Hughes raided the club, Judge Harry Fisher, he who had ruled dog racing to be legal, professed to view it as "an orderly private athletic club," and he enjoined the police "from annoying, molesting or in any manner interfering with the complainant in its lawful conduct of its members."

A year later, following the decline of Moran's prestige, Hughes' successor, Russell, directed another raid. This time the club stayed dark for a year before Kaufman and Brooks, with Moran's backing, determined to reopen it. Engraved invitations to the first night— June 9—were sent to the old clientele. Lingle had demanded a 50 percent cut. The partners refused. "If this joint is opened up," Lingle was reported to have said, "you'll see more squad cars in front ready to raid it than you ever saw before in your life."

So they decided to kill him. Jack Zuta, the whoremonger, who had become Moran's business manager, supposedly supervised the details, paying the labor racketeer Simon Gorman $20,000 to recruit a killer from among his cohorts. The choice, according to Roche's source, fell on one James "Red" Forsythe, who vanished immediately after the murder.

Zuta was a familiar figure around the detective bureau. He had been brought there frequently. Whining and servile, he was thought capable, if sufficiently frightened, of sacrificing his own mother. Captain Stege once reduced him to quaking terror by saying: "You're doomed. I've told that to 14 other hoodlums who have sat on that same chair you're sitting on and all of them are dead."

The North Siders despised Zuta for his cowardice, yet tolerated him because, next to Jake Guzik, he probably had the best business brains in the underworld. When, on June 30, the police arrested him along with a woman companion, Leona Bernstein, and two men,

Solly Vision and Albert Bratz, and took them to Roche, a tremor of apprehension ran through the gang. Though Zuta did not, in fact, incriminate anybody during the twenty-four hours he was detained, reports to the contrary leaked out of the bureau. He sensed as much, for when freed at 10:30 P.M. on a writ of habeas corpus, he implored a detective, Lieutenant George Barker, to escort him and his companions to safety. Because one was a woman, Barker agreed to drive them in his Pontiac through the Loop to the El station on Lake Street, thirteen blocks north. Bratz and Leona Bernstein sat in the front seat. Solly Vision sat behind with Zuta.

They were edging slowly into the Loop, by night as bright as high noon with its million dollars' worth of newly installed candlepower, when Zuta's fear took shape. Peering out the rear window, he saw a blue sedan bearing down on them. On the running board stood a man wearing a tan suit, a boutonniere and a Panama hat. "They're after us!" Zuta screamed, flinging himself to the floor. Bratz vaulted the front seat and crouched next to him. As the sedan drew alongside, the man on the running board took a .45-caliber automatic from a shoulder holster and emptied it into the tonneau of the Pontiac, while the driver and another gunman in the rear seat fired revolvers at the windows. Jamming on his brakes, Barker leaped to the street, gun in hand. The sedan halted, too, and as the summer nighttime strollers scattered in panic, gangsters and detective traded shots. Stray bullets hit a bank guard and a motorman, whose streetcar had been blocked by the besieged Pontiac. The motorman died in the hospital. (G. K. Chesterton was less than accurate when, six months later, following a visit to Chicago, he glibly wrote in the *New York Times Magazine:* "Chicago has many beauties, including the fastidiousness and good taste to assassinate nobody except assassins.")

Ammunition exhausted, the driver of the sedan shifted into first and started north up State Street. Barker stepped back into his car. His three passengers had vanished. He sped after the gunmen, but with a trick new to gang combat, they escaped him. Through a specially installed injection pump they forced massive quantities of oil into the intake manifold, thus laying down from the exhaust a dense, black smoke screen that covered the street from sidewalk to sidewalk. By the time Barker had crawled through it they were gone.

In the middle of State Street he spotted a revolver that one of the killers had thrown from the sedan. Delivered to the Goddard laboratory, it told an interesting story. A month earlier Sam "Golf Bag" Hunt had been arrested for trying to shoot Leo Mongoven, Public Enemy No. 27 and a Moran bodyguard. Searching the receptacle that gave Hunt his sobriquet, they confiscated a shotgun, a .38-caliber revolver mounted on a .45-caliber frame and shells for both weapons. To obliterate the serial numbers, the symbol # had been stamped over them, a Caponian technique. The revolver discarded on State Street bore the same symbol.

Zuta stayed out of sight for a month. He finally surfaced under the alias J. H. Goodman at the Lake View Hotel, a roadhouse by the shore of Upper Nemahbin Lake, in Wisconsin, 25 miles west of Milwaukee. The barroom had a coin-operated player piano, and on the evening of August 1 Zuta was idly feeding it nickels while half a dozen couples lindy hopped around the dance floor. Five men came in, Indian file, the first holding a tommy gun, the others sawed-off shotguns and revolvers. Zuta had just popped another nickel into the slot, causing the piano to thump out a hit of the hour—"Good for You, Bad for Me." The fusillade slammed him against the keys.

Sixteen bullets were extracted from Zuta's body. Several proved to be of a type used almost exclusively in the model of the revolver removed from Sam Hunt's golf bag. Applying his etching process to the Hunt weapon, Goddard discovered the number, communicated it to the manufacturer, and shortly established, as the ultimate consignee, the Capone organization. At the same time a frequenter of the Lake View Hotel identified Ted Newberry from photographs as one of Zuta's assassins. Though neither piece of evidence proved sufficient to bring the turncoat gangster to trial, both added weight to the theory that Capone had ordered the killing. (On the fatal evening Capone presided at a banquet in Cicero's Western Hotel for a hundred of his loyalists.) But the motive—whether to avenge Lingle or to prevent Zuta from telling what he knew about the assassination—remained forever obscure.

Zuta, a methodical man, had kept records of his business transactions under aliases in safe-deposit boxes at different banks. Roche's inquiries led him to two of them, and he obtained warrants to open them. Chicagoans had long been inured to revelations of politico-criminal chicanery, but what Zuta's caches disgorged dumbfounded the most blasé. They included canceled checks, ranging in amounts from $50 to $5,500—a total of $8,950—payable to two judges and

Judge Harry Fisher's brother, Louis, the dog track lawyer; two state senators; two police officers; a chief deputy coroner; an assistant business manager of the Board of Education; a city editor; and the William Hale Thompson Republican Club. There was a letter from Evanston's Chief of Police William O. Freeman.

> DEAR JACK:
>   I am temporarily in need of four "C's" for a couple of months. Can you let me have it? The bearer does not know what it is, so put it in an envelope and seal it and address it to me.
>
> Your old pal,
BILL FREEMAN
>
> P.S. Will let you know the night of the party, so be sure and come.

A card signed by Charles E. Graydon, sheriff of Cook County, notified whomever it might concern that "The bearer, J. Zuta, is extended the courtesies of all departments." Letters dated June, 1927, from an ex-Caponeite, Louis La Cava, who had been banished when he attempted to appropriate Cicero territory, suggested another reason why Capone might have wished to eliminate Zuta.

> I'd help you organize a strong business organization capable of coping with theirs in Cicero. You know you have lots of virgin territory on the north side limits border line and they are going to try and prevent me from lining up with you and thereby starving me out, until I go back to them, begging for mercy. . . . I have heard the Big Boy is stopping my brothers from making a living. . . .

A balance sheet showed the North Siders' gross revenue from gambling at their apogee, before the St. Valentine's Day massacre. In a single week (November 6–12, 1927) it totaled $429,146. Roughly a fourth of that went for police protection.

During the four months since Lingle's death the police, casting a dragnet over the Chicago underworld, had hauled in and questioned about 700 criminals of record. Rathbun and Roche followed dozens of trails to their dead ends. Again and again the compass needle of suspicion had swung back to Capone. Lingle took $50,000 from him (so it was whispered along the grapevine) as the price of official sanction for a new dog track on the West Side but never delivered, a capital offense in Capone's domain. The reporter's considerable knowledge of Capone's financial transactions—if, as Frank Wilson had thought possible, he could have been persuaded to share it with the government—would have constituted another reason for killing him. But no evidence supported any of these hypotheses.

Rathbun and Roche decided upon a campaign of relentless, daily harassment of gangland, hoping that somebody somewhere would eventually crack under the pressure and furnish a lead. Accordingly, the detectives assigned to them by the state's attorney, armed with axes, sledgehammers and crowbars, proceeded to raid and wreck every brothel, gambling dive and speakeasy they could find in Chicago and its suburbs and to arrest everybody on the premises. At the same time Rathbun and Roche strove to have old forgotten charges against the Public Enemies revived, parole violators reimprisoned, and pending cases hastened to trial. Judge Lyle did his bit by setting bail so high, whenever gangsters were brought into his Felony Court, that they preferred to await the outcome in jail. Thus, many important members of the Capone organization and its subsidiaries were immobilized, among them George "Red" Barker, boss of the Chicago Teamsters' Union, who was returned to jail to complete a sentence for robbery; his fellow labor racketeers James "Fur" Sammons, jailed again as a parole violator with an unexpired sentence for murder, and Danny Stanton, extradited to Wisconsin under a murder indictment; Three-Fingered Jack White, tried for killing a policeman in 1924, convicted, freed on appeal, and now resentenced; Claude Maddox, booked for vagrancy. . . .

Judge Lyle had also invoked a long-disused vagrancy law that defined as a vagrant one without visible means of support, regularly pursuing illicit enterprises, and provided penalties of up to six months' imprisonment or a fine of up to $200 or both. "I had within me a warm, tingling feeling," the judge recalled later, "as I reviewed the possibilities in the law in the case of, let us say, Al Capone. If Capone, arrested on a vagrancy warrant, declined to answer questions, he would automatically fail to disprove the allegations. I could find him guilty of vagrancy and fine him $200. If he tried to pay the fine he would have to explain where the money had come from. He could be sentenced to the House of Corrections to work out the fine. Were he to recite the sources of his income he would be opening the door to criminal charges. And any claim to legitimate employment would launch an investigation that could conceivably result in perjury charges."

The first warrant he issued named Capone, who appeared in Felony Court on September 16, 1930, with Nash's svelte law partner, Michael Ahern. "The People of the State of Illinois against Alphonse Capone alias Scarface Al Brown," the clerk of the court intoned. With fame and fortune the gang leader had grown increasingly sensitive about his scars and was planning to undergo plastic surgery. "Your Honor," said Ahern, "I ask that the epithet be stricken from the record."

Capone did not take lightly the disturbance to his organization. In hopes of ending it he requested, through a go-between, a confidential talk with Rathbun and Roche. They refused to meet with him themselves, but sent an emissary, identified in the records only as "Operative No. 1," to hear what he had to say.

At the morgue to which the police carried Lingle's body his billfold was found to contain fourteen $100 notes. The *Tribune*'s John Boettiger—the first reporter on the scene of the murder—fearing that so much cash might give rise to nasty gossip, somehow persuaded the police to let him take charge of it. He turned it over to his city editor. Such discretion commended itself to McCormick, and he chose Boettiger to work with the investigative committee. From this vantage point the reporter gathered material for a book published a year later, *Jake Lingle or Chicago on the Spot*, which put McCormick and the *Tribune* in the best possible light.* One chapter reproduced the exchange between Capone and Operative Number 1.

> "Here's what I want to tell you, and I won't be long about it," said Capone. "I can't stand the gaff of these raids and pinches. If it's going to keep up, I'll have to pack up and get out of Chicago."
> Operative Number 1 replied:
> "So far as I can tell, the gaff is on for keeps. This town has been burning up since Jake Lingle was murdered."
> "Well, I didn't kill Jake Lingle, did I?"
> "We don't know who killed him."
> "Why didn't you ask me? Maybe I can find out for you."
> "I have heard that Lingle was involved in the attempts of the North Side gangsters to open a dog track in the Stadium. . . .

* Later assigned to the *Tribune*'s Washington bureau, Boettiger married President Roosevelt's daughter, Anna, quit the *Tribune*, and eventually became publisher of Hearst's Seattle *Post-Intelligencer*.

I have been told that Lingle was asked by the Zuta crowd to see to it that the police and the state's attorney would not bother them, and that Lingle was paid $30,000. . . .

". . . When the gang saw that they could not go they blamed Jake Lingle, and I think that's why he was pushed." [A story Rathbun and Roche had heard before, but with the difference that Capone was the supposed dupe.]

"But I don't know who they used to do the job; it must have been some fellow from out of town. I'll try to find out."

"You can do this if you want to, Capone," said Operative Number 1, "but I don't think it'll help you with Pat Roche."

If Capone himself did not order Lingle's murder, he very likely knew who fired the fatal shot. He told Jake Guzik as much during a talk at the Lexington Hotel, which the great masquerader, Special Agent Mike Malone, overheard. Malone also heard Capone tell Guzik that he had no intention of delivering the real murderer. A few days later he asked Operative No. 1 whether Rathbun and Roche would take the killer dead. Had they risen to the bait, had they called off their incessant raids and arrests, Capone might conceivably have fabricated evidence against some triggerman, had him slain, and the body left for the police to find. The response to his question was flat. "You can tell Capone," Roche instructed Operative No. 1, "that we know he has been bluffing and that he can go to hell."

The official solution, when Rathbun and Roche finally announced it in December, 1930, left a good many people unconvinced. In October, having exhausted every other means, the investigators hired a purportedly reformed bank robber, beer runner and former associate of the Gennas named John Hagan to reenter gangland as their undercover operator. Hagan shortly ingratiated himself with a garrulous old hoodlum, Pat Hogan, whom underworld gossip vaguely connected with the Lingle murder. Taken to cabarets by Hagan night after night, plied with food and drink, Hogan finally let fall a nickname—Buster. This Buster, a friend and partner in crime, he drunkenly disclosed a few nights later, was Lingle's actual slayer. Hiding out broke in Chicago, he needed to bring off a robbery or two. Would Hagan care to team up with him? Hagan agreed, and Hogan promised to arrange a meeting.

Weeks passed while Rathbun and Roche waited for Buster to

show his hand. Eventually, they learned through Hogan's confidences to their prize stool pigeon that Buster was living under the alias Leo Bader, at the Lake Crest Drive Apartments. There, on December 21, Roche, Rathbun, four detectives and John Boettiger captured a tall blond man.

His real name was Leo Vincent Brothers. A labor-union terrorist, thirty-one years old, he came from St. Louis, where he was wanted for robbery, arson, bombing and murder. Of the fourteen witnesses to the flight of Lingle's murderer, seven now testified that they recognized Brothers and seven that they didn't. Arraigned before Chief Justice John P. McGoorty and asked how he pleaded, Brothers replied: "On the advice of my attorneys I stand mute."

The *Tribune* congratulated Rathbun, Roche and itself and later paid John Hagan the $25,000 reward. But the majority of the Chicago newspapers doubted Brothers' guilt, an attitude that Boettiger ascribed to professional jealousy. "[They] sought to obstruct the prosecution of a murderer who had been trailed and caught by an agency set up and supported by the *Tribune*." Some members of the opposition press insinuated that Brothers was the victim of a frame-up, either an innocent victim or one who allowed himself to be framed for money.

His trial, which lasted from March 16 to April 2, 1931, almost ended in a hung jury, so evenly balanced was the evidence presented for and against him. Though seven prosecution witnesses identified him as the man they saw fleeing from the Michigan Avenue tunnel, not one testified that he saw Brothers shoot Lingle. After deliberating for twenty-seven hours, the jury delivered a compromise verdict. They found Brothers guilty, but instead of the death penalty, as first-degree homicide normally called for, they imposed the minimum sentence of fourteen years' imprisonment, commutable for good behavior in eight. "I can do that standing on my head," was Brothers' comment.

In its issue of April 11 *Editor and Publisher* ran a dispatch from its Chicago correspondent, Edwin Johnson, who was also a staff member of the Chicago *Daily News*.

> The verdict . . . brought a torrent of denunciation upon Chicago courts in newspaper comments from other cities.
> The very fact that Brothers received the minimum sentence has given critics a basis for charges which have persisted since the

announcement of the arrest. The utter certainty of officials that Brothers was the man who killed Lingle and the fact that not one witness testified he saw Lingle slain, presents at least a groundwork for the ugly rumors that have been circulated.

. . . it is held unreasonable that a jury, finding a man guilty of the cold-blooded murder of Lingle, could impose the minimum sentence on the evidence presented.

It is a question in the mind of the police at large as to the guilt of Brothers.

The Tribune has, from the first, maintained that Brothers is the man. This persistence, in the face of an unwillingness on the part of either the newspaper or officials to strip the case bare, show a motive, reveal gang connections, and thus prove to the world that Brothers had a reason for killing Lingle and did so, has engendered a belief among newspapermen that Brothers is the man who killed Lingle, but it cannot be legitimately proved without entailing a scandal which would prove so devastating as to render the game not worth the candle.

. . . Those dissatisfied with the verdict are of the opinion that from a point of general good, Brothers belongs in jail but they hold that there is still the question left unanswered, "who killed 'Jake' Lingle, and why?"

A furious protest from McCormick moved the editor of the magazine, Marlen Pew, to print a retraction and an apology. But many a Chicago newspaperman continued to share Johnson's view.

At eleven o'clock on the night of April 29, four months after Brothers entered the penitentiary, the old whoremaster Mike de Pike Heitler telephoned the woman with whom he had been living for two decades and asked her to look up a number in his address book. When she picked up the receiver again, a strange voice said: "What the hell do you want?" and disconnected.

Late that night, on a country road eight miles west of the Chicago city limits, an automobile was set on fire. The heat discharged a pistol in a side pocket, bringing a farmer to the spot. He ran for the police. The car had been stripped of its license plates. They were spotted next day in the shallows of the Des Plaines River at River Grove, on the outskirts of the city. The next day, too, in the smoldering wreckage of a house in Barrington, twelve miles to the northwest, two boys found the charred remains of a human torso. Car, license plates and torso were all identified as Heitler's.

In his advanced age the pander had been reduced to a relatively humble position in the Capone syndicate. Reckless with resentment, he addressed an anonymous letter to State's Attorney Swanson, disclosing everything he knew about Capone's bordello operations. Not long after, Capone summoned him to the Lexington. On his desk lay the letter, how obtained Heitler never discovered. "Only you could have done this," said Capone. "You're through."

Heitler wrote a second letter, repeating and enlarging upon the first. This letter he entrusted to his daughter with instructions, should he die an unnatural death, to deliver it to Pat Roche. Upon the identification of his remains she did so. Though the posthumous testimony of such as Heitler furnished grounds too shaky for legal action, it strengthened one widely held theory about Lingle's death. First, the letter named eight gangsters as conspirators in the Lingle murder, all of them Caponeites. Then the letter described a meeting at which Capone called Lingle a double crosser and promised: "Jake is going to get his."

22

" . . . regardez le gorille"

IN 1930 Chicago's Medill School of Journalism polled its students as to whom they considered the year's ten "outstanding personages of the world . . . the characters that actually made history." The majority vote went to Benito Mussolini, Colonel Charles A. Lindbergh, Admiral Richard E. Byrd, George Bernard Shaw, Bobby Jones, President Hoover, Mahatma Gandhi, Albert Einstein, Henry Ford and Alphonse Capone.

Professor Walter B. Pitkin of Columbia, publicizing his book *The Psychology of Achievement,* told a reporter: "Al Capone has achieved much more than Charles Evans Hughes simply because Hughes was so inherently brilliant that his rise to the heights in law was so much child's play to him. Of course, in measuring achievement morality is not being taken into consideration."

Neither the Secret Six nor the federal authorities, neither the Chicago Crime Commission's Public Enemy listing nor the philippics of Judge Lyle ("He deserves to die . . . a reptile") had eroded the popular image of Capone as folk hero. Ordinary citizens throughout the country tended to accept his own estimation of his activities. "I'm a public benefactor. . . . You can't cure thirst by law. They call Capone a bootlegger. Yes. It's bootleg while it's on the trucks, but when your host at the club, in the locker room or on the Gold Coast hands it to you on a silver platter, it's hospitality. What's Al done, then? He's supplied a legitimate demand. Some call it bootlegging. Some call it racketeering. I call it a business. They say I violate the prohibition law. Who doesn't?"

At the Charlestown, Indiana, racetrack thousands stood and cheered Capone when he appeared with his bodyguards, waving his clasped hands above his head like a prizefighter entering the ring. U.S. Attorney Johnson was appalled during the American Derby at Washington Park to hear the band strike up "This Is a Lonesome Town When You're Not Around" as Capone, a sunburst in yellow suit and yellow tie, took his seat and to see droves of race fans rush forward, eager to shake his hand. Capone had reserved a box for himself, his family and guests and a second box adjoining it for his bodyguards. His guest of honor on this occasion was the widow of the British heavyweight champion Bob Fitzsimmons. On another occasion, a Cubs baseball game at Wrigley Field, it was State Senator (later U.S. Congressman) Roland V. Libonati. A news photographer snapped him in smiling converse with the gang lord and Jack McGurn. "I was very proud when he asked me to speak to his son," was Libonati's stock apologia in after years. "I would still be proud to speak to any man's son."

During a football game between Northwestern and Nebraska universities Evanston's Dyche Stadium resounded with cries of "Yea, Al!" They arose from a Boy Scout troop with which Capone had supplied a ticket for every member. Among the other spectators approbation was not unanimous. When Capone, wearing a purple suit, lavender shirt and white fedora, left with McGurn after the third quarter, a crowd of about 400 undergraduates followed him to the gate, booing. McGurn paused long enough to turn and snarl at them. Then triggerman and boss took to their heels. In the next issue of the student newspaper, *The Daily Northwestern,* the editor wrote under the headline GET THIS, CAPONE: "You are not wanted at Dyche Stadium nor at Soldier Field when Northwestern is host. You are not getting away with anything and you are only impressing a moronic few who don't matter anyway."

It was to a Chicago reeling under the full impact of the Depression that Capone had returned from Florida in the fall of 1930. No major American city suffered more, for the nationwide economic disaster was here compounded by the prodigality of the third Thompson administration. That year it squandered $23,000,000 above what it could collect in taxes. Outraged citizens organized a tax strike. Fifteen hundred municipal employees, among them teachers, firemen and policemen, had to be dropped from the payrolls, and those kept on went weeks without pay. To make work for its unemployed members, the Chicago Typographical Union ordered those who had jobs to lay off two days a month. With state, county and city treasuries running dry, private groups passed the hat to keep the schools open. Teachers dug into their savings to feed their pupils. "For God's sake," the superintendent of schools implored Chicagoans, "help us feed these children during the summer!" A starving child died on admission to the Children's Memorial Hospital. "Why do we have to go naked and hungry?" cried a Negro mother, speaking for thousands in the Negro ghetto.

A Midwestern drought inflicted further hardship. Homeless families slept in underpasses and tunnels. Clusters of shacks called Hoovervilles made of packing cases, tin, tarpaper and cardboard dotted the outlying parts of town. The International Apple Shippers' Association was promoting the sale of surplus apples with the slogan "Buy an apple a day and send the Depression away," as men who had once held well-paid jobs stood on street corners, an upended crate for a counter, hawking the fruit at a nickel apiece. With exceptional luck an apple peddler might earn $6 in a day.

As public relief funds dwindled, bills were introduced in both the state legislature and Congress to raise taxes, a prospect that brought angry protests from the wealthy. For tax purposes Colonel McCormick reported his personal holdings as no more than $25,250.

"My brother," announced Ralph Capone, while at liberty pending the outcome of his appeal against his federal prison sentence, "is feeding 3,000 unemployed every day." A sign affixed to the front of a huge South Side building proclaimed FREE FOOD FOR THE WORKLESS, and there a soup kitchen, financed entirely by Al Capone, dispensed in six weeks 120,000 meals at a cost of $12,000. On Thanksgiving Day Capone donated 5,000 turkeys. At Christmas he gave a mammoth party for the poor of Little Italy. During those festivities an old woman knelt before him and kissed his hand.

The Capone legend was growing both at home and abroad, nourished by a multitude of journalists, radio commentators, preachers, novelists, playwrights, moviemakers. In the Bronx Dr. Jacob Katz, rabbi of Montefiore Synagogue, went through extraordinary intellectual contortions in an effort to establish a case for the Capone gang, or "Chicago firm," to use his expression, as a potentially constructive force. "Severity of punishment is a policy of expediency, which may be good for a while," he told his congregation. "[The Chicago firm's] action is based on a policy that may be good for all time and should become a forerunner for what society as a whole ought to do with its maladjusted and anti-social. They will simply have to be drafted into the social system, and by that I do not mean that we should have to be adjusted to their low standards. A classic example is that of King David drafting into his army the outcasts of his people with which army, historians tell us, he built the nation of Israel. Far-seeing states and statesmen-like governments will learn from King David and the Chicago firm that to rebuild the nations of the world they will have to draft those men who, after all, are only the products of our way of living. Thus only should we be taking the first step for the solution of the age-old problem of crime."

The Hawthorne Inn became a fixed feature of guided bus tours around Chicago and its environs. "Capone Castle!" the conductor would bellow through his megaphone.

Beginning with Edward Dean Sullivan's *Rattling the Cop on Chicago Crime,* seven books devoted largely or entirely to Capone were published between 1929 and 1931. Fawcett Publications, then situated in Minneapolis' Sexton Building, brought out a profusely illustrated one-shot magazine, among the first of its kind to flood the newsstands, priced at 50 cents, with the title *The Inside Story of Chicago's Master Criminal.* The title page carried one of Judge Lyle's fulminations: "We will send Al Capone to the chair if it is possible to do so!" and the anonymous author attributed most of the murders described in the text to Capone, though in many cases there was no connection. The entire Fawcett executive staff then went into hiding for fear of reprisals. But evidently Capone was more flattered than offended by such lavish attention. He bought 100 copies. The total sales came to about 750,000.

In Howard Hughes' Hollywood studios work began on *Scarface,* screenplay by Ben Hecht, starring Paul Muni. (First National had released the first major gangster film, *Little Caesar,* with Edward G. Robinson, early in 1930, followed by Warner's *Public Enemy,* with James Cagney, in 1931.) One midnight (as Hecht told the story years later) there came a knocking at the door of his Los Angeles hotel room. He opened to two hard-eyed strangers. They had somehow obtained a copy of his screenplay.

"You the guy who wrote this?" said the man who was carrying the script.

Hecht admitted he was.

"We read it."

"How did you like it?" the author asked.

"Is this stuff about Al Capone?"

"God, no!" said Hecht. "I don't even know Al." He named a few gangsters he had known as a reporter in Chicago—Colosimo, O'Banion, Hymie Weiss. . . .

"OK, then. We'll tell Al this stuff you wrote is about them other guys." As they started to leave, one of the callers had an afterthought. "If this stuff isn't about Al Capone, why are you calling it *Scarface?* Everybody'll think it's him."

"That's the reason. Al is one of the most famous and fascinating men of our time. If you call the movie *Scarface,* everybody will want to see it, figuring it's about Al. That's part of the racket we call showmanship."

"I'll tell Al. Who's this fella Howard Hughes?"

"He's got nothing to do with it. He's the sucker with the money."

"OK. The hell with him." And they left, satisfied.

In the theater Capone was impersonated by Crane Wilbur as Tony Perelli, the protagonist of Edgar Wallace's gangster melodrama *On the Spot.* After a successful London run, it opened on Broadway on October 29, 1930, and lasted 167 performances.

An editorial in a Viennese newspaper, quoted by the Chicago press, called Capone "the real mayor of Chicago," and satirically wondered why the voters did not make him so in law, as well as in fact. The notion sent one of his underlings into paroxysms of mirth; but Capone found nothing laughable about it, and the fellow's levity so infuriated him that he knocked him down.

Le Journal de Paris dispatched its celebrated crime expert, Georges London, to Chicago to study gangsterism. He was charmed by Capone, who talked to him through an interpreter in his Prairie Avenue house. *"On ne peut guère croire que c'est un monstre ayant à peu près cinquante crimes sur la conscience,"* London wrote, which the Chicago *Daily News* translated in a reprint of the interview as

"One can barely believe that he is a monster having about fifty crimes on his conscience."

"*Ajoutez,*" London went on, "*qu'il ne manque pas d'esprit et de ruse.*" ("Add that he doesn't lack humor and cunning.")

" '*Vous êtes venu,*' il dit, '*voir celui qu'on appelle le gorille. Eh bien, regardez le gorille.*' " (" 'You came,' says he, 'to see the one who is called a gorilla. Well, look at the gorilla.' ") . . .

" '*Est-ce très indiscret de vous demandait de quelles affaires vous vous occupez?*' " (" 'Is it very indiscreet to ask you in what sort of business you are?' ")

" '*Oh, gros malin! Vous le savez bien.*' " (" 'Oh, you cute fellow! You know it well.' ") . . . He deplored his countrymen's hypocrisy. Too many Americans, he said, voted dry and lived wet; too many politicians were crooks behind their mask of respectability. " '*Comment voulez-vous que je ne déteste pas ces personnes?*' " (" 'How can you expect me not to despise these persons?' ")

He urged the Frenchman to visit him in Florida that winter. " '*Vous verrez mes belles fleurs.*' " (" 'You'll see my beautiful flowers.' ")

"*Et l'homme au cinquante cadavres, toujours souriant, me donne sa main, fine et très blanche.*" ("And the man of fifty corpses, always smiling, gives me his hand, fine and very white.")

But few interviewers ever found Capone more captivating or found him more glamorous than Mrs. Eleanor "Cissy" Patterson, editor and later owner of the Washington *Herald*. "One of those prodigious Italians," she gushed after spending an hour or two with him on Palm Island. "Once I looked *at* his eyes. Ice-gray, ice-cold eyes. You can't anymore look *into* the eyes of Capone than you can look into the eyes of a tiger. . . ."

She listened sympathetically to his lament that neither society nor the law treated him fairly. "I don't interfere with big business," he told the multimillionaire editor. "None of the big business guys can say I ever took a dollar from 'em. . . . I only want to do business, you understand, with my own class. Why can't they let me alone? I don't interfere with them any. Get me? I don't interfere with their racket. They should let my racket be."

"Well, you're still—you're still czar of—" Mrs. Patterson faltered, groping for the tactful word.

"But they're forever after me. All the time trying to frame me. . . ."

Like Reporter London, the lady editor was impressed by Capone's hands. "Enormous. Powerful enough to tackle—well, almost anything, although superficially soft from lack of exposure." But the eyes disturbed her. "The stirring of the tiger. For just a second I went a little sick. I had to fight the impulse to jump up and run blindly away."

The unobtrusive efficiency of a servant responding to Capone's order for a round of lemonade fetched a sigh of envy from Mrs. Patterson. "My goodness," she said, "I wish I could get service like that at home."

On parting she wished Capone good luck "and I meant it sincerely."

"It has been said, with truth," she concluded, "that women have a special kind of sympathy for gangsters. If you don't understand why, consult Dr. Freud."

The prominent people wanting to meet Capone ranged widely from artistic celebrities to the castellans of Chicago's lakeshore manors, one of whom remarked: "Society would be a lot more fun if Al Capone would join in." When the Metropolitan Opera diva Lucrezia Bori learned that George Jessel, who had been introduced to her in a New York restaurant, knew Capone, she asked him if he could arrange a meeting the next time she sang in Chicago. Jessel wrote to the opera-loving gang leader. Whether a meeting ever took place is doubtful, but during one summer opera season in Ravinia Park she did receive a case of vintage champagne "with the compliments of Al Capone."

A good many Chicago gangsters, Capone among them, had been Jessel fans ever since 1926, when he plucked their heartstrings in that lachrymose drama of filial sacrifice, *The Jazz Singer*. In the last week of Hymie Weiss' life he accompanied his mother to the Harris Theater and by the third act was mingling his tears with hers. Capone, equally moved, sent Terry Druggan backstage to tell Jessel how much he wanted to shake his hand. "Call me Snorky," he said, when, after the performance a few nights later, curiosity brought the actor to the Metropole Hotel. Capone took him to supper at the Midnight Frolics. "Anything happens to you or any of your friends, you let me know," he said.

It was not an empty offer. With Bugs Moran's North Siders reduced by gunfire and jail sentences to a skeleton force and the Aiellos either dead or retired, no serious challenge to Capone's supremacy remained. Few gangsters now operated in Chicago without his knowledge, and fewer still without his approval. Thus, he was able to intervene when Jessel appealed to him in behalf of some colleague. Show folk were the natural prey of both extortioners who would threaten them with disfigurement unless they paid regular tribute, and of holdup men, who would lay in wait for them when they left the theater. Such victims, intended or actual, came to include Lou Holtz, Georgie Price, Rudy Vallee, Harry Richman—to name only a few.

Richman presented a particularly enticing target to predators, for he normally wore a small fortune in jewelry and carried at least one $1,000 bill with which it amused him to pay a restaurant or speakeasy tab and watch the waiter's eyebrows rise. During the Chicago run of *George White's Scandals of 1927* he was waylaid between the Erlanger Theater and his hotel not once, but repeatedly. The next day he would buy a new jeweled cigarette case, rings, a watch, only to be robbed again. He finally went to see Capone, an admirer who had burst into his dressing room opening night, clapped him on the back, and cried: "Richman, you're the greatest!" Whispering some order to a henchman, Capone took the entertainer for a drive along the lakeshore. When they got back to the Lexington, a package lay on the mahogany office desk. It contained the missing jewelry and several thousand dollars. Capone also handed Richman a note, saying: "Put this in your pocket, and if you get into any trouble, use it." The note read: "To whom it may concern—Harry Richman is a very good friend of mine. Al Capone." Richman had occasion to use it a few nights later. The holdup men he showed it to apologized and withdrew.

While the impressionist Georgie Price was playing a Chicago vaudeville engagement, the jewelry and cash he left in his hotel room vanished. After Jessel spoke to Capone, that loot, too, was returned.

But the most dramatic recovery of stolen goods Capone ever brought about followed the appeal of a woman who had done him a small service, a Miss Mary Lindsay, the manager of a Washington, D.C., hotel. Driving through the Midwest on vacation, she had come upon a Chicago-bound train stalled just outside the city. Among the passengers pacing the track was Al Capone, whom she failed to recognize when he asked her for a lift. She drove him to the Lexington. Not until she glanced at the card he gave her, as he urged her to call on him for any help she might need while in Chicago, did she realize who the hitchhiker was. A few days later her purse, containing all her cash and traveler's checks, was snatched. She turned to Capone. That night, following his instructions, Miss Lindsay dined in a West Side café, taking the table facing the first of a line of stone columns. Midway through the meal, her purse suddenly appeared on the chair next to the column. Not a penny was missing.

On December 14, 1930, John Maritote, a twenty-three-year-old motion-picture operator and the younger brother of Frank Maritote, alias Diamond, whose wife was Rose Capone, married Mafalda Capone, age nineteen. It appears to have been a marriage of convenience for which neither bride nor groom could summon much enthusiasm. According to his friends, Maritote, who had hardly ever spoken to Mafalda, loved another girl, while Mafalda's heart was supposedly set on a boy she met in Miami. The internal politics of the Capone organization dictated the union. Frank Diamond, having risen to the top echelon, was demanding a bigger voice, especially when it came to the division of profits from bootlegging. By this second union between the two families Capone hoped to prevent dissension. He promised the couple $50,000 and a house as wedding presents.

Not since Angelo Genna was joined to Lucille Spingola had gangland witnessed such glittering nuptials. Three thousand guests, including Alderman William V. Pacelli, City Sealer Daniel Serritella, Jack McGurn, Frank Rio and the three Guzik brothers, packed St. Mary's Church in Cicero, and despite heavy snow and sleet, a thousand onlookers waited outside. Al Capone did not attend. With a vagrancy warrant issued by Judge Lyle hanging over him, he had decided to return to Florida.

The matrons of honor, in pink duvetyn hats and pink chiffon gowns, were Mmes. Al and Ralph Capone. The bride, wearing a Lanvin model of ivory satin with a 25-foot train, walked down the aisle on the arm of brother Ralph. After the Reverend Crajkowski pronounced the couple man and wife, they adjourned with their families and guests to the Cotton Club, a Cicero nightclub that Ralph ran. The wedding cake, shaped like an ocean liner, measured 9 feet long, 4 feet high and 3 feet wide, and the prow bore the name in red icing of the newlyweds' honeymoon destination—Honolulu.

Only one slight contretemps had marred the proceedings. Detectives Mike Casey and Louis Capparelli from the state's attorney's office arrested five Caponeites claiming to be ushers. "Not ushers," said Casey, as they marched them off to the station house. "Shushers. They had guns in their pockets."

From Florida Capone submitted, through George Barker of the Teamsters' Union, a proposal to Chief Justice McGoorty, which the latter described, with signal restraint, as "cool effrontery." He offered to surrender on the vagrancy warrant, quit labor racketeering, leave Chicago, and operate his other enterprises by remote control. His conditions: dismissal of the vagrancy charge the moment he surrendered; no interference with his liquor business.

What the chief justice said to Barker is not recorded, but he told the grand jury: "[Capone's] most formidable competitors have been ruthlessly exterminated and his only apparent obstacle towards undisputed sway is the law. Such a trade is unthinkable. The time has come when the public must choose between the rule of the gangster and the rule of law."

23

Paper Chase

THE office space allocated to Wilson in the old Federal Building was a windowless cubicle so cramped that he could hardly stir without brushing against the filing cabinet or another agent. For weeks, during the summer of 1930, he had closeted himself there, combing through mountains of papers seized by the police in raids on various Capone establishments as far back as 1924, through bank records, through the memoranda of his assistant agents, in quest of evidence linking Capone to the source of his profits. Wilson, Tessem and Hodgins between them had examined close to 1,700,000 separate items.

It was past midnight. Exhausted, discouraged, his vision blurred, he began gathering up the material strewn over the desk, chairs and floor to return it to the filing cabinet. Bending over to retrieve a bundle of checks, he bumped into the cabinet, and the drawer flew shut, locking automatically. He couldn't find the key. In the corridor stood a row of dusty old filing cabinets and seeing an open drawer, he decided to store the material there temporarily. The drawer was partly filled by a large package tied up in brown paper, one of many turned over to him by the state's attorney, which he had somehow overlooked. He broke the string. Out tumbled three black ledgers with red corners. They were dated 1924–26. Leafing through them, he stopped, electrified, at a page in the second ledger. The columns were headed BIRD CAGE, 21, CRAPS, FARO, ROULETTE, HORSE BETS.

He was no longer exhausted. He carried the ledgers to his desk and began analyzing them entry by entry. They showed net profits totaling, in an eighteen-month period, more than $500,000. Every few pages a balance had been taken and divided among "A" (for Al, Wilson surmised), "R" (Ralph Capone), "J" (Jake Guzik), etc. A balance of $36,687 on December 2, 1924, had been divided as follows:

Town	$6,537.42	(paid)
Ralph	1,634.35	
Pete	1,634.35	
Frank	5,720.22	
J & A	5,720.22	
Lou	5,720.22	
D	5,720.22	

Wilson took "Town" to mean Cicero officials; "Pete," probably Pete Penovich, the first Smoke Shop manager; "Frank," Frankie Pope; "J & A," Jake and Al; "Lou," perhaps Louis La Cava; "D"? A notation at the foot of the page read: "Frank paid $17,500 for Al."

From the state's attorney's office, to which Wilson hastened in the morning, he learned that the ledgers were among those seized during the Smoke Shop raid after the McSwiggin murder in 1926. They were written in three different hands. Wilson and his teammates undertook the enormous task of comparing them with every specimen of gangsters' handwriting they could collect from such sources as the motor vehicle bureau and other licensing agencies, banks, bail bondsmen, the criminal courts. Eventually a bank deposit slip turned up with a signature that matched the writing in numerous ledger entries between 1924 and 1926. It belonged to Leslie Adelbert Shumway, familiarly called Lou, who had preceded Fred Ries as cashier at the Ship.

While Wilson was trying to track down Shumway, a tipster repeated to him the comment of a Capone lieutenant: "The big fellow's eating aspirin like it was peanuts so's he can get some sleep."

Mattingly and Wilson conferred several more times. The lawyer conceded that his client's enterprises had produced income, though a relatively modest one. Wilson asked him to specify just how much in writing. To his amazement and joy, Mattingly submitted this statement "Re Alphonse Capone":

Taxpayer became active as a principal with three associates at about the end of the year 1925. Because of the fact he had no capital to invest in their various undertakings, his participation during the entire year 1926 and the greater part of 1927 was limited. During the years 1928 and 1929, the profits of the organization of which he was a member were divided as follows: one-third to a group of regular employes and one-sixth to the taxpayer and three associates. . . .

I am of the opinion that his taxable income for the years 1926 and 1927 might be fairly fixed at not to exceed $26,000 and $40,000, respectively, and for the years 1928 and 1929, not to exceed $100,000 per year.

As Wilson knew, Capone spent more than $100,000 a year on high living alone. But however remote from the truth, here was a written admission of tax delinquency. Mattingly made it "without prejudice to the rights of the above named taxpayer in any proceedings that might be instituted against him. The facts stated are upon information and belief only." He miscalculated. No such stipulation was legally binding, and Wilson gleefully added the statement to Case Jacket SI-7085-F.

Harking back to the investigation many years later, Wilson revealed the identity of a man he considered to have been his single most valuable secret ally. This was the St. Louis lawyer and dog track operator Edward O'Hare. Their mutual friend, John Rogers of the St. Louis *Post-Dispatch,* brought them together at lunch in the Missouri Athletic Club. "He wanted to look you over," he told Wilson afterward. "He's satisfied," and he explained that O'Hare had decided to inform against Capone. His motive was paternal. With his son's heart set on Annapolis he hoped to smooth the way for him by helping the government topple Capone. Did he understand the risk? Wilson asked. If O'Hare had ten lives, Rogers replied, he would gladly risk them all for the boy.

Wilson heard frequently from O'Hare thereafter, either directly or through Rogers. It was O'Hare who told him where to look for Fred Ries, who exposed to him the structure of the Capone dog track management, who verified the true percentage of the gambling profits that went into Capone's pockets—not one-sixth, but more than half.

You be sure to take good care of yourself. The veiled warning echoed in Wilson's mind when O'Hare called him one morning toward the end of November. Fantastic as it sounded, Capone, he said, acting against the judgment of cooler heads, had imported five gunmen from New York with a contract to kill not only Wilson, but also Arthur Madden, the chief of the Chicago tax intelligence unit, Pat Roche and U.S. Attorney Johnson. Mike Malone confirmed the report. The contract called for payment of $25,000. The gunmen had arrived in a blue Chevrolet sedan with New York license plates.

Wilson took O'Hare's advice to move himself and his wife to another hotel immediately. "They know where you keep your automobile and what time you get home at night and what time you leave in the morning." Telling the Sheridan Plaza desk they were going to Kansas, the couple drove to the Union Station, then circled back and took a room at the Palmer House. A twenty-four-hour guard was assigned to them and to each intended victim.

Pat Roche ordered his detectives to bring in Capone, but forewarned by the Cook County police, he eluded them. Then Arthur Madden, hearing that Johnny Torrio was in Chicago, gave him a message for Capone: "If those hoodlums aren't out of town by tonight, I'm going after them myself with two guns." With the murder plot known to the authorities, the members of Capone's cabinet prevailed upon him to call it off. Torrio telephoned Madden. "They left an hour ago," he said.

Having abandoned wholesale murder as a solution of his tax problems, Capone tried bribery. In New York Joseph H. Callan, former special assistant to the Commissioner of Internal Revenue and now an executive of the Crucible Steel Company, received a visit from an emissary calling himself "Smith." He bore an offer from Capone for Elmer Irey and asked Callan to transmit it—$1,500,000 in cash if there was no conviction. Callan showed him the door.

In February, 1931, four months after Shumway had been identified as the keeper of the Ship books, John Rogers relayed a message from O'Hare that sent Wilson dashing off to Miami. Lou Shumway was working there as a cashier at either a horse or dog track. While looking for him, Wilson saw Capone at Hialeah, "a jeweled moll on either side of him [he wrote later] . . . occasionally raising huge binoculars to his eyes, greeting a parade of fawning sycophants who came to shake his hand—a veritable Shah of Persia. . . . Good God,

I thought. When a country constable wants a man, he just walks up and says, 'You're pinched.' Here I am with the whole U.S. Government behind me, as powerless as a canary."

He found Shumway, a pole-thin man, his hands unsteady, at the Biscayne Kennel Club. When, green with terror, he disclaimed any knowledge of the Ship ledgers, Wilson presented two alternatives. He could go on pretending ignorance, in which case a deputy sheriff would publicly and noisily hand him a subpoena, thereby letting the Capone gang know that he had been found. To ensure his permanent silence, Wilson added, they would probably kill him. Or he could cooperate with the government and rest assured of the same protection as Ries. Shumway chose the second alternative.

"Orders and directives relating to my work were issued to me by Frank Pope and Pete Penovich," he deposed. ". . . the only other person whom I recognized as an owner of the business was Mr. Alphonse Capone." He also described the raid that the West Suburban Citizens' Association forced the county police to stage against the Smoke Shop in 1925. This led Wilson to interview the Reverend Henry Hoover and Chester Bragg, the vigilante who had guarded the entrance to the gambling dive during the raid. Bragg swore to the self-incriminating words Capone let slip in his rage—"I own the place."

Two years had elapsed since the government charged Capone with contempt of court for failing to answer a subpoena summoning him to Chicago from Miami. Now at last, on the morning of February 25, he entered the Federal Court Building once again. His arrival caused a work stoppage. Hundreds of clerks and stenographers deserted their posts to steal up to the sixth-floor courtroom for a glimpse of him. "No, I'm not going into the movies," they heard him tell the reporters. He wore a bright-blue suit woven of material soft as cat's fur, a blue-and-white-striped tie and gray spats. His girth had swollen to 250 pounds. Phil D'Andrea stood warily at his side, clenched fists thrust into the pockets of his chesterfield. "Neither am I going to write my autobiography. I've been offered as high as two million dollars, but I'm not going into the literary business."

Having waived jury trial, Capone pleaded guilty before Judge Wilkerson. A short, bristle-browed, testy man, the judge listened to seven prosecution witnesses give the lie to the deposition signed by

Capone's Miami doctor to the effect that bronchial pneumonia prevented his patient from traveling. There was the airplane pilot who flew Capone to Bimini when he was supposedly confined to bed, the policeman who helped him park his car at the Hialeah racetrack, the steamboat officer who talked to him aboard a Nassau-bound pleasure craft. . . .

As Capone left the courtroom at the noon recess, two police sergeants arrested him on the vagrancy warrant issued by Judge Lyle. Taking him to the detective bureau, they gave him a sandwich and coffee, then fingerprinted him, photographed him, and asked him his occupation. "Real estate," said Capone. The hearing was set for March 2.

In Judge Wilkerson's court on February 27 Capone was approached by a blushing girl reporter. "I wanted to ask you a question," she said, "but I'm so flustered I can't remember what it was." Capone smiled encouragingly. "Oh, I remember, I wanted to ask you what you think of the American girl."

"Why, I think you're beautiful," said Capone.

The judge's secretary, equally flustered, rushed out of his chambers to tell the defendant, "London is on the wire."

"I'm sorry, lady," Capone said, "but there's nobody in London that would be calling me, not even King George."

Wilkerson found him guilty and later fixed the penalty at six months in the Cook County jail, releasing him on a bond, pending appeal. "I ain't worrying about a cell," said Capone. "I'm not there yet. There are other courts."

In the vagrancy case he proved to be right. Judge Lyle recalled bitterly: "Waiting until I was on temporary assignment in another court, Capone . . . appeared before a judge who had been a severe critic of my high bond policy. The mobster maintained his perfect batting average in Chicago courts. After three continuances the case was dismissed."

Before Wilson transferred Shumway to a safe hiding place, a federal grand jury quickly and secretly convened to hear the cashier's testimony. There was good reason for haste. The preponderance of his disclosures about Capone's income referred to the year 1924. Together with figures supplied by Ries and O'Hare, they showed a tax liability, not counting penalties, of $32,488.81 on a net income of

$123,102.89, but under a six-year statute of limitations tax offenses committed in 1924 would be barred from prosecution after March 15, 1931. The grand jury returned an indictment on March 13. At the request of U.S. Attorney Johnson it agreed not to make its verdict public until the investigation had been completed for the years 1925 to 1929.

The April mayoral elections brought final defeat to Capone's political idol, Big Bill Thompson. In the Republican primary he had won over Judge Lyle, a victory which moved Capone to exult: "Lyle tried to make me an issue and the public has given its answer." But Thompson lost to Anton J. Cermak, who modeled his Democratic machine on Tammany Hall, by 194,267 votes, the biggest majority in the history of the Chicago mayoralty. Cermak never attempted to purge Chicago of gangsterism, only of the Capone gang in favor of others who had supported his campaign. On February 15, 1933, immediately after greeting President Roosevelt in Miami, he was fatally shot by Giuseppe Zangara. Some historians have dismissed the general assumption that Zangara intended to assassinate Roosevelt but hit Cermak by accident. Disenfranchised Caponeites, they contend, guided Zangara's hand. It is a belief the victim himself expressed on his hospital deathbed.

The federal grand jury convened again on June 5, this time openly, and to its earlier indictment against Capone it added another with twenty-two counts covering the years 1925–1929. That fraction of his income for those years which Internal Revenue had been able to compute totaled $1,038,655.84. The tax assessment came to $219,260.12, and the penalties to $164,445.09.

A week later the grand jury returned yet a third indictment. Based on the evidence assembled by Eliot Ness and his raiders, it charged Capone and sixty-eight members of his gang with conspiring to violate the Volstead Act. Five thousand separate offenses were cited, 4,000 of them consisting of beer truck deliveries, 32 barrels to the truck. They went all the way back to 1922, when Capone bought a used truck for Torrio. The income-tax case, however, took precedence.

24

Aggiornamento

A SPIRIT of rebellion was stirring inside the Mafia. (Or the Syndicate, the Outfit, the Mob, Cosa Nostra. The terms are interchangeable, "almost a matter of semantics," as Attorney General Robert Kennedy once put it, each used in its time by the press or the police—if hardly ever by the members themselves—to designate the same loose-knit national confederacy of Italian and Sicilian gangster "families.") A conflict threatened between an old-world gang tradition and a businesslike, Americanized approach to organized crime, between the "Mustache Petes" and the "Young Turks."

For decades the American Mafia families had been ruled by stiff-collared Sicilian despots with handlebar mustaches, who styled themselves Boss and aspired to the national title of Boss of Bosses. Parochial and bellicose, they organized their families along military lines with underbosses and soldiers. They shunned alliances with non-Sicilian gangs and would admit no mainland Italians to their ranks. Giuseppe "Joe the Boss" Masseria, who headed the predominant New York family during the twenties and carried considerable weight among Sicilian gangs all over the country, typified the Mustache Petes. "An outfit runs on its own," he insisted, "and knocks off anybody in its way." He acknowledged Peter "the Clutching Hand" Morello as Boss of Bosses. Masseria allowed exceptions to the ban against non-Sicilians in the cases of Vito Genovese, a Neapolitan, and Frank Costello, a Calabrian, and one or two others, who rose high in his family, and he had a friendly understanding with Dutch Schultz, a Jew converted to Catholicism. Otherwise Joe the Boss observed strict orthodoxy.

The Young Turks wanted no Boss of Bosses. They preferred the American system of delegating authority, of rule by committee instead of dictum. They were prepared to welcome Italians as fellow Mafiosi whatever their native province (though none of these radicals ventured so far as to propose non-Italians for membership) and to ally themselves with other gangs regardless of ethnic differences. They rejected warfare, making allowance only for the liquidation of individuals who imperiled the common purpose. In sum, they stood for the kind of ecumenism Torrio had always urged and Capone had practiced when possible. Out of their insurgency evolved organized crime as it flourishes in America today, still dominated by Italians, but with a board of directors to determine national policy and numerous non-Italian associates participating.

By the late twenties nearly every Mafia family harbored its Young Turks. In the Masseria family they included Genovese, Costello and the Sicilian Lucky Luciano, whom Joe the Boss looked on as a son. Capone had maintained liaison with them ever since the Atlantic City conference.

Masseria and many members of his family were natives of Sciacca, a town on the west coast of Sicily. New York's second most important Mafia family came mainly from the region bordering the Gulf of Castellammare, on the northwestern coast. It was headed by Salvatore Maranzano, who conducted his business, principally bootlegging, behind an office door marked REAL ESTATE high up on the ninth floor of the Grand Central Building, overlooking Park Avenue. In February, 1930, Masseria moved to take over the Castellammarese by arranging the murder of one of their top men, Tom Reina, and foisting upon them a lieutenant from his own ranks, Joseph Pinzola. In reprisal both Pinzola and the Masseria-supported Boss of Bosses, Peter Morello, were killed. The feud, which lasted more than a year, is known to Mafiologists as the Castellammarese War. Frantic with fear and hatred, Masseria decreed the execution of every Castellammarese in the country. The casualties in both camps totaled about sixty, many of them occurring in Massachusetts, Ohio and Illinois, as well as in New York and New Jersey.

Luciano, Genovese and Costello reaffirmed their loyalty to Mas-

seria. Dutch Schultz and Ciro Terranova, the Bronx artichoke racketeer, also fought on his side, and Capone contributed money to his
war chest. But secretly they considered Maranzano the lesser of two
evils. Luciano paid him a visit.

For five months the Castellammarese had been trying to trap Masseria, but he stuck close to his heavily guarded redoubt at 65 Second
Avenue. It was his trusted Lucky Luciano who finally lured him
away by convincing him that he knew how to ambush Maranzano
and inviting him to a tactical discussion with Genovese and Terranova. On April 15, 1931, they took him for lunch in Terranova's
car to his favorite Coney Island restaurant, Scarpato's. Terranova's
hand shook so when he pushed the key into the ignition (according
to what the Maranzano soldier Joseph Valachi told the McClellan
Committee thirty-two years later) that somebody else had to drive,
though apparently Masseria never noticed. As a result of his nervousness, the Artichoke King lost face with his co-conspirators. "Ever
since then," Valachi recalled, "Ciro Terranova was getting what was
called buckwheats, you know, like he was being stripped, you know,
a little at a time he was being taken, his power was being taken from
him. After a while he took it so hard he died from a broken heart."

Genovese and Terranova did not tarry long at Scarpato's. They left
before lunch. After eating lobster and sharing a bottle of wine, Luciano and Masseria played cards. By three thirty they were the only
customers in the place. Luciano excused himself to go to the men's
room. During his absence "persons unknown" entered. When he
rushed back, having heard gunfire, as he told the police, Joe the
Boss' blood was staining the tablecloth. He had been shot in the head
and back six times. His right hand held the ace of diamonds.

An armistice was declared, and to a hired hall in the Bronx flocked
almost 500 combatants from both camps to pay homage to the victorious Maranzano. It had been a costly war, and Maranzano gave a
series of five $6-a-plate banquets to raise money for his depleted
treasury. Luciano and Capone each bought $6,000 worth of tickets.
The total came to $115,000. But Maranzano committed a calamitous
diplomatic blunder. "Now it's going to be different," he promised.
"We are going to have—first we have the boss of all bosses, which is
myself."

The Young Turks had not obliterated one Mustache Pete only to
enthrone another. They could count as potential allies among the

Castellammarese a number of young, forward-looking future leaders like Giuseppe Profaci and Joseph "Joe Bananas" Bonanno. Maranzano recognized his danger. He told Valachi: "We have to go to the mattress again." (That is, carry mattresses from hideout to hideout to sleep on during the hostilities.) He handed him a list of the proscribed. Capone headed it, followed by Costello, Luciano, Genovese, Vincent Mangano, Joe Adonis, Dutch Schultz and four or five others.

But the rebels struck first. For executioners they went outside the Mafia to the Jewish gang chieftain Meyer Lansky, who assigned to them four killers. Shortly before two o'clock on the afternoon of September 11, the quartet, flashing fake detective badges and brushing aside the visitors crowding Maranzano's reception room, stepped into his office. They left the Boss of Bosses with four bullet holes in his body, six knife thrusts, and his throat cut. During the next forty-eight hours, in cities across the country, about forty Mafiosi of the old school were purged from the parent body.

The *coup d'état* brought Luciano to the top of the heap, and he lost no time instituting the reforms the Young Turks had fought for. Eschewing the title Boss of Bosses, he remodeled the whole system. Each family head would remain autonomous within his own district but would defer to a national commission when it came to issues affecting the common welfare. The old clannishness that had set Sicilians against mainland Italians gradually yielded to a spirit of cooperation. "Don Vitone" Genovese, a Neapolitan, was the second most prestigious figure, after Luciano, in the reorganized cartel. Though never technically members of the Mafia, many non-Italian gangsters became intimately affiliated with it, attaining positions of immense power. While Luciano took prostitution and narcotics as his special provinces, the major gambling concessions of Florida and the Bahamas fell to Meyer Lansky. His partner, Benjamin "Bugsy" Siegel, occupied the same spot in Nevada and California. Louis "Lepke" Buchalter largely controlled New York's garment district extortion racket; Dutch Schultz, its policy games; Frank Erickson, its bookmaking. Abner "Longy" Zwillman came to control practically every New Jersey racket. Under the generalship of Abe "Kid Twist" Reles, the gang known as Murder, Inc. frequently served as a punitive instrument for the Mafia. In Brooklyn alone it fulfilled scores of contracts. Give-and-take, strength in union, coexistence—these were the guiding principles in the new era of organized crime.

The winds of change promised to carry Capone to still greater heights. He was only thirty-one. His organizational skill and personal magic were recognized throughout the underworld. Luciano so valued his good opinion that he sent an emissary to Chicago to justify in Capone's eyes the murder of Maranzano. Unquestionably, there would have been a seat for Capone at the council table of the national commission. . . .

If only he had paid his income taxes.

25

The Reckoning

IF found guilty on every count in the three indictments, Capone faced a possible maximum prison sentence of thirty-four years. His legal staff comprised the flower of the Nash-Ahern firm. In addition to Thomas Nash and the elegant Ahern, it included foxy little Albert Fink, a Dickensian figure, round in the face and belly, with gold-rimmed eyeglasses riding the tip of his clever nose and a habit of exclaiming at critical moments, "Oh, my conscience!" They offered U.S. Attorney Johnson a compromise: their client would plead guilty if assured of a lighter sentence. After consulting Wilson, Irey, Attorney General William Mitchell and Secretary of the Treasury Ogden Mills, who had succeeded Mellon, Johnson agreed to recommend a sentence of two and a half years. The consensus had been that gang terrorism might yet prevent the government's star witnesses from testifying. Also, there was no certainty that the Supreme Court would uphold the six-year statute of limitations. If only a three-year limitation were applicable to tax evasion, as a U.S. District Court of Appeals had recently ruled, it would, in Capone's case, preclude prosecution for all the years covered by the indictments.

Capone's banana-yellow summer suit matched his bright spirits as he boarded the elevator in the Federal Court Building on the morning of June 16. A judge who tried to enter it at the same time was waved back by the operator. "You can't use this, bud," he said.

"It's reserved for Al Capone." Upon Capone's plea of guilty Judge Wilkerson adjourned the hearing until the thirtieth.

Taking for granted, as did the entire American press, that Capone would get off with a light sentence, the *New Republic* commented: ". . . the incident can only be described as a victory for its central figure. . . . The defeat is Chicago's." ". . . a devastating criticism of our legal machinery," said the St. Paul *News* and the Louisville *Courier-Journal:* "It is not conducive to American pride that gangsters, guilty of every abomination . . . should be found guilty only of failing to pay taxes on their ill-gotten gains." A cartoon by Daniel Fitzpatrick in the St. Louis *Post-Dispatch* showed a burglar jimmying a safe while Uncle Sam reminds him: "Don't fail to report this in your income tax."

On July 29, the day before his return to Judge Wilkerson's court, Capone, wearing white-bordered black silk pajamas, chatted amiably with reporters in his Hotel Lexington suite. Referring again to his offers from movie producers, he explained why he had turned them all down. "You know, these gang pictures—that's terrible kid stuff. Why, they ought to take them all and throw them into the lake. They're doing nothing but harm to the younger element of this country. I don't blame the censors for trying to bar them. Now, you take all these youngsters who go to the movies. You remember reading dime novels, maybe, when you were a kid. Well, you know how it made you want to get out and kill pirates and look for buried treasure—you know. Well, these gang movies are making a lot of kids want to be tough guys and they don't serve any useful purpose."

Contemplating his imprisonment, he observed: "I've been made an issue and I'm not complaining. But why don't they go after all these bankers who took the savings of thousands of poor people and lost them in bank failures? How about that? Isn't it lots worse to take the last few dollars some small family has saved—perhaps to live on while the head of a family is out of a job—than to sell a little beer, a little alky? Believe me, I can't see where the fellow who sells it is any worse off than the fellow who buys and drinks it."

He prophesied an end to gang warfare as a result of his efforts. "I have always been opposed to violence—to shootings. I have fought, yes, but fought for peace. And I believe I can take credit for the peace that now exists in the racket game in Chicago. I believe that the people can thank me for the fact that gang killings here are probably a thing of the past."

What would become of his gang during his absence? "It's really a shame to disabuse the public, to destroy one of their most popular myths. But, honestly, there is not, nor has there ever been what might be called a Capone gang."

That evening he gave a farewell dinner at the New Florence Restaurant. Mike Malone, still playing his role of fugitive gangster, was invited. "Sorry you're going away, Al," he said. But Capone was not downcast. A two-and-a-half-year sentence, with reduction for good behavior, seemed easy enough to bear, considering the alternatives. "Johnny'll look after things while I'm away," he said, hugging Torrio, who had come from New York to console his former protégé.

Pea green was the color of the linen suit Capone selected for his courtroom appearance on the thirtieth. Beaming on the spectators, he waited to hear the sentence. It never came. Instead, Judge Wilkerson, tense with repressed anger, announced: "The parties to a criminal case may not stipulate as to the judgment to be entered. . . . The Court may not now say to the defendant that it will enter the judgment suggested by the prosecution."

Ahern leaped to his feet. "We were led to believe that the recommendation would be approved by the Court," he protested. "Unless we had been confident that the Court would act according to the recommendation agreed upon the plea of guilty would never have been entered."

The judge's anger mounted. "The Court will listen . . . to the recommendation of the District Attorney. The Court will listen to the recommendation of the Attorney General. . . . But the thing the defendant cannot think, must not think, is that in the end the recommendation of the Attorney General and the Secretary of the Treasury, all considered, the Court is bound to enter judgment according to that recommendation. It is time for somebody to impress upon the defendant that it is utterly impossible to bargain with a federal court."

He permitted Capone to withdraw his plea of guilty and plead not guilty. He scheduled the trial for October.

On top of these ominous developments came a blow to Capone's professional standing. In its second roster of twenty-eight Public Enemies the Chicago Crime Commission assigned the No. 1 rank to his superintendent of breweries, Joe Fusco, and No. 2 to Ted New-berry. It did not even mention Capone.

By late summer Capone's optimism had returned, and he told the journalist Cornelius Vanderbilt, Jr.: "Oh, they are only trying to scare me. They know very well there'd be hell in this city if they put me away. Who else can keep the small-time racketeers from annoy-ing decent folks?"

He professed concern about the effect of the Depression upon the American way of life. "This is going to be a terrible winter. Us fellas has gotta open our pocketbooks, and keep on keeping them open, if we want any of us to survive. We can't wait for Congress or Mr. Hoover or anyone else. We *must* help to keep tummies filled and bodies warm. If we don't, it's all up with the way we've learned to live. Why, do you know, sir [here, one suspects, Vanderbilt substi-tuted his own ideas and vocabulary], America is on the verge of its greatest social upheaval? Bolshevism is knocking at our gates. We can't afford to let it in. . . . We must keep [the American worker] away from red literature, red ruses: we must see that his mind re-mains healthy. For, regardless of where he was born, he is now an American."

He deplored America's loss of ideals, or so Vanderbilt quoted him. "People respect nothing nowadays. Once we put honor, truth, and the law on a pedestal. Our children were brought up to respect these things. The war ended. We have had nearly twelve years to straighten ourselves out, and look what a mess we've made of our life!"

A week before the trial Wilson heard again from O'Hare. Capone, he reported, had procured the list of veniremen from which the jury would be chosen and his men were busy trying to bribe some of them with prizefight tickets, cash and job offers, and threatening to kill or maim others. O'Hare had copied ten names from the list—Nos. 30 through 39. Wilson showed them to Johnson, and together they took them to Wilkerson, who sent for the complete veniremen's list. The names of Nos. 30 through 39 tallied with those O'Hare had jotted down. "Bring your case into court as planned, gentlemen," said the judge. "Leave the rest to me."

O'Hare's activity as an undercover agent did not end with the Capone case. He developed a taste for the work. Despite his long, profitable association with gangsters, he had detested them from the first, and he went on informing against them to both county and state police, undaunted by Wilson's warning that some policeman in the pay of gangsters would betray him. At the same time, as president of the Sportsman's Park racetrack in Stickney, developer of legal dog tracks in Illinois, Massachusetts and Florida, manager of the Chicago Cardinals' pro football team, real estate investor, owner of an insurance company and two advertising agencies, he became a rich and respected business leader, the sins of his past forgotten.

Ensign Edward Henry O'Hare graduated from Annapolis in 1937. Five years later President Roosevelt awarded Lieutenant O'Hare the Congressional Medal of Honor for "one of the most daring single combat flights in the history of aviation." On February 20, 1942, piloting his Grumman Wildcat over the Pacific, he had brought down five Japanese medium bombers. The following year Lieutenant Commander O'Hare died in aerial combat. In 1949 Chicago's International Airport was renamed O'Hare Airport.

The hero's father lived to see none of these honors conferred. On November 8, 1939, while driving along Chicago's Ogden Avenue, he was killed by two men firing shotguns from a passing car. They were never identified. The objects the police removed from O'Hare's pockets included a rosary, a crucifix, a religious medallion, a note he had written in Italian and a doggerel verse clipped from a magazine. "Margy, Oh, Margy," the note read, *"Quanto tempo io penso per te. Fammi passar una notte insieme con te* [How often I think of you. Let me spend a night with you]." The verse went:

> The clock of life is wound but once
> And no man has the power
> To tell just when the hands will stop
> At late or early hour.
> Now is the only time you own.
> Live, love, toil with a will.
> Place no faith in time.
> For the clock may soon be still.

On the eve of the trial Damon Runyon, who was reporting it for Hearst's Universal Service, wandered into Colosimo's Café, saw Capone at a table with a group of gangsters, politicians and lawyers, and, having known him in Florida, joined the party. How did Capone estimate his chances? he asked. "I believe I've got at least an even break," replied the resilient gang lord.

He upbraided the press for its exaggerations. "It would have been utterly impossible for me to have done some of the things charged to me. Physically impossible. . . . Racketeer! Why, the real racketeers are the banks."

Runyon noted in his dispatch next day: "It is impossible to talk to Capone without conceding that he has that intangible attribute known as personality, or, as we say in the world of sport, 'color.' "

Tuesday, October 6

Squad cars carrying fourteen detectives convoy Capone the three miles from the Lexington Hotel north to the Federal Court Building. The lead car pauses at each intersection while its occupants survey the side streets for signs of friends or foes who might attempt to rescue or kill Capone. "Nobody's going to zuta anybody around here if we can help it," says the chief of detectives. Approaching the Federal Building, the motorcade turns into a tunnel, normally used only by delivery trucks, that ends at a basement entrance. The detectives guide Capone through an underground labyrinth to a freight elevator. The sixth-floor corridor is kept clear until he has entered the courtroom.

When the first venireman's name is called, Capone's face clouds. The name does not appear on the copy of the list he had obtained. At the last minute Wilkerson has nullified any possible subornation by the simple expedient of switching panels with a fellow judge.

As the selection of jurors proceeds, Capone bleakly studies the decor. A white marble dado, trimmed with gilt, rises halfway up the walls. Above them are murals depicting scenes from American colonial history. Behind the judge's bench Benjamin Franklin addresses the Continental Congress, his right hand outstretched toward George Washington. The windows are too high and narrow to admit enough light, and electric bulbs in the chandeliers and sconces burn all day. Phil D'Andrea fusses over Capone, when not glowering at the jurors, flicking a piece of lint from his master's mustard-brown suit, adjusting his chair closer to the counsel table.

Judge Wilkerson wears no robes over his dark-blue business suit. His iron-gray hair is tousled. As he questions each venireman at length, he sits on the extreme edge of his swivel chair. In striking contrast with his colleagues, U.S. Attorney George E. Q. Johnson (he adopted the "Q" to distinguish himself from innumerable George Johnsons) has the look of an esthete. His silken gray hair, parted straight as a ruler down the middle, lies on his high-domed head like birds' wings. His complexion is rosy, his mouth thin and sensitive. Four assistant U.S. attorneys sit at his table—William J. Froelich, Samuel G. Clawson, Jacob I. Grossman and Dwight H. Green (the last a future governor of Illinois) —and Johnson entrusts the examination of witnesses to them, content to remain the silent strategist.

By 4 P.M. the jury has been empaneled. It consists chiefly of small-town tradesmen, mechanics and farmers, who have sworn that they harbor no prejudice against the defendant, no wish to see him imprisoned.

Wednesday, October 7

The government's first witness, an Internal Revenue clerk, testifies that Capone filed no returns for the years 1924–1929. Chester Bragg follows him to the stand to repeat Capone's admission of ownership during the Smoke Shop raid. A pale, nervous Shumway then tabulates the Smoke Shop profits during his two years as its cashier. They exceeded $550,000.

Thursday, October 8

Assistant U.S. Attorney Clawson submits in evidence Lawyer Mattingly's foot-in-mouth letter to Agent Herrick. "A lawyer cannot confess for his client," objects the portly Fink. "When my client conferred power of attorney in this case to enable him to keep out of the penitentiary, it did not imply the power or authority to make statements that may get him into the penitentiary."

"It might have that effect ultimately," remarked the judge.

Oh, my conscience! In his dismay Fink mingles wrestling and Biblical allusions. "This is the last toe. They have got him nailed to the cross now. This is putting the last toe on him."

Ahern interjects: "The Supreme Court has often held that it is human nature to avoid tax. We had a Boston tea party—"

"I suppose," says the judge, "this is a Boston tea party."

But Capone's hopes still burn bright. How can lawyers who charge such fees, who have saved him time and again, fail him now? In the evening, at the Lexington, a tailor measures him for two lightweight suits. "You don't need to be ordering fancy duds," says Frankie Rio. "You're going to prison. Why don't you have a suit made with stripes on it?"

"The hell I am!" Capone retorts. "I'm going to Florida for a nice, long rest, and I need some new clothes before I go."

Friday, October 9

The wholesale price of alcohol has jumped from $30 to $32 per five-gallon can. The Chicago *Herald-Examiner* ascribes the rise to the cost of Capone's defense.

The public relations council for the Protestant Churches drops a hint to its clergymen: The reason they receive less publicity than Al Capone is because they are so much less picturesque.

A spectator advances to the counsel table and grasps Capone's hand. "I'm Benjamin Bachrach, public defender," he says.

An athlete from Kiel, Germany, pausing in Chicago on a round-the-world walking tour, asks Capone, through an obliging court attendant, if he will sign his "memory book." "I've signed too many things," says Capone. "Tell him no."

D'Andrea takes his customary seat behind Capone and fixes his dark, piercing eyes on the witness stand.

Dwight Green calls the government's first Florida witness, Parker Henderson. Squirming under D'Andrea's gaze, he testifies to the Western Union money orders he picked up for Capone, to the purchase of the Palm Island house and the addition of shrubbery, a boat dock and swimming pool. The small chalk-white man who mounts the stand next betrays intense anxiety. He is John Fotre, manager of the Western Union office in the Lexington Hotel, from which many of the money orders were telegraphed. Though cooperative in pretrial examination, he now claims he doesn't know who sent them. Judge Wilkerson speaks to him sharply: "You better think this over."

After the court recesses for the day, Wilson reproves the frightened witness. "What can you expect," says Fotre, "when they let one of Capone's hoodlums sit there with his hand on his gun?"

He has no need to name the hoodlum. Wilson details Sullivan and Mike Malone, who has finally dropped his disguise, to verify the charge.

Saturday, October 10

The two agents enter the crowded elevator behind D'Andrea. Malone brushes against him and nods to Sullivan. He has felt the contours of a revolver.

When the agents report to Wilkerson, he enjoins them from any action that might affect the witnesses yet to testify. They must handle D'Andrea outside the courtroom, and he will adjourn the trial for a few minutes during the morning session while they do so.

At a prearranged signal a bailiff notifies D'Andrea that a messenger is waiting in the corridor with a telegram for him. As the bodyguard leaves the courtroom, the agents, hard on his heels, hustle him into an antechamber, seize his revolver, and turn him over to the police. Claiming the right to carry concealed weapons, he flourishes deputy sheriff's credentials, such as those several Capone lieutenants carry.

"Your Honor," Ahern pleads later, trying to mollify Judge Wilkerson, "this defendant has taken care of his mother and sisters. To me, he is a high class boy. I like him. . . . If Your Honor understood D'Andrea's mind and his heart, you would know that he did not mean any affront to the Court."

Wilkerson finds D'Andrea guilty of contempt of court and sends him to jail for six months.

The procession of witnesses who have sold things to Capone and can contribute to the picture of his net worth and net expenditure is a long one, and their testimony consumes two all-day sessions. There are the butchers and bakers, the real estate agents, the decorators, furniture dealers, building contractors, tailors, jewelers. . . .

One of the Miami contractors, Curt Otto Koenitzer, settles himself into the witness chair, smoking a cigar. A deputy marshal takes it from him (laughter). After his brief testimony—Mrs. Capone paid him $6,000 for his work on the bathhouse and a garage—Koenitzer retrieves his cigar to the huge amusement of the audience and exits grinning.

In the corridor a pretty brunette witness from the Miami Western Union office expresses disenchantment with Chicago. She hardly considers the trip worth her time even at government expense. "What do y'all do for excitement up here?" she asks.

Tuesday, October 13

"When counsel speaks of Al," says Judge Wilkerson to Fink, "I assume he means the defendant."
"Yes. Is Your Honor affronted?"
"I think I should prefer the term defendant."
Fink feigns shock when the next witness, a former Internal Revenue agent, admits that in the course of investigating Capone he drank beer with him in a Cicero speakeasy. "Beer," he repeats without shame. "Good beer, too."

Wednesday, October 14

The Anglo-Italian historical novelist Rafael Sabatini, about to embark on an American lecture tour, concedes Capone to be "a center of that atmosphere of treachery, intrigue, shots in the dark and raw power in which historical romance best grows," but disqualifies him as a proper subject for the genre because "he seems really to have no ideals." The future writer of historical romances, Sabatini predicts, will probably find Mussolini the most inspiring personality of his day for "the power and the intrigue are there, and the ideal with them."

The last important prosecution witness is Fred Ries, who implicates Pete Penovich, Jimmy Mondi, Frank Pope, Jake Guzik and Ralph Capone, as well as the defendant, in the affairs of the Smoke Shop.

Thursday, October 15

A nonagenarian veteran of the Civil War, wearing his old blue uniform and medals, totters up to the bench with a bouquet of faded flowers for the judge. He is ushered to a front-row seat, where he soon falls asleep, not to awake until the adjournment.

The principal defense argument centers on Capone's misfortunes at the racetracks. As Fink tells it, no unluckier gambler ever placed a bet. He nearly always lost. Eight bookmakers estimate the increasingly large sums Capone paid them year after year, ranging from $12,000 in 1924 to $110,000 in 1929. It seems that practically all the money the government claims he made out of his gambling houses the bookies took away.

Oscar Gutter, a Chicago bookie, who keeps his derby on until the judge tells him to remove it, testifies to a $60,000 loss by Capone in 1927. Asked under cross-examination how he remembers, he replies: "My ledger showed that at the end of the season."

"I thought you didn't keep any books," says Green.

"Well, I kept them from month to month so I could pay my income tax." (Laughter)

"Why didn't you keep them permanently?"

"Well, it was an illegitimate business."

Joe Yario, a self-styled "gambling broker," operating in a Chicago "soft drink parlor" (his euphemism for "speakeasy"), refers airily to "two, three, ten thousand dollar losses," but cannot specify a single individual bet.

Judge Wilkerson: "Do you know what it is to remember anything?"

Yario: "I never kept no books."

Budd Gentry, a Hialeah bookie, is asked by Dwight Green to name the horses Capone backed in 1929 for a purported loss of about $10,000 each. He shakes his head.

"Can you give the name of just *one* horse that the defendant bet on?"

"I have five or six in mind, but they just won't come out."

In any event the argument is futile, a grasping at straws, for taxpayers may deduct gambling losses only from gambling winnings, and Capone's lawyers insist that he hardly ever won. All the bookies' testimony shows is that he did receive income totaling, during the year in question, at least $200,000. For the additional income, evidenced by his possessions and expenditures, the lawyers advance no plausible explanation.

Torrio, who has been sitting quietly apart since the first day, is expected to testify, but the defense counsel never calls him. Nor do they call Capone.

Friday, October 16

There is a flurry among the spectators as Beatrice Lillie, the chief attraction of *The Third Little Show,* playing at the Great Northern Theater, visits the courtroom with her husband, Lord Peel.

Prosecutors Grossman and Clawson between them recapitulate the government's evidence. Fink then leads off the defense summation. "Suppose Capone believed that money he received from so-called illegal transactions was not taxable," he asks the jury, "suppose he discovered to the contrary and tried to pay what he owed, would you say he ever had an intent to defraud the Government?" He paused and gazed fondly at his client. "No, and neither would I. Capone is the kind of man who never fails a friend."

The defendant swallows hard, and his eyes fill.

Ahern continues the summation with an historical analogy. "In Rome during the Punic Wars there lived a senator named Cato. Cato passed upon the morals of the people. He decided what they would wear, what they should drink, and what they should think. Carthage fell twice, but Carthage grew again and was once more powerful. Cato concluded every speech he made in the Senate by thundering, 'Carthage must be destroyed!' These censors of ours, these persecutors, the newspapers, all say, 'Capone must be destroyed!' The evidence in this case shows only one thing against Capone—that he was a spendthrift. . . ."

Saturday, October 17

Reporters and spectators have been impressed by the diversity, richness and colors of Capone's wardrobe. In the eleven days of the trial he has worn as many different ensembles, ranging from light browns through grays and blues to a climactic grass green on this, the final day.

Johnson, speaking at length for the first time, winds up the summation for the government. His winglike coiffure flapping with the vehemence of his emotions, he assails the Capone legend. "Who is this man who has become such a glamorous figure? Is he the little boy from the Second Reader who has found the pot of gold at the end of the rainbow that he can spend money so lavishly? He has been called Robin Hood by his counsel. Robin Hood took from the strong to feed the weak. Did this Robin Hood buy $8,000 worth of belt buckles for the unemployed? Was his $6,000 meat bill in a few weeks for the hungry? No, it went to the Capone home on Palm Island to feed the guests at nightly poker parties. Did he buy $27 shirts for the shivering men who sleep under Wacker Drive? . . ."

Capone casts despairing eyes around him, as if appealing to the audience against such gross injustice, he who has performed so many good works.

Without using the terms "net worth" or "net expenditure," Judge Wilkerson expounds the principles underlying them in his charge to the jury. Regarding the crucial Mattingly letter, he explains: "The statements of a duly authorized agent may be proof against the principal the same as if he had conducted in person the transaction in which the statements were made . . . if you find that under the power of attorney and the authority, if any, given at the interview in the revenue agents' office, considered with all the other facts and circumstances shown here in evidence, Mattingly was employed to get together information and to make an estimate and to give his opinion thereof to the bureau, then the fact that Mattingly made a statement as to what his opinion on that subject was is a fact to be considered by you. . . ."

The jury retires at 2:40 P.M.

Capone stands in the corridor, forcing a smile now and then at people who stare at him from behind a cordon of guards. When night falls and there is still no word from the jury, he decides to wait at the Lexington.

Watching the windows of the jury room from another section of the block-wide building, the reporters can see the shirt-sleeved jurors locked in debate. Shortly before eleven, almost eight hours since they entered the room, a burst of applause resounds through the sixth floor. The last dissenting juror has bowed to the majority.

Notified by phone, Capone bundles himself into his overcoat, slaps on his fedora, and hurries down to his limousine. By eleven o'clock he has returned to his seat at the counsel table, sweating from the exertion, and Judge Wilkerson is putting the question to the foreman of the jury, "Have you reached a verdict?" The foreman hands the bailiff a sheet of paper. The bailiff passes it to the clerk of the court, who reads it to the court.

The verdict indicates a considerable muddle in the minds of the jurors, and it confuses prosecution and defense alike. On the first indictment for 1924 they vote not guilty. On three of the twenty-two counts in the second indictment—Nos. 1, 5 and 9, charging tax evasion in 1925, 1926 and 1927—they vote guilty. Guilty also on counts 13 and 18, charging failure to file a return for 1928 and 1929. On the remaining counts, all charging tax evasion, not guilty. The confusion arises from mutually exclusive verdicts covering 1928 and 1929. The puzzled attorneys fail to understand how Capone can be guilty of filing no returns (13 and 18), yet at the same time be innocent of tax evasion (14 to 22). Nevertheless, after conferring with the judge, Johnson lets the verdict stand undisputed. The defense counsel will file an appeal with the U.S. Court for the Seventh District, arguing that the indictments had failed to specify sufficiently the means Capone employed to evade income tax.

Saturday, October 24

Flamboyant as ever in a heather-purple pinchback suit, Capone flashes an unnaturally wide smile at the audience, shakes Ahern's hand, and sinks heavily into his seat. He has cut his index finger, and it is bandaged. He jumps up a moment later, his hands locked behind his back, as Judge Wilkerson begins to read the sentence.

"It is the judgment of this court on count 1 that the defendant shall go to the penitentiary for five years, pay a fine of $10,000 and pay the cost of prosecution."

Capone's fingers twist and turn behind his back, but the forced smile lingers.

On counts 5 and 9 the judge imposes the same sentence; on counts 13 and 18, a year each in the county jail plus the same fines and court costs.

The smile fades at last.

"The sentence on counts 1 and 5 will run concurrently," the judge continues. "The sentence on count 13 will run concurrently with numbers 1 and 5, and count 18 will run consecutively." The earlier six-month sentence for contempt of court is also to run consecutively with count 1. The indictment for violation of the liquor laws is not pursued.

It adds up to eleven years' imprisonment, fines aggregating $50,-000 and court costs of $30,000—the stiffest penalty ever meted out to a tax evader (though there have been many stiffer ones since).

Wilkerson denies bail, pending the appeal, and asks U.S. marshal Henry Laubenheimer when he can remove Capone to Leavenworth. Capone gasps as Laubenheimer replies, "At six-fifteen tonight, Your Honor." But following Ahern's plea, Wilkerson agrees to let Capone stay temporarily in the Cook County Jail. "Good-bye, Al, old man," says Fink, his voice breaking. Silently and tearfully, Ahern clasps his client's hand.

As Capone leaves the courtroom, surrounded by deputy marshals, a little man prances up to him, brandishing an official-looking document. "Internal Revenue," he says. "I have a demand for liens on the property of Alphonse and Mae Capone." To prevent the couple from selling or transferring any assets before satisfying the tax claims, the bureau has frozen them with what it terms "a jeopardy assessment." Capone turns crimson, hurls an obscenity at the little man, and draws back his foot to kick him, but the deputy sheriffs march him into their office for fingerprinting. Recovering his self-control, he waggles his bandaged finger at the officer. "This is one finger the Government doesn't get."

In the freight elevator he finds himself next to the man he has known for two years as Mike Lepito, now revealed to him as Special Agent Malone. "The only thing that fooled me was your looks," he says without rancor. "You look like a wop." He manages another dim smile. "You took your chances and I took mine. I lost."

"Get enough, boys," he says to the news photographers. "You won't see me again for a long time." The deputy marshal assigned to take him to the jail in an unmarked car hangs back, fearing a rescue attempt. "I wouldn't go into that car for all the money in the world," he confides to Sullivan. So the revenue agent and a man from the narcotics bureau assume the risk.

To the reporters who have followed him to the jail, Capone says: "It was a blow below the belt, but what can you expect when the whole community is prejudiced against you?" The news photographers ask him to pose behind the bars of the receiving cell. "Please don't take my picture here, fellows," he pleads, retreating into a corner. "Think of my family."

His temper erupts again when, on the way to a fourth-floor cell, he hears a camera click. He spins around, grabs a tin bucket, and lunges at the offender, howling, "I'll knock your block off!"

The jail guards subdue him and rush him along to his cell, the reporters all following. As the turnkey opens the cell door, Capone finds two other occupants sitting on their cots. One is a Negro who, he learns shortly, has violated parole; the other, a skid-row bum unable to pay a $100 fine for disorderly conduct. Capone's sense of gesture reasserts itself. After questioning the bum, who is too awed by the legendary presence to utter a word in reply, he turns to the reporters. "I'm going to help this guy if I can," he announces, peeling off a $100 bill from the roll in his pocket and handing it to him.

The reporters leave. The guards take Capone to the jail hospital for the routine shower and medical examination, a humiliation that considerably deflates him.

But this was still Chicago, and to some of its officials Capone was still the "Big Fellow," capable of repaying favors with handsome rewards, and for a while they enabled him to run his organization from jail. Warden David Moneypenny moved him to a one-man cell on the fifth floor with a private shower. He let him make phone calls and send telegrams. In gratitude, when the warden had to go to Springfield, Capone arranged for him to borrow one of his chauffeur-driven Cadillacs. Capone's old political cronies aided him further by obtaining passes to visit him, then turning them over to members of his gang whom he wished to talk to, such as the new Public Enemy No. 1, Joe Fusco, Murray Humphreys, Johnny Torrio, Red Barker and Jake Guzik. Torrio raised the cash Capone needed for his lawyers' fees and other expenses. The prisoner dared not draw on the secret repositories of his own money lest Internal Revenue discover them and impound everything.

The most consequential gangsters to visit Capone during his months in the county jail were the New Yorkers Lucky Luciano and Dutch Schultz. Torrio brought them at Capone's insistence. The Dutchman had been challenging Luciano's claims to certain territorial monopolies, thereby endangering the general peace that had prevailed since the massacre of the Mustache Petes. Capone cast himself as arbitrator. He wanted the Italian and the Jew to reconcile their differences and work in amity with other gang leaders to revitalize the national organization, in which he himself expected one day to play a commanding role. For this conference Warden Moneypenny permitted the use of the death chamber, and it amused Capone to preside, sitting in the electric chair.

But the outcome was not satisfactory. The Dutchman infuriated Capone by his sweeping demands. He behaved as though the entire New York territory rightfully belonged to him. He clearly preferred his individual independence to any alliances—a Mustache Pete at heart, after all. "If I'd had him outside," Capone said years later, "I'd have shoved a gun against his guts." The conference broke up acrimoniously with nothing settled.

What troubled Capone even more was that Torrio, unaccountably, appeared to favor Schultz. Before his old mentor returned to New York, he conjured him to have nothing to do with the Dutchman. Torrio was noncommittal.

In December anonymous telegrams to the Department of Justice, describing Capone's privileged life in jail, put an end to it. After an investigation, U.S. Marshal Laubenheimer ordered Moneypenny to ban all visitors except the prisoner's mother, wife, son and lawyers. Capone was transferred to the hospital ward with a detail of deputy marshals assigned to twenty-four-hour guard duty. "I didn't want him to mingle with the other prisoners," said Moneypenny by way of explaining why he had maintained Capone in comfortable privacy. "I was afraid he'd be a bad influence on them."

On February 27 Capone was playing cards with two fellow inmates of the hospital ward, when a deputy warden called him to the door to tell him that the District Court of Appeals had rejected his appeal. He shrugged, rejoined his companions, and finished the game.

Three days later there occurred one of the most atrocious crimes of the century. To Capone, it suggested an opportunity to regain his freedom.

Ten days after Bruno Richard Hauptmann kidnapped the Lindbergh baby from his home in Hopewell, New Jersey, the Hearst columnist Arthur Brisbane, to whom Capone had got word that he could "do as much as anybody alive in getting the baby back," was given special permission to interview him.

"I don't want any favors if I am able to do anything for that baby," Capone told Brisbane. "If they will let me out of here, I will give any bond they require." He offered to leave his brother Mitzi in his place as hostage. "You don't suppose I would doublecross my own brother?" What, exactly, did he claim he could accomplish? "I have a good many angles and anybody that knows anything would know that he could trust me. There isn't a mob that wouldn't trust me to pay that money, if the relations of the kidnapped child wanted me to pay it, and there isn't anybody would think I would tell where I got the child, or who had it. . . .

"I would soon know whether the child is in the possession of any regular mob that I can connect with or in the possession of any individual working his own racket that would have sense enough to know that he could trust me, and know that it might not be a bad idea to do me a good turn." In the event of failure, "I would come back here, take my brother's place, and let justice go on with her racket."

The screaming Hearst headlines, together with the credulous Brisbane's endorsement ("It is possible that Alphonse Capone could do that which could not be done by others. . . . His power in whatever he undertakes is known to many. . . . This writer believes that whether he succeeded or failed, he would return") touched off a public clamor to free Capone. Republican Senator Hiram Bingham of Connecticut fostered the notion that the Capone gang had planned the kidnapping "for this very purpose."

No federal court would even discuss Capone's proposition and Lindbergh himself said, "I wouldn't ask for Capone's release even if it would save a life."

If the U.S. Supreme Court consents to review the decision of a District Court of Appeals, it grants the convict's application for a writ of certiorari (meaning it wishes to be "made certain") . The Supreme Court rejected Capone's application on May 2, and on May 4 he left the county jail. But his destination was no longer Leavenworth, as originally intended. Jake Guzik and other convicted Caponeites had started to serve their terms there, and the federal authorities thought it prudent to keep them far away from their leader. Capone, they decided, should go to the Atlanta Penitentiary.

The last day the guard was doubled outside the hospital ward, and

Capone was allowed to spend it with his family there instead of in the visitors' room, separated from them by a wire screen. They stayed until late afternoon, his mother, who brought an enormous dish of macaroni with cheese and tomato sauce, hot from her stove, speaking only Italian, Mae Capone and Sonny, all the brothers except Ralph (who had just been delivered to the McNeil Island Penitentiary) and the two sisters, by turns laughing, eating and weeping.

26

"Received . . . the body of the within named prisoner. . . . "

"**Y**OU'D think Mussolini was passing through," said Capone, as both the prisoners behind the jailyard fence and the crowd outside the gate hailed him. "Good-bye, Al . . . Good luck, Al . . . You got a bum break, Al. . . ." He gazed around him with evident satisfaction. "I'll bet Mussolini never got a send-off like this."

It was 10 P.M. when the U.S. marshal's car, accompanied by fifteen police cars, pulled out of the yard in a blaze of light from the Very flares that were fired to provide extra visibility in case of trouble. Capone sat in the back seat between a Secret Service agent and an automobile thief named Vito Morici, to whom he was handcuffed. Laubenheimer and a deputy marshal sat facing them on jump seats. At the Dearborn Station, where another crowd had gathered, Capone, indicating Morici's topcoat, said to him: "Throw it over your arm so nobody sees the handcuffs." Dan Serritella, who was on trial for his defalcations, and Matt and Mimi Capone walked with the prisoners as far as the train gate.

The Dixie Flyer carried five day coaches and three Pullman cars behind them. In Car 48, the second to last, Drawing Room A and an upper berth had been reserved for Capone and Morici. The latter, a thin, runty youth in a threadbare suit and scuffed shoes, was going through to Tampa, Florida, to face a federal trial for transporting a stolen car across state lines. Five deputy marshals, in addition to Laubenheimer, rode the train. As soon as the manacled prisoners took their seat, they were locked into leg irons. The Dixie Flyer left on schedule at eleven thirty.

Capone talked volubly to the guards, but the youth shackled to him, barely half his size, sat mute, overawed, all but blotted out by the older man's bulk. Capone talked mostly about Chicago. His organization, he told Laubenheimer, had been a boon to the city, for it had given jobs to men who would otherwise have been committing crimes. The handcuffs and leg irons were removed while the prisoners prepared for bed, Capone slipping into monogrammed sky-blue silk pajamas, but Laubenheimer then insisted on putting back the handcuffs, and so the two men had to occupy the same berth. The diminutive Morici lay awake all night, clinging fearfully to the edge lest Capone roll over and flatten him.

At every station stop next day a crowd of two to three hundred was waiting for a look at Capone through the train window. The sight never failed to lift his spirits. In the South the thermometer climbed to ninety, and he drank quarts of lemonade, ordered from the dining car. He bought soda pop for Morici.

The train steamed into Atlanta's Union Station at 7:46 P.M., only eleven minutes late. After Morici had been transferred to another car for the rest of his journey to Tampa, Car 48 was shunted to a siding to avoid reporters, and from there Laubenheimer and his prisoner were driven four miles to the penitentiary. The inmates, 3,000 of them packing cell blocks built to hold less than 2,000, somehow knew the instant the car entered the driveway and set up a tremendous clamor, banging the bars of their cells, some cheering the newcomer, others taunting him.

Warden Arthur C. Aderhold, a man devoted to ritual, called through the outer gate that was cut into a gray stone wall 30 feet high and 600 feet long: "Who are you?"

"Marshal Laubenheimer of Chicago," came the answer.

"Are you in charge of whoever is in your party?"

"I am."

The gate swung open. Stopping twenty paces farther on at an inner gate, the warden faced the prisoner. "What is your name?"

"Alphonse Capone."

"What is your sentence?"

"Eleven years."

Laubenheimer corrected him. "The sentence here is ten years. After that period has been served, the prisoner is to be returned to Chicago to serve a one-year sentence in the Cook County Jail."

"Your number is 40,822," Aderhold informed Capone.

The marshal handed the warden a paper, which he signed and handed back: "Received from H. C. W. Laubenheimer, United States Marshal for the Northern District of Illinois, the body of the within named prisoner. . . ."

In the receiving cell Capone was ordered to strip to the skin. A prison guard took away his clothes, leaving in their place a blue denim uniform. Fingerprinted and photographed, his hair cropped close to his skull, Capone was then consigned to the hospital ward for three to four weeks while the penitentiary physician, Dr. William Ossenfort, determined whether he carried any communicable disease.

A Wassermann test, which Capone took under protest, proved negative. He admitted that probably, three years before, he had contracted syphilis, but considered himself cured. The technique of analyzing a Wassermann being still somewhat crude, Ossenfort wanted to investigate further by making a spinal puncture and applying the test to the spinal fluid, as well as to the blood. This Capone would not hear of, and Ossenfort could not legally compel him to submit to it. Capone worried nevertheless. When, in the sizzling temperatures of the southern summer, he developed prickly heat, he wondered whether it might not be a symptom of syphilis after all. Ossenfort calmed his anxiety by showing him that he, too, had prickly heat.

"When not aroused," Ossenfort said later, "Capone was quiet, pleasant and fairly well spoken. He would have made a good administrator and a forceful leader."

The overcrowded penitentiary had no single cells, only two-man and eight-man cells. Capone was assigned to an eight-man cell, whose occupants included a wildcat promoter, a former judge convicted of using the mails to defraud, an Ohio criminal notorious for the variety of his offenses, and four mail robbers serving twenty-five years. One of the mail robbers came in from the recreation yard shortly after the guards brought Capone. He had flame-red hair and the accent of a Jewish vaudeville comedian. Capone recognized Red Rudensky, or Rusty, as he had always called him, the ace "mechanic" of the early bootleg days. Rudensky, who had long hero-worshiped the gang leader, warmly clasped his hand. "He still had that inner radiation of somebody who's been through it all," he recalled.

Capone couldn't sleep the first night. He roused Rudensky and sat on his bed. "Imagine," he said, "some creep gets me on a damn tax rap. Ain't that a helluva deal?" He suffered frequently from nightmares in the months that followed, yelling "No! No!" in his sleep and swearing. Rudensky would pummel him awake.

The other prisoners, by and large, admired Capone. When Rudensky, who stage-managed the occasional prison entertainments, introduced him, they gave him a standing ovation. There were deadly exceptions, however. "The little shots who wanted a crack at the big ones," as Rudensky remembered them. "I sent out word to lay off Big Al, but while ninety-nine percent would go along with anything I asked, there was always the creepy twenty-five or thirty cons waiting for a chance to make trouble. They had a healthy respect for Al, and figured that between us anyone who gave him trouble would get it back fast. Still, two hillbillies, both in on a morals charge, decided to put our strength to a test. I got the neck chop and the knee one day in the yard. Al was roughed up at chow. But inside twenty-four hours I had a revenge team take it out in spades. The two jackasses were pounded into bloody pulps during work hours. One wound up with a broken cheekbone and a fractured skull. The other never used his right arm again for work."

Rudensky's fondness for Capone grew. He arranged the smuggling of cash to him from the gang through a trusty who drove a supply truck. With this money Capone bought privileges from certain guards and loyalty and protection from his fellow prisoners. A corps of bodyguards surrounded him at work and at recreation. He seldom handled the cash himself. Rudensky frequently kept thousands of dollars for him in the hollowed-out handle of a broom. "A nod from Al in the yard was all it took for me to take care of those he wished to bestow largesse upon."

Capone worked eight hours a day cobbling shoes. For exercise he first tried baseball but proved to be a poor batter and a worse fielder. He switched to tennis. Money talked for him on the tennis courts, too. He never had to wait for a free court. If he wanted to play singles, he would point to the opponent he preferred, and the other player would retire; if doubles, one member of a team would give up his place. In his rages, when he muffed a shot, he broke a good many rackets.

The prisoners' families were allowed a thirty-minute visit once a fortnight, and Capone's family rarely failed to appear in a body. They sat with other visitors at a long table, conversing through a steel-mesh screen. Foreign languages were taboo, and so Capone's mother could only gaze at him and mumble a few broken words, while her sons and daughters talked. Capone kept photographs of all of them on the wall above his cot. He once asked Rudensky, pointing to a snapshot of Sonny, "How the hell can a fat dago like me have a son that good-looking?"

Not long after he entered the penitentiary, his brothers brought him bitter news. Torrio had formed a partnership with Dutch Schultz. Capone sent his lifelong friend a message, urging him to break up the partnership, return to Chicago, and resume leadership of the organization. There was no reply. Capone never forgave him. He ordered his wife to tear up the bonds Torrio had been buying for Sonny every birthday, now worth more than $80,000.

In August Teresa Capone retained one of the country's foremost attorneys, William E. Leahy of Washington, D.C., to get her son out of prison. With his younger associate, William J. Hughes, Jr., Leahy reopened the question of the statute of limitations. Strangely, the trial counsel had not pressed it at all, as the government feared they might (an omission which purportedly lost the Nash-Ahern firm its entire gangster clientele). The previous April the Supreme Court, ruling on a Boston tax case, had held that an attempt to evade a tax did not constitute fraud and that the three-year limitation, not six, should apply as in civil cases. Contending that Capone's case was parallel and that therefore he was illegally imprisoned, the attorneys petitioned the federal court in Atlanta, on September 21, for a writ of habeas corpus. The procedure governing such petitions required the presence of the prisoner, and so Capone emerged from the penitentiary to appear for half an hour before Judge E. Marvin Underwood. The judge took the petition under advisement.

On December 5, while Capone was still awaiting the judge's decision, an era came to an end—an era without precedent in the profits it produced for organized crime. President Roosevelt proclaimed the ratification of the repeal of the Eighteenth Amendment.

At Capone's next court appearance in January, Judge Underwood

cited a section of the federal statute of limitations whereby the time
the offender is absent from the district in which he committed the
offense "shall not be taken as any part of the time limited by law for
the commencement of proceedings." Between 1925 and 1931 Capone
was either in the Philadelphia jail or his Miami retreat for periods
totaling several years. The judge continued:

"If [trial counsel's] motion had put in issue the question of fact
as to whether or not petitioner had been within the district a sufficient length of time for the statute to establish a bar, then a denial
by the prosecution might have been necessary, but this was not done,
and the Court, according to the allegations of the petition, overruled the motion on the ground that the six-year limitation was applicable."

The ruling should have been challenged at the trial or on appeal,
Judge Underwood decided; the issue had no place in the habeas
corpus hearing. That the Supreme Court later declared the three-
year limitation applicable months after the Capone trial did not affect the hearing either. Finally: ". . . on habeas corpus, only the
jurisdiction of the court whose judgment is challenged can be called
in question. . . . Any other rule . . . would make a Federal Court
of a district where a penitentiary was located, a Court of Appeals to
retry all cases of prisoners who might apply for writs of habeas
corpus. . . ." He dismissed the petition, and the attorneys returned
to Washington.

"Overpaid dumb bastards," said Capone in his cell that night.
"They couldn't spring a pickpocket."

*Memorandum from U.S. Attorney General Homer S. Cummings to
Special Assistant Joseph B. Keenan, August 1, 1933:*

> . . . would it not be well to think of having a special prison
> for racketeers, kidnapers, and others guilty of predatory crimes,
> said prison to be in all respects a proper place of confinement. It
> would be in a remote place—on an island or in Alaska, so that the
> persons incarcerated would not be in constant communication
> with friends outside. . . .

*Memorandum from Sanford Bates, Director of the Bureau of Prisons,
to U.S. Attorney General Cummings, August 8, 1933:*

At your request, please find herewithin estimate of the probable maintenance charges at the prison at Alcatraz Island if operated by the Department of Justice on the basis of 200 prisoners. I am of the opinion that the removal of perhaps one hundred of the most desperate men in each Atlanta and Leavenworth would be a distinct benefit to those places and would aid in the prevention of threatened demonstrations. . . .

From a radio address by U.S. Attorney General Cummings on "The Recurring Problem of Crime," October 12, 1933:

For some time I have desired to obtain a place of confinement to which could be sent our more dangerous, intractable criminals. . . . You can appreciate, therefore, with what pleasure I make public the fact that such a place has been found. By negotiation with the War Department we have obtained the use of Alcatraz Prison, located on a precipitous island in San Francisco Bay, more than a mile from shore. The current is swift and escapes are practically impossible. It has secure cells for 600 persons. It is in excellent condition and admirably fitted for the purpose I had in mind. Here may be isolated the criminals of the vicious and irredeemable type so that their evil influence may not be extended to other prisoners who are disposed to rehabilitate themselves.

The Attorney General, accompanied by Mrs. Cummings, spent August 18 inspecting the former Army disciplinary barracks. The Army had left behind thirty short-term military prisoners, and the Bureau of Prisons had transferred the first batch of civilians from McNeil Island. The Cummings' guide was Warden James A. Johnston, a former banker, whose mild, avuncular manner concealed a talent for devising ways to break the toughest convict's spirit. Since January, when he took office, he had been transforming Alcatraz into the world's most redoubtable bastille.

Originally named by the eighteenth-century Spanish explorers *Isla de los Alcatraces* (Island of Pelicans) after the birds that then roosted there, Alcatraz has an area of 12 acres and rises steeply to 136 feet above the bay. At six points, commanding between them a view of every foot of the island, Johnston erected a guard tower equipped with a .30-caliber carbine and a high-powered rifle. A 12-foot-high cyclone fence, topped by barbed wire, enclosed the work sections. Barbed-wire barriers dotted the shoreline. All old sewer outlets and utility tunnels opening on the water were blocked. Not that any escapee, even if he could crawl through them, would be likely to reach the mainland $1\frac{1}{2}$ miles away, swimming in cold water against currents that often reached a velocity of almost 4 knots.

With special pride, Johnston explained to Mr. and Mrs. Cummings the three-door security system he had designed for the main entrance to the cell house on the crest of the island. It required two guards to operate. Before anybody could pass the first door, one of the guards, observing him through a glass panel, had to identify him. If satisfied, he would throw a switch, sliding back a steel plate that covered the lock. Only the second guard had the key. As soon as this guard had admitted the visitor, Guard No. 1 would send the steel plate gliding again over the lock. A few paces farther on the first of two inner doors with a vision panel barred the way. The Guard No. 2 would scan the corridors beyond and, if clear, unlock it, let the visitor through, lock it behind them, and advance to the third and last door. When the visitor left, the entire process would be repeated in reverse. To overpower the guard with the key, Johnston pointed out, would not help an escapee because the first guard operated the outer door from an impregnable sentry box of steel and bulletproof glass.

At four gates between the landing dock and the cell house, used by either prisoners or visitors, Johnston had installed "snitch boxes," oscillatory circuits, tuned to a certain electrostatic capacity which the presence of metal would disturb, activating a warning buzzer. To search the cells for hidden metal objects, there were portable electronic detectors.

In the three-tiered cell blocks, painted pink and red—Johnston's prescription for imparting a note of cheer—he had replaced the soft steel bars with toolproof steel. All the cells were one-man cells. Measuring 8 by 4 feet, they contained a fold-up bunk hooked to the wall, fold-up table and chair, shelf, washbasin, toilet, and a shaded ceiling light. The warden had designated cell block D as a disciplinary unit. Here were "light holes," ordinary cells, but set apart for solitary confinement, and *the* Hole, smaller cells with solid steel doors behind which the worst offenders were kept in total darkness. They had no furnishings other than a mattress, which a guard removed every morning. There was a so-called Oriental toilet, an opening in the floor, which could be flushed only from the outside of the cell.

"This prison is our pet project," said the Attorney General. "I am proud of the work you have done on it." In the mess hall, with its ceiling rack of tear-gas cylinders that could be opened at the touch of a wall button, Johnston showed Mrs. Cummings a sample menu. "M-m-m-m-m!" she burbled. "Why, we don't eat that much at home!"

A month earlier Cummings and J. Edgar Hoover visited the Atlanta Penitentiary ostensibly on a general inspection tour of all federal correctional establishments. But the explanation given convinced few inmates. They had heard and read too much about Alcatraz. They assumed the visitors were acting as "talent scouts" for the first trainloads to the island.

Capone, however, appeared unconcerned. "I've got things squared, Rusty," he assured his cellmate.

Rudensky was skeptical. "They'll never open that show without a name star."

"The fix is in," Capone insisted. "It cost plenty. I tell you I ain't going."

In the Atlanta Penitentiary, the day Warden Johnston was showing the Cummingses around Alcatraz, heat baked the cells. Sweat poured off the men in rivulets. At about 8 P.M. a guard known as Swede rattled his stick against the bars of Capone's cell. "Come on, Al," he said, "and leave your belongings behind." When he added that the order included the family photographs, Capone went berserk. It took three more guards to drag him out of the cell. "What are they doing to me, Rusty?" he yelled. "Where the hell are those dumb bastards who said I'd be out?"

Rudensky never saw him again. "I missed him very much," he recalled. "All of us did. I respected him for two reasons—he kept up his hopes to the end, and he never apologized. He was Capone, and there would never be another. What he'd done he'd done in a giant way." (Rudensky himself achieved total self-rehabilitation. As founder and editor of the prison paper the *Atlantian*, he attracted the interest of the Atlanta novelist Margaret Mitchell, of Ralph McGill, editor of the Atlanta *Constitution*, and of Eleanor Roosevelt. Freed after a total of almost thirty-five years behind bars, he was among the 200 ex-convicts employed by Charles Allen Ward, president of the St. Paul Advertising Agency, Brown & Bigelow, and himself an ex-convict. Rudensky became chief copy editor. In recent years the former safecracker has acted as consultant to lock manufacturing companies, banks and police departments. He never lost his admiration for Capone.)

27

Island of Pelicans

THE train was switched to a spur track and run through a sally port into the penitentiary yard. It comprised only six cars—two specially constructed prisoners' cars, baggage car, diner, sleeper for the prison personnel, and engine. Steel bars and steel mesh screens covered the windows of the prisoners' cars and boiler plate reinforced the flooring. Inside each of these cars Captain of the Guards Comer Head posted two of his men, unarmed to eliminate any possibility of a prisoner seizing their weapons, and at both ends, enclosed by a wire-screened cage, two men carrying shotguns. The air brake signal cord had been restrung in such a way that only the caged guards could reach it.

Fifty-three "incorrigibles" were prepared for the journey under the direction of Warden Aderhold, stripped and searched, their uniforms changed, their commitment papers verified, and their train seats assigned, two to a seat, shackled together. It was 5 A.M. when Aderhold finally climbed aboard, followed by Captain Head and Dr. Ossenfort.

For security the train followed a circuitous route known in advance only to a few railroad officials and federal authorities. Passing through Montgomery, Mobile, New Orleans, San Antonio, El Paso, Yuma, Los Angeles, it stopped only to change crews or take on water and fuel and then at unscheduled stations far from the passenger platforms. As Cummings wrote later in a congratulatory memorandum to Sanford Bates, "A slip-up or mistake, even an unfortunate happening of some kind, would have entailed unpleasant reactions and consequences. It was a difficult job. I do not believe that very many people realized how ticklish a job it was. . . ."

He tried to throw the press off the scent. "Capone is not headed for Alcatraz," he said, when the train was two days out of Atlanta. "That's one point on which all the newspapers were wrong."

The only adverse incident occurred near Yuma, when Capone, thrashing about in an effort to find a comfortable position, accidentally kicked open a radiator valve. The car, already steaming in the desert heat, became an inferno. Capone broke out in such a violent rash that Ossenfort had to sponge him down with alcohol.

During the four-day journey the prisoners ate and slept, if they slept at all, in their seats. Neither leg irons nor handcuffs were removed so that when a prisoner needed to use the toilet, his companion had to go with him.

In a final detour to preserve secrecy, the train was taken through Oakland to Napa Junction, 50 miles farther north, then switched to tracks winding south again to the rarely used bayside depot at Tiburon, a little yachting center across the water from San Francisco. No passenger car had stopped there for twenty-six years. Yet despite all the precautions, when the train pulled in at eight thirty on the morning of the twenty-second, about 200 people, nearly the entire population of Tiburon, were standing by the tracks while offshore hovered a launch full of reporters and cameramen. Railroad detectives and Department of Justice agents, brandishing rifles, kept the crowd at a distance. A small boy, seeing the grimy, stubbled faces through the car windows, called to one of the agents, "Are there men as bad as Al Capone on that train? Ma says there are." "Listen, Sonny," the agent replied, "there's no Capone or anybody by any name on that train. They may have been Capones once, but they're just numbers now." Such, in truth, was Warden Johnston's essential purpose—to destroy the prisoners' sense of identity.

The prisoners' cars were backed onto a barge with rails and detached from the rest of the train. Convoyed by a Coast Guard cutter, whose gun crew held their rifles at the ready, the barge moved behind a tugboat past rows of anchored yachts, out into the choppy bay. Low-lying clouds hid the sun and a light wind blew from the west. As the barge bumped against the Alcatraz dock, the Atlanta guards struck off the prisoners' leg irons, but not their handcuffs. Two by two they hobbled ashore, ankles swollen from the bite of the iron, every muscle stiff, stinking with the sweat and dirt of the long train ride. Walking between two files of Alcatraz guards, they started up the steep, spiraling roadway to the top of the island.

At the rear entrance to the cell house, Warden Johnston sat on one side of a desk, a deputy warden and Warden Aderhold on the other. As Johnston called out the names of each shackled pair of prisoners, a guard brought them inside from the yard and removed their handcuffs. Aderhold turned over their commitment papers to the deputy warden, who assigned them an identification number according to the order of their commitment. Capone was 85 (counting the military prisoners and those transferred from McNeil Island). "I could see him nudging the prisoners near him and slipping them some corner-of-the-mouth comment," Johnston wrote in his memoirs of Alcatraz. "As he walked toward me he flashed a big, wide smile. . . . It was apparent that he wanted to impress other prisoners by asking me questions as if he were their leader. I wanted to make sure that they didn't get any such idea. I handed him a ticket with his number, gave him the instructions I had given every other man, and told him to move along."

The guards led them to the bathhouse to be stripped, medically examined, and their ears, nostrils, mouth and rectum probed for contraband, such as narcotics or coiled watch springs, which, when straightened, could make an efficient saw or weapon. For weekday wear they were issued gray denim slacks and shirt; for Sundays, a blue denim uniform, and for cold weather, a wool-lined pea jacket. The fronts and backs bore their number stamped in letters legible at 20 yards. Finally, given sheets, a pillowcase, towel, comb and toothbrush, they were taken to their cells, where they would spend about fourteen hours out of every twenty-four, seven days a week. Capone drew the fifth cell from the right, third tier, block B. When the last prisoner had been locked up, Johnston wired Attorney General Cummings: FIFTY THREE CRATES FURNITURE FROM ATLANTA RECEIVED IN GOOD CONDITION INSTALLED NO BREAKAGE. Within a month, more than 100 more crates arrived from Leavenworth and Lewisburg, Pennsylvania.

It was Johnston's policy to listen to any prisoner who wished to talk to him, and when, the following day, Capone requested an interview, the warden had him brought to his office. "What can I do for you?" he asked blandly.

"Well, I don't know how to begin," said Capone, "but you're my warden now and I just thought I better tell you I have a lot of friends and I expect to have lots of visitors and I want to arrange to see my wife and my mother and my son and my brothers."

"You will be able to see your wife and your mother and your son," Johnston told him. "Your brothers may visit you, that is, all your brothers except Ralph who has a prison record [he had just been released from McNeil Island]. . . . You may receive one visit a month from blood relatives, but only two persons may visit you at the same time."

"Warden, I got a big family and they all want to see me and I want to see them all. I don't see why I can't have them all come at the same time."

"They cannot all come at the same time because the regulations limit the number of visitors to two relatives at one time. That rule will apply to you as it will govern all other prisoners."

"How about my friends, Warden, when can I see them?"

"Capone, your friends and associates will not be permitted to come here as visitors."

He smiled feebly. "It looks like Alcatraz has got me licked."

Johnston granted his request for another interview the next week. "Don't get me wrong, Warden," Capone began. "I'm not looking for any favors, but you know maybe some of these other cons ain't got any friends, but I gotta lot of friends. Maybe you don't know it, Warden, and maybe you won't believe it, but a lotta big businessmen used to be glad to be friends with me when I was on top and they wanted me to do things for them."

"What kind of businessmen conducting legitimate enterprises would need any help from you?"

Capone gave his version of the Chicago newsboys' strike and how, acting in behalf of Colonel McCormick, he ended it. "The big boys always sent for Al and they were glad to talk to Al when they needed Al, but they sure put the boots to me when they got me down."

"That is very interesting," said Johnston. "You may want to tell me some more sometime."

To gain the kind of leadership he had enjoyed at Atlanta, Capone tried to dispense favors to his fellow inmates. He offered to have money sent to their relatives, to buy musical instruments for those who, like himself, wanted to play in the prison band (he had taken up the tenor banjo). Johnston thwarted all such gestures. When it became apparent that Capone could not obtain the smallest special consideration, he lost face, as Johnston intended him to, especially among the small fry who composed the majority of the Alcatraz population. They mocked him to his face. They threatened him.

The men who conceived the Alcatraz prison did not even pay lip service to the principle of rehabilitation. What Cummings and Bates had in mind was a custodial and punitive institution. There would be no rewards for good behavior other than the usual reduction of sentence by ten days out of every forty served and work credits, no trusties, only punishment for breaking rules. A policy of maximum security, the Attorney General believed, combined with minimum privileges and total isolation from the mainland, would serve as a deterrent to Public Enemies and those who would emulate them. It deterred them no more than the prospect of the electric chair, the noose or the gas chamber reduced the homicide rate. In fact, despite the propaganda emanating from the Attorney General's office, comparatively few big-time gangsters ever went to Alcatraz. There were not enough of them to fill the cells. The "notorious mail robber" might be an obscure wretch who had broken into a postbox. Some inmates were first offenders. If the new prison profited anybody, it was the wardens of the old ones. Alcatraz took some of the strain off them. No court could sentence convicts to Alcatraz. Only those already serving terms could be transferred there, if the warden so recommended and the director of the Bureau of Prisons approved. During the thirties a decline was noted in prison mutinies, race riots, escapes, aggressive homosexuality, and killings, which Cummings ascribed to the prisoners' fear of ending up on "the Rock." ("I closed Alcatraz in 1963," wrote Bates' successor, James V. Bennett, in his autobiography, "because it was too costly to operate and too typical of the retributive justice that has no place in our philosophy.")

"It was necessary to admonish [Capone] several times, when he was being instructed in the rules and routine," Johnston recalled, "but no more than other inmates for they all found the regulations stricter than any to which they had been accustomed in other prisons. After the first tenseness was over he got in line and made an average adjustment in work and behavior."

His day began at 6:30 A.M. with the clanging of a bell and a burst of electric light. He had twenty minutes to dress and make his bed. To shave, he had to shove a matchbox through the bars of his cell. A guard would place a razor blade in it and allow three minutes before returning to reclaim it. At 6:50 the bell sounded again, the floor guard took the morning count. A third bell signaled that all prisoners were accounted for. Fourth bell: breakfast. The turnkeys, standing inside locked steel cages, pulled back a lever, and with the din of a cannonade all the heavy steel cell door bolts simultaneously shot back. Falling in between his neighbors, Capone shuffled toward the mess hall adjoining the cell blocks. The prisoners ate ten to a table, with the Negroes segregated. They all sat facing the same direction. Armed guards watched from a steel-barred gallery above. The prisoners ate in silence. Talking was forbidden not only in the mess hall, but in the cell blocks and the bathhouse. In the recreation yard during the morning and afternoon recesses they could talk for three minutes and on weekend afternoons for two hours. This rule of silence was later relaxed.

The food was served cafeteria-style from a steam table. Bad food had caused more prison riots than perhaps any other single factor, and Johnston was determined to provide three palatable meals a day with a calorie value of at least 3,100, 1,000 more than the Bureau of Prisons specified. Typical breakfast fare consisted of oatmeal with milk, fried bologna sausage, cottage fried potatoes, toast or bread with margarine, and coffee. Capone learned to clean his plate, for if a prisoner left a scrap, he got no food the next day. Recognizing the calmative properties of nicotine, Johnston also issued to each man three packs of cigarettes a week, and for heavy smokers he installed a tobacco and cigarette paper dispenser in every cell block so that they could roll their own. But he would not approve a commissary such as most prisons had, where the men could buy, with the few cents a day they earned in the workshops, candy, chewing gum, soda pop. At the 7 A.M. mess-hall bell the officer heading the guards' table raised his arm, and the prisoners rose. When he dropped his arm, they started back to their cells. A snitch box they passed on the way discouraged attempts to palm cutlery. It buzzed the first few times Capone passed it until the guards realized he was wearing metal arch supporters and replaced them with plastic ones.

No prisoner could wear a watch. Bells told the time. They rang for one reason or other about every half hour. After a brief interval in their cells, the prisoners were counted again and lined up according to their assigned workshop. Capone's first job was operating a mangle in the basement laundry room, to which the Army posts around the bay area sent their wash. (A private stationed on nearby Angel Island wrote home that his laundryman was none other than Al Capone.) Prisoners working outdoors or by a window endured the further torment of seeing ocean liners steaming through the Golden Gate, motor cruisers, sailboats and ferries skittering across the bay, the green and wooded hills of Marin County to the north and to the south, the San Francisco skyline—all within two miles.

Midmorning. Bell. Recess. Bell. Work. 11:30. Bell. Prisoners counted. Bell. Noon. Bell. Lunch. 1 P.M. Bell. Work. Midafternoon. Bell. Recess. Work. 4:30. Bell. Prisoners counted. Bell. 5:30. Bell. Supper. Bell. Back to cellblocks. Bell. Prisoners counted. Bell. 6:30. Bell. Lockup. 9:30. Bell. Lights out.

The routine was varied on the weekend to allow for religious worship Sunday morning, a weekly bath and two hours of leisure both Saturday and Sunday afternoons. The prisoners could spend their free hours exercising in the yard or pursuing a hobby indoors. Capone, who learned to read music and improvise, usually chose to play his banjo with a five-man combo he had organized. He sang, too, and composed a song entitled "Mother."

In their cells before lights out the prisoners could read books or magazines borrowed from the prison library, but to intensify their sense of isolation, Johnston denied them newspapers and radio. The deprivation led Capone to commit his first offense. He tried to bribe a guard to talk to him about the outside world. It cost him the loss of some good behavior credits.

Correspondence was also severely restricted. A prisoner could write one letter a week to a relative and from relatives receive no more than three. He could correspond with nobody outside his family except his lawyers. Censors read all incoming and outgoing mail, deleted any portion that did not confine itself to family affairs, and sent on a typed copy of what remained. The first letters Capone got from his wife were so drastically expurgated that he, not yet familiar with the system, upbraided her for her laziness when she visited him. "If you're too busy to write," he said, "don't send telegrams."

There were no fixed visiting days. Each monthly visit, limited to forty-five minutes, had to be arranged through Johnston, a pass issued and instructions given on where and when to board the island boat. A sheet of plate glass, floor to ceiling, separated visitor and prisoner. At head level ran two strips of steel a few inches apart, perforated by quarter-inch holes, with a thin sound diaphragm sandwiched between. The holes were staggered so that no object could pass through. To vibrate the diaphragm, voices had to be raised to normal speaking level. Thus, the guards present could hear every word exchanged and interrupt if forbidden topics were broached.

The first time Capone's mother came, accompanied by Mafalda, the buzzer sounded at the landing dock snitch box. The bewildered old woman was searched in vain. Only after the buzzer went off again, necessitating a second search, was the trouble traced. Mama Capone's old-fashioned corset had metal stays.

Wondering what message a letter contained before the censor got through with it or what a man's wife had been trying to tell him before the guards stopped her made for the sleepless "hell nights," as the prisoners called them. They were the harder to bear when, as happened almost every night, the guards could be heard practicing marksmanship in the yard. For targets they used man-shaped dummies, leaving them for the prisoners to see next day, a warning against trying to escape. Though Johnston forbade corporal punishment as a general rule, the guards did not hesitate, at a show of resistance, to knock a man senseless with water shot from a high-pressure hose, to break an arm or leg with their truncheons, or to truss him up for days in a straitjacket. The usual punishment, however, was solitary confinement, or the Hole, on a diet of bread and water with, twice a week, a "subsistence meal," such as a paper cup full of beets and potatoes mashed together. Nearly everybody committed to Alcatraz spent some time in the Hole. The limit of human endurance there was thought to be about nineteen days.

During Capone's years on Alcatraz several prisoners attempted suicide, and a few succeeded. Those who failed wound up in the Hole. A counterfeiter named John Standig made an attempt at suicide before he even got to Alcatraz by jumping from the train taking him there, but he suffered no mortal injury. On Alcatraz, where he later made another attempt, he told an inmate: "If you ever get out of here, tell them I wasn't trying to escape. I was trying to kill myself." A blood transfusion saved Jimmy Grove, an ex-GI imprisoned for raping an Army officer's daughter, after he cut the arteries in both arms. What amounted to suicide, the first successful one, was managed by Joe Bowers, a German-born criminal. In April, 1936, he was bandaged and taken to the Hole after he had broken his eyeglasses and slashed his throat with the jagged edges. Upon his release he scaled the steel fence surrounding the work area, knowing the guards would shoot him. The bullets dropped him 75 feet into the bay. The following year Ed Wutke, an ex-merchant marine, serving twenty-seven years for a murder at sea, was found dead in his cell, his jugular vein severed by a blade from a pencil sharpener.

Many prisoners went insane, fourteen of them violently so in 1937 alone, with innumerable others quietly "stir crazy." Mental illness was not a condition Johnston readily recognized. If capable of functioning physically, without disruption to the general routine, the madman was ignored; if uncontrollable, he was confined to the hospital ward. A consultant psychiatrist visited the island at irregular intervals, sometimes months apart. There was the prisoner from Leavenworth who screamed whenever a plane flew over the island, and the old prisoner who kept his head wrapped in towels as a defense against invisible tormentors. There was "Rabbit," a docile prisoner until he scooped up every movable object in his third-tier cell, wrapped his bedding around them, and the next time the door opened, hurled the bundle over the railing. Dragged away clawing and howling, he was never returned to the cell blocks. There was No. 284, Rube Persfal, assigned to the dock detail, who seized an ax, laid his left hand on a plank of wood and, laughing wildly, lopped off every finger. Still laughing, he laid his right hand next to it and begged a guard to chop it off. Though committed to the hospital, he was not officially declared insane.

Five men tried to escape during Capone's imprisonment. Before they could get off the island one was killed, one wounded, and one recaptured unhurt. Two others sawed through the bars of a workshop window, broke open a fence gate with a Stillson wrench, and dived into the water. They were never found dead or alive, but they could not have swum far against the riptide, with the dense fog then swathing the bay. Of the mutinies that erupted at the rate of about one a year, none lasted more than three days.

The laundry room, where Capone worked, was damp and badly ventilated, and when an Army transport anchored in the bay with an accumulation of wash, the work load became backbreaking. In January, 1935, Capone was at his usual station by the mangle when thirty-six of his co-workers walked out in protest. For every three prisoners Johnston employed one guard, a ratio two to three times higher than that maintained in most federal prisons. The strikers were quickly surrounded, separated, and removed to the Hole. Because Capone took no part, he aroused a good deal of enmity. A month later one of the strikers, Bill Collier, was catching laundry as Capone fed it into the mangle. He complained that it came through too fast and too wet. Capone paid no attention. So Collier picked up a sopping bundle and flung it into his face. Before the guards could stop the brawl, Capone blacked his attacker's eye. Both men spent eight days in the Hole.

Another strike, this time general, took place without Capone in January of the following year. The immediate provocation was the death of a prisoner with a stomach ulcer, whom Johnston had refused medical treatment because he thought him a malingerer. As Capone stuck to his post, the prison rang with cries of "Rat" and "Scab!" But it was not cowardice that kept him from joining the rebels. He knew the odds. "Those guys are crazy," he said. "They can't get anything out of this." He asked to be excused from work and allowed to remain in his cell until the strike ended. "I have to protect my skin, if I'm going to get out of here alive," he told the guards. He did not stand alone. Nearly all the prison "aristocrats"—the spectacular felons like Arthur "Doc" Barker, last surviving son of Ma Barker's murderous brood; the kidnappers George "Machine Gun" Kelly, Albert Bates and Harvey Bailey, who had collected a ransom of $200,000 for the Oklahoma oil magnate Charles Urschel; Roy Gardner, train bandit and escape artist—shared his prudence and likewise incurred the hatred of the mutineers.

Capone's request was granted. His first day back at work, the strikers having been starved into submission, an unknown hand hurled a sash weight at his head. Roy Gardner, seeing it coming, threw himself at Capone, shoving him aside. The missile struck Capone's arm, inflicting a deep cut. He was then shifted to the bathhouse cleaning squad.

The bathhouse adjoined the barbershop. On the morning of June 23, five months after the second strike, Jim Lucas, a Texas bank robber, reported for his monthly haircut. When he left, he seized a pair of scissors, crept up behind Capone, who was mopping the bathhouse floor, and drove the blades into his back. Capone recovered after a week in the hospital and Lucas went to the Hole.

A San Francisco lawyer, representing Mae Capone, appealed to the Attorney General to have Capone imprisoned elsewhere, but without result. Other attempts followed to kill or maim "the wop with the mop," as his enemies now referred to him. His friends exposed a plot to doctor his breakfast coffee with lye. On his way to the prison dentist one morning he was jumped and almost strangled before he broke his attacker's grip and floored him with a blow.

The chief medical officer who treated Capone's various injuries, Dr. George Hess, had formerly worked under Ossenfort at Atlanta and so knew the patient's aversion to a spinal puncture. He broached the subject again but did not press Capone when he recoiled. "Those sons of bitches!" Capone complained to Al Karpis, who had been transferred from Leavenworth in 1936 under a life sentence for kidnapping. "They told me they couldn't care less if that's what I wanted to die from." Yet he could not overcome his horror of the doctor's needle.

Perhaps more than anything except sexual relief, the prisoners craved news of their old haunts and associates. Their only hope lay in the newcomers, and they would maneuver tirelessly to get close to them and befriend them. The problem, if they succeeded, was to hold a conversation out of earshot of the guards. The first Sunday Karpis appeared in the recreation yard an inmate approached him quietly. "My name is Frank Del Bono," he said. "Al would like to talk to you. He knows a lot of people you know. He'd like to talk to you if it won't put any heat on you."

Karpis did not commit himself immediately. Before any involvement with Capone he wanted to find out how the Chicagoan stood in the eyes of other prisoners. He consulted those whom he considered the elite, a few of whom, like Doc Barker, had been his partners in bank robbery or kidnapping. "Everything I heard about Capone was good," he recalled after his release thirty-three years later. "The ones who hated him were mostly scum, white trash. I told Del Bono I'd talk to Al any time." During their initial encounter, sitting in the recreation yard, their backs to the cellhouse wall, Capone asked if he needed money. No, said Karpis, his people were taken care of. The kidnapper could play the guitar a little, and at Capone's suggestion he joined the band. They talked for the next few Sundays, as they bent their heads together over a music stand, pretending to study a score. Karpis was the first of several new arrivals who kept Capone abreast of developments in the underworld.

Capone learned that Machine Gun Jack McGurn was dead, killed in a bowling alley before a score of witnesses by two unidentified men. They killed him with machine guns on the eve of St. Valentine's Day, 1936, and left a comic valentine beside the body. It showed a couple who had literally lost their shirts, gazing dolefully at a sign— SALE OF HOUSEHOLD GOODS. The accompanying jingle described the state of McGurn's affairs at his death:

> You've lost your job,
> You've lost your dough,
> Your jewels and handsome houses.
> But things could be worse, you know.
> You haven't lost your trousers.

The organization that Capone built was still largely intact and moving into ever broader spheres. Jake Guzik, released from Leavenworth in 1935, and Ralph Capone had picked up where they left off as, respectively, general business manager and director of gambling and vice. Mitzi Capone was handling horse bets at a new Cicero dive, the Hi Ho Club, and also acting as contact man for loan sharks. Phil D'Andrea had succeeded to the presidency of the Italo-American National Union. With Guzik, Willie Bioff and others he had infiltrated the International Alliance of Theatrical Stage Employees and Motion Picture Operators, through which they extorted millions of dollars from the Hollywood studios by threatening labor trouble. Tony Accardo and Paul Ricca, but yesterday lowly Capone foot soldiers, were forging ahead fast as important Mafiosi. A new Cook County sheriff, John Toman, admitted the resurgence of the Caponeites. "But what can I do with only thirty-two-and-a-third deputies [sic] on a shift, and more than 400 square miles to cover?"

The news that Capone was allowed to receive from his family in the fall of 1936 chiefly concerned his wife's struggles to retain the Palm Island house. After payment of the trial lawyers' fees and part of the fines, court costs and taxes owed, her capital was meager. "Ralph is taking care of Mae's case," Mafalda wrote on October 31, "so, please, dear, relax." Ralph himself wrote two days later, following a visit to Alcatraz by Mae and Matt Capone.

. . . of course they didn't bring very good news but they didn't bring bad. The bad that I am referring to is the sale of the house in Florida. We had them beat until they served notice on Mae as transferee and we would have beat them only for the fact that when Mae was originally assessed in 1931, she did not protest the assessments. The law provides that the assessment must be protested within ninety days or lose the right to a hearing . . . she spoke to Ahern about it and he said not to pay any attention to it, so when she was named as transferee and a lien was placed on the place, the attorneys . . . discovered the unprotested assignment of 1931, so in spite of our efforts the place was advertised for sale. . . . I am sorry this had to be the final outcome of everything, but we did our best and it is all due to another mistake on the part of your attorneys.

But it was not the final outcome. On the tenth Ralph wrote:

Well you need have no more worries about the Florida home. I paid the whole thing in Jacksonville, last Saturday, the total amount was $52,103.30. We have obtained a complete release and there is no further claims against the home by the Gov. I obtained a mortgage on the house for $35,000. . . . I managed to borrow enough to make up the difference.

. . . everything points to a big season in Miami, in fact there are several tourists here now and they built 37 new hotels in the past six months. . . . Mae just arrived from Chicago. . . .

Among the first duties James Bennett set himself, after he succeeded Bates, was a tour of the prisons as an ombudsman. Upon arrival he would announce his willingness to interview any prisoner with a complaint. At Alcatraz a resentful Warden Johnston had a desk placed for him in a chilly, dim-lit corner of the cell house. Throughout each interview a guard stood facing the prisoner, pointing a rifle at his chest. "When I protested . . . ," Bennett wrote, "he explained that these were the most desperate men in the world . . . and they might regard it as an accomplishment to assault the prison director."

One of the first prisoners brought to Bennett was Capone. "I'm getting along all right," he said. "Capone can take care of himself. But I shouldn't be here. I'm here because of my reputation, because there's such a misunderstanding about me. People don't know the things I've done to be helpful." And once again he recounted his services to Colonel McCormick as a peacemaker in the newsboys' strike. If Bennett would remain on the island for two weeks, Capone offered, he would reveal to him everything he knew about the underworld, "and I'll throw in the movie rights." Bennett declined with a twinge of regret.

The mutiny that year, in September, nearly cost Johnston his life. When a majority of the prisoners (not including Capone) refused to work unless they could choose their workshop, the warden gave them a simple choice—unconditional obedience or starvation. About two-thirds of them soon resumed their tasks, while 100 remained locked in their cells a while longer. From the outset of his administration Johnston had observed a perilous custom because of its psychological value. At the end of each meal he would wait by the exit, alone and unarmed, with his back to the prisoners until the last man had marched out. On this occasion Barton "Whitey" Phillips, a young bank robber serving a life term, did not march out. As he passed close to Johnston, he felled him with a right fist to his jaw, and before the guards could reach the spot, stamped on his chest and head. Johnston survived, minus some teeth, but the beating Phillips took, followed by weeks in the Hole, left him a spiritless hulk.

In late January, 1938, his fourth year on Alcatraz, Capone received a visit from a familiar figure and one unknown to him. Special Agent Sullivan and Assistant U.S. Attorney Seymour Klein from the New York district had obtained permission to question him about Torrio.

A side effect of Capone's conviction, along with those of Druggan, Lake, Guzik, *et al.*, had been a rush of gangsters to the tax collector to pay up before disaster overtook them, too. The lesson, however, did not impress itself upon them indelibly. Before long many of them, aided by accountants and lawyers, concocted what they imagined to be unbeatable schemes to conceal income. The normally sagacious Torrio adopted such a scheme after Repeal. Labyrinthine in detail, it was simple enough in essence. He would declare only a small fraction of his income; the bulk of it he would invest through dummy partners in a legitimate New York wholesale liquor firm.

Sullivan and Klein were the first visitors ever allowed near an Alcatraz prisoner without supervision. At the start of the afternoon work period guards admitted them to Capone's cell, brought him back from his work, and, locking the cell door, left the trio alone.

Klein, a little man, grew increasingly apprehensive as the massive Capone, with his notoriously hot temper, paced the cell, and he kept as far away from him as possible, letting Sullivan conduct the interview. Capone talked. In his hunger for communication, he talked all that afternoon and the next. He philosophized. He reminisced. He reviewed his entire career from school days in Brooklyn to his conviction. He mentioned Torrio frequently ("I carried a gun for him; I'd go the limit for him"). He couldn't forgive him for his partnership with Dutch Schultz (since murdered by Luciano's order), but neither could he betray him. He responded to Sullivan's probing with generalities. Torrio made his money the same way Capone did; he'd been in the rackets twenty years longer—nothing usable as courtroom evidence. The investigators returned East emptyhanded.

Another year elapsed before Torrio stood trial, charged with evading taxes of $86,000 for the years 1933–35. The brilliant Max Steuer defended him and suffered one of his rare defeats. Midway through the trial Torrio changed his plea to guilty. He went to Leavenworth for two and a half years.

When the guards decided that the weather was cold enough for the prisoners to wear their pea jackets, they so indicated with three blasts of a whistle. February 5, 1938, dawned unseasonably warm, and no whistle blew. Capone nevertheless put on his pea jacket. For a year he had been on library duty, delivering and collecting books and magazines. Al Karpis, who occupied the second cell to the left of his and so always followed him in the line to the mess hall, had a magazine to return, and he tossed it into Capone's cell as he passed it. Seeing Capone still there, wearing full winter garb, including a cap and cotton work gloves, he called to him: "No jacket today." Capone seemed neither to hear nor to recognize him but stood staring vacantly ahead.

He failed to fall into line when ordered, a breach of discipline ordinarily punishable by removal to the Hole, but the guards, sensing something seriously wrong, watched without disturbing him. He finally left his cell and entered the mess hall last in line. A thread of spittle glistened on his chin. As he moved mechanically toward the steam table, a deputy warden, Ernest Miller, spoke to him quietly and patted his arm. Capone pointed meaninglessly out the window.

He started to retch. Miller led him to a locked gate across the hall and called to the guard on the other side to unlock it. They helped Capone up a flight of stairs ending at the hospital door.

To Dr. Hess and to the consultant psychiatrist he sent for, Dr. Edward Twitchell, Capone's symptoms suggested the damage to the central nervous system characteristic of advanced syphilis. When Capone, in a return of lucidity, understood this, he raised no more objections to a spinal puncture, and the fluid was rushed to the Marine Hospital in San Francisco for analysis. Warden Johnston, stopping by Capone's bedside, asked him: "What happened to you this morning?" "I dunno, Warden," Capone replied. "They tell me I acted like I was a little wacky."

The report from the Marine Hospital confirmed the doctors' diagnosis. Word of it reached the press, and front-page stories from coast to coast pictured Capone as a prisoner driven insane by the horrors of Alcatraz. Mae Capone telephoned Johnston, imploring him to free her husband, an act of clemency beyond his power. Capone was not seen again in the cell blocks or the mess hall. He spent the remaining year of his ten-year sentence (reduced to six years and five months for good behavior plus working credits) in the hospital ward, subjected to injections of arsphenamine, shock treatment and induced fever. The progress of the disease was retarded but not arrested. He alternated between periods of lucidity and confusion.

His last day on Alcatraz was January 6, 1939. For the misdemeanor of failing to file a tax return, he owed another year, reducible by good behavior to about ten months. In view of his deterioration, it was decided not to drag him halfway across the country and return him to Cook County Jail, as Judge Wilkerson originally decreed, but to let him serve the sentence in the newly opened Federal Correctional Institution at Terminal Island near Los Angeles. Deputy Warden Miller and three armed guards took him there by launch, train and automobile, with six weights added to his leg irons, a somewhat superfluous precaution, since he was partially paralyzed.

One Sunday the Harbor Region Ministerial Committee sent the Reverend Silas A. Thweat to Terminal Island to conduct a church service. "Do you feel the need of prayer?" the minister asked the seventy-five inmates who attended. Among the first to raise his hand was Capone. "Are any of you here feeling the need of a savior? If so, stand up before your fellows and confess the fact." Capone stood up.

The following November, after the last of the fines imposed by Judge Wilkerson had been paid through a Chicago gang lawyer, Capone was transferred to the U.S. penitentiary at Lewisburg, Pennsylvania. The day he arrived, November 16, Ralph and Mae Capone called for him and drove him to Baltimore's Union Memorial Hospital. Until spring he lived with Mae in Baltimore as an outpatient of the hospital under the care of Dr. Joseph Moore, a Johns Hopkins syphilologist.

In Chicago, reporters asked Jake Guzik if Capone was likely to return and take command again. "Al," he replied in language harsher than he intended, for his loyalty had never wavered, "is nutty as a fruitcake."

28

Tertiary Stage

IMAGINARY killers haunted him. The sight of an automobile, especially an automobile carrying men, would throw him into a panic. Only his own Pontiac and Sonny's Chevrolet were allowed beyond the gates. Ralph, moreover, had cautioned Mae against letting any outsiders near Al lest, in his befogged mental state, he babble about the organization.

The permanent household comprised, in addition to Sonny and his parents, Mae's sister, Muriel, and her husband, Louis Clark—"Uncle Louie"—and an aged but alert fox terrier who barked furiously at the approach of any stranger. The two Negro servants, "Brownie" Brown, cook and general utility man, and Rose, the maid, lived off the premises. Once a fortnight Steve from Steve's Barber Shop in the Grand Hotel, a Miami hangout of racketeers and gamblers, came to cut Capone's hair. Mae's brother, Danny, with his wife, Winifred, operated two establishments frequented by resident and visiting gangsters, Winnie's Waffle Shop and Winnie's Little Club, which between them grossed $500 to $700 a day. Danny Coughlin was also the business agent for the Miami Bartenders' and Waiters' Union.

At least four times a week Mae attended Mass at St. Patrick's Cathedral in Miami Beach. Capone never accompanied her, not wanting, as he explained, to embarrass the pastor, Monsignor William Barry. Sonny had gone to the private preparatory school run by the monsignor, who took a special interest in the shy, semideaf boy, trying to cultivate in him qualities that would help him rise above the stigma of his name. In 1937 Sonny had entered Notre Dame under his father's alias, Al Brown. He withdrew after freshman year, when his identity became known. He was now working toward a BS degree in business administration at the University of Miami.

Probably because Capone slept badly, the household kept strange hours, retiring at 10 P.M. and beginning to stir by 3 A.M. They spent most of the day around the pool. Capone, wearing pajamas and dressing gown, would sit for hours on the dock, smoking cigars, chewing Sen-Sen, and holding a fishing rod. Occasionally he would bat a tennis ball over a net stretched across the lawn. He hated solitude and always wanted many people around him, provided he recognized them as trusty old friends. He had grown obese and partly bald. He enjoyed gin rummy and pinochle; but the mental effort often proved too much for him, and the friends he played with would let him win. Once when an opponent forgot himself and scored a victory, Capone cried: "Get the boys. I want this wise guy taken care of."

In 1940 the family received astonishing news. They heard from the firstborn Capone brother, Jim, who had disappeared thirty-five years before. He was living in the town of Homer, Nebraska, under his legally adopted name of Richard James Hart. Broke, missing one eye, with a wife and children to support, he had written to Ralph, appealing for help. Ralph sent him $250 and had him come to Racap Lodge, his country place at Mercer, Wisconsin. Jim then stayed a month with Al in Miami. After he returned to Homer, Ralph sent him a check nearly every month.

According to the account he gave of himself, the long-lost James Capone had devoted most of his career to law enforcement. "Two-Gun Hart," he said the Nebraskans dubbed him because he carried a gun strapped to each hip and with either hand could shoot the cap off a beer bottle at a hundred feet. He lost an eye, he explained, in a gunfight with gangsters.

It was a story the newspapers later found irresistible and published without reservations—the white sheep of a black herd. The truth, however, as uncovered by government agents, who had occasion to look into Hart-Capone's activities, differed.

After running away from his boyhood home in Brooklyn, he had joined a circus as a roustabout and traveled with it all over the United States and Central America. In 1919 he dropped off a freight train passing through Homer and decided to settle there. He set up shop as a painter and paperhanger but proved too inexpert to prosper at it. He became friendly with a grocer named Winch and his daughter, Kathleen, whose lives he had saved in a flash flood. He told them he came from Oklahoma, left home in his early teens, worked on a railroad gang until he accidentally killed a man in a fight, and fled to Nebraska. During the World War, he said, he fought overseas. On the basis of this claim the local American Legion Post elected him commander. Toward the end of 1919 he married Kathleen Winch. They had four sons.

For two years Hart served as Homer's town marshal, then for a year as a state sheriff. In 1922 he became a special officer for the Indian Service, investigating the sales of liquor to the Winnebago and Omaha tribes, among whom he earned a reputation for brutality. Transferred to Sioux City, Iowa, he was arrested for the murder of an Indian in a saloon brawl. The victim, it appeared, had been a bootlegger, and Hart went free. The victim's relatives waylaid him, and it was in this melee that he lost an eye. Transferred to Coeur D'Alene, Idaho, he was charged with a second murder but never tried.

Reappointed town marshal of Homer, he was entrusted with the keys to various stores so that he could enter them, if necessary, when patrolling the town at night. The owners began to miss all kinds of merchandise. The marshal's own father-in-law found his stocks of canned goods mysteriously depleted. Hart was eventually relieved of both keys and his marshal's badge. As an American Legion commander he had often traveled to conventions, but when the local legionnaires finally thought to ask him for proof of his war service and he could produce none, they expelled him. Evicted from one house after the other for nonpayment of rent, the family went on relief. Not until Richard Hart came back from Miami did he tell his wife that he was Al Capone's oldest brother.

For once, on December 30, 1941, Capone overcame his reluctance to go to church. He went to St. Patrick's to witness his son's marriage to Diana Ruth Casey, a girl Sonny had first met in high school. The best man was his cousin, Ralph, Jr. After the honeymoon, the newlyweds lived on Northeast Tenth Avenue. Sonny had opened a florist shop the preceding September. During World War II, he was classified 4-F because of his defective hearing. He volunteered for civilian employment with the War Department and was assigned to the Miami Air Depot as a mechanic's learner. His wife bore him four children, all girls, on whom their grandfather doted, constantly giving them expensive toys and playing with them inexhaustibly in the Palm Island swimming pool. Sonny once said, mixing up folk heroes: "I want my father to be remembered as a kind of Jesse James who took from the rich and gave to the poor."

The course of neurosyphilis is unpredictable, the victim now seemingly normal, now disoriented, his speech unintelligible, a prey to tremors and epilepsylike seizures. In even his best periods Capone lacked mental and physical coordination. He would skip abruptly from subject to unrelated subject, whistling, humming and singing as he chattered. Despite his gross overweight, he walked rapidly, with jerky, automatonlike motions. By 1942 penicillin had become available, but in extremely limited supply, the War Production Board having imposed a tight quota. Dr. Moore of Johns Hopkins managed to procure dosages for Capone, who was thus one of the first syphilitics to be treated with antibiotics. Though no therapy could reverse the extensive damage to his brain, his condition was apparently stabilized.

On March 19, 1944, after suffering a humiliating defeat in the Republican gubernatorial primary, Big Bill Thompson died of pneumonia in his suite at the Blackstone Hotel.

In April the Chicago police were hunting Matt Capone, the sometime university student for whom Al had once entertained such glowing expectations. Matt ran the Hall of Fame Tavern in Cicero. The night of the eighteenth his two bartenders, Walter Sanders and Jens Larrison, fell to squabbling over a $5 bill missing from the cash register. About twenty people saw Sanders shove Larrison into a back room, saw Matt fumble for something in a drawer behind the bar and follow them, heard two shots. None of the three men reappeared. Larrison's body was found in an alley two miles from the tavern. Matt hid for a year, then surrendered. But the murder charge against him was dismissed because Sanders, the state's vital witness, never reappeared.

Within two weeks of Matt's surrender, Capone's old, reliable "Enforcer," Frank Nitti, faced with another term in Leavenworth for labor racketeering, put a bullet through his head.

It is doubtful that any of these events penetrated Capone's understanding. On January 19, 1947, at four o'clock in the morning, he collapsed with a brain hemorrhage. Dr. Kenneth Phillips arrived, followed by Monsignor Barry, who administered the last rites. The United Press reported Capone dead. But he rallied, and Phillips pronounced him out of danger. The following week he developed bronchial pneumonia. Reporters gathered in force outside the locked gate. As the hot day wore on, Ralph let them through and brought them iced beer. Saturday evening, the twenty-fifth, at the age of forty-eight, Capone died in the presence of his mother, his wife, his son, his brothers and sisters. Phillips tried without success to persuade the family to permit an autopsy "to make possible the study of the brain for medical history."

An icy wind shook the tent pitched on Plot 48 in Chicago's Mount Olivet Cemetery. Snow thickly covered the earth. The small band of mourners included, besides the immediate family, cousins Charlie and Rocco Fischetti, Jake Guzik, Sam Hunt, Murray Humphreys. Red Rudensky, a reformed character, had come from St. Paul. Torrio was not present. The archbishopric had forbidden a requiem mass or any elaborate ceremony but issued no injunction against burial in the same consecrated ground that held the remains of Capone's father and his brother Frank. Monsignor William Gorman explained to the reporters: "The Church never condones evil, nor the evil in any man's life. This very brief ceremony is to recognize his penitence and the fact he died fortified by the sacraments of the Church." The bronze casket was modest by gangster standards, as modest as the headstone later placed over it.

QUI RIPOSA
Alphonse Capone
Nato: Jan. 17, 1899
Morto: Jan. 25, 1947

The week before, Andrew Volstead had died at eighty-seven in Granite Falls, Minnesota, his belief unshaken to the end that "law does regulate morality."

Appendix: The Heritage

RALPH CAPONE NOW OVERLORD IN VICE

. . . in his own right [Ralph Capone] is now one of the overlords of the national syndicate which controls gambling, vice and
other rackets.

—United Press, July 28, 1950

From the report of the hearings, October, 1950, before the Special
Committee to Investigate Organized Crime in Interstate Commerce,
United States Senate (Chairman: Senator Estes Kefauver):

The roots of the criminal group operating in Chicago today go
back to the operations of the Torrio-Capone gang. . . .
Since the last reorganization of the [racing] wire service in the
Chicago area the city of Chicago has been serviced by the R. and
H. wire service owned by the Capone mobsters, Ray Jones, Phil
Katz, and Hymie Levin. . . .
The manufacture and distribution of slot machines has been
a lucrative field of operation for a number of Capone mobsters.
The Taylor Manufacturing Co. in Cicero, one of the largest manu-
facturers of gaming equipment in the country is partially owned by
Claude Maddox, a Capone mobster . . . and Joseph Aiuppa. . . .
Ed Vogel, old-time Capone henchman . . . is believed to con-
trol the distribution of slot machines in the North Side of Chicago
and in the northwest suburbs. . . .
Roland Libonati, Democratic State Senator from the West Side

and a close associate of Capone's, spearheaded the opposition to the reform legislation proposed by the Chicago Crime Commission and Governor Stevenson and backed by the bar. . . .

[In his book *Mafia*, published two years later, Ed Reid, a Pulitzer Prize-winning reporter, listed eighty-three Mafiosi by order of importance. He assigned forty-first place to Libonati.]

There is little doubt that members of the Capone syndicate use proceeds from their illegitimate activities to buy their way into hotels, restaurants, laundry services, dry-cleaning establishments, and wholesale and retail liquor businesses. . . .

Paul Ricca . . . one of the two or three leading figures in the Capone mob; Louis "Little New York" Campagna and Charlie "Cherry Nose" Gioe . . . were prominent in the mulcting of the movie industry. . . .

The two major crime syndicates in this country are the Accardo-Guzik-Fischetti syndicate, whose headquarters are in Chicago; and the Costello-Adonis-Lansky syndicate based in New York. Evidence of the Accardo-Guzik-Fischetti syndicate was found by the committee in such places as Chicago, Kansas City, Dallas, Miami, Las Vegas, and the west coast. . . .

The Kefauver Committee questioned both Ralph and Matt Capone at great length. A month later Ralph, Jr., or Ralph Gabriel, as he preferred to call himself, drank half a quart of scotch in his Chicago apartment, swallowed a quantity of cold tablets from a bottle whose label warned against mixing them with alcohol, and began a letter to a girl he loved. The pills were his final solution to the problem of carrying the Capone name. Through school and college, marriage, fatherhood, and a long series of jobs, the name, always discovered sooner or later, had unfailingly brought him grief. It had tainted his relations with his girl, Jeanne Kerin, a nightclub singer. "Jeanie, my sweetheart," he wrote. "I love you. I love you. Jeanie only you I love. Only you. I'm gone—" He got no farther.

In 1952 James Capone died, totally blind, in Homer. The same year Teresa Capone died, aged eighty-five. She was buried not in Mount Olivet Cemetery, but in Mount Carmel, at the opposite end of the city. When the family realized how many tourists were coming to see the grave of Al Capone, they bought another plot in Mount Carmel and had the caskets reburied there. The marble shaft with the Capone names still stands in Mount Olivet, left behind to sidetrack tourists. The real graves in Mount Carmel are marked by small black marble stones, clustered around a granite slab, each bearing the words "My Jesus Mercy."

The fifties carried off a good many Caponian charter members— Sam Hunt, Terry Druggan, Claude Maddox, Phil D'Andrea, Jake Guzik, Louis Campagna, Frank Diamond—nearly all of them dying abed of a heart ailment. Diamond was an exception. He was killed by a shotgun blast. A coronary struck down Torrio in a Brooklyn barbershop on April 16, 1957, and he died soon after in the hospital. He was seventy-five. Bugs Moran, serving a ten-year sentence in Leavenworth for bank robbery, met the end he had often said he feared most: He died of lung cancer. Judge Lyle, who considered him the likeliest of all the gangsters he had ever observed to undergo a religious repentance, wrote to the Catholic prison chaplain, asking about Moran's last hours. "George Moran died a peaceful death," replied the chaplain, "and was strengthened with the full Last Rites (Penance—Extreme Unction—Holy Viaticum—Apostolic Blessing) of the Catholic Church while he was fully conscious. This happened some days before he died and was not a 'last ditch' stand. Your theory certainly proved out very satisfactory in his case. I am sure that God in his mercy was very kind to him in judgment."

From a tapped telephone conversation in November, 1957, between Sam Giancana, Capone-trained top boss of the Chicago syndicate, and Sam Magaddino, his Buffalo opposite number, concerning the arrest at Apalachin, New York, of sixty-three Mafia leaders:

MAGADDINO: It never would've happened in your place.
GIANCANA: You're fuckin' right it wouldn't. This is the safest territory in the world for a big meet. . . . We got three towns just outside of Chicago with the police chiefs in our pocket. We got this territory locked up tight.

Only once after Capone's death did his widow emerge from anonymity. This was in 1959 when the Columbia Broadcasting System televised *The Untouchables*, a two-part film, further sensationalizing Eliot Ness's sensational account of his gang-busting adventures. Mae Capone, Sonny and Mafalda jointly brought a $1,000,000 suit against the network, the producer of the film, Desilu Productions, and the sponsor, Westinghouse Electric, complaining that the dead man's name, likeness and personality were used for profit. They lost, and in the fall the American Broadcasting System launched *The Untouchables* as a weekly series.

Capone's last lawyer, Abraham Teitelbaum, probably did not overstate the case by much when he said: "I'm sure Al died penniless." Capone alone never owned the sources of his once vast wealth. He shared them with partners, with the organization, and when he could no longer function, the sources reverted to them. No doubt they provided the means for him to live his last years comfortably—Ralph and Jake Guzik would have seen to that—but his personal property was heavily mortgaged, and what cash the family could raise went chiefly to pay back taxes. Mae sold both the Palm Island and Prairie Avenue houses. For a time she and Sonny ran a restaurant in Miami Beach, the Grotto, she handling the cash register and Sonny working as headwaiter. The venture failed.

At last accounts Mae was dividing her time between Miami, Chicago and Ralph's Wisconsin retreat. Ralph himself was retired. Mafalda and her husband were operating a delicatessen-restaurant in Chicago. Their son was practicing law.

From *Organized Crime and Illicit Traffic in Narcotics*—Report of the hearings held in September and October, 1963, before the Permanent Subcommittee on Investigations (Chairman: Senator John L. McClellan) of the Committee on Government Operations, United States Senate:

> Captain William J. Duffy, director of Intelligence for the Chicago Police Department . . . estimated that there are 300 men in the Chicago area who devote their full efforts to organizing, directing, and controlling a far greater number of people involved in criminal activities like gambling, narcotics distribution, pandering, loan sharking, labor racketeering and terrorism. . . .
>
> Captain Duffy stated that his office believed that there are 26 men who lead 300 full-time gangsters in control of Chicago's organized crime. These men are divided by the Chicago police into two groups, one of which is known as the "Mafia" group. . . . The other group consists of the "Associates of the Italian Organization." . . .
>
> Prominent in his testimony about the first group were . . . Sam

"Mooney" Giancana; Anthony Accardo; Felice De Lucia (Paul "the Waiter") Ricca; and Rocco Fischetti. Among the associates he named Murray "the Camel" Humphreys and Gus Alex [a protégé of Jake Guzik]. . . .

He emphasized that the power of the Chicago organization rests in a single characteristic . . . —the ability of the group to commit murder and other acts of violence without fear of retribution. . . .

Chicago's Superintendent of Police Orlando W. Wilson had earlier reported to the committee that since 1919, 976 gangland murders had been committed in the Chicago area. Only two of the murderers were convicted.

In the rosters of the Chicago Mafia and its associates, submitted to the committee by Captain Duffy, all four surviving Capone brothers figured among the gangsters controlling the West Side.

A fifth black marble gravestone took its place in the Mount Carmel plot in February, 1967. After ailing for several years with a weak heart, Matt Capone was dead at fifty-nine.

CAPONE BROTHER RUNS S. W. SUBURB VICE RING

A man who reluctantly bears one of the most chilling names in the annals of crime—Capone—now reigns as overlord of a growing vice and gambling empire in the southwest suburbs. . . .

Leader of this crime syndicate expansion move is Alberto Capone, aging (62) brother of the late Al Capone.

Alberto uses the name Bert Novak. He has also gone by the name of Albert Rayola. . . .

Capone operates out of two bases in Suburban Hickory Hills—Castle Acres Motel . . . and Hickory Lodge Cocktail Lounge. . . .

Both places are within shouting distance of the Hickory Hills City Hall, seat of what is probably the shakiest suburban administration in the Chicago area, or perhaps the nation. . . .

Mayor Thomas Watson admitted that he lived in fear since his election in the 13,000 population suburb as a reform candidate in April, 1967.

Three days after Watson's election, early morning shotgun blasts damaged his parked auto. Watson has also received frequent terror-type anonymous phone calls. . . .

[The Better Government Association] is convinced that [Capone] is the principal syndicate man behind the rising tide of gambling and vice in such nearby suburbs as Crestwood, Alsip and Willow Springs. . . .

Chicago Sun-Times, January 19, 1969

An avid golfer, the last of the active Capone brothers would appear on the suburban links, wearing a golfing glove studded with costume jewelry.

Until 1970, the Hawthorne Inn, renamed the Towne Hotel, remained a meeting place of the Chicago syndicate. Rossmar Realty, Inc., whose president was Joseph Aiuppa, an early Capone triggerman and latterly the ranking Cicero Mafioso, owned the hotel, as well as the adjoining Turf Lounge, a gangster rendezvous since Capone's day. On May 24, 1964, the *Sun-Times* had reported under the headline STATE POLICE BREAK UP DICE GAME IN CICERO GAMING FORT:

> State police battered down steel doors to raid a barboot [Greek dice] game in a basement of a Cicero coffee house and arrested 15 men fleeing through a network of catacombs.
>
> The raiders, armed with crowbars, sledgehammers, axes and an FBI warrant, said it was the most impregnable gambling fortress they had ever broken into.
>
> When the officers, led by State Chief of Detectives John Newbold, entered the one-story coffee house at 2208 South Cicero (which runs at right angles to 22nd Street) in the suburb, it was empty.
>
> By tapping and pounding on the walls, the detectives turned up a secret door in a panel. This led to an empty back room. Here in the floor was a trapdoor encased in steel straps that was bolted shut from below.
>
> After several minutes of sledge-swinging, the raiders broke through and found themselves in an underground passage that led to another steel door.
>
> This door took another several minutes of similar ax and crowbar work before it yielded. Crashing through, the police found an elaborate barboot dice game layout. They arrested four men as keepers. . . .
>
> Spilling out into catacombs were 11 other men who were arrested as players. . . .
>
> It was the third time in slightly more than a year that the big barboot game had been knocked over.

King Features Syndicate, Inc.

Noon recess. On the steps of the Federal Building Capone forces a smile for the thousands who gathered in the streets.

Investigators and prosecutor. Left to right: Elmer L. Irey, chief of the Internal Revenue Service's enforcement branch; U.S. Attorney George E. Q. Johnson; Frank J. Wilson, who directed the investigation of Capone's tax delinquencies; and Arthur P. Madden, head of the Chicago tax intelligence unit.

The defendant and his counsel. Left: Michael Ahern; right: Albert Fink.

Capone on the eve of his trial.

The jury.

U. S. BUREAU OF INVESTIGATION, DEPARTMENT OF JUSTICE
WASHINGTON, D. C.

Institution _____ Located at _____

Received _____
From N. Ill - Chicago
Crime Vio Income Tax Law
Sentence: 10 yrs. ___ mos. ___ d
Date of sentence Oct 24 - 193
Sentence begins May 4 - 19
Sentence expires May 3 - 194
Good time sentence expires Jan 19 - 19
Date of birth 1 - 17 - 99 Occupation Dant
Birthplace ny Nationality
Age 33 Complexed fair
Height 5 - 10 ½ Eyes grey
Weight 255 Hair dark brown
Build Stout

Scars and marks oblique scar of 4" across cheek 2" in front Left ear Vertical scar of 2½" on left jaw — oblique scar of 2½" - 2" under Left ear

CRIMINAL HISTORY

NAME	NUMBER	CITY OR INSTITUTION	DATE	CHARGE	DISPOSITION OR SENTENCE
	C	ny City	1919	Dis Cond	Discharged
	D	Chicago Ill	1923	Traffic Vio	Dismissed
	E	Do	5-8-24	Murder Wit	Released
	H	Do	6-7-26	Vio NPA	Dismissed
	J	Do	7-28-26	Murder	Charge Withdr
	K	Do	10-1-26	Vio NPA	Dismissed
		Do	11-12-27	Refuse to Testify	Do
	L	Joliet Ill	12-22-27	Con Weapon	Fine $2600.
		Phila Pa	5-17-29	Do	Served
	M	Miami Fla	1928	Susp	Released
		Do	5-8-30	Do	Nolle prossed

other arrests See Declaration

(Please furnish all additional personal history and police record on separate sheet)

The raiders found an underground passageway leading to the Towne Hotel. . . .

On February 17, 1970, a fire, starting in the kitchen, totally destroyed the hotel. When state officials questioned Aiuppa about the ownership, he invoked the Fifth Amendment sixty times.

Since the mid-sixties, when Sam Giancana expatriated himself to avoid the attentions of the FBI, the head of the Chicago syndicate and a member of the Mafia's national council has been the Capone bodyguard, a suspected co-planner of the St. Valentine's Day massacre, Tony Accardo.

Sonny Capone's efforts to earn a living had not been rewarding. A man of unexceptionable ethics, he quit his first postwar job as a used car salesman in disgust over his employer's fraudulent practices, such as turning back speedometers. He next apprenticed himself, at $75 a week, to a printer, in whose shop he hoped to buy a half interest if he could persuade his mother to advance the money, but she decided against it. Through his brother-in-law, a detective in the Miami Police Department, he met several officers. They thought highly of him. A marksman of tournament quality, he joined their pistol team, became a member of the National Pistol Association of America and the Florida Peace Officers' Association. Of his wife, whom he taught to shoot, the society page of the Miami *News* carried this account (April 6, 1958) :

> Diana Capone, a slender, red-haired Miami Shores housewife, owns three pistols. She is an expert with each of them. To prove it she won 20 trophies in the recent Flamingo Open Pistol Shoot. . . .
> The soft-spoken, blue-eyed mother of four daughters does her big talking with a gun. She asks no odds from the men. . . .
> Diana often beats [her husband] in a match.
> "It makes Albert awfully proud . . . ," she says.

After the Grotto failed, they moved to Hollywood, Florida, where Sonny worked for a tire distributor. On the morning of August 7, 1965, he went shopping at the Kwik Chek Supermarket near his home. As he wheeled his groceries past a drug counter, an irresistible impulse overcame him. He pocketed two bottles of aspirin and a box of radio transistor batteries, costing all together $3.50, none of which he needed or wanted. A store detective saw the theft and arrested him.

"Do you know why you did it?" the judge asked when Sonny appeared in Criminal Court and pleaded *nolo contendere* to the charge of petty larceny. "No, Your Honor." Considering his exemplary past, the judge passed no sentence but put him on probation for two years. "Everybody has a little larceny in him, I guess," Sonny said with infinite sadness as he left the courtroom.

The supermarket manager had, meanwhile, kept his perishable purchases on ice. "I bet you have contempt for me," Sonny said, when he returned for them.

"No," the manager replied, "but I will have if you don't come back next week and get your groceries from me."

The following year Albert Francis Capone, only son of Alphonse Capone, changed his name.

Sources and Acknowledgments

For access to a mine of material about Al Capone and his associates, much of it unpublished, I am thankful to the Internal Revenue Service, which allowed me to examine its investigative files on Capone, Torrio and others, the Federal Bureau of Investigation, which turned over to me invaluable documentation and photographs; and the General Services Administration, which granted me permission to visit Alcatraz.

I am deeply indebted to Herman Kogan, John J. McPhaul and Ray Brennan of the Chicago *Sun-Times* for sharing with me their special knowledge of the Capone era;

Robert St. John, owner and editor of the Cicero *Tribune* during Capone's heyday;

Ralph Daigh, vice-president of Fawcett Publications;

James V. Bennett, former director of the U.S. Bureau of Prisons;

Morris "Red" Rudensky, reformed safecracker, who was Capone's cellmate in the Atlanta Penitentiary, and Alvin Karpis, Capone's fellow prisoner on Alcatraz; Dr. William E. Ossenfort, medical officer at Atlanta during Capone's term there; Loring P. Mills, former general administration manager of Alcatraz; John Hart, Alcatraz guard and latterly security contractor on the island for the General Services Administration;

The late Frank W. Wilson, the Special Agent of the Internal Revenue Service, who directed the investigation of Capone's tax delinquencies, and his colleagues Nels Tessem and James N. Sullivan;

William Makepeace, a member of the U.S. Attorney General's team that prosecuted John Torrio;

Captain William Duffy of the Chicago Police Department, Ralph Salerno, former sergeant of the New York Police Department, and Edward J. Allen, chief of police, Santa Ana, California, formerly chief of police, Youngstown, Ohio, three of the country's leading authorities on the Mafia;

William F. Parker, one of Capone's Miami lawyers, and George Bieber, the Chicago lawyer who represented Sam "Golf Bag" Hunt and George "Bugs" Moran;

Joe E. Lewis, one of Capone's favorite entertainers; George Jessel, who also came to know Capone when he played Chicago; Louis Armstrong, Eddie Condon, and Austin Mack, veterans of Chicago's great jazz era;

Marvin L. Hayman, owner of Chicago's New Michigan Hotel (formerly the Lexington), once Capone's Chicago headquarters, and Roy Fowler, the present owner of Capone's Miami Beach mansion;

And the numerous lawyers, prison officials and acquaintances of Capone who prefer to remain anonymous.

For their patient and generous help I wish to thank Miss Margaret Scriven of the Chicago Historical Society Library, Palmer Brynildsen of the Brooklyn Public Library and the staffs of the New York Public Library's American History, Local History and Genealogy, and Newspaper Microfilm divisions.

For allowing me to range at will through the libraries of their respective publications I wish to thank John G. Trezevant, executive vice-president of the Field Enterprises; John G. McCutcheon, Jr., editorial writer of the Chicago *Tribune;* Lawrence Jinks, editor of the Miami *Herald;* and Albert P. Govoni, president of True Detective Corporation.

I wish especially to thank my editor, William Targ of Putnam's, who taught me what creative editing means.

I am immensely grateful to my wife, Evelyn, for her tireless help in research and in the preparation of the final typescript.

BOOKS AND PAMPHLETS

ANONYMOUS, *Alcatraz.* San Francisco, E. Crowell Mensch, 1937.

ALLEN, EDWARD J., *Merchants of Menace—The Mafia.* Springfield, Ill., Charles C. Thomas, 1962.

ALLEN, FREDERICK LEWIS, *Only Yesterday.* New York, Harper & Brothers, 1957.

ALLSOP, KENNETH, *The Bootleggers.* London, Hutchinson, 1961.

ARMBRUSTER, EUGENE L., *Brooklyn's Eastern District.* Brooklyn, 1942.

ASBURY, HERBERT, *The Gangs of New York.* Garden City, Garden City Publishing Co., 1928.

——, *Gem of the Prairie: An Informal History of the Chicago Underworld.* New York, Alfred A. Knopf, 1940.

——, *The Great Illusion: An Informal History of Prohibition.* New York, Doubleday & Co., 1950.

AUDETT, JAMES HENRY ("Blackie"), *Rap Sheet.* New York, William Sloane Associates, 1954.

BENNETT, JAMES O'DONNELL, *Chicago Gangland.* Chicago *Tribune,* 1929.

BENNETT, JAMES V., *I Chose Prison.* New York, Alfred A. Knopf, 1970.

BERGER, MEYER, *The Eight Million.* New York, Simon and Schuster, 1942.

BIDDLE, FRANCIS, *In Brief Authority.* New York, Doubleday & Co., 1962.

BOETTIGER, JOHN, *Jake Lingle.* New York, E. P. Dutton & Co., 1931.

BURNS, WALTER NOBLE, *The One-Way Ride.* New York, Doubleday, Doran & Co., 1931.

BUSCH, FRANCIS X., *Enemies of the State.* New York, Bobbs-Merrill, 1954.

CASEY, ROBERT J., and DOUGLAS, W. A. S., *The Midwesterner—The Story of Dwight H. Green.* Chicago, Wilcox & Follett Co., 1948.

CHURCHILL, ALLEN, *A Pictorial History of American Crime.* New York, Holt, Rinehart & Winston, 1964.

COHN, ART, *The Joker Is Wild: The Story of Joe E. Lewis*. New York, Random House, 1955.

CONDON, EDDIE, *We Called It Music*. New York, Henry Holt & Co., 1947.

COOPER, COURTNEY RYLEY, *Ten Thousand Public Enemies*. New York, Blue Ribbon Books, 1935.

CRESSEY, DONALD R, *Theft of the Nation*. New York, Harper & Row, 1969.

CUMMINGS, HOMER, *Selected Papers*. New York, Charles Scribner's Sons, 1939.

DEDMON, EMMETT, *Fabulous Chicago*. New York, Random House, 1953.

DEMARIS, OVID, *Captive City*. New York, Lyle Stuart, 1969.

DOBYNS, FLETCHER, *The Underworld of American Politics*. New York, Fletcher Dobyns, Publisher, 1932.

ELLEN, MARY; MURPHY, MARK; and WELD, RALPH FOSTER, *A Treasury of Brooklyn*. New York, William Sloane Associates, 1949.

ELLIS, STEVE, *Alcatraz Number 1172*. Los Angeles, Holloway House Publishing Co., 1969.

ENRIGHT, RICHARD T. (Earl Buell), *Al Capone on the Spot*. Graphic Arts Corporation (Fawcett Publications), 1931.

FEDER, SID, and JOESTEN, JOACHIM, *The Luciano Story*. New York, David McKay Co., 1954.

FEDERAL WRITERS' PROJECT, *The Italians in New York*. New York, Random House, 1938.

GLAZER, NATHAN, and MOYNIHAN, DANIEL PATRICK, *Beyond the Melting Pot*. Cambridge, Mass., M.I.T. Press, 1963.

GODWIN, JOHN, *Alcatraz 1868–1963*. New York, Doubleday & Co., 1963.

Hearings Before the Permanent Subcommittee on Investigations. Organized Crime and Illicit Traffic in Narcotics. U.S. Senate, 1963.

Hearings Before the Special Committee to Investigate Organized Crime in Interstate Commerce. U.S. Senate, 1950.

HECHT, BEN, *A Child of the Century*. New York, Simon & Schuster, 1954.

HELMER, WILLIAM J., *The Gun That Made the Twenties Roar*. New York, Macmillan Co., 1969.

HYND, ALAN, *The Giant Killers*. New York, Robert M. McBride & Co., 1945.

IREY, ELMER L. (as told to William J. Slocum), *The Tax Dodgers*. Garden City, Garden City Publishing Co., 1948.

JESSEL, GEORGE, *So Help Me*. New York, Random House, 1943.

JOHNSTON, JAMES A., *Alcatraz Island Prison*. New York, Charles Scribner's Sons, 1949.

KEFAUVER, ESTES, *Crime in America*. New York, Doubleday & Co., 1951.

LANDESCO, JOHN, *Organized Crime in Chicago*. Part III of the Illinois Crime Survey. Chicago, University of Chicago Press, 1929.

LEWIS, LLOYD, and SMITH, HENRY JUSTIN, *Chicago: The History of Its Reputation*. New York, Harcourt, Brace and Co., 1929.

LYLE, JOHN H., *The Dry and Lawless Years*. Englewood Cliffs, N.J., Prentice-Hall, 1960.

LYNCH, DENIS TILDEN, *Criminals and Politicians*. New York, Macmillan Co., 1932.

MAAS, PETER, *The Valachi Papers*. New York, G. P. Putnam's Sons, 1968.

MARIANO, JOHN HORACE, *The Second Generation of Italians in New York*. Boston, Christopher Publishing House, 1921.

MATTFELD, JULIUS, *Variety Music Cavalcade*. New York, Prentice-Hall, 1952.

McClellan, John L., *Crime Without Punishment*. New York, Duell, Sloan & Pearce, 1962.

McPhaul, John J., *Deadlines & Monkeyshines: The Fabled World of Chicago Journalism*. Englewood Cliffs, N.J., Prentice-Hall, 1962.

Merz, Charles, *The Dry Decade*. New York, Doubleday, Doran & Co., 1931.

Messick, Hank, *The Silent Syndicate*. New York, Macmillan Co., 1967.

———, *Secret File*. New York, G. P. Putnam's Sons, 1969.

Mezzrow, Milton ("Mezz"), and Wolfe, Bernard, *Really the Blues*. New York, Random House, 1946.

National Commission on Law Observance and Enforcement. *Report on the Enforcement of the Prohibition Laws of the U.S.*, 1931.

Ness, Eliot (with Oscar Fraley), *The Untouchables*. New York, Julian Messner, 1957.

Pasley, Fred D., *Al Capone: The Biography of a Self-Made Man*. New York, Ives Washburn, 1930.

———, *Muscling In*. New York, Ives Washburn, 1931.

Peterson, Virgil, *Barbarians in Our Midst*. Boston, Little, Brown & Co., 1952.

Redston, George, and Crossen, Kendell F., *The Conspiracy of Death*. New York, Bobbs-Merrill Co., 1965.

Reid, Ed, *Mafia*. New York, Random House, 1952.

———, *The Grim Reapers*. Chicago, Henry Regnery Co., 1969.

Richman, Harry (with Richard Gehman), *A Hell of a Life*. New York, Duell, Sloan & Pearce, 1966.

Ross, Robert, *The Trial of Al Capone*. Chicago, Robert Ross, Publisher, 1933.

Rudensky, Morris, *My Keeper's Brother*. An unpublished manuscript.

Rudensky, Morris (Red), and Riley, Don, *The Goniff*. Blue Earth, Minn., 1970.

St. John, Robert, *This Was My World*. New York, Doubleday & Co., 1953.

Salerno, Ralph, and Tompkins, John, *The Crime Confederation*. New York, Doubleday & Co., 1969.

Sann, Paul, *The Lawless Decade*. New York, Crown Publishers, 1957.

Shapiro, Nat, and Hentoff, Nat, *Hear Me Talkin' to Ya: The Story of Jazz and the Men Who Made It*. New York, Rinehart & Co., 1955.

Smith, Alson J., *Syndicate City*. Chicago, Henry Regnery Co., 1954.

Sondern, Frederic, Jr., *Brotherhood of Evil: The Mafia*. New York, Farrar, Straus & Cudahy, 1959.

Sullivan, Edward Dean, *Chicago Surrenders*. New York, Vanguard Press, 1930.

———, *Rattling the Cup on Chicago Crime*. New York, Vanguard Press, 1929.

———, *The Snatch Racket*, New York, Vanguard Press, 1932.

Thompson, Craig, and Raymond, Allen, *Gang Rule in New York*. New York, Dial Press, 1940.

Thrasher, Frederic M., *The Gang: A Study of 1,313 Gangs in Chicago*. Chicago, University of Chicago Press, 1927.

Toland, John, *The Dillinger Days*. New York, Random-House, 1963.

Touhy, Roger, with Ray Brennan, *The Stolen Years*. Cleveland, Pennington Press, 1959.

Turkus, Burton B., and Feder, Sid, *Murder, Inc.* New York, Farrar, Straus and Young, 1951.

Vanderbilt, Cornelius, Jr., *Farewell to Fifth Avenue*. New York, Simon and Schuster, 1935.

VITRAY, LAURA, *The Great Lindbergh Hullabaloo: An Unorthodox Account.* New York, Wm. Faro, 1932.

WALDROP, FRANK, *McCormick of Chicago.* Englewood Cliffs, N.J., Prentice-Hall, 1966.

WALLER, IRLE, *Chicago Uncensored.* New York, Exposition Press, 1965.

WENDT, LLOYD, and KOGAN, HERMAN, *Lords of the Levee.* New York, Bobbs-Merrill Co., 1943.

——, *Big Bill of Chicago.* New York, Bobbs-Merrill Co., 1953.

WHITEHEAD, DON, *The FBI Story.* New York, Random House, 1956.

WHYTE, WILLIAM FOOTE, *Street Corner Society.* Chicago, University of Chicago Press, 1943.

WILSON, FRANK J., and DAY, BETH, *Special Agent.* New York, Holt, Rinehart & Winston, 1965.

ZORBAUGH, HARVEY W., *The Gold Coast and the Slum.* Chicago, University of Chicago Press, 1929.

PERIODICALS

ANONYMOUS, "Mild-Mannered Mr. Volstead, the 'Goat' of the Wets." *Literary Digest,* Dec. 27, 1919.

——, "Philadelphia Justice for Chicago's Al Capone." *Literary Digest,* June 15, 1929.

——, "Capone's Amazing Proposal." *Literary Digest,* November 22, 1930.

——, "Capone Caught for Contempt." *Literary Digest,* March 14, 1931.

——, "Uncle Sam Taking Capone for a Ride." *Literary Digest,* June 27, 1931.

——, "Gangdom's King Guilty as a Tax Dodger." *Literary Digest,* October 31, 1931.

——, "Al Capone's Victory." *The New Republic,* September 9, 1931.

—— (RAY BRENNAN), "The Capone I Knew." *True Detective,* June, 1947.

ASBURY, HERBERT, "The St. Valentine's Day Massacre." *'47 The Magazine of the Year,* September.

BECHDOLT, FREDERICK, "The Rock," *Saturday Evening Post,* November 2, 1935.

BETTS, LILLIAN W., "The Italians in New York." *University Settlement Studies,* October 1905–January, 1906.

BRANNON, W. T., "The Modest Mr. Guzik." *True Detective,* April, 1946.

BRENNAN, RAY, "Al Capone." *True Detective,* August, 1961.

——, "Dion O'Banion." *True Detective,* June, 1961.

CHILDS, M. W., "The Inside Story of the Federal Government's Secret Operations in Convicting Al Capone." *St. Louis Post-Dispatch Sunday Magazine,* September 25, 1932.

CONWAY, BRYAN (as told to T. H. Alexander), "20 Months in Alcatraz." *Saturday Evening Post,* February 19, 1938.

CUMMINGS, HOMER, "Why Alcatraz Is a Success." *Collier's,* July 29, 1939.

DAVIDSON, BILL, "How the Mobs Control Chicago." *Saturday Evening Post,* November 9, 1963.

DE LACY, CHARLES (ed., *13–13:* Official Organ of the Chicago Police Department), "The Inside on Chicago's Notorious St. Valentine's Day Massacre." *True Detective Mysteries,* March–April, 1931.

DILLARD, JACK (R. A. Faherty), "How the U.S. Govt. Caught Al Capone!" *The Master Detective,* February, 1932.

FUCHS, DANIEL, "Where Al Capone Grew Up." *The New Republic,* September 9, 1931.

GENTILE, NICOLO, A series of interviews of *Paese Sera,* Rome, September, 1963.

GUNTHER, JOHN, "The High Cost of Hoodlums." *Harper's Monthly Magazine,* October, 1929.

HALLGREN, MAURITZ A., "Chicago Goes Tammany." *The Nation,* April 22, 1931.

HOSTETTER, GORDON L., and BEESLEY, THOMAS QUINN, "The Rising Tide of Racketeering." *The Political Quarterly,* London, July–September, 1933.

MANGIL, WILLIAM, "Torrio 'the Immune.' " *True Detective,* September, 1940.

MARTIN, JOHN BARTLOW, "Al Capone's Successors." *American Mercury,* June, 1949.

MURRAY, WENDELL, " 'When I Get Out of Prison . . .' Al Capone Talks." *Look,* October 24, 1939.

NELLI, HUMBERT S., "Italians and Crime in Chicago: The Formative Years, 1890–1920." *The American Journal of Sociology,* January, 1969.

PETERSON, VIRGIL W., "Nation-Wide Implications of Organized Crime." *Criminal Justice,* September, 1948.

——, "Rackets in America." *The Journal of Criminal Law, Criminology and Police Science,* April, 1959.

——, "The Career of a Syndicate Boss (Tony Accardo)." *Crime and Delinquency,* October, 1962.

——, "Chicago: Shades of Al Capone." *The Annals of the American Academy of Political and Social Science,* May, 1963.

PRINGLE, HENRY F., "Obscure Mr. Volstead." *World's Work,* July, 1919.

RANDOLPH, COLONEL ROBERT ISHAM, "How to Wreck Capone's Gang." *Collier's,* March 7, 1931.

RODANN, CURTIS (Charles Remsberg), " 'Big Daddy' of the Underworld (James Colosimo) ." *True Detective,* August, 1960.

SHEPHERD, WILLIAM G., "Can Capone Beat Washington, Too?" *Collier's,* Oct. 16, 1931.

STURM, J. E. THOMPSON, A three-part series on the Thompson submachine gun. *The New York Daily Mirror,* August 7, 14 and 21, 1932.

SULLIVAN, EDWARD DEAN, "I Know You, Al." *North American Review,* September, 1929.

——, "The Mystery of the Underworld King." *Liberty,* March 22, 1930.

TAYLOR, FRANK J., "Trouble House." *Collier's,* July 25, 1936.

TRAIN, ARTHUR, "Imported Crime: The Story of the Camorra in America." *McClure's Magazine,* May, 1912.

TURANO, ANTHONY M., "America's Torture Chamber." *American Mercury,* September, 1938.

VANDERBILT, CORNELIUS, JR., "Interview with Al Capone." *Liberty,* October 17, 1931.

WHITE, OWEN P., "Machine Guns for Sale." *Collier's,* December 4, 1926.

WILSON, FRANK J. (as told to Howard Whitman) , "How We Trapped Capone." *Collier's,* April 26, 1947.

——, "The Al Capone Story." *Retirement Life,* October, 1954.

WOLFE, EDGAR FOREST (R. H. Faherty) , "The Real Truth About Al Capone." *The Master Detective,* September, 1930.

SUTHERLAND, SIDNEY, "The Machine-Gunning of McSwiggin and What Led Up to It." Liberty, July 3–Aug. 7, 1926.

I drew heavily upon the files of the following newspapers:

In New York, the Brooklyn *Eagle,* the *Daily News,* the *World-Telegram, Herald Tribune* and *Times.*

In Miami, the *Herald* and the *Daily News.*

In Atlanta, the *Constitution.*

In Chicago, the *Daily Times, Daily Tribune, Daily News, Herald-Examiner, Evening American, Evening Post,* and the *Sun-Times.*

In San Francisco, the *Chronicle* and the *Examiner.*

Index

Accardo, Antonino Leonardo (Joe Batters), 144, 249, 368, 383, 385
Adamo, Niccolo, 93
Adams, Fred A., 212
Aderhold, Arthur C., 348–49, 357, 359
Adonis, Joe, 326
Adonis Social Club, Brooklyn, 36, 163–165
Aducci, Mary, 53
Agoglia, "Fury," 164
Ahern, Michael J., 160, 212, 301, 328, 330, 334, 336, 339, 341, 342, 369
Aiello, Dominic, 207
Aiello, Joseph, 204, 205, 206, 207, 223, 226, 266 n.
Aiello, Tony, 207
Aiuppa, Joseph, 379, 384
Albin, David (Cockeye Mulligan), 232
Alcatraz Island Penitentiary, 353–55, 357–72
Alcock, Tom, 289
Aldermen's war, 91–95
Alex, Gus, 383
Allen, Lizzie, 41
Alterie, Louis "Two-Gun," 86, 95, 126, 127, 130, 131–32
Amateur Athletic Union, 61
Amatuna, Samuzzo "Samoots," 88, 93, 157, 158, 160
America First movement, 208, 221
American Broadcasting System, 382
American Notes (Dickens), 31
Annenberg, Max, 235
Annixter, Julius "Lovin' Putty," 39

Anselmi, Albert, 88, 132, 140, 157, 159, 160–61, 165, 166, 182, 195, 204, 250, 257–58
Anton, Theodore "the Greek," 199
Apalachin (N.Y.) conference, 381
Arresso, Tony, 274
Arrowhead Inn, Burnham, 146
Atlanta Penitentiary, 345, 348–56
Atlantic City conference, 260, 265, 324
Attanasio, Band Master, 24
Aurelio, Thomas, 22
Aurora, Illinois, 82

Bach, Mrs., 174
Bachrach, Benjamin, 335
Bagwell, Gladys, 87, 159
Bailey, Harvey, 366
Baldelli, Ecola "the Eagle," 88, 160, 165
Barasa, Bernard, 35, 203, 218
Barbara, Joe, 255
Barker, Arthur "Doc," 366, 367
Barker, George "Red," 266 n., 297–98, 300, 315, 343
Barko, Louis, 185, 186–87
Barn (Burnham), 76
Barry, William, 374–75, 378
Barrymore, John, 40
Barton, Robert, 136, 137, 276
Barton, Sylvester, 135
Bascone, Vito, 88, 160, 165
Bates, Albert, 366, 369
Bates, Sanford, 352–53, 361
Becker, Morris, 234–35

Becker, Theodore, 234
Bed Bug Row, Chicago, 41, 44
Beer war massacres, 106–8
Belcastro, James, 143, 221, 266 n.
Bella Napoli Café, Chicago, 95, 170, 194, 205, 217
Bennett, James V., 361, 369–70
Bernstein, Abe, 223
Bernstein, Leona, 296, 297
Bertche, Christian P. "Barney," 192, 193, 205
Bertucci, Joseph, 49
Berwyn, Illinois, 121, 148, 152, 174
Berwyn *Beacon*, 148
Better Government Association of Chicago and Cook County, 166, 169
Bilton, George, 120
Bimbooms, 29–31
Binford, Jessie, 112
Bingham, Hiram, 345
Binningham, Edward, 119
Bioff, Willie, 368
Birns, Stanley J., 58–59
Biscayne Kennel Club, 320
Black Belt, Chicago, 99
Black Hand, 47–50, 51, 53, 71, 87, 89, 93, 143
Black Mary's, Chicago, 41
Bloom, Ike, 73
Blue Island, Illinois, 76
Boettiger, Anna Roosevelt, 301 n.
Boettiger, John, 294, 301–2, 303
Bolton, Byron, 254 n.
Bombings in Chicago, 51, 167, 217, 218, 221
Bonanno, Joseph "Joe Bananas," 326
Bonaparte, Napoleon, 262–63
Bori, Lucrezia, 312
Bowers, Joe, 365
Bowler, James, 92–93
Boyle, Michael J. "Umbrella Mike," 78, 79
Bragg, Chester, 154, 155, 320
Bratz, Albert, 297
Brennan, Ray, 257 n.
Brichet, George, 250
Bridgeport, Connecticut, 55
Brisbane, Arthur, 344–45
Brooklyn *Daily Eagle*, 164
Brooks (Josephs), Joey, 296

Brooks, Joseph "Dynamite," 98
Brothers, Leo Vincent, 303–4
Brothers, William V., 161, 166, 176
Brown, "Brownie," 374
Brundige, Harry T., 292–95
Buchalsky, "Izzy the Rat," 39
Buchalter, Louis "Lepke," 326
Bucher, George "Sport," 105, 106–7, 108 ,111
Bulow, William J., 284
Bundesen, Herman N., 248, 250, 251, 253
Burke, Fred "Killer," 251, 253, 254
Burnham, Illinois, 55, 56, 76, 146
Burnham Inn, 56, 57, 64, 76
Burr Oak Hotel, Blue Island, 76
Busch, Clarence M., 216
Busse, Fred A., 54
Butler, Walker, 248
Byrd, Richard E., 306

Cadets' Protective Association, 43
Caesar, A. H., 286
Caesarino, Antonio, 38, 70–71
Cagney, James, 309
Caldwell, H. Wallace, 251
California, the (Chicago), 41
Callan, Joseph H., 319
Camorra, 21
Campagna, Louis "Little New York," 206–7, 227, 380, 381
Campanini, Cleofonte, 40
Campanini, Italo, 66
Campilla, Frank, 70–71
Campion, Patrolman, 115
Cantor, Eddie, 285
Capone, Al (Alphonse), alias of, 67; antique dealer, 101, 108, 120; appearance, 15; arrests, 33, 103–4, 163, 164, 259, 284, 301–2; assassination attempts, 134–35, 200, 205, 206–8, 366–67; beer war massacres and, 106–8; birth, 23; boyhood in Brooklyn, 23–36; Brooklyn revisited by, 162–65; Cicero operation conducted by, 113–18; death, 378; dog racing racket and, 236–38; early jobs, 27, 35–36; education, 24–25, 27; exiled from Chicago, 209–12; flight from New York to Chicago, 37; gang wars

in Chicago, 106–8, 124–33, 142–55, 172–75, 185–86, 189–91, 199, 240–54, 329–30; Genna gang and, 158–62; gonorrhea contracted by, 77; heritage, the, 379–86; income-tax evasion, 270–82, 321–22, 328–29, 341; indictment and sentence, 341–42; imprisonments, 259–64, 342–73; last years, 374–75, 377–78, 382; Lingle murder and, 293–95, 301–2, 305; Mafia and, 325–27; marriage of, 36–37; McSwiggin case and, 177–83; murder committed by, 118–21; neurosyphilis suffered by, 349, 372, 377; O'Donnell gang and, 172–75; organization, 142–46; partner with Torrio in Chicago, 67, 71, 73, 76, 87, 100, 101, 112, 124–33; petitions rejected, 351–52; political interests, 198–99, 200–3, 216–22, 228–30; popular image, 306–15; public benefactor, 208–10, 235–36, 306–15, 329–30, 331, 348, 369–70; racketeering in Chicago, 230–35; St. Valentine's Day massacre and, 240–54; Sherman Hotel treaty and, 191–95; SI-7085-F case, 276–82, 318; social position, 285; son of, 37; syndicate headed by, 139–55; Thompson and, 208; trial, 333–41

Capone, Albert Francis (Capone's son), 37, 162, 211, 246–47, 285, 346, 351, 374–75, 378, 381, 382, 385–86

Capone, Amadeo (John, "Mimi") (Capone's brother), 19, 103, 121, 146, 147, 283

Capone, Diana Ruth Casey, 376–77, 385

Capone, Gabriel (Capone's father), 18–19, 23, 27, 101–2, 378

Capone, Mae Coughlin (Capone's wife), 36–37, 162–63, 211, 213, 216, 228, 246, 261, 263, 269, 336, 346, 363, 367, 372, 373, 378, 381, 382, 385

Capone, Mafalda (Capone's sister), 19, 103, 261, 269, 314–15, 346, 364, 368, 381

Capone, Matthew Nicholas (Capone's brother), 19, 20, 103, 142, 146, 147–148, 261, 345, 347, 368, 369, 377, 380, 383–84

Capone, Ralph (Capone's brother), 19, 102, 103, 112, 122–23, 142, 151, 152, 153, 182, 192, 211, 262, 264–65, 266, 272–74, 276, 308, 314, 317, 360, 368–369, 373, 374, 375, 378, 379, 380

Capone, Ralph, Jr., 376, 380

Capone, Rose (Capone's sister), 19, 314, 346

Capone, Salvatore (Frank) (Capone's brother), 19, 103, 112, 114, 115–16, 378

Capone, Teresa Riolia (Capone's mother), 18, 19, 23, 102, 103, 162, 261, 346, 351, 364, 378, 380

Capone, Umberto (Albert John) (Capone's brother), 154, 261, 283

Capone, Velma Pheasant, 103

Capone, Vincenzo (James) (Capone's brother), 18, 26, 102, 142, 375–76, 380

Capparelli, Louis, 315

Carbonari, 21

Carlstrom, Oscar, 176, 177

Carlton, Doyle E., 283

Carmichael, Jack, 148, 153

Carozza, George, 164

Carozzo, "Dago Mike," 115

Carroll, James, 273

Caruso, Enrico, 66

Casey, Mike, 315

Casino, the (Chicago), 41

Cassin, Patrolman, 115

Castellammarese War, 324–26

Cermak, Anton J., 322

Chandler, Harry, 290

Charlestown, Indiana, 307

Chesterton, G. K., 297

Chicago *American,* 62, 73–74, 138, 139

Chicago Association of Commerce, 247, 266

Chicago Athletic Association, 60, 61

Chicago Crime Commission, 13, 218, 228, 231, 306, 330, 380

Chicago *Daily Journal,* 235

Chicago *Daily News,* 38, 48, 202, 310

Chicago *Evening Post,* 290

Chicago gangs, 76–100

Chicago *Herald-Examiner,* 83, 290, 335

Chicago *Journal of Commerce,* 230

Chicago Musical College, 66

Chicago Newspaper Publishers' Association, 290
Chicago Police Department Morals Squad, 57–59, 63
Chicago *Star,* 294
Chicago *Sun-Times,* 384
Chicago *Times,* 91
Chicago *Tribune,* 59, 116, 120, 130, 177, 197, 235–36, 287, 289–90, 292, 294, 303
Chicago Typographical Union, 308
Chicago Vice Commission, 45, 54, 56
Chillicothe, Illinois, 211
Cicero, Illinois, 17, 76, 109–23, 124, 148–55, 171, 173, 175, 179, 209, 273, 314, 368, 384
Cicero *Life,* 148
Cicero *Tribune,* 148–50, 151, 153–54
Cinene, Beneditto, 49
Circus gang, 145
Clark, James (Albert Kashellek), 85, 243, 245, 253
Clark, Louis, 374
Clark, Muriel Coughlin, 374
Clarke, Charles W., 276–77
Clawson, Samuel G., 334, 339
Clements, Hilary, 199
Cleveland, Grover, 227
Cleveland, Ohio, 256
Cliffe, Adam, 136, 138
Cochran, Frank, 96
Cohan, George M., 40
Cohen, Danny, 144–45
Coldwater, Kansas, 82
Collier, Bill, 366
Collier's magazine, 96
Collins, Morgan A., 79, 111–12, 125–27, 130, 190
Colosimo, Dale Winter, 65–66, 71, 72–73, 75
Colosimo, James "Big Jim," 37, 38–39, 40, 43–45, 46, 47, 51, 52–53, 55, 56, 57, 58, 60, 63, 64–65, 67, 69, 70–75, 80, 92
Colosimo, Luigi, 43, 53, 75
Colosimo, Victoria Moresco, 66, 70, 71, 75
Colosimo's Café, Chicago, 38–40, 43, 53, 65, 73, 75, 332
Committee of Fourteen, 33

Coney Island Café, Burnham, 76
Congress Hotel, Chicago, 184
Conley, Thomas, 137
Consentino, Louis, 112
Converse, Clarence, 274, 277, 280
Conway, Michael, 157
Coolidge, Calvin, 168, 208, 283
Cooney, Dennis "the Duke," 39
Cooper, Courtney Ryley, 67
Corcoran, John, 211
Corrigan, Phil, 108
Cosmano, Vincenzo "Sunny Jim," 39, 52, 71, 78
Costello, Frank, 22, 23, 258, 323, 324
Costello, Tom, 63
Cotillo, Salvatore A., 22
Coughlin, Anna, 37
Coughlin, Bridget Gorman, 36
Coughlin, Danny, 374
Coughlin, John Joseph "Bathhouse John," 39, 44, 53, 59, 64, 69, 73, 76, 203
Coughlin, Michael, 36
Coughlin, Winifred, 374
Count, Reigh, 279, 280
Cowan, Louis, 143, 149, 151, 153, 154, 235, 283
Cox, James M., 284
Craikowski, Reverend, 314
Creedon, John, 259, 261
Crowe, Dorsey R., 200
Crowe, Robert E., 108, 151, 158, 167–170, 171, 172, 175–76, 177, 180, 181, 182, 183, 197, 208, 217, 218, 222
Crutchfield, William, 128, 129
Cuiringione (Rossi), Tommy, 135–36, 184, 199
Cummings, Homer S., 352, 353, 355, 357–58, 359, 361
Cuneo, Candida, 168
Cuneo, Lawrence, 217
Cusick, Detective Sergeant, 115
Czarneck, Anthony, 203

Daily Northwestern, 307
Daley, Richard, 196
Damato, Ralph, 164
D'Andrea, Anthony, 91–94, 225
D'Andrea, Horace, 92

D'Andrea, Joey, 39, 92
D'Andrea, Phil, 143, 202, 226, 279, 320, 333, 335, 336, 368, 381
Dannenberg, W. C., 57, 58, 59
Darrow, Clarence, 63, 111, 234
Dawes, Charles G., 166–67
Day, Edith, 75
Dead Man's Tree, 91
Dead Rabbits gang, 31
De Amato, James Finesy, 224
Death Corner, Chicago, 83, 94
Défrère, Désiré, 165
De Grazio, Orchell, 205
Delagi, Michael, 22
Delaney, James J., 37
Del Bono, Frank, 367
De Lucia, Felice (Paul "the Waiter" Ricca), 144, 368, 380, 383
Deneen, Charles S., 95, 172, 197, 217, 218, 220
Depression, 266, 291, 307–8, 331
De Sapio, Carmine, 22
Desilu Products, 382
Desso, Tony, 164
De Stefano, Rocco, 70, 71, 72
Dever, William E., 111, 112, 114, 119, 132, 140, 168–69, 196
De Vico, James, 37
Diamond (Maritote), Frank, 127, 178, 266 n., 314, 381
Dickens, Charles, 31
Dillon, William "Porky," 121–22
Ditchburne, Harry, 267–68
Dog racing, 236–38
Doherty, Jim, 117, 118, 171, 172, 173, 175, 180, 182
Doody, Mrs. Michael, 248
Dore, Harry, 246
Dreher, Judge, 155
Drucci, Vincent "Schemer," 83, 85, 127, 130, 135, 156, 157, 159, 161, 184–85, 186, 191, 200–1
Druggan, Terry, 95, 104, 138–39, 266 n., 271, 272, 284, 312, 381
Druggan-Lake gang, 124
Dry and Lawless Years, The (Lyle), 46
Duffy, Henry, 75
Duffy, Tom "Red," 171, 172, 174–75, 182
Duffy, William J., 382–83

Dunlap, Albert, 173
Dunn, "Sonny," 57

Eastern Penitentiary, 262–64
Editor and Publisher, 303–4
Egan, John, 247–49
Egan, William "Shorty," 107
Egan's Rats, 223, 249
Eighteenth Amendment, 351
Einstein, Albert, 306
Eisen, Maxie, 130, 191, 192, 231
Eller, Morris, 138, 184, 201, 221
Ellis, Oliver, 273
Ellison, James "Biff," 32, 33
Employers' Association of Chicago, 231
Enright, Maurice "Mossy," 78
Enright, Tommy, 57
Erbstein, Charles, 63, 111
Erickson, Frank, 326
Esposito, Carmela, 217
Esposito, Gaetano, 93
Esposito, Giuseppe "Diamond Joe," 95, 133, 170, 194, 217
Ettelson, Samuel, 201, 222
Evans, Dan, 283, 284
Everleigh, Ada and Minna, 41–43, 44, 54–55
Everleigh Club, Chicago, 41–43, 54
Extortion in Chicago, 47–51, 53, 230–35

Fairview Kennel Club, Cicero, 238, 243
Fancher, Thad, 96
Fanelli, Rocco, 266 n.
Fawcett Publications, 309
Federated Protestant Churches, 54
Ferraro, Joseph, 225
Ferry, Cornelius "Needles," 163, 164
Fifth Amendment, 271
Finalli, Tony, 88, 165
Fink, Albert, 328, 334, 337, 338, 342
Fischetti, Charles, 102, 112, 115, 116, 142, 146, 224, 244, 285, 378
Fischetti, Rocco, 102, 112, 285, 378, 383
Fish Fan Club, Chicago, 196
Fisher, Emil, 116
Fisher, Harry, 237
Fisher, John S., 264
Fisher, Louis, 237, 299
Fitzmorris, Charles C., 69, 169, 201, 217
Fitzpatrick, Daniel, 329

Fitzpatrick, Mac (W. E. Frazier), 51, 58
Fitzsimmons, Bob, 307
Five Pointers gang, 26, 31, 35
Fogarty, "Dandy Joe," 57
Foley, John "Mitters," 182, 188, 191
Ford, Henry, 306
Forest View, Illinois, 121–23
Forsythe, James "Red," 296
Forty Little Thieves gang, 32
Forty Thieves gang, 31
Foss, Tom, 148
Foster, Frank, 294, 295
Fotre, John, 335–36
Four Deuces, Chicago, 67, 87, 100, 101, 102, 111, 118, 119, 141
Franche, Jim "Duffy the Goat," 58, 59
Frantzius, Peter von, 146, 224, 250, 295
Freeman, Clyde, 186
Freeman, William O., 299
French Emma's, Chicago, 41
Freschi, John J., 22
Friedman, Max Motel (Morris Rudensky), 139–40
Friendly Friends, 43
Froelich, William J., 334
Funkhouser, Metellius I. C., 57, 59, 63
Fusco, Joe, 331, 343

Galli, Ugo, 203
Galli-Curci, Amelita, 40
Galluccio, Frank, 36, 164
Gambino, Frank "Don Chick," 93
Gandhi, Mahatma, 306
Gang wars in Chicago, 106–8, 124–33, 142–55, 172–75, 184–95, 199, 240–54, 329–30
Garden, Mary, 40
Gardner, Roy, 366
Garofalo, Gioachino, 23, 24
Garrity, John J., 71
Gary, Indiana, 161
Gaskin, Ruth, 241, 244
Gavin, Michael, 114
Geary, Gene, 79
Genero, Joseph "Peppy," 266 n.
Genite, Joseph, 48
Genker, Charlie "Monkey Face," 39
Genna, Angelo "Bloody Angelo," 87, 93, 94, 127, 128, 135, 156, 159, 223, 314

Genna, Antonio "Tony the Gentleman," 87
Genna, Lucille Spingola, 134, 314
Genna, Mike "Mike the Devil," 87, 133, 157–58, 159
Genna, Pete, 159
Genna, Sam, 87, 159
Genna, Vincenzo "Jim," 87, 93, 128, 159, 170
Genna brothers gang, 87–95, 105, 124, 125, 127, 133, 142, 156–70
Genovese, Vito, 323, 324, 325, 326
Gentry, Budd, 338
George White Scandals of 1927, 313
Gest, Morris, 66
Giambastiani, Father Louis, 94
Giancana, Sam "Mooney," 144, 381, 383, 385
Giblin, Vincent, 284
Gioe, Charlie "Cherry Nose," 380
Giovanni, Tutino, 24
Giunta, Giuseppe "Hop Toad," 204, 250, 255
Gleason, Chief of Police, 59
Gnolfo, Felipe, 88, 165–66
Goddard, Calvin H., 252, 253
Goddard, Herbert M., 263, 298
Goldet, Benjamin M., 262
Goldstein, Abraham "Bummy," 160
Gopher gang, 33
Gordon & Giblin, 284
Gorman, Charles, 169
Gorman, George E., 182
Gorman, Simon J., 232, 296
Gorman, William, 378
Gorysko, Nick, 106
Grabiner, "Jew Kid," 51, 56
Grady, Michael, 125
Granady, Octavius, 221
Graterford, Pennsylvania, 264
Gray, "Blubber Bob," 41
Gray, Therese, 41
Graydon, Charles E., 299
Green, Dwight H., 334, 335, 338
Greenberg, "Young," 109
Grogan, Patrolman, 115
Grossman, Jacob I., 334, 339
Grotto, the (Miami Beach), 382
Grove, Jimmy, 364
Guardino, Johnny "Two-Gun," 93

Guilfoyle, Martin, 145, 193
Guilfoyle gang, 145
Gullet, "Chicken Harry," 51, 57
Gusenberg, Frank, 130, 156, 186, 238, 243, 245, 246
Gusenberg, Henry, 187, 238, 244
Gusenberg, Pete, 187, 243, 245, 246
Gutter, Oscar, 338
Guzik, Alma, 76, 77–78, 79
Guzik, Harry, 76, 77–78, 79, 112, 142, 314
Guzik, Jake "Greasy Thumb," 14, 112, 118–20, 136, 142, 192, 212, 224, 235, 239, 243, 258, 262, 266, 275, 276, 280, 302, 314, 317, 337, 343, 345, 368, 373, 378, 381
Gypsum, Colorado, 86

Hagan, John, 302, 303
Haggerty, Cornelius, Jr., 259
Hammond, Indiana, 258
Hanley, Edward, 173, 174
Harlem Inn, Stickney, 121, 279
Harms, Aaron, 163, 164
Harrison, Carter H., Jr., 54–55, 57, 58, 59, 60, 168
Hart, James, 163, 164–65
Hart, Kathleen Winch, 376
Hart, Richard James (Vincenzo Capone), 375–76
Harvard Inn, Brooklyn, 35, 36
Hasmiller, Harry, 105
Hastings, Mary, 45
Hauptmann, Bruno Richard, 344
Hawthorne Inn, Cicero, 17, 113–14, 116, 148, 172, 185–87, 193, 202, 257, 266, 309, 384–85
Hawthorne Kennel Club, Cicero, 236, 237, 238, 282
Hawthorne Park Café, Cicero, 109
Hawthorne Smoke Shop, Cicero, 116–117, 142, 154, 155, 179, 282, 317, 320, 337
Hayes, Howard, 119
Head, Comer, 357
Healey, Charles C., 63
Healy, Dan, 200
Hearst, William Randolph, 208
Hecht, Ben, 38, 309–10
Heeney, Willie, 178

Heitler, "Mike de Pike," 39, 63, 67, 142, 304–5
Henagow, Isaac, 57, 59
Henderson, Parker, 215, 216, 222, 224, 241, 242, 244, 277, 335
Henderson, Parker, Jr., 214
Henshaw, C. A., 215
Herrick, C. W., 281, 334
Herrick, Genevieve Forbes, 268–69
Hertz, John D., 284
Hess, George, 367, 372
Hevemeyer Streeters, 28
Heyer, Adam (John Snyder), 238, 243, 245
Hi Ho Club, Cicero, 368
Hitchcock, Frank, 147
Hodgins, William, 277, 281, 282, 316
Hoff, Max "Boo Boo," 223, 258
Hoffman, Peter B., 110, 138, 139, 151, 154, 169
Hoffman, Samuel, 175, 225
Hogan, Pat, 302
Holmesburg County Prison, 262
Holtz, Lou, 313
Homer, Nebraska, 375, 376, 380
Hoover, Henry C., 151, 154–55, 320
Hoover, Herbert C., 229–30, 270, 271, 279, 306
Hoover, J. Edgar, 355
House of All Nations, Chicago, 41
Howard, Joe "Ragtime," 119–20, 121, 126, 163
Hoyne, State's Attorney, 59
Hubacek, Charlie "Big Hayes," 199
Hughes, Charles Evans, 306
Hughes, Howard, 309, 310
Hughes, Michael, 80, 120, 201, 202, 208, 210, 296
Hughes, William J., Jr., 351
Humphreys, Murray, 343, 378, 383
Hunt, Samuel McPherson "Golf Bag," 143, 298, 378, 381

Illinois Association for Criminal Justice, 96, 113
Illinois Crime Survey, 74–75, 170, 183
Inside Story of Chicago's Master Criminal, The, 309
Insull, Samuel, 201

Internal Revenue Bureau, 240–41, 266, 270, 271–82, 316–22, 342, 343
International Apple Shippers' Association, 308
International Longshoremen's Association, AFL, 33
Irene (play), 75
Irey, Elmer I., 53, 271–73, 276, 277, 319, 328
Irish street gangs, 27, 163–64
Issigson, Edward, 158
Italian immigrants, 19–23, 113
Italo-American National Union (Unione Siciliane), 34–36, 39, 125, 127, 128, 142, 158, 160, 162, 204–5, 223, 225–26, 250, 255–56, 259, 368

Jacobs, Benny, 188, 189
Jacobs, Heinie, 120
Jake Lingle or Chicago on the Spot (Boettiger), 301
James Street gang, 33, 55
Jarecki, Edward K., 115
Jazz Singer, The (play), 312
Jessel, George, 285, 312–13
Jewish street gangs, 27–28
Joffre, Ferdinand, 69
Johnson, Edwin, 303–4
Johnson, Enoch J. "Nucky," 258
Johnson, George E. O., 269, 307, 319, 322, 328, 331, 334, 339–40, 341
Johnson, Jack, 62
Johnston, James A., 353–55, 358, 359–361, 362, 363, 364, 365, 366, 369, 370, 372
Joliet, Illinois, 211–12
Jolson, Al, 40, 285
Jones, Bobby, 306
Jones, Roy, 57–58, 379
Journal de Paris, Le, 310
Justice Department, U.S., 270, 271, 344
Juvenile Protective Association, 112

Karpis, Al (Francis Albin Karpaviecz), 140, 254 n., 367–68, 371
Kastel, Phil, 230
Katz, Jacob, 308–9
Katz, Phil, 379
Kaufman, Julian "Potatoes," 115, 192, 296

Keane, Morrie, 107, 108
Kebel, Arnold, 201
Keeler, Harry Stephen, 187
Keenan, Joseph B., 352
Kefauver, Estes, 379
Kefauver Committee, 379–80
Kelly, Charlie, 146
Kelly, George "Machine Gun," 366
Kelly, Harry Eugene, 175, 180
Kelly, Paul (Paolo Antonini Vaccarelli), 32–33, 37
Kenna, Michael "Hinky Dink," 39, 44, 53, 59, 64, 69, 73, 76, 203, 206
Kennedy, Robert F., 323
Kerin, Jeanne, 380
Kiepka, Joe, 106
Kilgubbin, Chicago, 82
Klein, Seymour, 370–71
Klenha, Joseph Z., 109, 114, 116, 148, 151
Klimas, Leo, 117
Knox, Frank, 270
Koenitzer, Curt Otto, 336
Kofoed, Jack, 247
Kolb, Matt, 145
Koncil, Frank "Lefty," 182, 188, 194, 199
Korocek, Alex, 146, 173
Krause, Fred, 103

Labriola, Paul, 93, 94
La Cava, Joseph, 112
La Cava, Louis, 112, 299, 317
Lait, Jack, 65, 75
Lake, Frank, 95, 104, 138–39, 266 n., 271, 272
Landesco, John, 112–13
Landesman, Mrs. Max, 243–44, 245
Lane, Clem, 257 n.
Lansky, Meyer, 326
Larrison, Jens, 377
Lasker, Albert D., 284
Laspisa, Joe, 94
Laubenheimer, Henry C. W., 342, 344, 347, 348–49
Lauderback's, Cicero, 117
Lawndale Kennel Club, 237
Lazar, Sam, 258
Leahy, William F., 351

Leathers, Billy, 51
Leavenworth Penitentiary, 342, 359, 371, 381
Lederer, George, 65
Lee, Edward T., 169
Lee, Ivy, 229
Lemisch, Bernard L., 259, 262
Levee, the (Chicago), 38, 39, 41–43, 53–54, 55, 57–59, 60, 61, 62, 66–67, 73, 76
Levine, Hymie "Loud Mouth," 142, 379
Lewis, Elmer, 242, 243
Lewis, Joe E., 144–45, 230, 285
Lewisburg (Pa.) Penitentiary, 359, 373
Lexington Hotel, Chicago, 13–14, 227–228, 268, 329, 340
Libby, Josephine, 84, 85
Libonati, Roland V., 307, 379–80
Lightnin' magazine, 238
Lillie, Beatrice, 339
Lindbergh, Charles A., 306, 345
Lindbergh kidnap case, 344–45
Lindsay, Mary, 313–14
Lindsay, William, 137
Lingle, Alfred "Jake," 203, 264–65, 282, 286, 287–92, 293, 295–96, 299, 301
Lingle, Alfred, Jr., 288
Lingle, Dolores, 288
Lingle, Helen Sullivan, 288
Lipschutz, Louis, 275
Litsinger, Edward R., 197, 218–19
Little Bohemia, Chicago, 95
Little Caesar (movie), 309
Little Dead Rabbits gang, 32
Little Hell, Chicago, 82–83
Little Hellions gang, 83
Little Italy, Chicago, 87–95, 105, 158, 160, 308
Little Whyos gang, 32
Loesch, Frank, 13, 14, 15, 16, 228, 229, 266
Logan, Thomas, 123
Lolordo, Aleina, 226
Lolordo, Joseph, 225, 250–51
Lolordo, Pasquale, 225, 226, 238, 255
Lo Mantio, Angelo, 206
Lombardo, Tony, 142, 159–60, 162, 187, 191, 192, 204, 206, 223, 225
London, Georges, 310–11

Lonergan, Richard "Peg-Leg," 163–64, 261
Los Angeles, California, 210
Los Angeles *Times,* 290
Louisville *Courier-Journal,* 329
Loverdo, Agostino, 226
Lovett, Anna, 164
Lovett, "Wild Bill," 163, 164
Lucas, Jim, 366–67
Luciano, Lucky (Salvatore Luciana), 25, 31, 162, 185, 258, 324–25, 327, 343–344, 371
Lummis, John Newton, 214, 215, 216
Lundin, Fred, 61–62, 110–11, 167
Lundin, Oscar, 187–88
Lupo, Mrs. Joseph, 47–48
Lyle, John H., 46, 67, 73, 85, 129, 131, 300, 306, 309, 314, 321, 322, 381
Lynch, Thomas J., 181, 182, 183

Mack, Austin, 230
Madden, Arthur P., 273, 319
Maddox, Claude, 145, 249, 254 n., 300, 379, 381
Mader, Fred "Frenchy," 169
Madigan, Harry, 98, 115, 173, 179
Madison, Illinois, 237
Madison Kennel Club, 237
Mafia, 21, 35, 47, 140, 142, 255, 323–27, 368, 381, 383, 384
Mafia (Reid), 380
Magaddino, Sam, 381
Magliocco, Joe, 255
Malato, Stephen, 94
Malloy, Father, 131
Malone, James "Shooey," 259
Malone, Michael F., 261, 277, 279–80, 282, 302, 319, 330, 336, 342
Maloney, Patrick "Happy," 163
Mancuso, Francis X., 22, 23
Mangano, Antonio, 20
Mangano, Lawrence "Dago Lawrence," 142, 266 n.
Mangano, Vincent, 255
Mann Act (1910), 45, 84
Maple Inn, Forest View, 123
Maranzano, Salvatore, 324, 325–26, 327
Marino, Joe, 93
Maritote, John, 314–15
Market Street gang, 83

Marks, Willie, 238, 241, 244
Marmion Military School, 103
Maroa, Illinois, 82
Marshfield Inn, Chicago, 79
Martin, Archie, 273, 274
Massee, Burt A., 251, 252
Masseria, Giuseppe "Joe the Boss," 323–25
Matrisciano, George "Martini," 51
Mattingly, Lawrence P., 275, 280, 281, 317–18, 334, 340
May, Johnnie, 242–43, 245
McAndrews, William, 198
McClain, Mayme, 117
McClellan, John L., 382
McClellan Committee, 325
McClure's magazine, 49
McCormack, John, 40
McCormick, Robert R., 235, 236, 282, 290, 291, 292, 301, 304, 308, 360, 370
McCullough, Bob, 178
McDonald, Charles A., 181, 182, 183, 194–95
McErlane, Frank, 96, 106, 107, 108, 146, 191, 258, 266 n.
McErlane, Vincent, 266 n.
McFall, Danny, 98, 106, 107, 108
McGill, Ralph, 355
McGlynn, Patrolman, 115
McGoorty, John P., 303, 315
McGovern, Hugh "Stubby," 98
McGurn, Jack "Machine Gun," 141, 144–45, 205, 238, 239, 250, 251, 257, 266 n., 283, 284, 307, 314, 368
McLaughlin, John J. "Boss," 295
McNeil Island Penitentiary, 346, 353, 359, 360
McPadden, William "Gunner," 98
McSwiggin, Anthony, 171, 172, 177–78, 182, 183
McSwiggin, William H. "Little Mac," 118, 120, 171–75, 176, 177, 179, 180, 181–83
Medill School of Journalism, 306
Meeghan, George, 105, 106–7, 108, 111
Mellon, Andrew, 270, 277
Merlo, Mike, 39, 125, 127–28, 158
Merriam, Charles F., 63, 64
Metropole Hotel, Chicago, 141, 200, 202–3, 312

Mezzrow, Milton "Mezz," 77, 146–48
Miami, Florida, 212, 213–16, 222–23, 229, 239, 242, 374–75, 283, 284–85, 382
Miami *Daily News,* 214, 215, 216, 284
Midnight Frolics, Chicago, 230, 312
Miller, "Big Hymie," 95
Miller, Davy "Yiddles," 80, 98
Miller, Ernest, 371–72
Miller, George, 116
Miller, Harry B., 194
Miller, Max, 80
Mills, Herbert S., 63
Mills, Ogden, 328
Mills Novelty Company, 62
Mitchell, Margaret, 355
Mitchell, William, 328
Modeni, Marino, 47, 48
Mondi, Jimmy, 112, 337
Moneypenny, David, 343, 344
Mongoven, Leo, 266 n., 298
Monoghan, John, 262
Mooney, Chief of Detectives, 71
Moonlight Café, Chicago Heights, 76
Moore, Eddie, 178
Moore, John Edward "Screwy." *See* Maddox, Claude
Moore, Joseph, 373, 377
Moran, George "Bugs," 85–86, 130, 135, 137, 156, 157, 186, 191, 192, 205, 238, 241, 244, 246, 247, 249, 256, 259, 266 n., 296, 381
Morano, Richard, 164
Morello, Peter "the Clutching Hand," 323, 324
Moresco, Joseph, 51, 60, 71
Moresco, Victoria, 44
Morgan, David, 154, 155
Morici, Agostino and Antonio, 165
Morici, Vito, 347–48
Morin, Mrs. Alphonse, 245
Morton, Samuel J. "Nails," 86
Mount Carmel Cemetery, Chicago, 131, 156, 159, 191, 200, 380–81, 383
Mount Olivet Cemetery, Chicago, 102, 116, 378, 380
Mulvaney, Sadie, 24–25
Mundelein, George, 72
Muni, Paul, 309
Municipal Voters' League, 60

Murder, Inc., 326
Murphy, "Big Tim," 52, 78, 113
Murray, Paddy, 188, 189
Mussolini, Benito, 306
"Mustache Petes," 323, 325

Nash, Thomas D., 182, 204, 212, 266–268, 328
Nerone, Giuseppe (Antonio Spano), 88, 159
Ness, Eliot, 265, 270, 271, 322, 381
Newberry, Ted, 241, 244, 295, 298, 331
Newbold, John, 384
Newmark, "Jew Ben," 78, 79
New Republic, 329
Newton, Frankie, 283
New York State Crime Commission, 22
New York Times Magazine, 297
Niemoth, Terry, 266 n.
Nitti, Frank "the Enforcer," 112, 127, 142, 258, 276, 280, 378
Nootbar, Max, 60
Nordi, Bruno, 49
Norris, George W., 218
Northwestern University crime detection laboratory, 252, 253
Nosek, Joseph W., 121–22
Notre Dame University, 375
Notte, Paul, 93
Nugent, "Crane Neck," 254 n.

Oak Park, Illinois, 121
O'Banion, Anna, 131
O'Banion, Dion, 39, 79–84, 85, 86, 95, 105, 112, 115, 116, 124–33, 141, 156, 159, 190, 201
O'Banion, Viola, 81
O'Banion gang, 195, 199, 200, 205
Oberlander, Mamie, 231
O'Berta, John "Dingbat," 96, 113, 191, 194
O'Brien, Father, 83
O'Brien, William W., 188, 189
O'Connor, Jerry, 106, 108
O'Connor, William, 205–6, 207
O'Donnell, Bernard, 87, 109
O'Donnell, Edward "Spike," 99–100, 105, 108, 266 n.
O'Donnell, Myles, 109, 117–18, 161, 172, 173, 179, 192, 266 n.

O'Donnell, Steve, 99, 100
O'Donnell, Tommy, 99, 106, 108
O'Donnell, Walter, 99, 106, 108
O'Donnell, William "Klondike," 87, 109, 110, 172, 173, 174, 179, 192, 266 n.
O'Donnell brothers gang, 87, 99–100, 105–8, 109, 110, 117–18, 142, 161, 171, 172–75, 179–80, 192, 193
O'Grady, Edward P., 58
O'Hara, Danny, 30
O'Hare, Edward Henry, 318–19, 321, 331–32
O'Hare, Edward J., 236–38
O'Hare Airport, Chicago, 332
Olean, New York, 261
Olson, Edwin A., 168–69, 204
Olson, Harold, 157
Olson, Walter E., 252
Omens, David V., 228
One of Us (play), 75
On the Spot (Wallace), 310
Organized Crime and Illicit Traffic in Narcotics, 382–83
Orvidson, Mrs. Frank, 248
Ossenfort, William, 349, 357, 358

Pacelli, William V., 314
Palm Island, Biscayne Bay, Florida, 215–16, 285, 311, 340, 368–69, 377, 382
Parker, William, 286
Parkway Tea Room, Chicago, 83
Parton, Johnny, 236
Patterson, Eleanor "Cissy," 311–12
Patton, John, 55, 146
Payette, Peter, 112, 179
Payne, Orval W., 166
Pecorara, Rose, 161
Peel, Lord, 339
Peller, Sam, 188, 189
Penney, J. C., 230
Penovich, Pete, 142, 317, 320, 337
Persfal, Rube, 365
Pew, Marlen, 304
Pflaum, William K., 114
Phillips, Barton "Whitey," 370
Phillips, Kenneth, 256, 378
Piazza, Frank, 164
Pinedo, Francisco de, 203

Pinkert State Bank, 275
Pinzola, Joseph, 324
Pitkin, Walter B., 306
Pizak, Pete, 151, 152
Plug Uglies gang, 31
Pony Inn, Cicero, 98, 115, 173, 174
Pope, Frank, 112, 116, 142, 282, 290, 317, 320, 337
Pope, Generoso, 22
Pope, Generoso, Jr., 23
Popham, James, 216
Posen, Illinois, 76
Potzin, "Mike the Greek," 53, 75
Powers, John "Johnny de Pow," 91, 92–93
Price, Georgie, 313
Price, Joseph, 115
Profaci, Giuseppe, 255, 326
Prohibition, 104, 109, 125, 167, 168, 221, 230
Prohibition Unit, Chicago police, 68
Prostitution, 41–45, 54, 110, 121, 280, 326
Psychology of Achievement (Pitkin), 306
Public Enemy (movie), 309
Purple Gang, 248, 249
Putnam, Mrs. James, 137

Quigg, Leslie, 214–15
Quinlan, Walter "the Runt," 95

Racial tension in Chicago, 99
Ragen, Frank, 97–99
Ragen's Colts, 97–99, 114, 115
Raimo, Joseph, 22
Raimondi, Frank, 92–93
Raimondi, Harry, 93
Randolph, Robert Isham, 266
Rapid City, South Dakota, 283
Rathbun, Charles F., 290, 291, 299, 300, 301, 302, 303
Rattling the Cop on Chicago Crime (Sullivan), 309
Ray, James, 251
Really the Blues (Mezzrow), 77
Reform movement in Chicago, 54–60, 110–12
Reid, Ed, 380
Reid, William H., 217

Reina, Tom, 324
Reles, Abe "Kid Twist," 326
Remus, George, 237
Rex Hotel, Chicago, 39
Richards School, Chicago, 103
Richman, Harry, 285, 313
Ries, Fred, 275–76, 317, 318, 321, 337
Rio, Frank (Frank Kline), 127, 178, 185–86, 257–58, 259–60, 266 n., 314, 335
Rizzito, Peter, 225, 226
Roach, Joseph, 176
Roamer Inn, Posen, 76–77
Robertson, John Dill, 197
Robinson, Edward G., 309
Roche, Patrick T., 181, 290, 291, 296, 298, 299, 300, 301, 302, 303, 305, 319
Rockefeller, John D., 229
Rogers, John T., 291, 318, 319
Rolfe, Louise, 250, 251
Roosevelt, Eleanor, 355
Roosevelt, Franklin D., 322, 332, 351
Roosevelt, Theodore, 92
Rossmar Realty, Inc., 384
Rotariu, Anna, 187
Rubin, Sam, 234
Rudensky, Red, 145, 349–50, 351, 355–356, 378
Ruffo, Titta, 156
Runelsbeck, David, 120
Runyon, Damon, 332–33
Russell, William P., 202, 247, 288, 291, 296
Russo, Tony, 205
Ryan, John J., 83
Ryan, Michael F., 57, 59, 60
Ryan, "Paddy the Bear," 95

Sabatini, Rafael, 337
Sabetta, Guido, 49
Saietta, Ignazio "Lupo the Wolf," 34–35
St. John, Archer, 148, 152
St. John, Robert, 148–54
St. Louis *Post-Dispatch*, 291, 329
St. Paul *News*, 329
St. Valentine's Day massacre, 240–54, 257, 258, 267, 385
Saltis, Joe "Polock Joe," 96, 113, 182, 188, 191, 194, 199, 258, 266 n.

Saltis-McErlane gang, 96–97, 105, 106, 124, 142, 193

Sammons, Jack "Fur," 266 n., 300

Sanders, Walter, 377

Sanitary Cleaning Shops, Chicago, 235

Santa Maria II (hydroplane), 203

Sappho, the (Chicago), 41

Saratoga, the (Chicago), 44, 53

Savage, Joe, 191

Saverra, Francesco, 22

Sbarbaro, John, 184, 191, 217

Scalise, John, 88, 132, 140, 157, 158, 159, 160–61, 165, 166, 182, 195, 204, 250, 257–58

Scarface (Hecht), 309–10

Schipa, Tito, 156

Schoemaker, William, 129, 158, 173, 175, 180, 182, 186, 190, 200

Schofield, Lemuel B., 128, 259, 260–61

Schofield, William, 80, 81 n., 187

Schultz, Dutch (Arthur Flegenheimer), 258, 324, 325, 326, 343–44, 351, 371

Schultz, Mrs. Theodore, 188

Schwartz, Charles, 258

Schwimmer, Reinhardt H., 243, 245, 253

Scotti, Paolo, 24

Secret Service, U.S., 35

Senaro, Alexander, 22

Senterfit, Ralph, 285, 286

Serritella, Daniel, 200, 201, 224, 235, 242, 278, 314, 347

Sewell, James, 216

Shadow Inn, Stickney, 76

Sharkey, Jack, 246

Shaw, George Bernard, 306

Sheldon, Frank, 146

Sheldon, Ralph, 98, 99, 192, 193, 199

Sheldon gang, 124, 142

Sheridan Wave Tournament Club, Chicago, 296

Sherman Hotel, Chicago, 192

Shirt Tails gang, 31

Shumway, Leslie Adelbert, 155, 317, 319, 320, 321, 334

Shupe, James "Bozo," 250

SI (Special Investigation)-7085-F, 276–282, 318

Sicilian street gangs, 27

Sieben Brewery, Chicago, 126, 136

Siegel, Benjamin "Bugsy," 326

Silloway, Frederick D., 247, 248

Silvani, Black Hander, 48

Simet, Martin, 117, 118

Sinacola, Joe, 94

Skelly, Charles, 252, 253

Skidmore, Billy, 63, 192, 193, 205

Sloop, John C., 58

Small, Len, 78–79, 100, 123, 168, 169, 197, 219, 222

Smith, Alfred E., 229

Smith, Frank L., 219

Smith, Gipsy, 53–54

Smith, Herbert B., 262, 264

Smith, Oliver P., 236

Spagony, Giacomo, 165

Speedway Inn, Burnham, 56, 76

Spencer, Georgie, 41, 44

Speringa, Michael, 279

Spicuzza, Vincent, 205

Spingola, Henry, 89, 134, 165

Spingola, Lucille, 89

Sports, Inc., 146

Sportsmen's Club, 63

Sprague, Albert A., 80

Springer, Joseph, 289

Stabile (Stickum), Jack, 164

Standard Beverage Corporation, Chicago, 138, 271

Standard Oil Building, Chicago, battles of, 184–85

Standig, John, 364

Stanton, Danny, 266 n., 300

Steffens, Lincoln, 50

Stege, John, 90, 131, 175, 178, 257 n., 265, 267–68, 284, 288, 291, 296

Stella, Antonio, 20

Stenson, Joseph, 104, 126

Sterns, Mrs., 213

Steuer, Max, 371

Stevens, Walter, 106, 107

Stevenson, Adlai E., 380

Stickney, Illinois, 66, 76, 121, 131, 165

Stockade, the (Cicero), 178, 179

Street gangs, 27–34

Stribling, "Young," 246

Sullivan, Edward Dean, 79, 186, 309

Sullivan, James N., 277, 279, 280, 336, 342, 370–71

Sullivan, Manly, 271

Sullivan, Roger, 59
Sullivan Law (1911), 97
Summers, Gregory, 128, 129
Supreme Court, U.S., 271, 272, 278, 328, 345, 352
Svoboda, Theodore, 151
Swanson, John A., 217, 218, 295, 305
Sweeney, Clarence, 246
Sweeney, William, 157, 158, 160
Sweitzer, Robert W., 62, 80
Swerling, Jo, 75

Tammany Hall, 33
Tancl, Eddie, 109, 110, 115, 117–18, 161, 172
Taylor, Robert, 240–42, 243
Taylor Manufacturing Company, 379
Tennes, Mont, 39, 63, 111
Terminal Island (Calif.) Federal Correction Institution, 372
Terranova, Ciro, 34, 325
Tessem, Nels E., 273, 274, 275, 280, 316
Tetrazzini, Luisa, 40, 156
Thiel, Theodore, 177–78
Thompson, Frank H., 250
Thompson, John T., 96–97
Thompson, William Hale "Big Bill," 15, 60–63, 64, 69, 110–11, 156, 168, 169, 196–208, 212, 217, 218–22, 229, 235, 236, 291, 307, 322, 377
Thompson submachine gun, 96–97, 146, 173, 224
Thrasher, Frederic, 29
Thurston, Harry, 43
Thweat, Silas A., 372
Tiburon, California, 358
Toman, John, 368
Torchio, Tony, 205
Torrio, Ann, 64, 134, 136
Torrio, John, 26–27, 31, 33, 36, 37, 52–53, 55, 56, 57, 58, 64–65, 66–67, 68–69, 71, 72, 76, 77–78, 87, 99, 100, 101, 104–5, 107, 109, 110–13, 114, 116, 117, 119, 121, 124–28, 130, 132, 133, 134, 136–38, 139, 142, 158, 161, 190, 230, 256, 258, 259, 281, 319, 330, 338–39, 343, 344, 351, 370, 371, 378, 381
Torrio, Marie Caputa, 52–53
Train, Arthur, 49

Tropea, Orazio "the Scourge," 88, 160, 165
Tucker, Sophie, 40
Tunney, Gene, 198
Turf, the (Chicago), 58
Tuttle, William H., 178
Twitchell, Edward, 372

Underwood, E. Marvin, 351–52
Union League Club, 175
Unione Siciliane. *See* Italo-American National Union
Untouchables, The, 381–82
Urschel, Charles, 366
Utopia, the (Chicago), 41

Vacco, Carmen, 128
Vadis, Arthur, 79
Valachi, Joseph, 21–22, 325
Valenti, Louis A., 22
Vallee, Rudy, 313
Valley gang, 95
Van Bever, Julia, 46, 53, 57
Van Bever, Maurice, 46, 53, 57, 60
Vanderbilt, Cornelius, Jr., 331
Vanilli, Roxie, 57, 58, 60
Varain, Leland. *See* Alterie, Louis
Varchetti, Ralph and Joe, 217
Veesaert, Peter, 137
Victoria, the (Chicago), 44
Villani, Antonio, 70
Villanova University, 103, 261
Vision, Solly, 297
Vitale, Albert A., 22
Vitello, Constantino, 35
Viviani, René, 69
Vogel, Eddie, 109, 110, 114, 116, 192, 379
Volpi, Tony "Mops," 112, 266
Volstead, Andrew, 378
Volstead Act, 68, 69, 168, 179, 271, 322

Walkoff, David, 231
Wallace, Edgar, 310
Walsh, Charles, 157, 161, 204
Walsh, John E., 261–62
Ward, Charles Allen, 356
War of the Sicilian Succession, 204–5, 225

Washington *Herald,* 311
Waters, Eddie, 272
Watson, Thomas, 383
Wayman, John E. W., 56, 168
Weil, Milton, 197–98
Weinshank, Alfred, 238, 243, 245, 249
Weiss, Earl "Little Hymie," 81, 83, 84–85, 86
Weiss, Ed, 41
Weiss, Frank, 85
Weiss, Hymie, 115, 126, 127, 130, 133, 134, 135, 136, 140, 142, 156, 157, 184–85, 186, 187, 188, 189, 190–91, 194, 257, 312
West Suburban Citizens' Association, 151, 154, 155, 178, 320
Westbrook, Wesley, 138
Westinghouse Electric Company, 382
Whalen, Grover, 224
White, William Jack "Three-Fingered," 143, 266 n., 300
White Hand Society, 49–50, 163, 164
White slavery, 43, 45–47, 50, 53, 54, 55, 77–78
Whyos gang, 31–32
Wilbur, Crane, 310
Wilkerson, James H., 138, 257, 272, 274, 320, 321, 329, 330, 331, 333–34, 335, 337, 338, 340–42, 372, 373

Willard, Jess, 62
Williams, Elmer T., 169, 238
Wilson, Frank J., 272, 275, 277, 278, 279, 280–82, 290–91, 300, 316–20, 321, 328, 331, 332, 335, 336
Wilson, Judith Barbaux, 272
Wilson, Orlando W., 383
Winge, Al, 145
Winkler, Gus, 254 n.
Wisniewski, Steve, 84
Wolff, Oscar, 176–77, 180
Wolfson, Abraham, 93–94
World War I, 69
Wutke, Ed, 365
Wyman, State's Attorney, 59

Yale, Frank (Frank Uale), 33–34, 35, 37, 72, 127, 132–33, 162, 223–25, 253, 256, 267
Yario, Joe, 338
"Young Turks," 323, 324, 325, 326

Zangara, Giuseppe, 322
Ziegfeld, Florenz, 66
Ziegler, George, 254 n.
Zion, Eddie, 160, 162
Zuta, Jack, 200, 205, 266 n., 296–97, 298–300
Zwillman, Abner "Longy," 326

Other titles of interest